High Assurance Services Computing

T0138063

Jing Dong · Raymond Paul · Liang-Jie Zhang
Editors

High Assurance Services Computing

 Springer

Editors
Jing Dong
Department of Computer Science
University of Texas, Dallas
2601 N. Floyd Road
P.O. Box 830688
Richardson TX 75083
USA
jdong@utdallas.edu

Liang-Jie Zhang
IBM Research
19 Skyline Dr.
Hawthorne NY 10532
USA
zhanglj@us.ibm.com

Raymond Paul
Department of Defense
4502 7th St. NE.,
Washington DC 20017
USA
raymond.paul@osd.mil

ISBN 978-1-4419-4684-3   e-ISBN 978-0-387-87658-0
DOI 10.1007/978-0-387-87658-0
Springer Dordrecht Heidelberg London New York

Printed on acid-free paper

Springer is part of Springer Science+Business Media (www.springer.com)

Table of Contents

Preface VII

Chapter 1 Translucent Replication for Service Level Assurance 1
Vladimir Stantchev and Miroslaw Malek

**Chapter 2 Trustworthiness Assessment Framework for Net-Centric
Systems** 19
Raymond Paul, Jing Dong, I-Ling Yen, and Farokh Bastani

Chapter 3 A Trust Monitoring Architecture for Service-Based Software 45
Mohammad Gias Uddin and Mohammad Zulkernine

**Chapter 4 Human Interoperability Enterprise for High-Assurance
Systems** 65
Raymond Paul, Stefania Brown-VanHoozer, and Arif Ghafoor

Chapter 5 Service Composition Quality Evaluation in SPICE Platform 89
Paolo Falcarin

Chapter 6 High-Assurance Service Systems 103
Jay Bayne

**Chapter 7 A Graph Grammar Approach to Behavior Verification
of Web Services**.. 127
Chunying Zhao, Kang Zhang

**Chapter 8 A Formal Framework for Developing High Assurance Event
Driven Service-Oriented Systems** 145
Manuel Peralta, Supratik Mukhpadhyay, and Ramesh Bharadwaj

**Chapter 9 Towards A Dependable Software Paradigm
for Service-Oriented Computing**.. 163
Xiaoxing Ma, S.C. Cheung, Chun Cao, Feng Xu, Jian Lu

**Chapter 10 Developing Dependable Systems by Maximizing Component
Diversity** 193
Jeff Tian, Suku Nair, LiGuo Huang, Nasser Alaeddine and Michael F. Siok

Chapter 11 High Assurance BPEL Process Models 219
Mark Robinson, Hui Shen, Jianwei Niu

Chapter 12 Specifying Enterprise Web-Oriented Architecture................... 241
Longji Tang, Yajing Zhao, Jing Dong

Chapter 13 Designing an SOA for P2P On-Demand Video Delivery 261
Zhenghua Fu, Jun-Jang Jeng, Hui Lei, and Chao Liang

**Chapter 14 A Coverage Relationship Model for Test Case Selection
and Ranking for Multi-version Software** 285
Wei-Tek Tsai, Xinyu Zhou, Raymond A. Paul, Yinong Chen, Xiaoying Bai

About the Editors 313

About the Authors.. 315

Index.. 323

Preface

Services computing is an emerging discipline cross-cutting the science, engineering and technology. It bridges the gap between Business Services and IT Services. The scope of services computing covers the whole lifecycle of services innovation research and practice that includes services modeling, creation, deployment, discovery, composition, analysis, and management. The goal of services computing is to facilitate the application of loosely-coupled services and computing technology for building systems more efficiently and effectively. The core technology suite includes Service-Oriented Architecture (SOA) and Web services. SOA is a common platform for implementing large scale distributed applications by composing services, which are platform independent components running on different hosts of a network. It offers native capabilities, such as publication, discovery, selection and binding for creating new applications by combining services as basic building blocks. A repository of existing services independent of the underlying infrastructures can be discovered and composed in an application. The requester and the provider exchange messages via the network through standard protocols.

SOA is now being deployed in mission-critical applications in domains that include space, health-care, electronic commerce, telecommunication, and military. Many critical systems require multiple high assurance, including reliability, safety, dependability, security, and availability. Failures of such systems may cause the loss of human lives and finance. For example, the reliability of aircraft/spacecraft navigation and guidance control systems can affect human lives; the correctness and timeliness of military command and control systems can be crucial to the success of defense missions; the failure of a medical process-control system can cause death or injury to the patient; the failure of a banking system can cause property losses for many clients; the failure of a security management system in a network server can cause chaos and result in financial or intellectual property losses; the failure of railroad control systems can cause delays and subsequent financial losses or can even lead to catastrophic life threatening failures. In modern human society, our reliance on computer systems can be observed in our daily lives. From the current trend, our reliance on high assurance systems will grow at an increasing pace. Thus, there is a pressing need for developing computer systems whose quality can be guaranteed to a high degree; otherwise, we will risk the well-being of societies at the hands of computer hardware and software failures or misuses by human intruders. Existing methods dealing with such constraints may be not readily applied in service-oriented environment. Different from traditional computer-based systems, services are typically third-part entities. There is no standard way to define high assurance properties in service specifications. Service interfaces normally focus on the descriptions of functional aspects, such as input, output, pre/post conditions (IOPE). The high assurance properties of a service are generally unclear or defined in an ad hoc manner in the service interfaces. This poses new challenges on service discoveries with high assurance requirements.

A successful service needs to provide the required functionality and the necessary Quality of Service (QoS). The QoS parameters are typically specified in service level agreements (SLAs) that the service provider needs to guarantee and their violation will be penalized appropriately. The QoS constraints that a service provider guarantees may include run-time properties, such as timeliness, transaction rate, and availability, as well as design-time properties, such as language of service and compliance. Such high assurance guarantees are difficult to ensure when services are spatially distributed over a network subject to active attacks, network congestion, and link delays, which may pose a formidable challenge in delivering services that meet the SLAs.

There are a number of important issues in high assurance services computing:

- How to describe, assess, and ensure Quality of Service in service-oriented systems?
- How to manage and evaluate dependability of service compositions from individual services?
- How to analyze and assess the trustworthiness of service requestors and service providers?
- How to facilitate service creations and executions?
- How to verify service behavior and service level agreement?
- How to engineer service-oriented systems?
- How to test service applications?

This book is a collection of fourteen chapters solving some of these problems.

About This Volume

Chapter 1 defines separate levels of Quality of Service (QoS) assurance within a service-oriented architecture. Each of these levels includes replication options that can bring substantial benefits toward high assurance of run-time related non-functional properties (NFP) in complex environments. Experimental results based on architectural translucency in health care applications showed an increase of 50% on the NFP levels with more stable QoS levels. The NFP representation has been formalized for automating runtime assurance and matching between required and provided QoS levels. System reconfiguration techniques for the different levels within an SOA will dynamically adapt the architecture so that it provides QoS assurance at different loads.

Chapter 2 considers the challenges of assessing highly critical net-centric systems. A trustworthiness ontology is developed to capture the trustworthiness aspects and their correlations as well as to model various classes of system entities and their integrations. The ontology provides information to guide the trustworthiness analysis and data collection. Based on the ontology, a trustworthiness assessment framework is developed. In the framework, systematic steps are formulated to achieve trustworthiness assessments. Techniques and tools to perform the assessments in each step are incorporated in the ontology to allow the actual analysis and derivation of assessment results. A holistic assessment technique is developed to provide a single overall measure of the trustworthiness of a system or a subsystem.

Chapter 3 presents a monitoring architecture for managing trust rules in service interactions. The trust rules identify the contexts of trust concerns and snapshot system events encapsulating a service outcome that is crucial to the target system. The proposed architecture, called Trust Architecture for Monitoring, may reside in each service provider, which allows the analysis of the trustworthiness of users based on trust rules and calculation schemes. A service requestor is penalized for the violation of trust rules and rewarded otherwise, which thus facilitates the quantification of its trustworthiness. Incorporating the recommendations from similar service providers may help collaborative decision making. The performance overhead of the architecture has been evaluated based on the monitoring of a prototype trust-aware file-sharing grid.

Chapter 4 addresses the key policy challenges of human interoperability enterprise (HIE) and highlights major steps that can lead to the development of a holistic interoperability policy framework for engineering high-assurance systems. The human performance criteria for high-assurance and trustworthy systems are elaborated. The HIE systems are designed by integrating core technology components and methodologies drawn from the area of human cognitive engineering. The key challenges and elicit solutions of HIE systems are closely related to the technological areas including Human-Centered Computing, Information, Knowledge and Intelligence Management, service-oriented architecture, and behavioral sciences.

Chapter 5 describes the architecture of the Service Execution Environment that hides the complexity of the communication environment and the Service Creation Environment to help service developer in evaluating the quality of an orchestration of telecom-IT services. Both static and dynamic non-functional properties are aggregated by the Aggregator service that calculates the overall aggregated non-functional properties of a service composition designed by the developer, relying also on the Monitor manager which provides live values of dynamic non-functional properties such as response time.

Chapter 6 introduces a performance measurement framework for cyberphysical systems. The framework includes a cyberspatial reference model for establishing the identity and location of servers and clients in distributed high-assurance service systems. It also defines a set of service performance indices to measure the reliability, availability, safety, security and timeliness properties. An application neutral, yet operational definition of value useful in high assurance service systems is developed for defining their respective value propositions.

Chapter 7 applies graph grammars for verifying the behavior of service-oriented systems. The behavior verification problem is cast to a visual language parsing problem. A behavior graph is parsed with user-specified rule-based constraints/properties expressed by a graph grammar. A parsing result indicates whether the observed behavior satisfies its requirements or not. A parsing error represents a potential problem in the service behavior. The approach allows developers to check the acceptable sequence of message exchanges between services confirming to some requirements/specifications.

Chapter 8 provides a distributed service-oriented asynchronous framework in an event-driven formal synchronous programming environment. This model-driven framework is based on a synchronous programming language SOL (Secure Operations Language) that has capabilities of handling service invocations asynchronously and provides strong typing to ensure enforcement of information flow and security policies. The clients' requirements and the service level agreements can be ensured in the service-oriented systems that have been formally verified. An infrastructure for deploying and protecting time- and mission-critical applications on a distributed computing platform is developed especially in a hostile computing environment, such as the Internet, where critical information is conveyed to principals in a manner that is secure, safe, timely, and reliable.

Chapter 9 offers a coordination model for building dynamically adaptive service oriented systems. Each service is situated in and coordinated by an active architectural context, which mediates the interactions among the services. The architecture of service oriented applications is self-adaptive for bridging the gaps between environment, system and application goals with an ontology-based approach. An access control model is proposed for secure service coordination logic as well as keeping service autonomy discretionarily with a decentralized authorization mechanism. Three classes of trust relationships are also identified for a trust management framework to help the understanding and assurance of the trustworthiness of service oriented applications.

Chapter 10 develops a generalized and comprehensive framework to evaluate and maximize diversity for general service-oriented systems. The dependability attributes of individual service components under diverse operational conditions are evaluated. The internal assessments of services are linked to their external dependability attributes. The preferences of a specific set of stakeholders can also be used to assess the relative importance and trade-off among dependability attributes. The evaluation framework also includes an overall methodology that maximizes system diversity using a mathematical optimization technique for ensuring system dependability via diversity maximization that combines collective strengths of individual services while avoid, complement, or tolerate individual flaws or weaknesses.

Chapter 11 transforms the BPEL processes into Unified Modeling Language (UML) sequence diagrams for consistency analysis. Since sequence diagrams are intuitive and show temporal-based execution naturally, they help to ease the learning curve of BPEL's nomenclature and reduce errors. Two examples have demonstrated the discovery of certain errors in the sequence diagrams with tool support.

Chapter 12 specifies both structurally and behaviorally the Enterprise Web-Oriented Architecture (EWOA) and analyzes its software quality attributes. The specification of the EWOA is based on a generic model of the Enterprise Service-Oriented Architecture. The EWOA style consists of a set of design principals based on REST and Web 2.0, a set of architectural elements of infrastructure, management, process, and a set of software quality attributes. Based on the analysis of the security and manageability issues of EWOA, the pure RESTful system architecture with RESTful QoS governance and a hybrid approach with both REST and SOAP for enterprise are proposed.

Chapter 13 outlines a service oriented architecture for the Peer-Assisted ConTent Service (PACTS) that is a video on demand streaming system. The PACTS organizes elements of traditional video streaming and peer to peer computing into loosely-coupled composable middleware services and distributing them among participating entities for high-quality low-cost video streaming at a large scale and in real time. The implementation of PACTS has demonstrates effectively offload server's bandwidth demand without sacrificing the service quality and in dynamic settings with system churns. It shows significantly reduces bandwidth utilization at the server by leveraging peer assistance. The service level agreement specification is modeled to differentiate QoS to end users based on their bandwidth contributions to the system to derive the minimum and maximum QoS level given a bandwidth budget at the server side.

Chapter 14 proposes a Model-based Adaptive Test (MAT) for multi-versioned software based on the Coverage Relationship Model (CRM) for case selection and ranking technique to eliminate redundant test cases and rank the test cases according to their potency and coverage. It can be applied in various domains, such as web service group testing, n-version applications, regression testing, and specification-based application testing. Two adaptive test cases ranking algorithms are provided by using the coverage probability. Experiments are conducted using the proposed techniques. The experiment results indicate that the CRM-based test case selection algorithm can eliminate redundant test cases while maintaining the quality and effectiveness of testing.

This book is intended particularly for practitioners, researchers, and scientists in services computing, high assurance system engineering, dependable and secure systems, and software engineering. The book can also be used either as a textbook for advanced undergraduate or graduate students in a software engineering or a services computing course, or as a reference book for advanced training courses in the field.

Acknowledgements

We would like to take this opportunity to express our sincere appreciation to all the authors for their contributions and cooperation, and to all the reviewers for their support and professionalism. We are grateful to Springer Publishing Editor Susan Lagerstrom-Fife and her assistant Sharon Palleschi for their assistance in publishing this volume.

Jing Dong
Raymond A. Paul
Liang-Jie Zhang

Chapter 1

Translucent Replication for Service Level Assurance

Vladimir Stantchev*[1] and Miroslaw Malek**

* International Computer Science Institute, Berkeley, California (vstantch@icsi.berkeley.edu)

** Humboldt-University at Berlin, Germany

Abstract: Web services are emerging as the technology of choice for providing functionality in distributed computing environments. They facilitate the integration of different systems to seamless IT supporting infrastructure for business processes. Designing a service-oriented architecture (SOA) for this task provides a set of technical services and composition techniques that offer business services from them. There are two basic aspects of a successful service offering: to provide the needed functionality and to provide the needed Quality of Service (QoS). Mission-critical applications in health care require high and stable QoS levels. The complexity of different web service platforms and integration aspects make the high assurance of such run-time related nonfunctional properties (NFPs) a nontrivial task. Experimental approaches such as architectural translucency can provide better understanding of optimized reconfigurations and assure high and stable QoS levels in mission-critical clinical environments.

1. Introduction

Web services are emerging as a dominating technology for providing and combining functionality in distributed systems. A service-oriented architecture (SOA) offers native capabilities, such as publication, discovery, selection and binding [1]. Since services are basic building blocks for the creation of new applications, the area of composite services is introduced on top of native capabilities. It governs the way applications are developed from basic services. Here, richer interface de-

---

[1] Vladimir Stantchev is also a senior lecturer at the Fachhochschule fuer Oekonomie und Management in Berlin, Germany

J. Dong et al. (eds.), *High Assurance Services Computing*,
DOI 10.1007/978-0-387-87658-0_1, © Springer Science+Business Media, LLC 2009

finitions than the Web Service Description Language (WSDL) are needed and they can be provided in the form of contracts [2, 3].

There are two basic aspects of a successful service offering: to provide the needed functionality and to provide the needed Quality of Service (QoS). QoS parameters are part of the nonfunctional properties (NFPs) of a service, typically specified in service level agreements (SLAs). We distinguish between runtime related and design-time related NFPs. Run-time related NFPs are performance oriented. Examples are response time, transaction rate, availability. Design-time related NFPs such as language of service and compliance are typically set during design time and do not change during runtime. Run-time related NFPs can change during runtime when service usage patterns differ (times of extensive usage by many users are followed by times of rare usage), or when failures occur. Such failures can occur within the service, as well as in the network components that lie between user and service. NFPs and QoS are regarded (together with semantics) as topics that encompass all three levels of services within an SOA (basic services, composite services, managed services) [1].

Formalization and specification of NFPs and their SLAs is currently a very active research field. The enforcement of these levels for runtime-related NFPs cannot be done automatically a priori, due to the changes in service usage and network availability. An approach to dynamically adapt service performance to these changes can ensure continuous meeting of service levels. Providing such dynamically reconfigurable runtime architectures is regarded as one of the main research challenges in the area of service foundations [1]. Such approach should employ service reconfiguration at runtime, as changes in source code of a service are not a feasible option. One approach to identify possible reconfigurations in an SOA and evaluate their implication is called architectural translucency [4]. It describes the notion that different levels in an SOA can have different implications to service levels of NFPs and that understanding these implications is key to provide service level assurance. A central aspect of this approach is to evaluate different replication configurations at the operating system (OS) and serviceware (SW) level and how they affect web service performance.

Health care applications often require high and stable QoS levels. This is particularly true for clinical environments where mission-critical IT systems support life-saving activities.

In order to apply architectural translucency to address high assurance of NFPs in such clinical environments, several questions arise. First, what is the relation between replication and assured service levels, especially concerning runtime related NFPs (Section 2) and how can we formally represent performance aspects (Section 3). Second, what methods are well suited to research this relation and to recommend optimized replication configurations (Section 4). Finally, what are the possibilities to integrate automated assurance of service levels in a clinical environment based on these recommendations (Section 5).

2. Service Level Assurance of Performance

This section describes the effect of web service replication on performance, presents architectural translucency as approach to decide optimized reconfigurations and the importance of the OS and SW levels as places for possible replications.

2.1 Replication and Performance

Performance, more specifically transaction rate, is defined as the system output $\omega(\delta)$ that represents the number of successfully served requests from a total of input $\iota(\delta)$ requests during a period of time δ. This is a generalized view of the equation model presented in [5], where it is referred to as throughput Xa.

$$\omega(\delta) = f(\iota(\delta))$$

The performance of a serial composed service chain is determined by the service with the lowest performance. If that service is Service N then its performance can be defined as follows:

$$\omega^{ServiceN} = f^{ServiceN}(\iota_1)$$

The performance of a serial composed service chain that includes Service N would be:

$$\omega^{ServiceChain} \leq f^{ServiceN}(\iota_1)$$

The performance of replicated composed service chain that includes Service N would be:

$$\omega^{ServiceChain} \leq 2 * f^{ServiceN}(\iota_1)$$

This definition corresponds to transaction rate as NFP.

Another typical run-time related NFP is response time. The average response time can be derived from the transaction rate as follows:

$$RT_{avg} = \frac{1}{\omega}$$

Therefore, replication has advantageous effects on service chain performance when no replica synchronization is required. This applies to transaction rate and response time as NFPs in a SOA.

The traditional view of availability is as a binary metric that describes status. Status can be "up" or "down" at a single point of time. A well-known extension is to compute the percentage of time, on average, that a system is available during a certain period. This results in statements where a system is described as having 99.99% availability, for example.

There are several extended definitions of availability that address the inherent limitations of this definition – availability should be considered as a spectrum, rather as a binary metric. It should also reflect QoS aspects. One possibility is to measure availability by examining variations in system QoS metrics over time [6]. Therefore, assurance of stable QoS metrics leads to better availability.

2.2 Architectural Translucency

The complexity involved in providing a single web service is often underestimated. A look at hardware platforms, even commodity hardware, reveals complex microprocessors and processing architecture. Standard OSs are far away from microkernel designs and contain a large number of OS extensions. These are called *modules* in a Linux system and *drivers* in a Windows system. Beside typical device drivers, extensions include network protocol implementations, file systems and virus detectors. Typical component environments such as .NET and J2EE often serve as the middleware for providing web services [7], here referred to as serviceware. A look at the application programming interfaces of these environments reveals their complexity.

One general problem in such complex environments is where to introduce a certain measure (e.g., replication), so that the system can assure optimized performance at certain loads.

Much work has been done in the area of QoS-aware web service discovery [8], QoS-aware platforms and middleware [9,10,11,12], and context-aware services [13]. However, all of these approaches do not address assurance of service levels by a single service, but rather deal with the composition of services where aggregated NFP levels would satisfy a specific requirement.

The existing standards for specification of QoS characteristics in a service-oriented environment can be grouped according to their main focus: software design/process description (e.g. UML Profile for QoS and QML - QoS Modeling

Language) [14], service/component description (e.g. WS-Policy) and SLA-centric approaches (e.g. WSLA - Web Service Level Agreements [15], WSOL - Web Service Offerings Language [16], SLAng - Service Level Agreement definition language [17] and WS-Agreement [18]).

Extensive research concerning NFPs exists in the field of CORBA (Common Object Request Broker Architecture), particularly in the areas of real-time support [19,20], replication as approach for dependability [21,22,23,24], adaptivity and reflection [25,26], as well as mobility [27,28]. Similar approaches involving replication have been proposed for J2EE-based web services [29,30,31].

To the best of the authors' knowledge, there are no other published works that address the question where and how an optimized reconfiguration can be introduced in the complex of hardware, OS and component environment in order to optimize the NFPs of web services. Of particular interest is to evaluate whether reconfigurations at one level are generally more advantageous than others. This is the main objective of architectural translucency as an approach for service level improvement and assurance. The approach is an extension of architectural approaches that aim to improve NFPs in one location, e.g., reliability at the OS level [32], scalability by clustering of web servers [33] or email servers, as well as introducing software RAID approaches [6]. Architectural translucency defines levels that encompass these approaches and compares replication configurations at the different levels. These levels are: hardware, operating system and serviceware.

Failures at the network level lead to network partitions. There is currently no convincing way to mathematically model network partitions [34]. Furthermore, it is NP-hard to derive a partition model from link and node failure models [35]. Currently, architectural translucency does not address questions of network availability and performance. Nevertheless, there are several promising approaches that can be combined with architectural translucency in order to incorporate network availability in overall availability of distributed systems. One possible way is to incorporate network failures in availability metrics that define $Avail_{client} = Avail_{network} \times Avail_{service}$ [34]. Better assignment of object replicas to nodes can further improve availability in such settings [36].

2.3 Experimental Computer Science

Architectural translucency can be classified in the field of experimental computer science [37]. There are three key ideas in experimental computer science – a hypothesis to be tested, an apparatus to be measured, and systematic analysis of the data to see whether it supports the hypothesis [37]. The hypothesis is that replications at different levels and in different ways have different effect on web service run-time related NFPs (specifically performance). The apparatus consists of typical platforms for web services (Windows Server with .NET and Internet Information Server (IIS), UNIX with WebSphere) and web service benchmarks. Tools like

Microsoft Application Center Test (ACT) and HP LoadRunner allow for automated testing of web services during long periods and with different loads. They also facilitate the gathering of large amounts of test data. Statistical tools such as SPSS [38] and R [39] are well suited to further analyze this data.

3. Performance Models

Some approaches to model performance-related aspects of a system are described in [40,41,42,43]. One promising approach to analytically model multi-tier Internet applications was recently published in [44]. The model is based on a network of queues where the queues represent different application tiers. This research effort is similar to efforts of Kounev and Buchmann [45] and, more recently, Bennani and Menasce [46]. The second work is based on previous research published in [47,5,48,49,50]. Kounev and Buchmann also use a network of queues to predict performance of a specific two tier application and solve the model numerically using existing analysis software. Bennani and Menasce model a multi-tier Internet service that serves multiple types of transactions. The model is again based on a network of queues with customers belonging to multiple classes.

There are some other recent efforts to model multitier applications. These are often extensions of single-tier models. One approach [51] considers server provisioning only for the Java application tier and uses an M/G/1/PS model for each server in this particular tier. Another approach [52] models the same tier as a G/G/N queue. Other works have modeled an entire multi-tier application using a single queue (e.g., a M/GI/1/PS queue in [53]).

Various works describe complex queuing models. Such models can capture simultaneous resource demands and parallel subpaths within a tier of a multitier application. One example is Layered Queuing Networks (LQNs). They are an adaptation of Extended Queuing Networks which account for the fact that software servers run atop of other layers of servers, thus giving complex combinations of simultaneous resource requests [54,55,56,57,58]. The focus of these works lies primarily on Enterprise Java Beans-based application tiers.

Extensive work exists in the area of modeling of single-tier Internet applications, most commonly HTTP servers. One of the early works [59] introduced a network of four queues to model static HTTP servers. Two of the queues model the web server, and two – the Internet communication network. Another approach [60] also presented a queuing model and related average response time to available resources. A GPS-based (Generalized Processor Sharing) queuing model of a single resource (e.g., CPU) at a web server was proposed in [61,62]. A G/G/1 queuing model was suggested in [63], a M/M/1 queuing model to compute web request response times – in [64]. One web server model with performance control as objective was introduced in [65]. Menasce [66] presented in 2003 a combination of a Markov chain and a queuing network model, an idea originally presented in [67]. Despite these tremendous developments such models still cannot fully reflect the complexity of the three layers of web service platforms concerning NFPs. Therefore, experimental methods can help to further enhance our knowledge of optimized configurations in such complex settings.

4. Translucent Replication

In service-oriented computing (SOC) a node receives a stream of requests, processes them and sends back a stream of results. From an operating system point of view there exist two general strategies for request processing – threaded request processing and event-driven request processing. There are two questions that architectural translucency can address in this context:

1. Are there ways to introduce (or alter default) replication settings at the OS and SW level?
2. Can a system assure optimized performance (or other QoS) by reconfiguring such OS or SW settings?

4.1 Threaded Request Processing

When implementing pure threaded request processing an OS creates a thread for each client request. The whole request and maybe its subsequent ones from the same client are processed in the context of this newly created thread. This approach offers good parallelization of request processing and good utilization of available resources. Main disadvantage is the large overhead of the thread lifecycle (creation, management, deletion). Modern OSs address this by employing thread pools – a specific number of request processing threads are created in advance and left idle. The OS can then dynamically assign them to incoming requests. Implementations differ in handling new requests if all worker threads are busy.

4.2 Event-driven Request Processing

With pure event-driven request processing the OS processes all requests within a single worker thread. Arriving requests are stored in a queue which is used as input for the worker thread. The worker fetches and processes the requests one at a time. The per request overhead here is minimal (managing the request queue) and a queuing policy with request priorities can be introduced. The approach is nevertheless contradictory with a key goal of architectural translucency – to ensure high resource utilization. The low degree of parallelism can result in longer idle times.

4.3 Thread and Process Replication

At operating system level there are two general ways for functional replication – replication of threads and replication of processes. While in the former a node creates a new thread to process a client request, in the latter it creates a new process to handle an incoming request. Generally, it can be assumed that a per-thread replication should be more favorable to performance as per-process replication, as the overhead of process management is larger from an OS point of view. The research of this hypothesis requires knowledge about the mechanisms to control this type of replication at the OS level of typical platforms for web services.

4.4 Levels

The hypothesis is that there are different levels (HW, OS, SW) where a service provider can introduce replication and different ways to replicate at each level. Furthermore, there are differences in web service performance when the provider applies them. The objective is to define these different ways of replication and find reconfiguration techniques for them. High assurance during runtime often makes hardware changes unfeasible or costly. Therefore, in this chapter we focus on architectural translucency aspects at the OS and SW level.

4.4.1 Operating System Level

When working with typical OS/Middleware configurations for SOC (Windows Server 2003 with IIS 6 and the .NET Framework, or UNIX and IBM WebSphere) a service provider has to consider several specifics.

Pure threaded or event-driven implementations are rare. There are different design patterns for hybrid implementations (staged request processing, thread pools, reactor pattern).

Windows 2003 with IIS 6 uses the thread pools pattern – when deploying a web service in IIS 6 it creates one process for the service that also contains a number of precreated threads. While IIS 5 allowed only changing the number of these threads per web service process (number specified in the configuration file machine.config), IIS 6 allows also specifying the number of process replicas to serve multiple requests. Furthermore, IIS 6 ignores threading parameters known from IIS 5 such as maxWorkerThreads and minFreeThreads, as threading optimiza-

tion is automated. A test of replication alternatives at the OS level involves speci-fying a higher number of process replicas for a web service (see Figure 1).
WebSphere also uses the tread pools pattern; configuration settings are accessible via the *application server* menu. The menu item *Thread-Pools* contains an over-view of the existing thread pools within the application server. By selecting *Web Container* the specific parameters of the thread pool can be configured. The set-tings for processes and the Java Virtual Machine (JVM) are accessible in the group *Java and Process Management*, menu *Process Definition*.

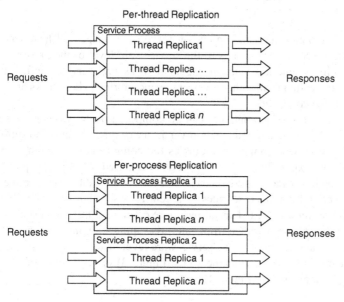

Fig. 1. Replication at OS Level: Per-process Replication vs. Per-thread Replication

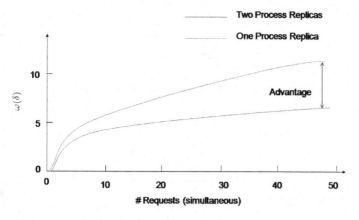

Fig. 2. Replication at OS Level: Advantage of Per-process Replication vs. Per-thread Replication

Tests have demonstrated that having two process replicas per web service instead of one can lead to throughput increases of up to 50% under higher loads (more than 40 simultaneous client requests, see Figure 2). This applies to services that are already optimized using asynchronous requests and minimizing need for exclusive hardware access (e.g., hard disk). Performance is also far more stable with confidence intervals of 99%.

4.4.2 Serviceware Level

Nodes in SOC typically use an application server to manage and host services. Such application server corresponds to the serviceware level of the presented approach. It simplifies generic service management tasks, e.g., service configuration, deployment, connection (with other services) or monitoring. These tasks are often done using service containers.

Services within a service container can be composed using two general structures: direct composition and composition via a service bus. Direct composition of services within a service container resembles the component programming paradigm: services are explicitly connected with other required services at deployment time. As precondition the required services must be available. The service bus concept connects all deployed services to a central bus which is responsible for request routing to the services. This allows more complex interactions such as the publish/subscribe approach known from enterprise application integration.

When looking at replication at the serviceware level there are two basic alternatives – replication of service containers (see Figure 3) or replication of services within service containers (see Figure 4).

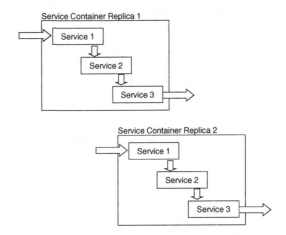

Fig. 3. Replication of a Service Container

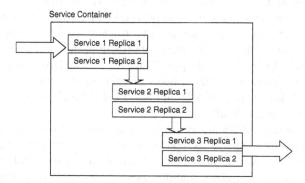

Fig. 4. Replication of Services within a Service Container

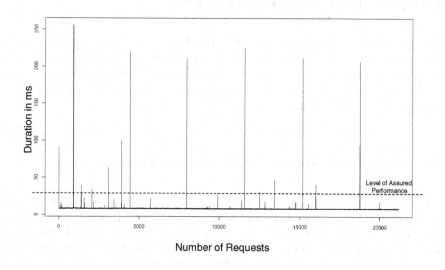

Fig. 5. High Assurance through Serviceware Replication

From an object-oriented point of view both these alternatives can be implemented by instantiating new service or container objects. An objective of architectural translucency is to allow for such reconfigurations without reprogramming.

When dealing with replication at the serviceware level using WebSphere, the question is how to distribute instances in different Web Containers (Web Containers serve as service containers in WebSphere). Possible ways are to use another main context or to change the main context manually within the EARs. Manual change is done by editing the file application.xml in the META-INF directory. The service provider has to edit the pairs of names so that there is no match within a pair, especially concerning the elements display-name, web-uri and context-root. Names of web archive (WAR) files also have to be adapted accordingly before packing the EAR with jar.

Our results here show distinct performance advantages for replication within a service container as compared to replication of service containers. Furthermore, when we focus on aspects of high assurance we observe substantially higher confidence intervals in performance stability, as shown exemplarily in Figure 5. The required response time (30ms) is assured for all but 16 requests from 22 000 requests overall, resulting in an assurance rate higher than 99.9 percent. Our framework deals also with these delayed requests by a resubmission after a certain timeframe expires.

5. High Assurance in the Operating Room

The application scenario focuses on the surgical sector. It is not only one of the largest cost factors in health care but also a place where failures to provide timely needed information can be perilous, endangering life and health of a patient.

Pre- and postoperative processes are key factor for the effective and safe utilization of the surgical sector.

5.1 Perioperative and Postoperative Processes

The perioperative processes start with a notification from an operating room nurse or an anesthesia nurse, that the staff should transport the next patient to the operating room. Then a transport service or a nurse moves the patient from the ward to the operating room area. In the main registration area clinicians transfer the patient from the ward bed to an operating room table. Afterward the patient resides in the induction area, where he is anesthetized. Then clinicians move the patient to the operating room, where the preparation for the operation starts, for example operation specific bedding, sterile coverage etc. The surgery starts with the cut and finishes with the suture. After the surgery clinicians transport the patient to the post anesthesia recovery unit, where he is moved again to the ward bed and recovers from anesthesia. After the recovery the staff transports the patient back to the ward.

There is an extensive usage and movement of things (devices, instruments, beds) related with these processes. Furthermore, such devices and instruments need a preparation (e.g., disinfection) prior to usage. Proximity of clinicians to such things typically indicates intended or current usage. Therefore, position information is a key input for the planning and steering process.

Furthermore, there are high requirements regarding performance and other NFPs that the IT infrastructure needs to satisfy.

5.2 Technology Environment and Architectural Approach

There exist a variety of position sensing systems than are suited for deployment in such environments [68]. An integration of such system, together with a hospital information system (HIS) and enterprise resource planning system (ERP) can provide the needed functionality to optimize surgical processes.

Figure 6 shows our integration approach within an SOA. Here the WLAN positioning system, the HIS and the ERP system are integrated in the SOA with wrappers that provide web service interfaces to the enterprise service bus (ESB). Clinicians are using Tablet PCs as mobile devices; Devices and patients are equipped with WLAN tags.

The usage of an SOA in such mission-critical environments depends heavily on the high assurance of run-time related NFPs. For example, data about position of monitored objects (more than 10000) has to be available within 5 seconds. The AT engine is responsible for service QoS assurance by monitoring and management. In a first step, it measures performance of services in their standard configurations at the OS and serviceware levels. We then import the QoS requirements and evaluate them. We presented a structure for their formalization in [69]. Using these formalized requirements, the AT engine configures the proper settings at each service platform. During runtime, when the engine notices that for example a service is experiencing higher loads, it dynamically reconfigures the replication settings of the service platform to further provide the expected QoS.

Representation and further information processing are depicted in the upper part of the figure. The system provides portal-based access to process-related information. Examples are electronic patient records (EPRs) or case definitions that are extracted from the HIS and visualized on the Tablet PC. Which patient record or case definition is visualized depends on the current location of the Tablet PC and otherWLAN-enabled objects that surround it (e.g., patient tags).

Furthermore, the system offers more complex planning, steering and evaluation functions. These are provided by composite services.

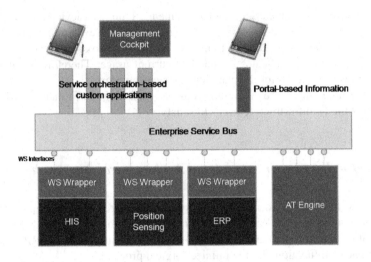

Fig. 6. Architectural view of the solution. HIS - hospital information system, ERP - enterprise resource planning system, AT - architectural translucency

6. Summary

Mission-critical environments in clinics require high assurance of performance and other run-time related NFPs. Typical platforms for providing web services are complex and hardly predictable. Seamless IT support of processes often requires integration of different *off-the-shelf* systems such as HIS and ERP. Location awareness can optimize usage planning, monitoring and steering of resources in clinical environments. Position sensing systems based on radio technology (e.g., RFID, WLAN) provide such information and are key components of clinical IT support. The design of an SOA is a promising approach to integrate these different systems. Such integration typically requires the development of web service wrappers around the interfaces of the systems and leads to further increases in complexity. This makes QoS assurance even more compelling. A definition and separation of levels within an SOA, as well as a look at replication options at these levels can bring substantial benefits toward high assurance of run-time related NFPs in such complex environments. Experimental approaches such as architectural translucency are well suited for this task and can increase assured NFP levels by 50%. They can also provide more stable QoS levels.

Automated run time assurance further requires formalization of NFP representation and matching between required and provided QoS levels. Furthermore, automated assurance systems need to provide integrated system reconfiguration techniques for the different levels within an SOA. Such run time reconfiguration will dynamically adapt the architecture so that it provides QoS assurance at different loads.

References

[1] Michael P. Papazoglou, Paolo Traverso, Schahram Dustdar, and Frank Leymann. Service-oriented computing: State of the art and research challenges. Computer, 40(11):38–45, Nov. 2007.

[2] Nikola Milanovic and Miroslaw Malek. Current solutions for web service composition. IEEE Internet Computing, 8(6):51–59, 2004.

[3] Francisco Curbera. Component contracts in service-oriented architectures. Computer, 40(11):74–80, Nov. 2007.

[4] Vladimir Stantchev and Miroslaw Malek. Architectural Translucency in Service-oriented Architectures. IEE Proceedings - Software, 153(1):31–37, February 2006.

[5] Daniel A. Menascé. QoS issues in Web services. Internet Computing, IEEE, 6(6):72–75, 2002.

[6] A. Brown and D.A. Patterson. Towards Availability Benchmarks: A Case Study of Software RAID Systems. Proceedings of the 2000 USENIX Annual Technical Conference, 2000.

[7] Gerry Miller. The web services debate: .net vs. j2ee. Commun. ACM, 46(6):64–67, 2003.

[8] Y. Makripoulias, C. Makris, Y. Panagis, E. Sakkopoulos, P. Adamopoulou, M. Pontikaki, and A. Tsakalidis. Towards Ubiquitous Computing with Quality of Web Service Support. Upgrade, The European Journal for the Informatics Professional, VI(5):29–34, 2005.

[9] S.S. Yau, Yu Wang, Dazhi Huang, and H.P. In. Situation-aware contract specification language for middleware for ubiquitous computing. Distributed Computing Systems, 2003. FTDCS 2003. Proceedings. The Ninth IEEE Workshop on Future Trends of, pages 93–99, 28-30 May 2003.

[10] L. Zeng, B. Benatallah, A.H.H. Ngu, M. Dumas, J. Kalagnanam, and H. Chang. QoS-aware middleware for Web services composition. IEEE Transactions on Software Engineering, 30(5):311–327, 2004.

[11] G. Canfora, M. Di Penta, R. Esposito, and M.L. Villani. An approach for QoS-aware service composition based on genetic algorithms. Proceedings of the 2005 conference on Genetic and evolutionary computation, pages 1069–1075, 2005.

[12] A. Solberg, S. Amundsen, J.Ø. Aagedal, and F. Eliassen. A Framework for QoS-Aware Service Composition. Proceedings of 2nd ACM International Conference on Service Oriented Computing, 2004.

[13] Y. Tokairin, K. Yamanaka, H. Takahashi, T. Suganuma, and N. Shiratori. An effective QoS control scheme for ubiquitous services based on context information management. cec-eee, 00:619–625, 2007.

[14] Svend Frolund and Jari Koistinen. Quality of services specification in distributed object systems design. In COOTS'98: Proceedings of the 4th USENIX Conference on Object-Oriented Technologies and Systems (COOTS), pages 1–1, Berkeley, CA, USA, 1998. USENIX Assoc.

[15] H. Ludwig, A. Keller, A. Dan, R.P. King, and R. Franck. Web Service Level Agreement (WSLA) Language Specification. IBM Corporation, 2002.

[16] V. Tosic, K. Patel, and B. Pagurek. WSOL-Web Service Offerings Language. Web Services, E-Business, and the Semantic Web: CAiSE 2002 International Workshop, WES 2002, Toronto, Canada, May 27-28, 2002: Revised Papers, 2002.

[17] D.D. Lamanna, J. Skene, and W. Emmerich. SLAng: A Language for Defining Service Level Agreements. Proc. of the 9th IEEE Workshop on Future Trends in Distributed Computing Systems-FTDCS, pages 100–106, 2003.

[18] A. Andrieux, K. Czajkowski, A. Dan, K. Keahey, H. Ludwig, J. Pruyne, J. Rofrano, S. Tuecke, and M. Xu. Web Services Agreement Specification (WS-Agreement). Global Grid Forum GRAAP-WG, Draft, August, 2004.

[19] A. Polze and L. Sha. Composite Objects: Real-Time Programming with CORBA. In Proceedings of 24th Euromicro Conference, Network Computing Workshop, Vol. II, pp.: 997–1004, Vaesteras, Sweden, August 1998.

[20] W. Feng. Dynamic client-side scheduling in a real-time corba system. In COMPSAC, pages 332–333. IEEE Computer Society, 1999.

[21] Pascal Felber, Rachid Guerraoui, and André Schiper. Replication of corba objects. In Sacha Krakowiak and Santosh K. Shrivastava, editors, Advances in Distributed Systems, volume 1752 of Lecture Notes in Computer Science, pages 254–276. Springer, 1999.

[22] V. Marangozova and D. Hagimont. An infrastructure for corba component replication. In Judith M. Bishop, editor, Component Deployment, volume 2370 of Lecture Notes in Computer Science, pages 222–232. Springer, 2002.

[23] M. Werner. Replikation in CORE. Bericht an das Graduiertenkolleg "Kommunikationsbasierte Systeme", Oct 1996.

[24] Pascal Felber and Priya Narasimhan. Reconciling replication and transactions for the end-to-end reliability of corba applications. In Meersman and Tari [70], pages 737–754.

[25] Pierre-Charles David and Thomas Ledoux. An infrastructure for adaptable middleware. In Meersman and Tari [70], pages 773–790.

[26] Sebastian Gutierrez-Nolasco and Nalini Venkatasubramanian. A reflective middleware framework for communication in dynamic environments. In Meersman and Tari [70], pages 791–808.

[27] Gregory Biegel, Vinny Cahill, and Mads Haahr. A dynamic proxy based architecture to support distributed java objects in a mobile environment. In Meersman and Tari [70], pages 809–826.

[28] Sandeep Adwankar. Mobile corba. In DOA '01: Proceedings of the Third International Symposium on Distributed Objects and Applications, page 52, Los Alamitos, CA, USA, 2001. IEEE Computer Society.

[29] O. Babaoglu, A. Bartoli, V. Maverick, S. Patarin, J. Vuckovic, and H. Wu. A Framework for Prototyping J2EE Replication Algorithms.

[30] Etienne Antoniutti Di Muro. A software architecture for translucent replication. In DSM '05: Proceedings of the 2nd international doctoral symposium on Middleware, pages 1–5, New York, NY, USA, 2005. ACM.

[31] Lei Gao, Mike Dahlin, Amol Nayate, Jiandan Zheng, and Arun Iyengar. Application specific data replication for edge services. In WWW '03: Proceedings of the 12th international conference on World Wide Web, pages 449–460, New York, NY, USA, 2003. ACM.

[32] Michael M. Swift, Brian N. Bershad, and Henry M. Levy. Improving the reliability of commodity operating systems. ACM Trans. Comput. Syst., 23(1):77–110, 2005.

[33] Armando Fox, Steven D. Gribble, Yatin Chawathe, Eric A. Brewer, and Paul Gauthier. Cluster-based scalable network services. In SOSP '97: Proceedings of the sixteenth ACM symposium on Operating systems principles, pages 78–91, New York, NY, USA, 1997. ACM.

[34] Haifeng Yu and Amin Vahdat. The costs and limits of availability for replicated services. ACM Trans. Comput. Syst., 24(1):70–113, 2006.

[35] A. Rosenthal. Computing the Reliability of Complex Networks. SIAM Journal on Applied Mathematics, 32(2):384–393, 1977.

[36] Haifeng Yu and Phillip B. Gibbons. Optimal inter-object correlation when replicating for availability. In PODC '07: Proceedings of the twenty-sixth annual ACM symposium on Principles of distributed computing, pages 254–263, New York, NY, USA, 2007. ACM.

[37] Peter J. Denning. Acm president's letter: What is experimental computer science? Commun. ACM, 23(10):543–544, 1980.

[38] M.J. Norušis and S. Inc. SPSS 11.0 Guide to Data Analysis. Prentice Hall, 2002.

[39] B.D. Ripley. The R project in statistical computing. MSOR Connections. The newsletter of the LTSN Maths, Stats & OR Network, 1(1):23–25, 2001.

[40] Ann T. Tai, William H. Sanders, Leon Alkalai, Savio N. Chau, and Kam S. Tso. Performability analysis of guarded-operation duration: a translation approach for reward model solutions. Perform. Eval., 56(1-4):249–276, 2004.

[41] Krishna R. Pattipati and Samir A. Shah. On the computational aspects of performability models of fault-tolerant computer systems. IEEE Trans. Computers, 39(6):832–836, 1990.

[42] Gianfranco Ciardo, Raymond A. Marie, Bruno Sericola, and Kishor S. Trivedi. Performability analysis using semi-markov reward processes. IEEE Trans. Computers, 39(10):1251–1264, 1990.

[43] Kishor S. Trivedi, Antonio Puliafito, and Dimitris Logothetis. From stochastic petri nets to markov regenerative stochastic petri nets. In Patrick W. Dowd and Erol Gelenbe, editors, MASCOTS, pages 194–198. IEEE Computer Society, 1995.

[44] Bhuvan Urgaonkar, Giovanni Pacifici, Prashant Shenoy, Mike Spreitzer, and Asser Tantawi. An analytical model for multi-tier internet services and its applications. In SIGMETRICS '05: Proceedings of the 2005 ACM SIGMETRICS international conference on Measurement and modeling of computer systems, pages 291–302, New York, NY, USA, 2005. ACM.

[45] S. Kounev and A. Buchmann. Performance Modeling and Evaluation of Large-Scale J2EE Applications. Proc. of the 29th International Conference of the Computer Measurement Group (CMG) on Resource Management and Performance Evaluation of Enterprise Computing Systems-CMG2003, 2003.

[46] Mohamed N. Bennani and Daniel A. Menascé. Resource allocation for autonomic data centers using analytic performance models. In ICAC '05: Proceedings of the Second International Conference on Autonomic Computing, pages 229–240, Washington, DC, USA, 2005. IEEE Computer Society.

[47] Daniel A. Menascé, Larry W. Dowdy, and Virgílio A.F. Almeida. Performance by Design: Computer Capacity Planning By Example. Prentice-Hall, Inc., Upper Saddle River, NJ, USA, 2004.

[48] Daniel A. Menascé, Virgílio A. F. Almeida, Rudolf Riedi, Flávia Ribeiro, Rodrigo Fonseca, and Jr. Wagner Meira. In search of invariants for e-business workloads. In EC '00: Proceedings of the 2nd ACM conference on Electronic commerce, pages 56–65, New York, NY, USA, 2000. ACM.

[49] Daniel A. Menascé and Virgílio A. F. Almeida. Scaling for e-business. Prentice Hall PTR Upper Saddle River, NJ, 2000.

[50] Daniel A. Menascé, Virgílio A.F. Almeida, and Larry W. Dowdy. Capacity Planning and Performance Modeling: From Mainframes to Client-Server Systems.Prentice-Hall, Inc., Upper Saddle River, NJ, USA, 1999.

[51] Daniel Villela, Prashant Pradhan, and Dan Rubenstein. Provisioning servers in the application tier for e-commerce systems. ACM Transactions on Internet Technology (TOIT), 7(1):7, 2007.

[52] S. Ranjan, J. Rolia, H. Fu, and E. Knightly. QoS-driven server migration for Internet data centers. Quality of Service, 2002. Tenth IEEE International Workshop on, pages 3–12, 2002.

[53] A. Kamra, V. Misra, and EM Nahum. Yaksha: a self-tuning controller for managing the performance of 3-tiered Web sites. Quality of Service, 2004. IWQOS 2004. Twelfth IEEE International Workshop on, pages 47–56, 2004.

[54] J.A. Rolia, K.C. Sevcik, et al. The Method of Layers. IEEE Transactions on Software Engineering, 21(8):689–700, 1995.

[55] E.D. Lazowska, J. Zahorjan, G.S. Graham, and K.C. Sevcik. Quantitative system performance: computer system analysis using queueing network models. Prentice-Hall, Inc. Upper Saddle River, NJ, USA, 1984.

[56] C.M. Woodside and G. Raghunath. General Bypass Architecture for High-Performance Distributed Applications. Proceedings of the Sixth IFIP WG6. 3 Conference on Performance of Computer Networks: Data Communications and their Performance, pages 51–65, 1996.

[57] Roy Gregory Franks. Performance analysis of distributed server systems. PhD thesis, Ottawa, Ont., Canada, Canada, 2000. Adviser-C. Murray Woodside.

[58] J. Xu, A. Oufimtsev, M. Woodside, and L. Murphy. Performance modeling and prediction of enterprise JavaBeans with layered queuing network templates. ACM SIGSOFT Software Engineering Notes, 31(2), 2005.

[59] Louis P. Slothouber. A model of web server performance. In Proceedings of the Fifth International World Wide Web Conference, 1996.

[60] R. Doyle, J. Chase, O. Asad, W. Jin, and A. Vahdat. Model-Based Resource Provisioning in a Web Service Utility. Proc. of the 4th USENIX Symp. on Internet Technologies and Systems.

[61] Abhishek Chandra, Weibo Gong, and Prashant Shenoy. Dynamic resource allocation for shared data centers using online measurements. In SIGMETRICS '03: Proceedings of the 2003 ACM SIGMETRICS international conference on Measurement and modeling of computer systems, pages 300–301, New York, NY, USA, 2003. ACM.

[62] A. Chandra, P. Goyal, and P. Shenoy. Quantifying the Benefits of Resource Multiplexing in On-Demand Data Centers. Proceedings of the First Workshop on Algorithms and Architectures for Self-Managing Systems, 2003.

[63] B. Urgaonkar and P. Shenoy. Cataclysm: Handling Extreme Overloads in Internet Services. Proceedings of the 23rd Annual ACM SIGACT-SIGOPS Symposium on Principles of Distributed Computing (PODC), 2004.

[64] R. Levy, J. Nagarajarao, G. Pacifici, A. Spreitzer, A. Tantawi, and A. Youssef. Performance management for cluster based Web services. Integrated Network Management, IFIP/IEEE Eighth International Symposium on, pages 247–261, 2003.

[65] Tarek F. Abdelzaher, Kang G. Shin, and Nina Bhatti. Performance guarantees for web server end-systems: A control-theoretical approach. IEEE Transactions on Parallel and Distributed Systems, 13(1):80–96, 2002.

[66] Daniel A. Menascé. Web server software architectures. Internet Computing, IEEE, 7(6):78–81, 2003.

[67] G. Bolch, S. Greiner, H. de Meer, and K.S. Trivedi. Queueing networks and Markov chains: modeling and performance evaluation with computer science applications. Wiley-Interscience New York, NY, USA, 1998.

[68] Vladimir Stantchev, Trung Dang Hoang, Tino Schulz, and Ilja Ratchinski. Optimizing clinical processes with position-sensing. IT Professional, 10(2):31–37, 2008.

[69] Vladimir Stantchev and Christian Schröpfer. Techniques for service level enforcement in web-services based systems. In The 10th International Conference on Information Integration and Web-based Applications and Services (iiWAS2008),New York, NY, USA, 11 2008. ACM.

[70] Robert Meersman and Zahir Tari, editors. On the Move to Meaningful Internet Systems, Confederated International Conferences DOA, CoopIS and ODBASE 2002, Irvine, California, USA, Proceedings, volume 2519 of Lecture Notes in Computer Science. Springer, 2002.

Chapter 2

Trustworthiness Assessment Framework for Net-Centric Systems

Raymond Paul**, Jing Dong*, I-Ling Yen*, and Farokh Bastani*,

*University of Texas at Dallas, Richardson, Texas, USA

**Department of Defense, USA

Abstract　Modern applications are becoming increasingly large-scale and net-work-centric, involving a variety of different types of system entities. Also, the assurance requirements for these systems are evolving due to the continuing emergence of new threats from new operational environments. To assure the trustworthiness of these systems to a sufficiently high degree of confidence is a challenging task. Most existing methods require different specialized assessment techniques for not only different types of system entities but also different trustworthiness aspects. Also, most existing techniques lack consideration of the overall system trustworthiness assessment from an integrated system perspective or fail to provide a holistic view. To address these problems, we develop an ontology-based approach to provide systematic guidelines for net-centric system assessment. The ontology-based approach captures evolving system trustworthiness aspects and effectively models their relationships and correlations. It can also organize system entities and associate appropriate assessment techniques for each class of system entities and their integrations.

1. Introduction

Due to the advances of computer and networking technologies, many applications are becoming large-scale and network-centric. A net-centric system (NCS) typically involves a distributed set of sensors, actuators, processors, software, along with a variety of other resources interconnected together by a network and interacting with and controlled by end users. Operational scenarios range from tele-control and tele-monitoring systems to distributed coordination and communication systems, command and control systems, emergency response, and other areas.

J. Dong et al. (eds.), *High Assurance Services Computing*,
DOI 10.1007/978-0-387-87658-0_2, © Springer Science+Business Media, LLC 2009

All these domains are mission- and/or safety-critical since these systems interact with the physical world and failures could potentially have catastrophic consequences. Hence, it is imperative to be able to build ultra dependable and trustworthy NCS and to be able to certify the trustworthiness of these systems to a high degree of confidence before deploying them in the field.

Many techniques have been developed to achieve high assurance and trustworthiness. But almost all of these techniques focus on one or a few trustworthiness aspects. When designing a high assurance system, it does not have to be the invention of new techniques for every part of the system. Rather, it is mostly a decision process to determine which technique to use to achieve certain desired properties in a subsystem. There are many existing techniques that can be considered and adopted. However, how to know which technique is the best to use for a part of the system. The general solution is to use analysis techniques to determine whether a certain combination of techniques does result in a system that satisfies high assurance requirements. Thus, assessment techniques play an important role for the design as well as the assessment phases of mission- and safety- critical systems.

There are significant challenges in trustworthiness assessment for NCS [19]. In general, it is very expensive to assess the trustworthiness of software systems to a high degree of confidence. Considering just the reliability aspect, it has been shown that it would take hundreds of years of testing to achieve adequate confidence in the reliability of a safety-critical system. Net-centric systems face numerous other challenges, including security, usability, and performance issues that require even more time and effort for high-confidence assessment. Compounding these challenges is the fact that these systems are mission-specific and likely to be dynamically composed from existing COTS (commercial off the shelf) and GOTS (government off the shelf) hardware and software components and services [17,18]. Due to the potential lack of complete information regarding the development history of COTS components and their exact implementation details, they can pose severe but difficult-to-detect security and reliability threats, including the potential for embedded "Trojan horses" and other malicious logic designed to trigger rare failures during critical periods. These make it difficult to achieve high confidence in the assurance levels of COTS hardware and software components. In addition, while compositional assessment methods are widely used for certifying hardware systems by, for example, calculating the reliability of a complex system from the reliability of its constituent components, this type of assessment technique has in general proven to be difficult to achieve for software. The reason is that hardware assessment typically focuses on problems due to wear-and-tear and other degradations that impact components independently of each other. This is not the case for software where reliability problems are predominantly due to specification, design, development, and implementation faults. The reliability of the system depends on the way one component uses another component. Because of this, it is possible to build a system where some components are faulty but yet the system is highly reliable since those faults are not triggered due to the way the components are used in the system. Likewise, it is possible to build a system using components that are individually highly reliable but that collectively lead to poor reliability due to unexpected interactions between the components [3].

Besides the complexity in trustworthiness assessment techniques, assessment time and cost are also major concerns. Mission-specific systems must typically be built and deployed rapidly since the mission requirements may change dynamically. Thus, there is a need to be able to rapidly and dynamically certify the trustworthiness of the system systems to a high degree of confidence. This is difficult to do using solely testing or verification methods.

In this chapter, we consider the challenges of assessing highly critical NCS systems and develop technical solutions to address the numerous and interdependent issues involved. We use ontology to capture the evolving trustworthiness metrics and increasing varieties of NCS system entities and their correlations. Based on the ontology, we develop systematic steps to guide trustworthiness assessment. Various assessment techniques are associated with the ontology nodes to facilitate systematic or even semi-automated assessment data collection, integration, and analysis.

A large number of techniques have been developed over the past years for trustworthiness and dependability assessment and most of these methods can be associated with the ontology to assist with NCS assessment. However, there are still many missing links in such techniques. For example, security assessment domain is still in its infancy. A major area in trustworthiness assessment that is missing is that of holistic evaluation. Almost all of the assessment techniques focus on a single aspect, such as software reliability, data security, system performance, etc.; however, this is not always adequate as can be seen by considering some scenarios. For example, when a commander in a battlefield needs to compose a plan to accomplish one or multiple missions, it is desirable to know whether the plan is good enough in terms of accomplishing the missions. It would also be interesting if there are multiple plans and the goal is to assess them to determine which plan is the best for the given missions. In this case, it is desirable to offer a single score for each plan, i.e., the probability that a given plan can successfully accomplish the specified missions. This requires the integration of the evaluations of various trustworthiness aspects of the system and provides a holistic measurement. Thus, in this paper, we also develop techniques for integration in an attempt to provide holistic assessments.

The rest of the chapter is organized as follows. In Section 2, the ontology for trustworthiness assessment, including the system entities dimension and the trustworthiness aspects dimension, is presented. Section 3 introduces an integrated assessment framework that provides systematic assessment procedures based on the trustworthiness assessment ontology. A holistic assessment technique is introduced in Section 4. Section 5 concludes the chapter and identifies some future research directions.

2. Ontology for Trustworthiness Assessment

To deal with trustworthiness assessment of high assurance NCS, we need to deal with two dimensions of complexity. First, the NCS is highly complex, consisting of systems of systems. Each subsystem and the constituent system entities and components can be of very different characteristics. Techniques for assurance and assessment of different system entities and components can be very different. For example, methods for hardware and software reliability assurance and assessment are significantly different. Similarly, assurance and assessment of security for data and for software components involve the use of different techniques. Also, the techniques for compositional assessment of different types of components may also be different. To facilitate the management of techniques for dealing with different entities and their integrations, we construct an evolving ontology of system entities and integrations and associate various high-confidence assurance and assessment techniques with the ontology nodes.

Another complex dimension in high assurance and trustworthiness assessment is the set of metrics to be used. The requirements for achieving "high assurance, ultra dependability, and trustworthiness" for critical applications have been evolving along with the continuing advances in computer and communication environments. In the early era, hardware and software reliability, system availability, and real-time concerns were the major focus in high-assurance systems engineering. In [3], the definition of dependability is clearly elaborated. However, with the growth of computing environments, some new requirements for high-assurance systems have emerged. For example, with advances in data and knowledge mining, the concept of "privacy-preserving" capabilities has been introduced and is an increasingly essential property for high-assurance information systems. Also, Internet applications are moving toward open environments and "trust" is increasingly becoming another measure that is important in dependable computing. To cope with this problem, we develop an ontology to capture the evolving requirements in high-assurance systems. Ontology facilitates easy evolution. To differentiate from conventional dependability definitions, we use *trustworthiness* to include dependability as well as other high-assurance attributes.

Most of the trustworthiness aspects are directly or indirectly related to each other to some extent. Frequently, techniques that improve one aspect may impact some other aspects. Thus, when building the ontology of trustworthiness aspects, it is necessary to express the interdependencies and correlations among the aspects. However, existing works on categorizing dependability/trustworthiness aspects do not consider such correlations. Consider an example of the correlations between trustworthiness aspects. Redundancy is always required for achieving reliability, availability, and survivability. A higher degree of redundancy implies a higher level of reliability, availability, and survivability. On the other hand, a higher degree of redundancy can lead to more points in the system that may be vulnerable to security attacks and a higher probability that one weak point becomes compromised and, hence, results in a system having weaker security. However, this only indicates the correlations among reliability, availability, survivability, and security, but they are not directly dependent upon each other. Instead, all these aspects are dependent on redundancy. To provide a clear view of the correlations of the trustworthiness aspects in the ontology, we further define an ontology of trustworthiness evidences. The trustworthiness evidences are quantitatively or qualitatively measurable properties of the system or system entities and they are orthogonal to each other. For example, the level of redundancy and software logical correctness can be trustworthiness evidences of the system. The trustworthiness evidence ontology facilitates the expression of the correlations of trustworthiness aspects and can help optimally balance various conflicting trustworthiness aspects in the design of high-assurance systems.

Overall, we consider an integrated ontology that spans the dimension of system entities and integrations and the dimension of trustworthiness aspects with a subontology of trustworthiness evidences. The two dimensions can evolve independently and can be used together to provide a fine-grained guidance for trustworthy assessment. Trustworthiness assessment and assurance techniques can be associated with the corresponding nodes in the ontology. Current assessment techniques focus on individual types of components, such as reliability assessment for software versus reliability assessment for hardware, software aging models versus hardware degradation models, assessment of the efficacy of hardware redundancy methods versus those for software redundancy, etc. The merged ontology with associated assessment techniques can provide an organized view to link existing techniques together. It can also reveal the missing links in assessment techniques. Based on the ontology, a systematic and well guided trustworthiness assessment and verification process can be developed for large-scale NCS.

In the following subsections, the two dimensions of the ontology are discussed in detail.

2.1 Ontology of the Trustworthiness Aspects Dimension

2.1.1 Trustworthiness Aspects

A variety of trustworthiness aspects have been proposed in the literature for high-assurance systems. The fundamental requirement of any high assurance system should include reliability and availability [3].

- **Reliability:** The reliability of a system for a time interval (0,t) is the probability that the system continuously operates correctly for the entire time interval given that it is available at the start of the time interval [4, 14].

- **Availability:** The availability of a system is the probability that the system is ready for correct service when needed.

The increasing use of computing systems in automation and control applications where failures can potentially have catastrophic consequences has led to the formulation of additional trustworthiness requirements for safety-critical systems. While reliability and availability measures are concerned with the "good" or "desirable" things that the system should do, safety concerns address the "bad" things that should not happen during the operation of the system. Safety analysis techniques were first used in Inter-Continental Ballistic Missile (ICBM)-based weapon systems to ensure the absence of scenarios that could potentially lead to disastrous failures [12]. System safety is defined as follows:

- **Safety:** The safety of a system is the probability that it does not result in any catastrophic consequences for the user(s) or the environment.

With the advent of networked systems and the growing concern about cyber attacks, concerns about other "bad" things that should not happen during the operation of a system have been investigated in the context of system security. Unlike reliability, availability, and safety issues, security is an umbrella term that covers several more specific trustworthiness issues, including system integrity, confidentiality, privacy, trust, authenticity, nonrepudiability, and credibility:

- **Security:** The security of a system is the probability that it can operate correctly in spite of intentional efforts to cause it to do otherwise. It consists of several additional aspects:

  - **Integrity:** The integrity of a system is the probability that it does not have any unauthorized system alterations.
  - **Confidentiality:** The confidentiality of the system is the probability that it does not allow unauthorized disclosure of information.
  - **Privacy:** The privacy of the system is the probability that private information will not be disclosed in spite of potential inferences from multiple information sources [1, 7].
  - **Authenticity:** The authenticity of a system is the probability with which it can assure the integrity of specified data items, including the integrity of the actual content of the information as well as auxiliary associated information such as the creator of the information or its creation time.
  - **Nonrepudiability:** The nonrepudiability characteristic of a system is the probability with which it can assure the availability and integrity of information regarding the creator of a data item as well as the availability and integrity of information regarding those who access that item [8].
  - **Credibility:** The credibility of a computer system is the probability that its operation is trustworthy (i.e., well-intentioned, truthful, unbiased) and reflects adequate expertise (i.e., knowledgeable, experienced, competent) [9].

Another umbrella term in trustworthiness is system maintainability. In its original hardware context, system maintainability was a measure of the ease with which the system can be repaired in the event of a failure. This was captured by the repairability measure of the system. With software playing an increasingly important role in computer systems, maintainability now also includes other factors as described below.

- **Maintainability:** The maintainability of a system is the probability that it has the ability to undergo repairs and modifications. Maintainability can be decomposed into the following attributes:

  - **Modifiability:** The modifiability of a system is the probability that its design and implementation can be updated to add new capabilities or alter existing capabilities.
  - **Repairability:** The repairability of a system is the probability that detected faults in the system, whether due to latent development defects or due to failures caused by physical wear and tear, can be successfully corrected to restore the system to its correct operational state.
  - **Configurability:** The configurability of the system is the probability that it has adjustable parameters that can be set during its operation to enable it to function correctly under different operational situations.
  - **Adaptability:** The adaptability of a system is the probability that its design and/or implementation can be rapidly altered to enable it to function correctly under different operating conditions.
  - **Autonomy:** The autonomy of a system is the probability that the system can correctly adapt to different operating conditions by itself.

Another set of quality factors is the performance of the system, including temporal and spatial measures. These are defined as follows:

- **Performance:** There is usually a range of acceptable values for each performance attribute. The specification of the acceptable range of values for an attribute can sometimes be a fuzzy quantity [10]. For example, for hard real-time systems, such as missile control systems, the system fails if it cannot meet complete its task within a specified deadline. For soft real-time applications, however, such as net-centric conferencing systems, some missed deadlines can be tolerated [15]. In the latter case, the range is a fuzzy value.

  - **Timeliness:** This is a measure of the time taken by the system to complete its task. This is especially critical for real-time systems [5, 11].
  - **Precision:** This is a measure of the quantity of data present in the output of the system, e.g., the number of bits in a numerical value [10].
  - **Accuracy:** This is a measure of the deviation of the output of the system from the correct output [10].

Though reliability, availability, and security address several major aspects of trustworthiness, the design issues concerning these aspects generally do not scale up to catastrophic failures or attacks. With some specific types of redundancy, survivability can be an additional aspect that specifically addresses catastrophic failures or attacks.

- **Survivability:** This is defined as the probability that the system can complete its mission in a timely manner in spite of attacks, failures, and catastrophic natural disasters. It integrates security assurance techniques with risk management strategies to protect the core capabilities, such as essential services, of a net-centric system even under adverse conditions [13, 16].

A higher level grouping of these aspects includes dependability, resilience, and trustworthiness.

- **Dependability:** The dependability of a system is the probability that it delivers service that can be justifiably depended on, i.e., the probability that it will perform correctly under the specified operational and environmental conditions over a specified time period [3]. Dependability includes availability, reliability, safety, integrity, confidentiality, and maintainability.
- **Resilience:** The resilience of a system is the probability with which it can bring itself back to a correct state from an incorrect or failed state and then resume normal operation [2]. It is related to conventional fault-tolerant computing methods. Resilience aspects include maintainability and survivability.
- **Trustworthiness:** The trustworthiness of a system is the degree to which one can justifiably accept or rely upon the operation of the system [3]. Trustworthiness is a comprehensive system quality measure that includes all the dependability and resilience as well as security and performance attributes. Based on the individual trustworthiness aspects and group of aspects listed above, the ontology along the trustworthiness aspect dimension can be described above and illustrated as shown in Fig. 1.

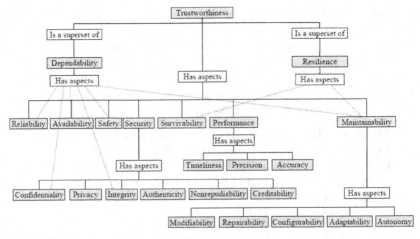

Fig. 1. High level ontology of trustworthiness aspects.

2.1.2 Trustworthiness Evidences

Many of the trustworthiness aspects are correlated. However, it is difficult to describe such correlations since it is not the case that one aspect is directly dependent on another; rather, the system trustworthiness evidences that these aspects are dependent on define the correlations among the trustworthiness aspects. We propose a novel and effective way to observe the correlations among trustworthiness aspects by defining a trustworthiness evidences ontology.

Each trustworthiness evidence defines a set of observable as well as quantitatively or qualitatively measurable properties of the system or system entities and the trustworthiness evidences are orthogonal to each other. We build different categories of trustworthiness evidences. At the top level, the trustworthiness evidence is partitioned into:

- Positive trustworthiness evidences. Positive trustworthiness evidences can be classified into many categories. Each trustworthiness evidence may be further decomposed into finer-grained trustworthiness evidences. Trustworthiness evidence can be collected to facilitate high assurance, dependability, trustworthiness assessment.
- Negative trustworthiness evidences. Negative trustworthiness evidences describe external evidences that are not within the system but may impact the system assurance. For example, faults and threats are negative trustworthiness evidences. In [3], a thorough taxonomy of faults and threats has been constructed, which can be used as the negative evidences.

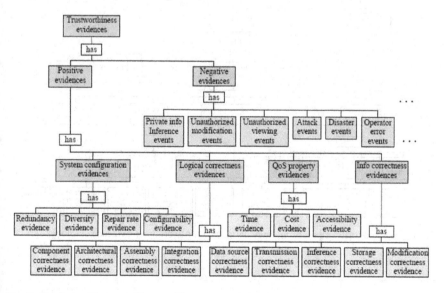

Fig. 2. Ontology of trustworthiness evidences.

The ontology of trustworthiness evidences can be quite extensive. The granularity of the evidences is determined based on whether it is possible for evidence data collection at the leaf nodes. A partial ontology is shown in Fig. 2. In this figure, some major faulty and attack evidences are included in the negative trustworthiness evidences. The positive evidences are divided into the system configuration, software logical correctness, information correctness, and QoS properties evidence sets. These positive evidences are further divided into finer grained evidences.

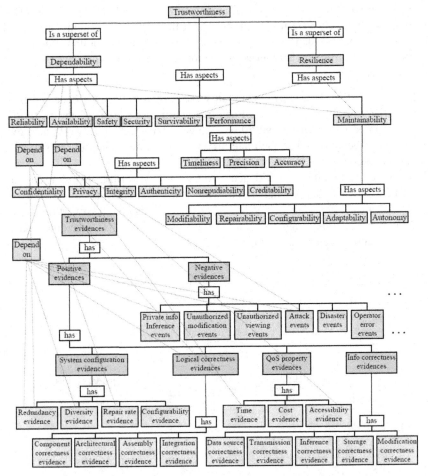

Fig. 3. Integrated trustworthiness ontology defined on trustworthiness evidence ontology.

2.1.3 Trustworthiness Ontology

The dependencies of the trustworthiness aspects on the trustworthiness evidences can be constructed by merging the high level trustworthiness aspects ontology given in Fig. 1 and the ontology of trustworthiness evidences given in Fig. 2 and drawing the dependency links from each trustworthiness aspect to the related trustworthiness evidences. The merged ontology is shown in Fig. 3.

The dependency definitions for the trustworthiness aspects given in Fig. 3 are partial and are shown only for two trustworthiness aspects, namely, availability and confidentiality. The relationship of the two trustworthiness aspects can be observed from the ontology. Some examples are as follows:

- Redundancy evidence contributes to the assessment of the availability, reliability, and confidentiality aspects. In other words, these aspects are correlated in terms of the redundancy evidence. In reality, the higher the level of redundancy, the higher will be the likelihood of a subsystem or a system entity being available. But the higher the redundancy level, the higher is the probability that one weak point in the system may be compromised.
- Attack evidences can result in unauthorized viewing evidences and unauthorized modification evidences. Thus, confidentiality and availability are both impacted due to attacks.
- Confidentiality and availability do not appear to share other trustworthiness evidences.

2.2 Ontology of the System Entities Dimension

With the rapid advances in computer and communication technologies, many application systems are shifting into the network-centric paradigm. A network-centric system typically involves a distributed set of sensors, actuators, processors, software, along with a variety of other resources interconnected together by a network and interacting with and controlled by end users. The system entities in a network-centric application can have a significant impact on the types of faults and threats and on the trustworthiness analysis. Here we define the ontology for the system entities and the relationships of their trustworthiness evidences (as shown in Fig. 4). A subsystem consists of multiple system entities and their interactions. Similarly, a system consists of subsystems and system entities and their interactions. System entities can be categorized into:

- **Computer platforms**. Each computer platform consists of the hardware and many systems software components, such as operating systems and system utilities. In this chapter, we assume that the computer platforms are connected through public or private networks.

- **Devices**. Physical devices are of many different varieties, such as various sensors and actuators, robots, unmanned or crew controlled vehicles, etc. Some devices are equipped with software control units and/or communication capabilities.
- **Communication channels**. Communication channels provide the connectivity among computer platforms, devices, and human operators and users. They can be wired, wireless, or operate across some other medium.
- **Application software and policies**. Generally, in a large-scale system, there may be a lot of application software for achieving various tasks. They may run on a single computer platform or across multiple computer platforms and devices. Also, with the network-centric nature of many modern applications, the systems are becoming multi-institutional or even multi-national. Different policies must be defined in the system to govern the system operations and resource accesses.
- **Information**. Information category can be further decomposed into raw data, metadata, semantic information, inferred knowledge, etc.
- **Human**. Humans always play an important role in large-scale systems. Most of the system interactions involve operators and users.

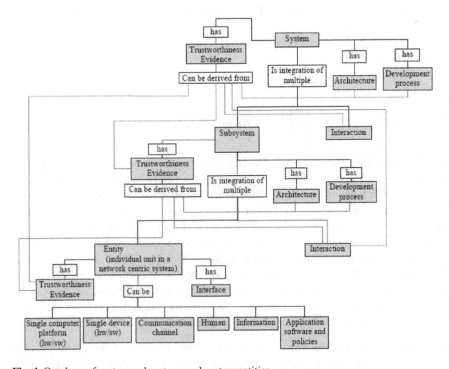

Fig. 4. Ontology of system, subsystem, and system entities.

We separate the hardware components into computer platforms and devices, though it is difficult to draw a clear line between these entities. Generally computer platforms have higher computation and storage power and have a common system structure, including the hardware, operating systems, etc., and are capable of hosting a variety of application software. On the other hand, devices are mostly specialized for specific purposes, are frequently mobile, and can vary greatly in their power. Software and policies are highly important in modern systems and they can have substantial variations. They are being placed in the same category since most policies are realized through software.

The interactions among system entities can have significant impact on the overall system trustworthiness analysis and assessment. In the literature, the analysis techniques for interactions among multiple system components have not been widely studied. This is especially true for different types of system entities. Thus, it is important to understand the possible interactions to facilitate systematic analysis and to ensure that all parts of an integrated system are covered in the assessment process. Each system entity can have interactions with another system entity. For example, software and hardware components may have close interactions. Successful completion of critical tasks requires both software and hardware to have correct behavior. Software techniques are frequently used to mask hardware failures. Hardware techniques can be used to detect and isolate software faults. Standalone subsystems interact with each other through communication channels. When delivering information via communication channels, the subsystem needs to process the information to make it suitable for delivery. Human interaction with other system entities is also a critical issue in high-assurance systems. Many system failures can be traced back to human errors [6]. Thus, it is important to investigate the human entity in high assurance systems.

System level trustworthiness evidences are defined based on the trustworthiness evidences of its entities. Methods for such derivations can be associated with the corresponding nodes in the ontology. Some of these methods can be very difficult to derive. For example, the reliability of the system depends on the way one system entity uses another. A system can be highly reliable even if some entities are faulty as long as those faults are not triggered under the system interaction patterns. Likewise, even if individual entities are highly reliable, collectively the system may lead to poor reliability due to unexpected interactions between the entities [3].

Consider an example information subsystem in a net-centric application. The system offers data, metadata, and semantics of the data and knowledge. An information system also needs to manage the access rights and host information processing software and environment. Thus, the information subsystem can consist of the following system entities.

- Devices:

  - Sensor networks that serve as one type of information sources.

- Platforms:

  - Server platforms that interface with the operators for entry of information from various sources.
  - Storage platforms that host raw data and metadata.
  - Platforms for access control management and authentication, such as certification authorities.
  - Platforms hosting data processing and knowledge inference.

- Policies:

  - Access control policies.
  - Data management and interoperation policies.

- Software:

  - Access control and authentication software.
  - Data management software.
  - Data processing software.

- Human:

  - Users who own the viewing and/or modification privileges for all or a subset of the data sets.
  - System administrators who manage the platforms, file systems, or databases.
  - System operators.

- Communication channels

  - Wireless and wired networks and communication software that link all platforms and devices together.

Besides the system entities, interactions among the system entities can also be defined. Based on these subsystems and system entities in each of the categories and interactions among the system entities, the ontology of system entities can be expanded. Some partial expansion for the example information subsystem is shown in Fig. 5.

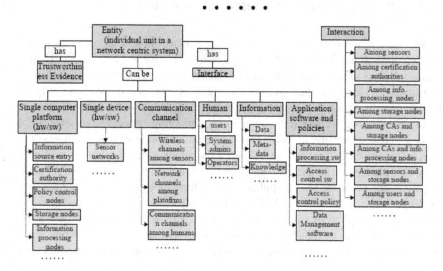

Fig. 5. Expanded ontology along the system entities dimension.

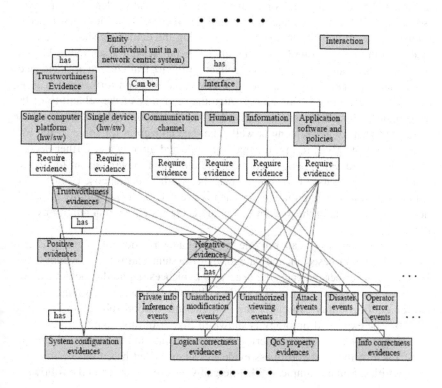

Fig. 6. Merging trustworthiness ontology and system entities ontology.

3. An Ontology-based Integrated Assessment Framework

We have developed ontologies along the trustworthiness aspects and system entities dimensions. These ontologies can be merged together to facilitate rigorous trustworthiness analysis. Merging ontologies requires the expansion of each trustworthiness evidences at the leaves of the ontology based on the system entity ontology to include the relevant system entities.

In this section, we illustrate the ontology merging process in several steps. First, a partial expansion at lower levels (system entities and trustworthiness evidences) is shown in Fig. 6. For example, the attack evidence can be applied to computer platforms, devices, software, and communication channels. An unauthorized viewing evidence can be applied to the information entity. The operator error evidence can only be applied to the human entity. The logical correctness evidence can be applied to software and policies. The information correctness evidence requires the verification of the information sources, such as from sensor networks (devices), existing information (information), or human operators and users.

The ontology can provide a clear categorization of negative evidences (faults and threats) based on the categories of system entities and evidences themselves. Also, it further indicates the necessary evidences required to achieve assurance of various system entities. Techniques for collecting the evidences should be associated with the merged ontology to facilitate overall system assessment. For example, there are many techniques for collecting the logical correctness evidences for software and hardware components, including testing and formal verification. Based on the testing or verification results, the reliability of the reliability of the corresponding component can be derived. The logical correctness evidences can be used for security assessment as well. The data collection for some of the evidences and events given in Fig. 6 cannot be collected directly and further decomposition is needed. For example, consider the undesired viewing event for the information components. This event can be further decomposed into node "compromisation" event, policy inconsistency event, etc. The probability of occurrence of these events in the system can be used for system confidentiality assessment.

The merged ontology can provide a clear categorization of negative events (faults and threats) based on the categories of system entities and events themselves. Also, it further indicates the necessary evidences required to achieve assurance of various system entities. To further illustrate the merged ontology, we expand the confidentiality aspect for the example information subsystem described in Fig. 5. The expanded ontology is shown in Fig. 7. In this example, the expansion is done partially, only considering the attack events and unauthorized viewing events. Each of the trustworthiness evidences is expanded based on the involved system entities. Some examples of the merged view are discussed in the following.

- The attack event may be applicable to platforms, devices, and communication channels. The platforms could be storage platforms, certification authorities, and nodes for data entries. Thus, for assessing confidentiality of the subsystem, trustworthiness evidence, the attack probability, for the storage platforms, the certification authority platforms, and the communication channels among them are to be considered.
- The unauthorized viewing event can be due to a compromised platform, a compromised device subsystem, a compromised communication channel, or an untrustworthy human. Also, incorrect software and policies can cause information breaches as well.

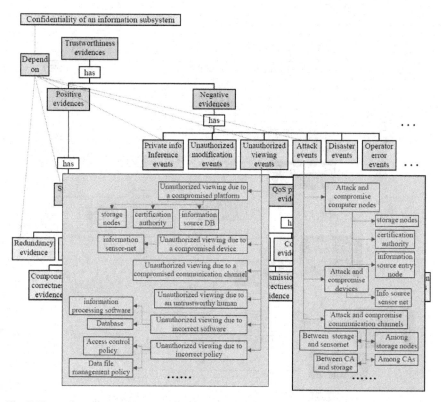

Fig. 7. Expanding trustworthiness evidences based on system entity ontology.

The merged ontology clearly indicates the evidence data to be collected for each system entity. Based on the merged ontology, the system analysis can be done in a well guided manner.

The discussion above (including Fig. 6 and 7) focuses on ontology merge of the system entities and the trustworthiness evidences. Consider the upper levels in the merged ontology. Each trustworthiness aspect of the system depends on the trustworthiness evidences of the system. The trustworthiness evidences of the system can be derived from the trustworthiness evidences of the subsystems and individual system entities. The trustworthiness of the subsystem and individual system entities can also be derived from the trustworthiness evidences of the subsystems and individual system entities, respectively. Such derivations form the basis of the ontology-driven trustworthiness evidence based integrated trustworthiness assessment technology. In Fig. 8, the derivation of trustworthiness at various levels is illustrated.

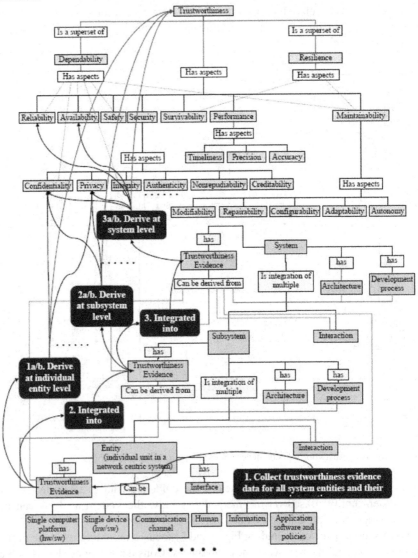

Fig. 8. Trustworthiness evidence based assessment procedure.

Based on the ontology, a systematic procedure can be used to guide system assessment and it is illustrated in the following.

- System entity level trustworthiness assessment.

  o **Step 1**: Collect trustworthiness evidence data. The first step for all trustworthiness assessment is to collect trustworthiness evidence data for each system entities. Note that earlier discussions (Fig. 6 and 7) offer more detailed guidelines for data collection for various system entities and various trustworthiness evidences.
    - If the goal is to assess the system entity level trustworthiness, then go to Step 1a.
    - If the goal is to assess the individual trustworthiness aspects at the system entity level, then go to Step 1b.
    - If the goal is to assess trustworthiness at a higher level, then go to Step 2.
  o **Step 1a**: The single trustworthiness measurement. This measurement can be derived from trustworthiness evidence collected for the system entity.
  o **Step 1b**: Measurements of each trustworthiness aspect.

- Integrated assessment for a subsystem.

  o **Step 2**: Collect or derive trustworthiness evidence data. Trustworthiness evidence data of the subsystem can be derived from the trustworthiness evidence data of the constituting system entities and the architecture that specifies the interactions among the entities. For some trustworthiness evidences, the data can be collected directly. The derivation algorithm is evidence set dependent.
    - If the goal is to assess the subsystem level trustworthiness, then go to Step 2a.
    - If the goal is to assess the individual trustworthiness aspects at the subsystem level, then go to Step 2b.
    - If the goal is to assess trustworthiness only at the overall system level, then go to Step 3.
  o **Step 2a**: The single trustworthiness measurement. This measurement can be derived from trustworthiness evidence of the subsystem.
  o **Step 2b**: Measurements of each trustworthiness aspect. The derivation formula for the measurements is aspect dependent.

- Integrated assessment for the overall system.

  o **Step 3**: Collect or derive trustworthiness evidence data. Trustworthiness evidence data of the system can be derived from the trustworthiness evidence data of the constituting subsystems and the architecture that specifies the interactions among the subsystems. The derivation algorithm is evidence type dependent.

- If the goal is to assess the system level trustworthiness, then go to Step 3a.
- If the goal is to assess the individual trustworthiness aspects at the system level, then go to Step 3b.
  o **Step 3a**: The single trustworthiness measurement. This measurement can be derived from trustworthiness evidence of the subsystem.
  o **Step 3b**: Measurements of each trustworthiness aspect.

The steps discussed above, including assessment data collection for individual system entities regarding various trustworthiness evidences, integration of the evidence data from system entities level to subsystem level and to system level, and derivation of trustworthiness aspect assessment results from the evidence data, involve various assessment techniques. To complete the framework, the merged ontology should be further expanded to include the assessment techniques. In Step 1, the techniques for evidence collection can be associated with the corresponding nodes in the merged ontology. In Steps 2 and 3, assessment of a subsystem or the overall system can be done directly at the system level. For example, testing can be conducted at the overall system level to collect evidences of its behavior and subsequently assess its trustworthiness properties. In some situations, such subsystem or system level testing and verification is infeasible. For example, in a large-scale system that is widely distributed, it may be difficult to simulate the realistic environment for testing. Also, such testing could be too costly. Further, at design time, it may often be difficult to understand the impact of selecting a certain technique or component in the overall system behavior. Since many different compositions may have to be considered, the testing of each composition is simply not possible. Thus, it is necessary to derive the system level properties from subsystem level and component level evidences. Such derivation techniques are highly challenging. Techniques for many different types of integrations are still to be investigated.

An example ontology with the assessment techniques is given in Fig. 9. The assessment techniques shown in the figure are for the reliability aspect. We consider the techniques for the integration of the trustworthiness evidences at the system entity level into the evidences at the subsystem level and direct assessment techniques at the subsystem level. For the integration of multiple system entities of the same type, we need to consider integration of software entities, integration of hardware entities, integration of communication channels, and integration of information sources (though some are not shown in the figure). In cyber world, we disregard human-human interactions and only consider humans interacting with the cyber world (mainly with software). We also consider integration of system entities of different types, such as integrating hardware and software, software and human, software and information, human and information, etc. Most of the existing techniques in reliability assurance and assessment are based on integrated testing.

The integrated assessment framework is flexible and expandable. Each dimension has its own ontology which can evolve independently. Expansion from the nodes in the merged ontology can be linked to the nodes in the individual ontologies. The ontologies can be customized to fit the needs of the special applications.

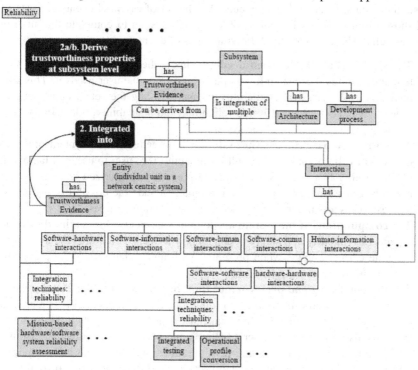

Fig. 9. Ontology with integrated assessment techniques.

4. Holistic Assessment Techniques

The goal of the framework discussed in Section 3 is to provide a comprehensive guidance toward systematic assessment of integrated systems considering various trustworthiness aspects. One important assessment that is frequently demanded is a holistic view of the overall system or subsystem. For example, a commander may demand a single "score" to represent the trustworthiness of a system. When a third party delivers a product, the manager may want to know the level of assurance in a holistic view, instead individual aspects. It is difficult to give such a single "score" in a rigorous way. In this section, we define a mission-driven integration method to integrate multiple aspects into one single measure of the trustworthiness of the NCS, which indicates the probability of success of the given missions. The assessment is based on a collection of events that can impact the degree to which one can use the system to successfully accomplish all the specified mission objectives. These events are classified into two categories, namely, essential events, E, and adverse events, A. The set of essential events consists of all those events that must occur in order for the system to complete the mission successfully. These include the following types of events:

- **The system is available when needed:** This is the first step in using the system and requires the system to be operational when the user needs it. This corresponds to the classical availability measure among the set of dependability aspects. It is also affected by the reliability, maintainability, adaptability, and reconfigurability qualities of the system.
- **An authorized user can use the system when needed:** This event ensures that the system will not make it difficult for an authorized user to use it. It factors in the possibility that security measures to prevent unauthorized accesses could pose obstacles for legitimate users. Examples include the possibility of forgotten passwords and failures of biometric authentication systems.
- **The computations of the system are logically correct:** This is related to some aspects of reliability and safety dependability aspects. It requires the system to generate correct outputs when presented with inputs that satisfy the preconditions of the system.
- **The system timing and performance qualities are acceptable:** This is related to performance issues in addition to reliability and safety issues. It is a critical requirement for real-time systems that must generate outputs in a timely manner. It is also important in other situations and encompasses classical termination requirements, i.e., the requirement that the system must not have any infinite loops or be susceptible to deadlocks, livelocks, etc. In terms of real-time performance, it may be possible to specify the tolerance of missed deadlines, as well as the tolerance of the quality of a result to meet deadlines.
- **The cost and resource requirements of the system are acceptable:** This corresponds to the practicality of the system. For example, if the system requires too many processors in order to complete its computations on time, then it may be reliable but not practical.

The second class of events is the set of adverse events, i.e., events that should probably not occur if the system is to be able to complete its mission successfully. The occurrence of an adverse event does not automatically mean that the system will not be able to complete its mission successfully for the specified mission. Instead, it decreases the probability that the system will be successful. The potential adverse events are as follows:

- **Unauthorized users can access the system:** This is a part of the security requirements of the system. For safety-critical system, it can also lead to safety assurance issues since a malicious unauthorized user could deliberately lead the system to an unsafe state. In practice, the authentication problem is more complicated since an authorized user for some capabilities of the system may be an unauthorized user for other features. For example, an authorized user of the system may be able to view and update some confidential information in the system but may not be allowed to reconfigure the system while another authorized user (such as a system administrator) may be able to reconfigure the system but may not be allowed to access any confidential information in the system.

- **The system triggers operator or user errors:** This is related to the usability aspects of the system. Human errors are often significant causes of failures of systems. These can be prevented by better human factors design as well as the use of sanity checks and other methods of detecting potential user errors. Increasing the system autonomy, as in the design of autonomic or self-stabilizing systems, can help alleviate the stress on the users and, hence, reduce human errors, especially with regard to system adaptation and configuration changes.

- **The system or the environment enters an unsafe state:** Malfunctions in systems that control the physical world via actuators can potentially lead to catastrophic losses of lives and/or property. Such systems are called safety-critical systems and must be designed and certified to be highly safe. Safety is independent of reliability. A classical example is that of a stalled car parked in an area that is away from other traffic. It is fully unreliable but it is safe. Likewise, a car being controlled by a small child can be very reliable but can also be very unsafe.

- **The system information regarding the state, input, output, or code can be viewed by others:** This is a security related attribute and corresponds to the confidentiality and privacy dependability assurance properties of the system. Methods such as data partitioning, code obfuscation, data encryption, etc., can be used to prevent retrieval of confidential or private information by hackers and other adversaries.

- **System information regarding the state, input, output, or code can be changed by others:** This is a security and resilience related aspect corresponding to integrity aspects of the system. Depending on the potential threats, as well as the sources of these threats, various mechanisms can be used to protect the integrity of the system. These include the use of redundancies, error detection codes, write-once memory devices, continuous monitoring, proof carrying codes, etc.

- **The system provides additional functionalities:** This is also a security related issue and corresponds to embedded malicious logic, "Trojan horses", and other extra functions, i.e., functions that are in addition to the ones specified in the requirements specification document. These are difficult to detect, especially if embedded by insiders during the development process. The system can be verified to be logically correct and shown to meet all non-functional requirements, but it may contain additional capabilities that could be exploited to subvert the system. An example is an extra functionality in the system that causes it to transmit a lot of redundant data at critical occasions, thereby overloading the network and other computers.

The integrated assessment of a system for a specific mission requires the following information:

- For each essential event, methods have to be used to determine the probability of occurrence of that event. For example, consider the event, "The system is available when needed." In this case, the corresponding probability that must be determined is the probability that the system is available when needed. For some of the events, formal methods, including verification and analysis techniques, can be used to fully guarantee the occurrence of that event, in which case the corresponding probability is 1.0.
- For each adverse event, various methods have to be used to determine the probability of occurrence of that event. The probability of occurrence of an adverse event depends not only on the intrinsic capabilities of the system and the platform but also the likelihood of the sources of the corresponding threats. For example, the probability that an unauthorized user will be able to access the system is 0 if it can be guaranteed that there are no unauthorized users in the environment. A specific example would be a system deployed in a highly secure building that is protected by guards and locked doors.
- For each adverse event, determine the "criticality" of the event. The criticality of an adverse event ranges from 0 to 1. It is 0 if the event is fully acceptable, i.e., if the occurrence of the event has no consequence on the successful completion of the mission. It is 1 if the event is fully unacceptable, i.e., if the occurrence of the event will definitely lead to a failure of the system. The criticality of each event is a fuzzy quantity and must be specified as part of the requirements for the mission.

The overall assurance level of the system for the specified mission is given by the probability that the mission will be completed successfully after factoring in all the possible essential and adverse events:

P{the specified mission will be completed successfully} =

$$\prod_{i=1}^{n} P(e_i \mid e_i \in \mathbf{E}) * \prod_{j=1}^{m} \{1 - \sigma_j * P(e_j \mid e_j \in \mathbf{A})\},$$

where σ_j is the criticality of adverse event e_j, for $1 \leq j \leq m$. σ_j ranges from 0 to 1 with 0 indicating that the occurrence of event e_j will not have any adverse consequences for the specified mission and 1 indicating that the occurrence of the event will definitely lead to failure of the mission. The overall result is one number that characterizes the overall effectiveness or assurance level of the system for accomplishing a given mission. This can be used to rank the potential candidates for implementing the system to enable the selection of the best candidate, i.e., the one that has the highest chance of success.

Often, it is necessary to be able to rank a collection of assets that are predeployed with the goal of supporting a range of potential missions that may arise in the future rather than any given specific mission. In this case, the integrated assessment is based on the expected (average) value of the capability of the asset to support the specified set of possible missions. This yields,

P(the asset can support the set of specified missions) =

$$\Sigma_{k=1}^{n} \text{ P(mission k can be completed successfully using the asset)}|(\text{mission k occurs}).$$

The overall result can then be used to select between different candidate set of assets, i.e., the one that is the most capable in supporting the specified set of missions.

5. Summary and Future Research Directions

We have introduced the concept of trustworthiness to include dependability and a comprehensive set of other high assurance attributes. A trustworthiness ontology is developed to capture the trustworthiness aspects and their correlations as well as to model various classes of system entities and their integrations. The ontology provides information to guide the trustworthiness analysis and data collection. Based on the ontology, a trustworthiness assessment framework is developed. In the framework, systematic steps are formulated to achieve trustworthiness assessments. Techniques and tools to perform the assessments in each step are incorporated in the ontology to allow the actual analysis and derivation of assessment results.

We have also identified some missing links in assessments techniques and developed a holistic assessment technique to provide a single overall measure of the trustworthiness of a system or a subsystem.

Future research includes two major directions. First, we plan to analyze the current techniques and tools for each step of the trustworthiness assessment. Based on the ontology, we will identify areas that require further research for new or better analysis techniques. Second, we plan to develop integration based assessment techniques to facilitate assessment of large-scale systems from trustworthiness attributes of their individual subsystems with known trustworthiness assessment. We also plan to develop assessment techniques with holistic views for different levels of NCS systems.

References

1. Mark S. Ackerman, Lorrie Faith Cranor, Joseph Reagle, "Privacy in e-commerce: examining user scenarios and privacy preferences," Proceedings of the 1st ACM conference on Electronic commerce, Denver, Colorado, 1999, pp. 1-8.
2. T. Anderson, *Resilient Computing Systems*, John-Wiley, New York, 1985.

3. A. Avizienis, J.-C. Laprie, B. Randell, and C. Landwehr, "Basic concepts and taxonomy of dependable and secure computing," *IEEE Trans. on Dependable and Secure Computing*, Vol. 1, No. 1, Jan.-Mar. 2004, pp. 11-33.

4. F. B. Bastani and A. Pasquini, "Assessment of a sampling method for measuring safety-critical software reliability," *Proceedings of 5th International Symposium on Software Reliability Engineering*, November 1994, pp. 93-102.

5. A.M.K. Cheng, Real-Time Systems: Scheduling, Analysis, and Verification, Wiley Interscience, 2002.

6. Mike Chen, Emre Kıcıman, Eugene Fratkin, Eric Brewer, and Armando Fox, "Pinpoint: Problem determination in large, dynamic Internet services," Dependable Systems and Networks, 2002.

7. Julie E. Cohen, "DRM and privacy," Communications of the ACM (Special issue on digital rights management and fair use by design), Vol. 46, No. 4, April 2003, pp. 46-49

8. Riccardo Focardi, Fabio Martinelli, "A uniform approach for the definition of security properties," World Congress on Formal Methods, 1999.

9. B.J. Fogg and H. Tseng, "The elements of computer credibility," Proc. 1999 SIGCHI Conf. on Human Factors in Computing Systems, Pittsburgh, PA, 1999, pp. 80-87.

10. T.F. Lawrence, "The quality of service model and high assurance," Proc. 1997 IEEE High-Assurance Systems Engineering Workshop, Washington, DC, Aug. 1997, pp. 38-39.

11. E. A. Lee and S. Edwards., "Precision Timed (PRET) Computation in Cyber-Physical System", National Workshop on High Confidence Software Platforms for Cyber-Physical Systems: Research Needs and Roadmap, November, 2006.

12. N. Leveson, Software: System Safety and Computers, Addison Wesley, New York, 1995.

13. H.F. Lipson and D.A. Fisher, "Survivability - A new technical and business perspective on security," Proc. 1999 workshop on New security Paradigms, Caledon Hills, Ontario, Canada, 1999, pp. 33-39.

14. B. Littlewood and L. Strigini, "Software reliability and dependability: A roadmap," *Proceedings of the 22nd International Conference on Software Engineering*, Limerick, Ireland, A. Finkelstein (ed), June 2000, pp. 177-188.

15. J.W.S. Liu, Real-Time Systems, Prentice Hall, 2000.

16. J. McDermott, "Attack-potential-based survivability modeling for high-consequence systems," 2005. Proc. 3rd IEEE Intl. Work. on Information Assurance (IWIA'05), March 2005, pp. 119-130.

17. R. A. Paul, "DoD towards software services," *Proceedings of the 10th IEEE International Workshop on Object-Oriented Real-Time Dependable Systems*, February 2005, pp. 3-6.

18. G. Vecellio and W. M. Thomas, "Issues in the assurance of component-based software," Proc. 2000 IEEE Intl. Work.on Component-Based Software Engineering, Limerick, Ireland, Jun. 2000.

19. J. Voas, "Certifying software for high-assurance environments," IEEE Software, Vol. 16, No. 4, Jul./Aug. 1999, pp. 48-54.

Chapter 3

A Trust Monitoring Architecture for Service-Based Software

Mohammad Gias Uddin* and Mohammad Zulkernine**

* Dept. of Electrical and Computer Engineering, Queen's University,

Kingston, Canada K7L 3N6. Email: gias@cs.queensu.ca

** School of Computing, Queen's University,

Kingston, Canada K7L 3N6. Email: mzulker@cs.queensu.ca

Abstract. Service-based software can be misused by potentially untrustworthy service requestors while providing services. A service-based system is usually dynamic due to mutual collaboration among stakeholders to achieve goals, perform tasks and manage resources. However, it lacks the presence of a central authority to monitor the trustworthiness of service users. In this chapter, we propose a trust monitoring architecture, called TrAM (**Tr**ust **A**rchitecture for **M**onitoring) to monitor the trustworthiness of service users at run-time, facilitating the analysis of interactions from trust perspectives. Monitoring allows the enforcement of corrective actions that may protect the software by mitigating major unwanted incidents. The performance of the architecture has been evaluated by monitoring a prototype file-sharing grid.

1. Introduction

In service-based software systems, stakeholders are scattered across different organizational domains, and they can join and leave the systems at any time. A service-based system usually operates through spontaneous interactions with limited reliance on a specific central control authority. This inherent nature of decentralization introduces security concerns as software may be exploited by potentially untrustworthy stakeholders on whom the software has minimal or no control. Uncertainty is prevalent due to its open nature, so it may not be always sufficient to use '*hard security*' mechanisms to protect services from malicious and unwanted incidents. For example, illegal access to resources can be avoided using access control mechanisms. However, a malicious user with access to system resources from several administrative boundaries can still use different services that may

J. Dong et al. (eds.), *High Assurance Services Computing*,

DOI 10.1007/978-0-387-87658-0_3, © Springer Science+Business Media, LLC 2009

provide that user with ample opportunities to break into the system. Given that, a trust monitoring architecture is necessary for the run-time analysis of the services based on the trustworthiness of the service requesters.

Trust is considered as 'soft security' and it is "a particular level of the subjective probability with which an agent assesses that another agent or group of agents will perform a particular action" [1, 2]. Trust incorporates risk analysis to examine potential risks or opportunities the interactions may invite to the total system. In this chapter, we present a monitoring architecture for analyzing service interactions from trust perspectives by identifying the contexts of trust concerns in trust rules that are prevalent in such interactions. A trust rule snapshots system events encapsulating a service outcome that is crucial to the target system from trust perspectives [6]. The proposed architecture is called TrAM (**T**rust **A**rchitecture for **M**onitoring), and it may reside in each service providing software. The architecture allows the analysis of the trustworthiness of users based on trust rules and calculation schemes [6, 7]. A service requestor is penalized for the violation of trust rules and rewarded for no such violations, which thus facilitates the quantification of the trustworthiness of the corresponding entities. Collaborative decision making is introduced by incorporating the recommendations from similar service providers. The performance overhead of the architecture has been evaluated based on the monitoring of a prototype trust-aware file-sharing grid.

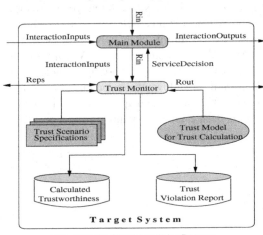

Rin = Incoming Recommendation Requests
Rout = Outgoing Recommendation Requests
Reps = Recommendation Replies

Fig. 1. Working environment of the monitoring architecture

Fig. 1 presents an overview of the trust monitoring architecture, where the target system is any service provider. An interaction is initiated when a service user requests a service. The events received from requestors by the Main Module of a provider are called *InteractionInputs*. The provider uses the Trust Monitor to analyze the interactions with the requestors which are forwarded to it by the Main Module. For a service request, the Trust Monitor provides a decision (*ServiceDe-*

cision) on whether to grant the service or not. Upon the granting of services, the monitor analyzes interaction events related to the corresponding session based on trust scenario specifications represented as trust rules at run-time. Based on this analysis, the trust monitor provides another *ServiceDecision* specifying whether the interaction is successful or not. The Main Module sends replies in the form of *InteractionOutputs* to the requestors according to the *ServiceDecision*. The requestor is penalized with a distrust value if any trust rule is violated in one of the interaction events, while it is awarded a trust value if no such violation occurs. The Main Module receives incoming recommendation requests (*Rin*) from other service providers and forwards those to the Trust Monitor which can send recommendation requests to others through *Rout*. Moreover, the Trust Monitor receives or sends recommendation replies through *Reps*. The calculated trust values are stored in the repositories. Alert reports are generated and logged for any violation of a trust rule.

The rest of the chapter is organized as follows. The monitoring architecture is described in detail in Section 2. Section 3 provides the implementation and evaluation. In Section 4, the proposed architecture is compared and contrasted with the related work. Section 5 identifies the limitations and future research directions.

2. TrAM: The Trust Architecture for Monitoring

TrAM (Trust Architecture for Monitoring) is composed of a number of modules to analyze and calculate the trustworthiness of stakeholders and make trust-based run-time decisions. The architecture is presented in Fig. 2, and the modules and the related entities are described in detail in this section.

InteractionInputs are service request events (*sRQ*) or service session events (*sSN*). Upon the granting of a service to a user by a provider, a service session is initiated, during which the user and the provider exchange information related to the granted service. The events related to the session are called service session events (*sSN*). The Event Dispatcher of the Main Module receives the *sRQ* and the *sSN* as primary inputs. A provider makes a recommendation request (*rRQ*) to other providers about the requestor and receives recommendation replies (*rRP*) from other providers. The secondary inputs to the Event Dispatcher are the recommendation requests from other service providers through *Rin*.

The *sRQ*s are forwarded to the Trust Engine, and *sSN*s to the Trust State Analyzer of the Trust Monitor. The *Rin*s are forwarded to the Recommendation Engine, from where *rRQ*s are sent as *Rout* to other providers. The replies to recommendat- ion requests (*rRP*) are received and sent by the Recommendation Engine through *Reps*. The Trust Engine provides decisions to grant or reject service request (*i.e.*, *sRQ*s), while the Trust State Analyzer checks *sSN*s against possible trust rules and provides decisions based on the state of the risk outcomes of the interaction. The Trust Decision Notifier forwards decisions from the Trust Engine and the Trust State Analyzer to the Trust Actions of the Main Module, from which service replies are provided as *sRP*s through *InteractionOutputs* to requestors. Every provider has a `ServiceDescriptor.xml` file to describe provided services and a `ServiceTrustContext.xml` file to designate corresponding trust rules.

A snippet of `ServiceDescriptor.xml` is provided in Fig. 3. The target system is a provider with ID *sp1*, offering file sharing services (*i.e.*, file upload, search, open, and download) to requestors. One of the provided services is *UploadDoc-File* to upload documents to the server. The required parameters (*i.e.*, `service-param`) are *fileName*, *fileSize*, *fileType* and *fileContents*. *sp1* employs constraints on this service which users need to follow while uploading documents. The constraints are specified in the `ServiceConstraints` tag, such as *fileSize.maxPOST* which limits the maximum file-size in the server, lest malicious users upload files of very large size to waste server space, possibly making the upload service unavailable to other users. The trust rules follow the corresponding `ServiceConstraints` in the corresponding risk state space construction.

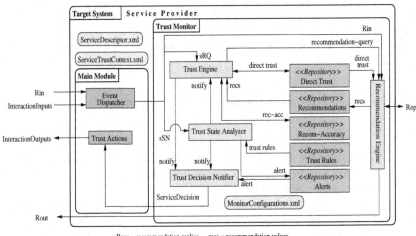

Fig. 2. TrAM : Trust Architecture for Monitoring

```
<?xml version = "1.0" encoding = "UTF-8"?>
<TargetSystem name = "FileServer" id = "sp1">
  <ProvidedServices>
    <ProvidedService
        service-params = "fileName, fileSize, fileType, fileContents">UploadDocFile
    </ProvidedService>
    ...
  </ProvidedServices>
  <ServiceConstraints>
    <ServiceConstraint fileSize.maxPOST = "100MB">UploadDocFile</ServiceConstraint>
    ...
  </ServiceConstraints>
</TargetSystem>
```

Fig. 3. A snippet of ServiceDescriptor.xml

A snippet of `ServiceTrustContext.xml` is presented in Fig. 4. The `interac-tion- threshold` is used to denote the minimum trust value necessary for a user to be of fered the service; in this case, if the user has a previous total trust value greater than or equal to 0.52, the *UploadDocFile* service will be granted to the user. The trust rules to analyze the *UploadDocFile* service are "`FileExcess`", "`FileHarmful`" and "`UploadCompletion`". The `class-ids` in each of the trust rules designate the corresponding module used to deploy the corresponding trust rule. The `FileExcess` trust rule checks whether the uploaded file meets the server maximum file size constraint (*i.e.*, `fileSize.maxPOST`). A user may accidentally try to upload such large file once or twice. However, if the user executes such attempts beyond an acceptable limit, it surely is untrustworthy and should be considered carefully before granting any further uploading service. If this rule is violated, the requestor is penalized by a *disbelief* value of *medium* as denoted by `category` and `importance` respectively. The `AccpetableLimit` of such misbehavior is 3, *i.e.*, the user will be warned (`action = "WARNING"`) for such misbehavior up to three times, after which the service will not offered to the corresponding user anymore for the particular interaction[1]. The "`FileHarmful`" trust rule examines the uploaded file for any harmful contents (e.g., virus-infected file or the presence of any objectionable contents in the *fileContents*) and has `importance` value set as *high* with `action` as *terminate* and `AcceptableLimit` as 1, interpreted as follows: the service offering of uploading doc file will be terminated (`action = "TERMINATE"`) to the corresponding user as soon as (`AcceptableLimit = "1"`) the uploaded file is detected as harmful, and also the user will be penalized a disbelief value (`category = "disbelief"`) of high for such misbehavior (`importance = "high"`). The "`UploadCompletion`" trust rule checks for the successful completion of the service. This trust rule is not violated if the user uploads files maintaining all the service constraints; that is, if the `FileExcess` and the `FileHarmful` trust rules are not violated. If this trust rule (*i.e.*, `UploadCompletion`) is not violated, the requestor is awarded a belief (`category = "belief"`) value of high (`importance = "high"`). Moreover, the interaction with the user will be considered as trustworthy as soon as (`AcceptableLimit = "1"`) the user uploads legitimate doc file, and will be sent a notification of successful interaction (`action = "SUCCESSFUL"`).

The Main Module has two parts: Event Dispatcher and Trust Actions. All the incoming events are received by the Event Dispatcher and forwarded to the different modules of the Trust Monitor. The incoming events to the Event Dispatcher are of three types: service requests (*sRQ*), service sessions (*sSN*), and recommendation requests (*rRQ*). Upon receipt of an event, the module delegates a *sRQ* to the Trust Engine, *sSN* to the trust state analyzer, and *rRQ* to the Recommendation Engine of the Trust Monitor. The Trust Actions module provides service replies to requestors by following the *ServiceDecisions* obtained from the Trust Decision Notifier of the Trust Monitor. For example, based on a *sRQ*, the module can offer or reject services, or based on an *sSN*, the module can terminate an unsatisfactory interaction.

---

[1] The values of different attributes and constants will depend on the corresponding target system.

```
<?xml version = "1.0" encoding = "UTF-8"?>
<ServiceTrustContexts>
    <Service name = "UploadDocFile" interaction-threshold = "0.52">
        <trust-rules>
            <trust-rule class-id = "ChkFileExcess"
                category = "disbelief" importance = "MEDIUM"
                AcceptableLimit = "3" action = "WARNING">FileExcess</trust-rule>
            <trust-rule class-id = "ChkFileHarmful"
                category= "disbelief" importance = "HIGH"
                AcceptableLimit = "1" action = "TERMINATE">FileHarmful</trust-rule>
            <trust-rule class-id = "SuccessfulDocUpload"
                category= "belief" importance = "HIGH"
                AcceptableLimit = "1" action = "SUCCESSFUL">UploadCompletion</trust-rule>
        </trust-rules>
    </Service>
    ...
</ServiceTrustContexts>
```

Fig. 4. A snippet of ServiceTrustContext.xml

The Trust Monitor analyzes interactions, calculates the trustworthiness of the interacting entities and makes decisions. It has four basic sub-modules: the Trust State Analyzer, the Trust Engine, the Recommendation Engine, and the Trust Decision Notifier. The sub-modules are discussed in the following subsections. To substantiate these discussions, we show three most prevalent scenarios using sequence diagrams: user requesting a service (Fig. 5), user violating a trust rule (Fig. 6), and user performing a trustworthy interaction (Fig. 7).

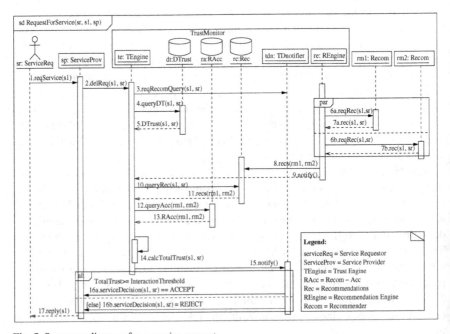

Fig. 5. Sequence diagram for a service request

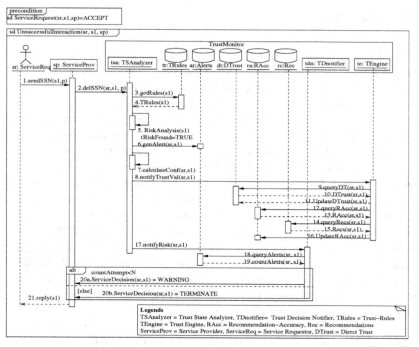

Fig. 6. Sequence diagram for a user violating a trust rule

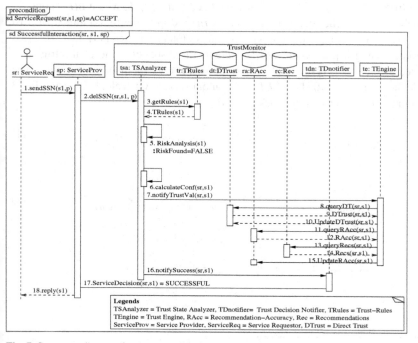

Fig. 7. Sequence diagram for a user performing trustworthy interactions

2.1 Trust State Analyzer

This module constructs trust-based risk state space to analyze service session events (sSNs) using trust rules from the Trust Rules repository. Upon the arrival of a service session event, this module checks the event outcome against all possible trust rules. Based on the result of the check, the module notifies the Trust Engine about the confidence (μ) it has gained from the interaction. Whenever a trust rule is violated, this module generates an alert in the Alerts repository. An alert has the form {sr, s_i, r, sID, t_{alert}}, where sr is the requestor, s_i is the requested service, r is the trust rule that is being violated, sID is the ID of the session in which the violation was detected, and t_{alert} is the time when alert was generated based on the identification of potential risks in the corresponding interactions.. If a trust rule is violated the corresponding interaction is determined as unsatisfactory; otherwise, it is considered as satisfactory. The Trust Decision Notifier is notified of this potential risk-state info in the interaction status and makes decisions accordingly. The Trust Engine is notified of a confidence value only when a potential risk state is confirmed through the convergence to a confirmed untrustworthy state. However, the user is warned each time a potential risk is found in the corresponding interaction that is deemed as suspicious but requires further analysis. The Trust Decision Notifier is notified of any potential risk state information. In addition, the Trust Decision Notifier is notified of any successful interaction with service users. The total belief (I_b) (range [0, 1]) of provider E1 on requestor E2 for service s_i at time t from interaction I (i.e., sRQ) is calculated using Eq. 1, where B(rn) contains the belief value of the trust rule indexed as rn, and n_b is the total number of trust rule(s) related to belief outcome(s)[2]. Similarly, total disbelief I_d (range [0, 1]) is calculated using Eq. 2, where D(rn) contains the disbelief value of the trust rule indexed as rn, and n_d is the total number of trust rules with disbelief outcome. The confidence (μ) (range [0, 1]) of E1 on E2 about service s_i is calculated using Eq. 3 (w_b (range [0, 1]) as the weight assigned to I_b.)

$$I_b(E1, E2, s_i, t) = \frac{d(E1, E2, s_i, t)}{n_d}, where \ d(E1, E2, s_i, t) = \sum_{rn=0}^{n_d} B(rn) \tag{1}$$

$$I_b(E1, E2, s, t) = \frac{b(E1, E2, s, t)}{n_b}, where \ b(E1, E2, s, t) = \sum_{rn=0}^{n_b} B(rn) \tag{2}$$

$$\mu(E1, E2, s_i, t) = w_b I_b(E1, E2, s_i, t) + (1 - w_b) I_d(E1, E2, s_i, t) \tag{3}$$

---

[2] For the sake of simplicity, we denote both the provider and the requestor as entities (E).

2.2 Trust Engine

This module performs two tasks. First, based on the feedback on confidence (μ) from the Trust State Analyzer, it calculates and updates direct trust and the corresponding recommendation accuracies. Second, it calculates total trust using direct trust, recommendations and recommendation accuracies that are used by the Trust Decision Notifier to provide decisions on service requests (sRQ). Whenever the Trust State Analyzer provides confidence from an interaction, direct trust is calculated, updated, and stored in the Direct Trust repository. The previous direct trust value is retrieved from the repository, updated based on the new confidence value and then stored into the repository. This new direct trust is the compared against the previous recommendations from the Recommendations repository that were used to make service granting decision to the corresponding service user. The comparison facilitates the understanding of the provider on the accuracies of the corresponding recommendations in its decision making phases. The recommendation accuracies are stored in the Recom-Accuracy repository. If the measured accuracy falls below a pre-determined recommendation-accuracy accuracy threshold, the corresponding recommendation is considered as unreliable for the particular type of interactions. However, it should be noted that the measure of recommendation accuracy is not used as determining the trustworthiness of the corresponding recommenders; rather its purpose is to identify the reliability of recommendations in a particular provider decision state space. In following the context-awareness nature of trust [7] that "a recommender $r1$ may not be reliable to a provider $sp1$ for a service s_i, but it may still be considered as reliable for another service s_j ($i \neq j$)" and "based on the deployment of a recommendation accuracy in different providers, a recommender $r1$ may considered as unreliable in provider $sp1$ for service s_i, but it may still be regarded as reliable in the provider $sp2$ for the same service". The direct trust T_D (range [0, 1]) of $E1$ on $E2$ for service s_i at time t is calculated using Eq. (4), where δ (range [0, 1]) is a weighting factor. The value of T_D thus changes after each interaction based on the outcome of the interaction.

$$T_D(E1, E2, s_i, t) = \delta T_D(E1, E2, s_i, t-1) + (1-\delta)\mu(E1, E2, s_i, t) \qquad (4)$$

The accuracy (A) (range [0, 1]) of a recommender $E3$ in providing a recommendation to a provider $E1$ about requestor $E2$ regarding service s_i is calculated using Eq. 5, where $\Delta R(E3, E1, E2, s_i, t)$ calculates the difference between the provided recommendation and the calculated direct trust. The calculation of recommendation-accuracy follows [8], but tailored to service attributes in TrAM. $R(E3, E1, E2, s_i, t)$ denotes the recommendation value provided by $E3$ to $E1$ about $E2$ regarding service s_i at time t. Each provider keeps an accuracy table (AT) in the Recom-Accuracy repository, where it updates the accuracy of every recommendation after the corresponding interaction. The accuracy of $E3$ to $E1$ about $E2$ regarding service s_i at time t in the AT is denoted by $AT(E3, E1, E2, s_i, t)$. The update in the *AT* is performed using Eq. 6 by considering previous recommendation accuracy (*AT (E3, E1, E2, s_i, t−1)*) and new recommendation accuracy (*A (E3, E1, E2, s_i, t)*). ζ (Range [1, 0]) weights the importance of previous and current accuracies. Using Eq. 5, and 6, unreliable recommendations are detected. A recommender is considered as most reliable with accuracy 1 and most unreliable with accuracy 0.

$$A(E3, E1, E2, s_i, t) = 1 - \Delta R(E3, E1, E2, s_i, t),$$ (5)

$$where, \nabla R(E1, E2, s_i, t) = | R(E3, E1, E2, s_i, t) - T_D(E1, E2, s_i, t)|$$

$$AT(E3, E1, E2, si, t) = \zeta AT(E3, E1, E2, s_i, t - 1) + (1 - \zeta)A(E3, E1, E2, s_i, t)$$ (6)

The calculation of total trust is a function of direct trust, recommendation and recommendation-accuracy [7,8], and is used to make the trust-based service granting decision for an *sRQ*. The Trust Decision Notifier is informed of this trust value.

2.3 Recommendation Engine

This module provides a recommendation reply (*rRP*) in response to a recommendation request (*rRQ*), receives recommendations from other providers, and stores the recommendation values in the Recommendations repository. A recommendation value is at most equal to the corresponding direct trust value to avoid any overstating about users in the system [8]. For example, if a provider has a direct trust value of 0.8 on a user about a particular service, it should provide a recommendation value no greater than 0.8.

2.4 Trust Decision Notifier

This module provides the Trust Actions module the *ServiceDecicion* it obtains from the Trust Engine and Trust State Analyzer. A service request is granted if the calculated total trust value from the Trust Engine is at least equal to the interaction threshold of the requested service, otherwise the request is rejected. A *ServiceDecision* is constructed as {*sr, s_i,* Accept, *t*}, if the request for service s_i from requestor *sr* is accepted at time *t*, or as {*sr, s,*Reject, *t*} if it is rejected. Based on the notification of any potential risk outcome in an interaction, such as the detection of file uploading beyond the server allowed maximum file size using the FileExcess trust rule, the Trust Decision Notifier queries the Alerts database to determine the total number of such misbehavior from the corresponding user for the particular service. This total number is then compared against sever allowed such maximum attempts (*i.e.*, `AcceptableLimit`) in `ServiceTrustContext.xml` (recall Fig. 4). If the total number of such misbehavior falls below the acceptable limit, the Trust Decision Notifier constructs a *ServiceDecision* as {*sr*, s_i, *Unsatisfactory*, `WARNING`, `FileExcess`, *sID*, *t*} to give warning to the corresponding requestor *sr* of the unsatisfactory interaction between them, but continues to offer the s_i service to the user (*i.e.*, *UploadDocFile*). Here, *sr* is service- user; *sID* is the ID of the corresponding session that was initiated between the provider and requestor for the service s_i. However, if the number of such attempts reaches the acceptable limit, the interaction with the user for the particular service usage is terminated by providing a *ServiceDecision* as {*sr*, s_i, *Unsatisfactory*, `TERMINATE`, `FileExcess`, *sID*, *t*}. A *ServiceDecision* is constructed as {*sr*, *s*, *Satisfactory*, *sID*, *t*} if the interaction was successful without violating any trust rules.

```
<?xml version = "1.0" encoding = "UTF-8"?>
<Configuration Version = "1.0">
    <RecommenderList>
        <Service name = "UploadDocFile" last-modified = "2008-07-31">
            <Recommender-id>sp2</Recommender-id>
            <Recommender-id>sp3</Recommender-id>
            <Recommender-id>sp4</Recommender-id>
        </Service>
    </RecommenderList>
    <Constants>
        <EquationConstants>
            <EquationConstant wb = "0.8" wd ="0.2">Confidence</EquationConstant>
            <EquationConstant delta = "0.8">DirectTrust</EquationConstant>
            <EquationConstant delta = "0.8">DirectTrust</EquationConstant>
            <EquationConstant zeta = "0.8">Recommendation-Accuracy</EquationConstant>
        </EquationConstants>
    </Constants>
</Configuration>
```

Fig. 8. A snippet of MonitorConfigurations.xml

The `MonitorConfigurations.xml` file denotes the list of recommenders and the constant values used in the trust equations. A snippet of the `MonitorConfigurati ions.xml` is provided in Fig. 8. The `RecommenderList` tag shows the list of recommenders to whom *sp1* asks for recommendations for a particular service, such as *UploadDocFile*. The provider continuously refreshes its database to update the list of such recommenders (as identified by `last-modified`) and identifies the recommenders by their IDs in the system, such as *sp2*, *sp3* and *sp4*. The `Constants` tag includes the constant values used in the trust calculations. For example, the value of w_b in calculating confidence (Eq. 3) is 0.8.

3. Implementation and Experimental Evaluation

We develop a prototype file sharing grid [9] in Jade (Java Agent Development Environment) [10], by focusing on three types of file sharing services: file upload, open and search. The trust scenarios are modeled using UMLtrust [6] and converted to trust rules. The `Trust Rules` repository is developed based on the different trust scenarios [6] (see Table 1). The other repositories (i.e., `Direct Trust`, `Recommendations`, `Recom-Accuracy`, and `Alerts`) are developed as database tables in MySQL 5.0 [11]. The providers and requestors are implemented as Jade agents. Events are generated by employing the `ACLMessage` (Agent Communication Language Message), with the different modules of the architecture as 'behaviours' of Jade. The summary of the implementation environment is provided as follows:

- System Configuration: Pentium 1.886 GHz Dell machine. 1 GB RAM.
- Development Languages: Java, XML, MySQL 5.0 [11].
- Development Platform: Jade 3.5 [10], Eclipse IDE 3.2.

The service providers employ the monitor to analyze interactions and decide accordingly. Experimental results show that the proposed architecture can analyze service-based interactions from trust perspectives, measure trustworthiness, and make automatic decisions. The performance of the service provider is measured while analyzing service session, service request, and recommendation requests events. However, the monitor creates some performance overhead also. The overheads discussed in the next subsections are of three types, delay in providing a decision on a service request event (sRQ), delay in analyzing a service session event (sSN), and delay in a long recommendation chain.

Table 1. Elicited trust scenarios for a file sharing server

Trust Scenarios	Description
File Excess	Requestors may upload files beyond the limit of the server and thus make the upload service unavailable for others.
File Spamming	Requestors may upload illegal and insignificant files to waste storage space on the server.
File Harmful	Requestors may upload files containing malicious scripts which can harm other users.
Illegal Access Attempt	Requestors may try to access others' personal files in the resource database by manipulating the file search service.
Remote File Inclusion	Requestors may manipulate the file open service to open malicious files remotely and to execute them on the server.

3.1 Delay in Providing Decision on a Service Request Event (sRQ)

A provider retrieves previous direct trust value with the requestor for the service from the `Direct Trust` repository, and handles recommendations from other providers. The handling of recommendations includes the requests for recommendations and the receipt of the corresponding replies. In a service-based system without the trust monitor, these two tasks would not be present. The delay is calculated by taking the difference between the sending time of a service request event and the receipt time of the corresponding decision in a service reply. In the experimental setup, we use one service provider (*sp1*) to provide services, three providers (*sp2, sp3,* and *sp4*) for recommendations. We vary the number of service requests from 10 to 100 from a requestor *sr1*. We run the experiment for each setup 10 times and take the average to minimize errors. (see Fig. 9). The system without the trust monitor just receives the *sRQ* event and provides *sRP* randomly (*i.e.,* without using any trust-based analysis), while the system with the trust monitor employs trust-based analysis before providing *sRP*. The result shows that the trust-based processing of a *sRQ* introduces some delay in providing the corresponding service decision. However, the result is encouraging since the delay does not increase with the increase of the number of service requests, *i.e.,* scalability will not be an issue as the number of requesters grow. The response from a provider without the trust monitor requires almost constant time (in the range of 30-40 milliseconds), while the response from a provider with the trust monitor also requires an almost static time (in the range of 500–600 milliseconds). The reason for this is as follows. All of the modules in our provider software are implemented as specific behaviors (*i.e.,* threads) in the Jade platform. With the arrival of each service request, the provider creates new instance of different modules of the monitor. For example, for 100 service requests at a time, the provider creates 100 instances of each working module. The creation times of these instances are almost constant, so the total time required to create 100 instances of working modules is almost the same as the time required to create 10 instances. Therefore, the execution is performed in parallel for each service request.

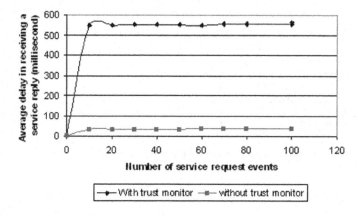

Fig. 9. The average delay in receiving a service reply for a service request

3.2 Delay in Analyzing a Service Session Event (sSN)

TrAM analyzes a service session (*sSN*) event in two steps: compare *sSN* against trust rules, and update direct trust, recommendation, and recommendation accuracies. The delay is calculated by taking the difference between the sending time of an *sSN* event and the corresponding reply time. To examine the overhead, we send a number of *sSN*s to the *sp1* varying from 10 to 100, where the requested service is *UploadDocFile*. Fig.10 provides the results which show that the analysis of an *sSN* introduces some delay; however, the delay remains almost constant with the increase in events. The delay in providing a service reply without the trust monitor remains almost constant in the range of 30–40 milliseconds, while the delay with the trust monitor also remains almost constant in the range of 80–90 milliseconds. The reason is the same as the processing of service request events discussed in the previous subsection. However, the monitor does not need to send or receive recommendations to analyze an *sSN*. Therefore, the delay occurred is only due to the analysis of trust rules and the accessing of the database for the retrieval and update of trust values. Nevertheless, the slight increase in average delay with the increase in service session events is due to the synchronized accessing of shared database tables by individual instances. The combined analysis of Figs. 9 and 10 shows that the average delay is in the range of 500–600 milliseconds for *sRQ*, while it is in the range of 80–90 milliseconds for *sSN*, having the average difference as 420–520 milliseconds. The major difference in handling a *sRQ* and an *sSN* is the handling of recommendations.

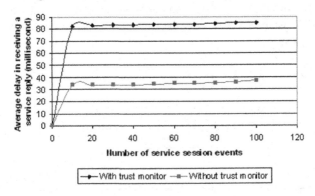

Fig. 10. The average delay in receiving a service reply for a service session

3.3 Delays in Long Recommendation Chains

Since recommendations are handled as sending of recommendation requests and receiving of the corresponding replies, there is some delay in providing runtime decisions on a *sRQ*. However, while analyzing the delay on a *sRQ*, we only considered direct recommendations (*i.e*, the recommendations from immediate neighbors [7]). Since we allow both direct and indirect recommendations in our system, we were interested to see the impact of handling recommendations with long chain, *i.e.*, when the path-length for indirect recommendations varies. To do this experiment, we assumed a long chain from *sp1* to *sp10*, where *sp1* asks *sp2* for recommendation, *sp2* to *sp3*, and so on. We further assumed that a provider can ask for recommendations to only one another provider, *i.e.*, *sp1* only to *sp2* and *sp2* only to *sp3*. We varied the number of recommenders from 1 to 9 (*i.e.*, *sp2* to *sp10*), and send recommendation requests from *sp1* to calculate the difference between a recommendation request and the corresponding reply. Fig. 11 presents the results which show that the delay in receiving a recommendation reply increases almost linearly with the increase of path-length in a chain.

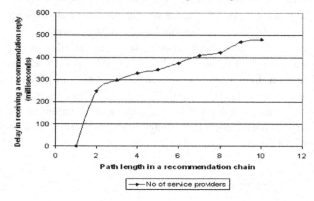

Fig. 11. The average delay in receiving a recommendation reply.

3.4 Monitoring Overhead

The first experiment concludes that there is some delay in providing trust-based service granting decision on service request events, although the average delay remains almost constant with the increase in service requests. The second experiment shows that the run-time monitoring and analysis of service-based interactions does not create that much overhead. It should be noted that the purpose of this measurement is to show that the performance overheads remain almost static, which makes the architecture applicable for large-scale systems. Therefore, the focus of the first two experiments was not to show the differences between the two response time delays that occur in the system with and without the monitor. The third experiment confirms that a large recommendation chain is probably not a good idea when there is a need for prompt reply to service request events.

4. Related Work

Many trust-based approaches are proposed by focusing on trust-based policy management [3-5, 24-32]. The monitoring of the trustworthiness of service requestors has not been adequately addressed so far. English et al. [4] neither support any trust rules to perform automatic trust monitoring of service-based software nor they present any calculation schemes to quantify the trustworthiness of stakeholders. Trust-based spam detection [24] and reputation-based social network systems [25, 26] assume that the trust values are available, hence necessitating the incorporation of a monitor like ours in their systems. Since we establish dynamic trust relationships between service providers and requestors based on the automatic monitoring of service usage, our architecture can be applicable in any social network-based systems that require sharing of resources. Unlike our XML-based service and trust monitor configuration, facts from past interactions are used in [27, 28]. Some other trust-based access control mechanisms [3, 5, 29-32] define the syntax and semantics of the corresponding policy languages, and the deployment of the policy languages in the target system requires language-based parsers and compilers. We compare and contrast those work in Table 2.

Table 2. Trust-based monitoring approaches

Work	Domain	Trust Mechanism
TBRM [3]	Information system	Policy-based access control
SPM [4]	Ubiquitous system	Interaction-based system monitoring
TRBAC [5]	Information system	Policy-based access control
SureMsg [24]	Email services	Reputation-based email exchanging
EigenTrust [25]	Peer-to-peer system	Reputation-based trust negotiation
FuzzyTrust [26]	Semantic web	Social network-based trust formation
FuzzyWeb [27]	Web services	Rule-based service access
TAP [28]	Service-based software	Policy-based software access control
ICTM [29]	Information system	Policy-based access control
ATN [30]	Open grid system	Trust negotiation, access control
TBAC [31]	Information system	Policy-based access control
TrustBack [32]	Information system	Role-based access control
Our work	Service-based software	Interaction-based service monitoring

A number of monitoring architectures exist for service quality analysis and automatic service composition [12–23]. We quantify the trustworthiness of requestors by monitoring their service usages, while the existing architectures monitor service providers to improve service quality to end users. Table 3 summarizes those research with respect to our work.

Table 3. Selected work on service monitoring

Work	Monitored Attributes	Monitored Entity	Trust Quantification
FQoS [12]	Service quality in user feedback	Provider	N
AMR [13]	Service accountability in composition	Provider	N
SMC [14]	Errors in service execution	Provider	N
MSLA [15]	Service constraints for mutual safety	provider, user	N
RM [16]	Service quality using requirements	Provider	N
WSR [17]	Exceptions in web service for quality	Provider	N
ZAS [18]	Service timeliness, type checking	Provider	N
WSN [19]	Errors in service execution	Provider	N
AGSM [20]	Quality of service in grid	Provider	N
GSM [21]	Quality of service for end users	Provider	N
SGR [22]	Resource allocation status	Provider	N
IBS [23]	Quality in service execution	Provider	N
Our work	Service safety in trust concerns	Requestor	Y

5. Conclusions and Future Work

Due to the pervasiveness of software in our everyday activities, it is important to monitor trust relationships between the users and the system to analyze the vulnerabilities and opportunities the relationships may invite to the system. In this chapter, we present a trust monitoring architecture called TrAM, to automatically analyze service-based interactions from trust perspectives. TrAM employs trust rules to analyze such interactions and uses trust calculation schemes to quantify the trustworthiness of service users. TrAM not only makes run-time decision for service provision but also employs dynamic decision on the risk status of the service that may suggest the premature termination of an interaction to protect the corresponding stakeholders. The proposed architecture is implemented in a trust-aware file sharing grid and evaluated under different trust conditions and performance overhead related concerns. Our future enhancements to the system will concentrate on addressing the following limitations. While specifying a trust scenario, we assumed that the identity of a trustee is properly resolved. It was also assumed that the network is secure from false recommenders. However, in real situations, this might not be the case always.

Acknowledgments

This research is partially funded by the Natural Sciences and Engineering Research Council of Canada (NSERC).

References

[1] Gambetta D (1988) Can we trust trust? In: Trust: Making and Breaking Cooperative Relations. Chapter 13. University of Oxford: 213–237.

[2] Yu B, Singh MP (2002) An evidential model of distributed reputation mechanism. In: Proc. of the 1st Intl. Joint Conf. on Autonomous Agents and multi-agent systems. Italy. ACM Press: 294–301.

[3] Lin C, Varadharajan V (2006) Trust based risk management for distributed system security - a new approach. In: Proc. of the 1st International Conference on Availability, Reliability and Security. Vienna, Austria. IEEE CS Press: 6–13.

[4] English C, Terzis S, Nixon P (2005) Towards self-protecting ubiquitous systems: monitoring trust-based interactions. In: Personal and Ubiquitous Computing 10(1). Springer: 50–54.

[5] Dimmock N, Bacon J, Ingram D, Moody K (2005) Risk models for trust-based access control (TBAC). In: Proc. of the 3rd Annual Conference on Trust Management (LNCS v3477). France. Springer: 364–371.

[6] Uddin MG, Zulkernine M (2008) UMLtrust: Towards developing trust-aware software. In: Proc. of the 23rd ACM Symposium on Applied Computing. Brazil. ACM Press: 831–836.

[7] Uddin MG, Zulkernine M, Ahamed SI (2008) CAT: A context-aware trust model for open and dynamic systems. In: Proc. of the 23rd Annual ACM Symposium on Applied Computing. Fortaleza, Brazil. ACM Press: 2024–2029.

[8] Azzedin F, Maheswaran M (2003) Trust modeling for peer-to-peer based computing systems. In: Proc. of the International Symposium on Parallel and Distributed Processing. USA. IEEE CS Press: 10pp.

[9] Deng Y, Wang F (2007) A heterogeneous storage grid enabled by grid service. In: ACM SIGOPS Operating Systems Review 41(1). ACM Press: 7–13.

[10] Bellifemine F, Caire G, Poggi A, Rimassa G (2003) Jade: A white paper. In: EXP in Search of Innovation 3(3): 14pp.

[11] MySQL 5.0 Reference Manual (2008). In: MySQL Enterprise Server.

[12] Jurca R, Faltings B, Binder W (2007) Reliable QoS monitoring based on client feedback. In: Proc. of the 16th Intl. Conference on World Wide Web. Canada. ACM Press: 1003–1012.

[13] Zhang Y, Lin K, Hsu J (2007) Accountability monitoring and reasoning in service-oriented architectures. In: Journal of Service Oriented Computing and Applications 1(1). Springer: 35–50.

[14] Baresi L, Ghezzi C, Guinea S (2004) Smart monitors for composed services. In: Proc. of the 2nd International Conference on Service-Oriented Computing. USA. ACM Press: 193–202.

[15] Skene J, Skene A, Crampton J, Emmerich W (2007) The monitorability of service-level agreements for application-service provision. In: Proc. of the 6th International Workshop on Software and Performance. Buenos Aires, Argentina. ACM Press: 3–14.

[16] Spanoudakis G, Mahbub K (2004) Requirements monitoring for service–based systems: towards a framework based on event calculus. In: Proc. of the 19th International Conference on Automated Software Engineering. Linz, Austria. IEEE CS Press: 379–384.

[17] Robinson WN (2003) Monitoring web service requirements. In: Proc. of the 11th IEEE International Conference on Requirements Engineering. Japan. IEEE CS Press: 65–74.

[18] Letia T, Marginean A, Groza A (2007) Z-based agents for service-oriented computing. In: Proc. of the Service-Oriented Computing: Agents, Semantics, and Engineering (LNCS v4504). Honolulu, HI, USA. Springer: 160–174.

[19] Yan Y, Cordier MO, Pencole Y, Grastien A (2005) Monitoring Web service networks in a model-based approach. In: Proc. of the 3rd European Conference on Web Services. Vaxj, Sweden. IEEE CS Press: 192–203.

[20] Rochford K, Coghlan B, Walsh J (2006) An agent-based approach to grid service monitoring. In: Proc. of the 5th Intl. Symposium on Parallel and Distributed Computing. Romania. IEEE CS Press: 345–351.

[21] Peng L, Koh M, Song J, See S (2006) Grid service monitoring for grid market framework. In: Proc. of the 14th IEEE International Conf. on Networks. Singapore. IEEE CS Press: 1–6.

[22] Mao H, Hunag L, Li M (2005) Service-based grid resource monitoring with common information model. In: Proc. of the IFIP International Conf on Network and Parallel Computing (LNCS v3779). Beijing, China. Springer: 80–83.

[23] Sahai A, Machiraju V, Wursterl K (2001) Monitoring and controlling internet-based e-services. In: Proc. of 2nd Workshop on Internet Applications. USA. IEEE CS Press: 41–48.

[24] Zhang W, Bi J, Wu J, Qin Z (2007) An approach to optimize local trust algorithm for SureMsg service. In: Proc. of the ECSIS Symposium on Bio-inspired, Learning, and Intelligent Systems for Security. Edinburgh, UK. IEEE CS Press: 51–54.

[25] Kamvar SD, Schlosser MT, Molina-Garcia H (2003) The eigentrust algorithm for reputation management in P2P networks. In: Proc. of the 12th International Conference on World Wide Web. Budapest, Hungary. ACM Press: 640–651.

[26] Lesani M, Bagheri S (2006) Applying and inferring fuzzy trust in semantic web social networks, in Proc. of the Canadian Semantic Web. Quebec City, Canada. Springer: 23–43.

[27] Sherchan W, Loke S, Krishnaswamy S (2006) A fuzzy model for reasoning about reputation in web services. In: Proc. of 21st Annual ACM Symposium on Applied Computing. Dijon, France. ACM Press: 1886–1892.

[28] Rajbhandari S, Contes A, Rana OF, Deora V, Wootten I (2006) Trust assessment using provenance in service oriented applications. In: Proc. of the 10th IEEE on Intl. Enterprise Distributed Object Computing Conference Workshops. Hong Kong. IEEE CS Press: 65–72.

[29] Etalle S, Winsborough W (2005) Integrity constraints in trust management. In: Proc. of the 10th Symposium on Access Control Models and Technologies, Sweden. ACM Press: 1–10.

[30] Ryutov T, Zhou L, Neuman C, Foukia N, Leithead T, Seamons K (2005) Adaptive trust negotiation and access control for grids. In: Proc. of the 6th IEEE/ACM International Workshop on Grid Computing. Washington, USA. IEEE CS Press: 55–62.

[31] Chakraborty S, Ray I (2006) TrustBAC: Integrating trust relationships into the RBAC model for access control in open systems. In: Proc. of the 11th ACM Symposium on Access Control Models and Technologies. California, USA. ACM Press: 49–58.

[32] Dimmock N, Belokosztolszki A, Eyers D, Bacon J, Ingram D, Moody K (2004) Using trust and risk in role-based access control policies. In: Proc. of the 9th ACM Symposium on Access Control Models and Technologies, New York, USA. ACM Press: 156–162.

Chapter 4

Human Interoperability Enterprise for High-Assurance Systems

Raymond Paul*, Stefania Brown-VanHoozer*, and Arif Ghafoor**

*US Department of Defense

**Purdue University, West Lafayette, IN 47907

Abstract. Development of dependable high-assurance systems requires policies and standards essential for improving human interoperability among collaborating individuals and organizations. Such systems facilitate unfettered strategic communication flow to all the stakeholders, while supporting intelligent interfaces in a manner that reinforces the collaboration through cooperative and coordinated cognitive activities of the participants. In essence, these activities elucidate a *group sense making* process that allows creation/recreation of distributed and similar knowledge among group members through sharing and interpreting of information. This chapter elaborates on key human interoperability enterprise policy challenges and the role of coordinated human behavior and human cognition for developing high-assurance systems. In addition, the chapter provides a roadmap for developing an interoperability policy framework and engineering economically viable high-assurance systems to support missions where people play a key role.

1. Introduction

Emerging mission critical and non-mission critical applications are exhibiting increasing reliance on high-assurance systems which are trusted systems that perform their functions reliably and dependably [1]. These systems often operate in a large-scale service-oriented network-enabled environment that connects geographically dispersed personnel, resources, and data. Examples of such applications abound in the domains of emergency response systems, banking, finance, and airlines, as well as military and critical national infrastructures. These systems are built based on traditional approaches drawn from the discipline of system engineering. However, as advances in network-enabled environments are allowing

J. Dong et al. (eds.), *High Assurance Services Computing*,
DOI 10.1007/978-0-387-87658-0_4, © Springer Science+Business Media, LLC 2009

collaboration among diverse community of users, *human interoperability enterprise* (HIE) has become an emergent paradigm which is aimed *to achieve high quality value chain for the users of high assurance systems starting with data and moving over to information, knowledge and services to awareness.*

HIE poses a unique set of challenges that have been overlooked in the area of traditional system engineering. The effectiveness of high-assurance systems needs to be treated as a function of collaborative capacities for coordinating, communicating and processing information that entail acquiring data, fusing and correlating data streams with available knowledge, projecting outcomes, weighing alternatives, deciding a course of action, enacting the decision, and coordinating the process of enactment. As a result, progress in building high-assurance systems will be driven by the development of optimum communications, decision making and sharing of knowledge among humans and computers. The quality of shared awareness in such a human-centric environment is explicitly placed in the cognitive domain and critically depends on the human cognitive performance and degree of trustworthiness among human operators and systems. These environments are heavily dependent on the end users' assessments of the value and integrity of the information, trust, and the quality of decisions [2,3,4,5,29]. Human interactions in these environments can include:

- Operating and maintaining complex cyber physical infrastructures, computer-controlled combat systems, weapon systems, and command-and-control systems;
- Remotely controlling large number of sensors and actuators, such as unmanned drones, or a swarm of robots, a group of autonomous airborne/underwater/space vehicles;
- Collaborating and visualizing current environment through the control of sensors and information processing;
- Interacting with cyber interfaces on desktop or mobile handheld devices to integrate information, make command and control decisions, and provide coordination plans.

Failure to achieve seamless interoperation among systems and human operators in a high assurance environment can have drastic consequences that can translate directly to financial losses, loss of prestige, or endangerment of lives. For example, the statistics collected over the last several decades have raveled that the human error is the major cause for airline accidents [6]. Aviation control is a complex and dynamic system intended to provide a high assurance environment. However, errors can occur in this environment on the part of any number of people, including air traffic controllers, flight crew, and maintenance crew. An error can entail a wrong decision or poor judgment in taking an appropriate action in an emergency situation or a distraction that results in a flaw being overlooked. Lack of training or fatigue can be the additional causes of poor human cognitive performance.

The challenge of human interoperability and human cognitive performance exacerbates while developing high-assurance collaborative systems at the global level connecting coalition partners, organizations and nations. The goal of such global systems is to facilitate unfettered strategic communication flow to all the stakeholders, while supporting intelligent interfaces in a manner that reinforces the collaboration through cooperative and coordinated cognition activities. Such activities elucidate a group sense making process that allows creation/recreation of distributed and similar knowledge among group members through sharing, processing and interpreting of information [7,8]. These collaborations are generally formed in a dynamic manner during missions and potentially conflicting interoperability policies among partners may require mediation to synergize operational capabilities. Such synergy can be achieved through enhanced human cognitive matching, trust building and improved collective intelligent of diverse team members. However, assessment of human cognitive performance on the operational capabilities of these systems poses daunting HIE challenges because interoperability policies and methodologies for decision makers within and across organizational boundaries can be ad-hoc and the human/social behavior can vary drastically across national/racial boundaries.

A leading example of a global collaborative endeavor is the STAR-TIDE project aimed at providing economic development, humanitarian assistance, disaster relief, and post-war stabilization across the globe [9]. The goal of this project is to empower decision-makers and other human operators in the field to carry out their missions through "knowledge on demand". Currently, the HIE challenges in this project are being addressed using social networking and trust management methodologies.

Another example of collaborative system is the Eagle-1 project by Microsoft [10]. It is an extensive data-driven system being designed to support interactive collaboration among various agencies for disaster management.

We view such projects and case studies as important stepping-stones on the path to the development and management of high assurance systems. In essence, a rigorous HIE framework is vital to the development and evolution of such systems. It is, therefore, imperative that issues dealing with an HIE framework should be well understood and incorporated during all the phases of high assurance system development lifecycle. In this chapter we addresses the key HIE policy challenges and highlight major steps that can lead to the development of a holistic interoperability policy framework for engineering high-assurance systems. The design philosophy of such systems is based on integrating core technology components and methodologies drawn from the area of human cognitive engineering. In addition, we elaborate on human performance criteria for high-assurance and trustworthy systems. The goal is to highlight key HIE challenges and elicit solutions from relevant technological areas including Human-Centered Computing (HCC), Information, Knowledge and Intelligence Management (IKIM), service-oriented architecture (SOA), and service and behavioral sciences [11,12].

2. Human Interoperability Enterprise Challenges for High Assurance Systems

HIE involves numerous dimensions including: human-machine interaction, human-human collaboration and cooperation, group dynamics, and integrated human-system engineering including human-system requirement engineering, composable and re-composable system architecture, modeling and simulation, dynamic system deployment, dynamic system monitoring, and dynamic policy enforcement. These dimensions need to be considered collectively for:

1. developing, operating and maintaining highly complex mission-critical autonomous systems that are economically and operationally viable, and
2. ensuring a high degree of integration, interoperability, collaborative interaction, integrity, interdependence and trustworthiness between the human operators/users and the network-enabled systems to achieve high quality of shared awareness and decision making capabilities.

These challenges not only depend on technology; but also on many other factors at *macro*-level such as:

- Policy and doctrines controlling the degree of interoperation
- Complexity associated with the federation of distributed collaborative enterprises
- Autonomy of such enterprises
- Organizational structures of individual enterprise
- Social networking
- Formation of teams, and
- Rank/skill parity of distributed enterprises

Less obvious but equally crucial are the *micro*-level factors representing the underlying human interoperability processes related to [13]:

- Trust and reputation
- Behavior and cognitive capabilities of team members
- Emotion during operation; and
- Social technology that maps the skills and needs of users to share critical information across a variety of domains

These human factors strongly impact the overall effectiveness of high assurance systems due to cultural and/or social disparity that may exist among the team members. As a result, progress in innovation of new approaches to high assurance environments will be driven by the development of optimum provenance based on human communications and emergent "into" networks such as decision making, sharing of Data, Information, Services and Knowledge (DISK) among humans and the evolution of new types of networks and automated human-centric systems.

2.1 DISK Interoperability

Any large organization with a mission to design and develop dependable high-assurance systems needs a set of well-defined requirements for systems engineering and a process plan to deal with the challenges that arise from human-human, human to organization, human to systems and human-machine and machine-machine collaborative interactions. Human capabilities, skills, and needs must be considered early in the design and development phases, and must be continuously reviewed throughout the development lifecycle to maximize "cognitive matching[1]". Such inclusion of the human cognitive-behavioral aspects provides the interoperability requirements for the development of high-assurance systems. These requirements are formalized through an HIE policy framework which enables an organization to reduce the lifecycle cost and increase the efficiency, effectiveness, usability, trustworthiness, and quality of its high-assurance systems.

Figure 1 shows some of HIE tenets that affect the development of high-assurance systems. This paradigm highlights the role played by these tenets in service provision for applications and missions and supporting E2E sharing of DISK across organizational boundaries. These tenets support the overall business and interoperation process and policies; the underlying IT and networking infrastructure, architectures and protocols for controlling quality of service and aligning human cognitive/behavioral factors, such as situation assessment and judgment, with DISK. All components of this paradigm need to be in harmony and aligned for interoperation to remain effective and efficient in supporting high-assurance applications and services.

As shown in Figure 1, the HIE tenets are categorized along the following three overlapping dimensions.

- End user experience and behavior
- Technology and architecture; and
- Organizational processes and policies such as Service-Level Agreement (SLA)

(U) **End user experience and behavior**: Tenets in this group describe how the end users such as operators, warfighters, and decision makers collaborate, cooperate and react while operating in a network-enabled environment.

(T) **Technology and architecture**: These tenets are related to the underlying design and implementation technology, and deal with the technical issues such as how the technological advances affect human operators and decision makers in performing their missions.

(O) **Organizational processes and policies**: A complex system does not operate by individuals without an organization or a set of processes. Large organizations often have a disciplined process to ensure proper execution of their doctrines and policies.

---

[1] The meaning of the communication elicited is the same as that intended.

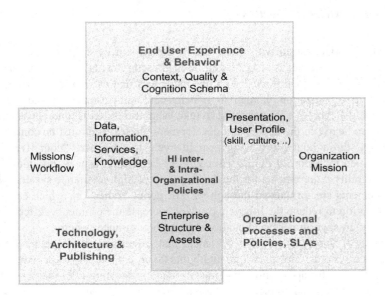

Fig. 1. HIE Tenets for High-assurance Systems

These three dimensions overlap and interact with each other. For example, presentations and user profiles are common to both (U) and (O) dimensions; DISK is common to both (U) and (T) dimensions; and the enterprise structure and assets are common to both (T) and (O) dimensions. HIE policies, which are shared by all the dimensions, encompass the following sub-dimensions dictating the required capabilities of a high-assurance system:

- Provide integration protocols among many different, disparate and distributed DISK sources belonging to autonomous enterprises;
- Support automated discovery protocols of new DISK sources while allowing both push and pull mode of sharing;
- Facilitate integration and interoperation among enterprises in terms of configuration, management and maintenance of their network-enabled DISK sources;
- Facilitate sharing of DISK and provision of services to the end users and across enterprise boundaries by incorporating environmental contexts and user's preferences, and accordingly, streamline the coordinated cognition activities;
- Enhance the end-user cognition capability for situation awareness, sharing of information, sharing of behaviors in establishing trust to facilitate quality judgment in decision-making and understanding of the messages being delivered through shared knowledge.

In essence, the HIE policy enunciates the rules and regulations that promote and support efficient and effective human collaboration and cooperation for network-centric systems. A clear requirements definition is needed elucidating: (a) the benefits of participating in HIE framework, (b) the limits on the inconvenience; and (c) a transformation plan for data stewardship in providing the incentive for relevant users to participate. Moreover, interoperability among pre-existing (legacy or 'stove-pipe') systems is by definition a post-hoc, i.e., post-development, requirement imposed on each system. Since legacy systems are not originally designed to fulfill the interoperability requirements, the high-assurance performance of these systems with respect to the HIE requirements must be assessed and analyzed. Any performance gaps must be identified and decision must be made that whether or not these systems can evolve over time or should be eliminated.

Note, each participant in a network-enabled interoperability environment must be considered as an autonomous federated participant in the sense of having a full control on local DISK assets, policies and processes. Consequently, there should be clearly defined tradeoffs between the benefits reaped from coordination efforts and sacrificing of autonomy by each participant through mediation, if such need arises. Subsequently, federation's operational and mediation rules on how to overlay the participation must be established at the time of formation of the federation.

2.2 DISK Interoperability

DISK interoperability can be classified at the following levels:

Level 1: Communication or Protocol Interoperability: This type of interoperability implies that two parties can communicate with each other and exchange messages using a common protocol such as SOAP that is understood by both parties. This is the minimum level of interoperability.

Level 2: Data Integration: This interoperability entails that two parties not only can send message to each other, they can also understand the meaning of data in the message. For example, if message are sent in XML format, and both parties understand XML and can process XML schema, they should be able to understand the meaning of the transmitted data.

Level 3: Application & Data Integration: This interoperability implies that the two parties not only can exchange message with each other and understand the meaning of data, they can also use the data for service calling, such as method calls.

Level 4: Process & Service Integration: This type of interoperability implies that two collaborating parties are acquainted with each other so well that they know each other's processes allowing them to establish collaboration protocols at runtime. SoA DCP is one such example [14].

Level 5: Knowledge Sharing & Collaboration: Interoperability at this level means two parties not only know each other's processes, they also know the detailed knowledge and expertise of each other. For example, when two physicians communicate with each other, their interaction is carried out at a level that can be drastically different from the one when a physician interacts with a layman. Interaction between two physicians is based on their domain knowledge related to the field of medicine.

Through DISK, we assess the current state of technology and the overall goals that must be achieved by building high-assurance systems while incorporating the HIE policy requirements. The overall intent of the HIE framework is to integrate technology evolution with human cognitive engineering during the design phase of high-assurance systems delineated in terms of the following HIE policy objectives:

- Providing new network-enabled requirements definition about the integration and co-evolution of social interchange and systems engineering, integration and collaborative interaction, and in particular emphasize those collaborative areas that have the potential to transform data to information, understanding, learning, discovery and enhance quality of capability, presentation, and knowledge of human operators including decision makers;
- Increasing the knowledge base of understanding to enhance cognitive capabilities of human while sharing of information across organizations and communicating to machines to create, discover and reason with knowledge. Advancing the interactive ability to represent, collect, store, organize, visualize, and communicate data and information is of paramount importance. At the same the resulting growth and complexity of the overall system need to be managed.
- Advancing knowledge through coordinated cognition process elucidating the process through which high-assurance systems perform tasks autonomously, robustly, and flexibly while incorporating human interoperability; and
- Advancing the state of the practice and state of the art in the application of human interoperability and intelligent information system technologies, such as human centered computing and information/knowledge management in specific contexts.

3. HIE and the Role of Cognitive Engineering

Development of an HIE policy framework for high-assurance systems starts with the specification of key performance parameters for sharing DISK among diverse set of operators (humans, organizations, groups) and identify issues in cognitive-behavioral aspects of such sharing. In addition, performance of an HIE framework should be assessed with respect to aforementioned HIE policy objectives. Figure 2 delineates a view illustrating these objectives in terms of establishing critical performance factors and assessing the effectiveness of an HIE policy framework for high-assurance systems.

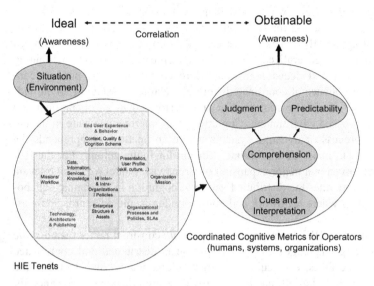

Fig. 2. Role of HIE Tenets and Metrics-Based Cognitive Assessment Framework in High-assurance System Development

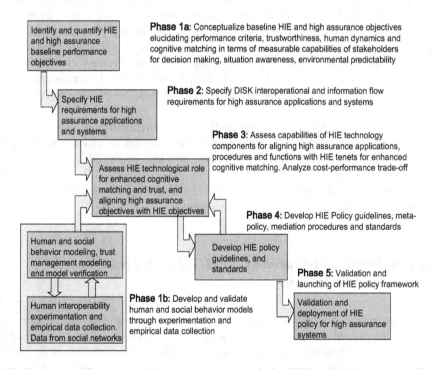

Fig. 3. Roadmap for Integrated Development Framework for HIE-Based High-Assurance Systems

According to this view, which is a major extension of the Brunswick lens model and its generalization for situation awareness (SA) [15,16,17], various operators as well as the HIE tenets can be viewed as constituents of a coordinated cognitive system. The generalized lens model conceptualizes processes pertaining to human judgment and decision making. Here cognition is the product constructed as a consequence of coordinated work elucidating the state of an individual's engagement within the context of a task performed in an operational and possibly a group-based environment. Cognition is an intermediate state in the decision-making process of dynamic systems where an operator comprehends the situation in order to make an appropriate decision for future actions. For the HIE framework, we envision a major expansion of Brunswick model (or other relevant models) that incorporates the distributed nature of cognition in a dynamic collaborative environment where teamwork and non-individual-centered approach are essential.

As cognition in an HIE environment is a *dynamic* construct rather than a *static* feature, the vexing challenges are how cognition is distributed and coordinated across various interfaces, e.g., cultural, infrastructure, policy, and doctrine, and how coordinated cognition ultimately can provide a high degree of assurance for systems used in SA, as depicted in Figure 2.

It is important to note that the individual is not abandoned but rather the individuals' roles "provide the internal structures that are required to build the external structures into co-ordination with another [18]". Accordingly, several human-centered cognitive performance metrics (discussed in Section 3.2) are needed to assess the effectiveness and formation of the HIE policy framework. The role played by the HIE tenets must be clearly understood and the dependence of the cognition metrics on the underlying "invariants" of these tenets need to be analyzed.

In Figure 2, the correlation between the actual environmental and situation conditions as comprehended by a human operator provides an assessment of the effectiveness of HIE on the level of assurance provided by the DISK technology deployed for the network-enabled system.

The following subsections elaborate the challenges of the view presented in Figure 2 and outline an approach to address them.

3.1 Development Methodology for HIE Policy Framework for High Assurance Systems

The development of a high assurance system incorporating an HIE policy framework for distributed coordination and cognition, as depicted in Figure 2, requires a rigorous methodological plan. The roadmap in Figure 3 outlines this plan. The roadmap, comprising of multiple phases, captures the core processes pertaining to requirement specifications, technology selection, human dimensions captured through experimentation and modeling, and HIE policy development process. Details about the various phases of this roadmap are given below:

1. Phase 1a delineates the critical baseline HIE and high assurance system's performance objectives corresponding to the DISK and cognition metrics discussed in the following section. These metrics pertain to two major components (represented by two circles) in Figure 2.
2. Phase 1b, which can be pursued concurrently with Phase 1a, describes the development and validation processes for human and social behavior models. This phase consists of two iterative activities consisting of empirical data collection via experimentation and subsequent development and validation of robust behavior models. These models are subsequently used for developing high assurance systems.
3. The second phase specifies the overall DISK sharing operational requirements of high-assurance applications and their alignment with the HIE performance objectives. This phase uses the baseline performance objectives and the behavioral models developed in Phase 1a and Phase 1b, respectively.
4. During the third phase various HIE technologies, methodologies, and capabilities are evaluated and the results can then be compared against the requirements established in Phase 2.
5. During Phase 4, a set of HIE policy guidelines and standards are produced and deployed.
6. In Phase 5, the policies and guidelines developed are evaluated with respect to the overall goals and requirements established for the HIE policy framework and the applications supported by the DISK system.

The following subsections discuss these phases. Note that alternative HIE policy development processes can also be used.

3.2 Identifying and Quantifying HIE Baseline Performance Criteria

Phase 1a, as shown in Figure 3, consists of identifying the key DISK tenets belonging to various levels of interoperability, as summarized in Section 2.2, and establishing the baseline performance criteria for high-assurance systems while incorporating the HIE policy framework. The baseline criteria elucidate numerous human dynamics due to human-to-human, human-to-groups, human-to-systems, and system-to-system interoperations. The criteria can be expressed in terms of both qualitative and quantitative cognition capability metrics that capture comprehension of information and knowledge, use of this knowledge to assess emerging scenarios and situation awareness, environmental predictability, and exhibiting quality of judgment under various contexts by human operators. The overall metrics can be broadly classified into the following two categories:

- The first category comprises of technology-driven metrics specific to DISK.
- The second category of metrics quantifies coordinated cognition capabilities of operators as shown in Figure 2.

These two categories of metrics are described below.

DISK and technical performance metrics for HIE: These metrics specifically deal with the qualitative aspects of the technology deployed for high assurance systems. Some relevant system-centric metrics that fall in this category are the traditional high assurance metrics that include the following:

- **Readiness**: Meeting the needs of mission-oriented requirements for all users under various contexts;
- **Timeliness**: Deliverance of DISK to all participating users in a timely manner under all circumstances;
- **Trustworthiness**: Ensuring a high degree of trustworthiness for all DISK sources;
- **Usability**: Ensuring information and knowledge for various modes of interoperability that are user-centric and facilitate ready comprehension, added perspective, and immediate usage. Also, ensuring that system interoperability is compatible with the user capabilities for receiving, manipulating, comprehending and storing the information;
- **Relevance**: Ensuring information and knowledge are meeting the end-user requirements, with potential consequences and significance of the information made explicit to the user's context.

Coordinated cognition metrics for HIE: These metrics are specific to cognition domain and are related to operator's enhanced capability as a result of coordinated cognition based on the elicitation of knowledge by individuals participating in a team. The main metrics in this category, as depicted in Figure 2, include:

- Interpretability and comprehensiveness of shared knowledge
- Degree of quality of judgment, and
- Environmental predictability

The aforementioned metrics of both the categories are context specific and are generally statistical in nature [19]. For example, the team knowledge and the resulting coordinated cognition can vary due to the changing dynamics of a fleeting situation. Note, the metrics in the second category are highly dependent upon the DISK and technology-based performance metrics belonging to the first category. Identifying and analyzing such dependency poses an important challenge for developing a viable high assurance system that incorporates an HIE policy framework.

The two sets of metrics collectively define the degree of assurance for a network-enabled high assurance system.

The consistency and the correlation of the resulting degree of situation awareness with respect to the ideal awareness can vary drastically with respect to the key common "invariants" of the overall HIE tenets (technology and human cognition components in Figure 2). An important challenge here is to identify these common "invariants" on which the aforementioned metrics might depend. An example of a possible invariant is the plausibility of the mission's domain knowledge as such knowledge can directly or indirectly affects most of the aforementioned metrics. Another possible invariant is the skill level and the experience of human operators. A related challenge is to analyze dependency of metrics on such invariants.

3.3 Human-Social Behavior and Trust Management Modeling

The objective of Phase 1b is to develop and validate human and social behavior models within the context of HIE. This phase consists of two iterative activities focused on collecting empirical data through experimentation designed to study human behavior under various scenarios and subsequently develop and validate robust behavior models. In essence, through modeling we need to understand and capture the processes by which individuals, groups and organizations establish rapport to form a basis of trusted environment to share information and exhibit behavior to allow prudent problem solving and decision making capabilities. These processes should represent the actual and highly complex human cognitive activities which are heavily influenced by prevailing contexts and the state by which the individuals operate in those contexts to establish the trust required for sharing information among the group members, the collaborative partners and systems. Most of the existing human and social behavior models are agent-based and cooperative behavior models, respectively. From HIE and high assurance system's perspective both human and group behaviors need to be driven based on well formed outcomes.

The key challenge in human modeling for high assurance environment is to capture the role of the aforementioned DISK and human cognitive metrics, including operational context, in a comprehensive manner. As human behavior may range from deterministic to holistic with respect to specific context, it is imperative that human behavior models must be stochastic and adaptive in nature to represent variations in behavior in diverse operational environment. Agent-based modeling is one of the leading paradigms to capture human behavior. However, these models lack advanced cognition features such as learning, perceptual computing, and pattern matching.

In a collaborative environment involving groups and services, trust plays significant role [20] which can directly impact the collective cognitive performance of the all the participants. Reasons can emerge that can hinder an individual's willingness to voluntarily share sensitive information and knowledge which can result in dwindling trust among partners and can eventually lead to the failure of missions [21]. Computational trust management models to predict trustworthiness parameter still need to be developed to understand and train the processes for cooperative behaviors in social networks. Existing approaches for trust management and trust propagation [22,23] in social networking can be extended towards the HIE framework.

A primary challenge is the validation of human and social models for their plausibility using a wide range of empirical data. Once the models are accepted, the training of these models is necessary for individuals, groups and organizations to establish trust in contexts requiring reliable and compatible social networks.

Experimentation, collection of empirical data and behavior modeling should be well-formed activities. These activities must include the following steps:

1. Identify the behavioral and consequential data to be collected and based on the results, establish data collection procedures. Some basic data to be collected include the characteristics of the users, the characteristics of the network-enabled systems that require human interactions, and the effect of the interoperations.
2. Develop repositories to facilitate the storage, categorization, management, and privacy-preserving sharing of the collected data.
3. Apply data mining and analysis techniques on the data collected across multiple applications and multiple systems. Establish models for statistically predicting human behaviors and impact of human interoperations.
4. Validate the accuracy of the prediction models. Examine the effectiveness of the collected data on behavioral predictions. Identify the missing factors. Based on the analysis, recalibrate the data collection procedures of Step 1.
5. Perform trustworthiness analysis. Based on the data collected and the prediction models established, the next step is to carry out trustworthiness analysis of individual human entities as well as the overall system, as discussed below:

   – One technique for trustworthiness analysis is to simulate human entities in the network-enabled workflows. The simulation model should be built upon the collected data and established behavioral prediction models. Through simulation it is relatively easier to analyze large scale systems and measure the impact and risk factors.
   – Trustworthiness analysis results can be used to (a) determine human entity requirements and human interoperation policies to achieve the maximal mission success probability, (b) understand the impact of end users on the overall system, including the potential risks and pitfalls that may occur due to end-user problems, (c) help with the system design to facilitate a human-error-resistant environment.

3.4 Technologies for HIE and High Assurance System

Central to the roadmap of Figure 3 is Phase 3 aimed at analyzing the potential role played by core technology, the underlying scientific methodologies and the emerging interoperability standards. The key technologies and methodologies to be considered include:

- Human-Centered Computing (HCC)
- Information, Knowledge and Intelligence Management (IKIM) and
- Service-oriented Architecture (SoA)
- Social and Behavior Sciences (discussed in Phase 1b)

HCC encompasses themes of software engineering, computer science, and information technology, all of which are united by a common thread that human beings, whether as individual, teams, or organizations, assume participatory and integral roles for carrying out their missions. HCC technology can enhance human insight and creativity through highly interactive visual interfaces coupled with interoperability tools and techniques that enable people to synthesize information, to derive insight from massive, dynamic, and often conflicting data, information and knowledge, to detect the expected and discover the unexpected. The HIE framework heavily depends on this technology whereby human operators and decision makers can work collaboratively across collaborative heterogeneous enterprises.

The IKIM technology deals with the transformation of contents from disparate DISK sources into cognitive capabilities through collaboration. Such collaboration subsequently provides intelligent perception, communication and reasoning capacities that are not constrained to address a single problem in isolation or in one particular context. This technology can allow integration of heterogeneous knowledge and reasoning methodologies in complementary as well as supplementary ways.

3.4.1 Service-Oriented Architecture

SoA technology plays a vital role for supporting interoperability across multiple organizations and provides the backbone infrastructure for distributed services [1]. In the following sections, we provide an assessment of SoA in terms of its potential role in developing high-assurance systems that explicitly incorporate HIE requirements.

Recently, many US government agencies including the Department of Defense have adopted SoA and Service-Oriented Computing (SoC) for its mission-critical systems to address the first HIE challenge mentioned in Section 2 [1, 24]. New software applications are offered as services for network-enabled environments that meet the high assurance standards entailing security, dependability, trustworthiness of the hardware and software, and scalability. In this regard, each service publishes its "definite range of behavior" as to what it can and cannot perform [25].

SoA not only affects systems and technology, but can also influence numerous other entities and factors listed below:

- **Human operators/actors**: Human operators may need to discover new services, compose them into applications, and deploy the newly orchestrated applications for execution. Thus, SoA system operators need to be system designers and analysts in addition to being operators.
- **Decision makers**: SoA offers decisions makers the choice of re-designing the system to meet the new environmental and operational requirements at runtime. While such new capabilities offer significant advantages over conventional rigid systems due to their adaptability and reconfigurability, these new capabilities also may need decision makers to examine more choices and options in real time to make optimal decisions.
- **Policies**: As SoA offers dynamic service discovery and capability for system composition, operators and decision makers can have more options and choices. While such flexibility offers significant advantages, it is necessary to have more rigorous policies to regulate the kind of actions that can be performed through SoA systems at runtime.
- **Doctrines**: Operational doctrines often depend on the technology that can be used. For example, the warfighting doctrines used in World War II were significantly different from the warfighting doctrines of World War I as mechanical devices such as tanks and high-speed airplanes were available in the former case. With dynamic service discovery and system composition, SoA offers a greater flexibility for selecting assets and resources.
- **Management**: SoA development practices follow a model-driven approach consisting of multiple phases such as modeling, assembling, deployment, and management. They are distinct from the conventional system development methodologies commonly practiced by the US Department of Defense for many years. To support the new kind of SoA system development that incorporates the desired HIE requirements, new system development infrastructures need to be developed, such as sample infrastructure that includes repositories of reliable and dependable services that can be reused for application development, and repositories of SoA modeling, design, code generation, and testing techniques.
- **Decision processes**: Network-enabled high assurance system users such as decision makers and operators need to consider many factors and issues during the decision making process pertaining to operations.

The SoA paradigm is still evolving and numerous issues still remain open. While interoperability has been a key concept behind this paradigm, such interoperability has different meaning. The current state of the SoA technology allows DISK interoperability only at Level 3 of application and data integration, discussed in Section 2.2. It is expected that this technology will take at least five or more years to reach the next level.

3.4.2 Human Interoperability in SoA

The HIE challenge arises at Level 4 and beyond of DISK interoperability (Section 2.2) that specifically deal with human-computer interaction, human-computer interface, human-human interaction, cognition, and organization process and protocols which can be modeled and incorporated as an integral part of a high assurance system. Note, all the key components of an SoA architecture can be changed simultaneously. For example, on the system side, an existing service can be replaced by a new service, an existing workflow can be updated, and the overall system architecture can be changed at runtime to meet any runtime requirement. On the other hand, operators can be replaced in case the original operator is unavailable, or new commanders employ a new tactical warfighting plan and decide to change both the personnel and the system at the same time, or a new policy from senior decision makers is issued requiring a change in the operational plan.

When a group of autonomous operators (humans, systems, organizations) participate in a SoA-based collaborative effort, there is a need to assess that a service is being provided to the level agreed upon, and ensure that the service continues to be provided at the agreed level. The following concepts are important to handle these two high-assurance issues:

- Quality of Service (QoS): Numerous QoS metrics for measuring the performance of services, at the negotiated level of service must be specified. Some of the DISK related metrics, discussed in Section 3.2, also fall in this category.
- Service-Level Agreements (SLA) or 'contracts' provide a formal mechanism governing the collaboration among various autonomous enterprises providing services. SLAs constitute a core component of an HIE policy and mediation framework.

These two concepts are part of the HIE tenets (Figure 1) and any formulation of data interoperability policy needs to consider these two concepts.

3.4.3 Existing HIE and DISK Technology Approaches

HCC, IKI and SoA technologies as well as methodologies for modeling human and social behavior and trust management can enable users at different levels of an organization to take full advantage of the benefits of these technologies. These technologies are designed to empower human operators to participate fully in the pervasive information world and establish and maintain social relationships while keeping their autonomy.

Several public and private enterprises have adopted SoA design philosophy for the network-enabled environment. Noted among them are the DISA's Net Enterprise Command Capability (NECC) and Marine Corps Enterprise Information Technology Services (MCEITS) [26]. In addition, numerous programs in human interoperability management and traditional human factor engineering have been pursued by several agencies. These include the NASA's Space Human Factors Engineering (SHFE) project [27] and Air Force's Cognitive Engineering effort for information dominance [28]. These efforts provide examples of how human factor engineering, and human systems integration can significantly improve the human interoperability effectiveness of mission-oriented high-assurance systems under various constraints. However, these projects do not address the broad set of challenges related to system complexity and human interoperability for developing network-enabled high assurance cyber infrastructure. For example, the SHFE project has been primarily focused on individualistic cognitive models for human-system interaction used for situation awareness and decision making under uncertainty of individual or organizational responses. Similarly, the traditional cognitive engineering effort by the Air Force does not address the interoperability aspects for group or organizational based collaboration dealing with situation awareness.

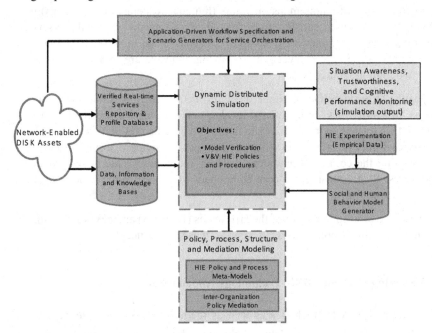

Fig. 4. Simulation-based Validation of HIE Policy Framework for High Assurance System (Phase 5)

3.5 HIE Evaluation and Validation

As described in Section 2, an effective HIE policy framework for developing high assurance systems must consider various dimensions, including technology, organization and process, and end-user issues. Further, the approach for developing such a framework must inherently be iterative and incremental in nature, with stakeholder's feedback built into the process. Phase 5 of Figure 3 is focused on analyzing the effectiveness of such a framework for high assurance systems and validating it through an extensive modeling and simulation environment which is depicted in Figure 4. This environment comprises of two main components providing modeling and simulation functionalities. These components are discussed below.

1. Modeling of all the HIE entities and includes the following steps:

   – Incorporating social and human behavioral models (from Phase 1b), including trust management and propagation in a group-based collaboration.
   – Meta-models for interoperability policies and processes governing interaction with network-enabled DISK assets within organizational structures and across organization boundaries (Phases 1a, 2, 3). This component should also include modeling of mediation techniques for merging heterogeneous interoperability policies belonging to autonomous organizations and agencies.
   – Models for SoA, that include any real-time and QoS-based requirements, for specification and orchestration of end-to-end application workflows and scenario generators for high assurance systems

2. Dynamic Distributed Simulation component. This component is driven by the aforementioned models and the end-to-end workflow-based scenarios generated from the high level application requirements. The distributed nature of the simulation is essential to correctly model network-enabled services. Goal of the simulation is to provide an understanding of dynamics and interaction exhibited by the endogenous building blocks of the HIE policy framework on the face of complexity associated with network-centric systems. It will facilitate identifying recurring patterns within alternate configurations that seem to perform well over an ensemble of plausible scenarios.

In particular, the simulation and validation phase entails performing a broad range of measurements and analyses that include:

• Performing a comparative assessment of various behavioral models within and across organizational interactions for high assurance systems and analyzing the impact of collaboration on high assurance applications. In particular, the implications that arise from the evolutionary nature (calling for a dynamic response measure) and emergence (non-monotonic behavior, implies that the "whole is greater than the sum of the parts") should be analyzed.

- Measuring the effectiveness of various policies, processes and alternative "network-enabled system views" on the cognitive performance of team members in terms of the quality of their decision-making capabilities, predictability and appropriateness of response in diverse and dynamic environments. The objective is to streamline policies and processes in a manner that maximizes human cognitive performance both at the individual level as well in a collaborative environment.
- Measuring various HIE-oriented related metrics (identified in Phase 1a of Figure 3)
- Performing trustworthiness analysis of the overall system, as elaborated in Step 5 of Section 3.3.
- Evaluating the impact of emerging DISK and workflow technologies on the overall performance of high assurance systems.

4. Summary of HIE Challenges for High-Assurance Systems

The overarching objective of an HIE policy framework is to establish a foundation for effective human networks that are cost effective and provide robust environment for policy, legal, cultural, infrastructure and technological solutions. Traditionally, the discipline of system engineering for developing high-assurance network-enabled systems has ignored the role of human interoperability and its impact on the design, maintenance and complexity of these systems. Undoubtedly, the complexity of system design increases tremendously as the role of HIE is incorporated in the development lifecycle.

In this chapter we have highlighted numerous challenges related to developing an HIE policy framework. In addition, a roadmap for developing high-assurance systems that expands the traditional system engineering design paradigm by integrating the role of the HIE policy framework has been presented. Within the context of HIE and high-assurance system development, several challenges have been identified which are listed below:

- How can intelligent interfaces and user behavioral models be incorporated during the high-assurance system's development lifecycle?
- What should be the design of collaborative architectures that control and coordinate actions and solve complex problems in network-enabled environments in a wide variety of domains? Such architectures should enable knowledge-intensive and dynamic interactions for innovation and knowledge generation across organizational boundaries.

- How can we develop viable models for effective computer-mediated human-human interaction under a variety of constraints, (e.g., video conferencing, collaboration across high vs. low bandwidth networks)?
- What should be the design requirements for interoperability and information integration methodologies and processes for heterogeneous and autonomous DISK sources? In addition, methodologies for personalizing, organizing, navigating, searching, interpreting, and presenting information of different types, using various modalities are needed which can enhance cognitive performance of human operators.
- What types of efficient computational models of human cognition, perception, and communication for commonsense or specialized domains and tasks, including acquisition and representation of ingredient knowledge would be needed?
- How can we deal with the complexity and scalability issues in managing and sharing cognitive knowledge and interoperability policies?
- An important related challenge is to analyze the tradeoff between the impact of the technological solution of the aforementioned issues on the performance and effectiveness of the HIE policy framework and the cost of its deployment.

The aforementioned challenges are the foremost representative requirements that need to be researched for the development of high-assurance systems while incorporating the role played by human operators into the design, development and maintenance of such systems. A simulation-based evaluation, discussed in Section 3.5, can provide some insight and preliminary answers to these challenges.

5. Conclusions

In this chapter we have elaborated several HIE policy challenges for developing high-assurance systems. Given the growing complexity of network-enabled systems, the role of human vis-à-vis interoperability with systems, groups and across organization boundaries is crucial for achieving a high degree of assurance for network-enabled applications and missions. We have presented two broad categories of high assurance metrics that are technology-driven and are related to the interoperability aspects of human operators. The role of numerous technologies included HCC, IKIM and SoA as well as methodologies from the disciplines of human and social behavioral sciences for developing HIE framework have been elaborated. Finally, key steps for developing an HIE policy framework for engineering economically viable high assurance systems have been outlined.

References

[1] C. Atkinson, D. Brenner, G. Falcone, and M. Juhasz, "Specifying High Assurance Services," IEEE Computer, August 2008, pp: 64-71

[2] G.A. Boy, "Perceived Complexity and Cognitive Stability in Human-Centered Design," D. Harris (Ed.): Engineering Psychology and Cognitive Ergonomics, HCII 2007, LNAI 4562, pp. 10–21, Springer-Verlag Berlin Heidelberg 2007

[3] H.A. Handley and R.J. Smillie, "Architecture Framework Human View: The NATO Approach,' Systems Engineering, 2008, pp: 156-164, Wiley Periodicals.

[4] M. Kasunic and W. Anderson, "Measuring Systems Interoperability: Challenges and Opportunities," Technical Note, CMU/SEI-2004-TN-003, April 2004

[5] L. Warne, A. Ali, D. Bopping, D. Hart, and C. Pascoe, "The Network Centric Warrior: The Human Dimension of Network Centric Warfare," Tech. Report DSTO-CR-0373, Defense System Analysis Division, Edinburgh, Australia, July 2004.

[6] http://www.planecrashinfo.com/cause.htm

[7] J. Nosek, "Exploring Group Cognition as a Basis for Supporting Group Knowledge Creation and Sharing" Proceedings of AMCIS 1998, Paper 164.

[8] B.M. Toaszewski and A.M. MacEachren, "A distributed Spatiotemporal Cognition Approach to Visualization in Support of Coordinated Group Activity," Proceedings of the 3rd International ISCRAM Conference, May 2006, Newark, NJ, pp:1-5.

[9] http://www.star-tides.net/

[10] http://www.networkworld.com/news/2008/120108-10-microsoft-research-projects.html?page=2

[11] A. Pentland and A. Liu, "Modeling and Prediction of Human Behavior'" Neural Computation, Vol. 11, 1999, pp: 229-242

[12] R.E. Wray, and J.E. Laird, "Variability in Human Behavior Modeling for Military Simulations," Proceedings of the 12th Conference on Behavior Representation in Modeling and Simulation, May 2003.

[13] E. Salas, C. Prince, D.P. Baker, and L. Shrestha, "Situation Awareness in Team Performance: Implications for Measurement and Training," *Human Factors, 37, pp:* 123-136.

[14] W.T. Tasil, Q. Huang, B. Xiao, Y. Chen, and X. Zhou, "Collaboration Policy Generation in Dynamic Collaborative SOA." Proceedings of the 8th International Symposium on Autonomous Decentralized Systems, March 2007, Page(s):33 - 42

[15] E. Brunswik, "Perception and the Representative Design of Psychological Experiments," University of California Press, Berkeley, 1956 CA.

[16] R.W. Cooksey and P. Freebody, 'Generalized Multivariate Lens Model Analysis for Complex Human Interface Tasks," Jour. Of Organizational Behavior and Human Decision Processes, Vol. 35, 1985, pp: 46-72.

[17] M.R. Endsley, "Direct Measurement of Situation Awareness: Validity and Use of SAGAT," In: Endsley, M.R., Garland, D.J. (Eds.), Situation Awareness Analysis and Measurement. 2000, Erlbaum, Mahwah, NJ, pp. 147–174.

[18] E. Hutchins, "The Technology of Team Navigation," in J. Galegher, R. E. Kraut & C. Egido (Eds.) *Intellectual Teamwork - Social and Technological Foundations of Cooperative Work.* 1990, pp:22-51, Hillsdale, NJ

[19] B. Fischhoff, "Debiasing," In Kahneman, D., Slovic, P. and Tversky, A. (eds), *Judgment under Uncertainty: Heuristics and biases,* New York: Cambridge University Press, 1982.

[20] R. Bhatti, E. Bertino, A. Ghafoor, "A Trust-based Context-Aware Access Control Model for Web Services," *International Distributed and Parallel Databases Journal, Special Issue on Web Services*, Vol. 18, No. 1, July 2005, pp: 83-105

[21] R.M. Kramer, "Trust and Distrust in Organizations: Emerging Perspectives, Enduring Questions'" Annual Review of Psychology, Vol. 50, 1999, pp: 569-598

[22] J.A. Golbeck, "Computing and Applying Trust in Web-based Social Networks," Ph.D. Dissertation, Dept. of Computer Science. University of Maryland, 2005.

[23] R. Guha, R. Kumar, P. Raghavan, and A. Tomkins, "Propagation of Trust and Distrust," Proceeding of the Thirteen International World Wide Web Conference, 2004, pp: 403-412.

[24] J. Dong, R.A. Paul, and L-J. Zhang, "High Assurance Service-Oriented Architecture", IEEE Computer, August 2008, pp: 27-28

[25] M.J. Carey, "SOA What," IEEE Computer, No. 3 March 2008, pp; 92-94

[26] www.mceits.usmc.mil

[27] www.shfe.jsc.nasa.gov

[28] R. D. Whitaker and G. C. Kuperman, 'Cognitive Engineering for Information Dominance: A Human Factors Perspective," AL/CF-TR-1996-0159, Wright-Patterson AFB, OH 45433-7022

[29] B. Best, and C. Lebiere, "Spatial Plans, Communication, and Teamwork in Synthetic MOUT Agents," Proceedings of the 12th Conference on Behavior Representation in Modeling and Simulation, May 2003

Chapter 5

Service Composition Quality Evaluation in SPICE Platform

Paolo Falcarin

Politecnico di Torino, Dipartimento di Automatica e Informatica (DAUIN)

C. Duca degli Abruzzi 24, I-10129, Torino (Italy), Paolo.Falcarin@polito.it

Abstract. The goal of the SPICE project is to develop an extendable overlay architecture and framework to support easy and quick creation, and deployment of Telecommunication and Information Services. The SPICE Service Creation Environment (SCE) is used by developers to create both basic services and complex service compositions, which are then deployed in the SPICE Service Execution Environment (SEE), which hide the complexity of the communication environment. Along with its functional interface, each service exposes its own non-functional properties (like Response Time, Cost, Availability, etc...) by means of the SPATEL service description language. These properties are defined in an ontology and this chapter will discuss how the SCE helps developers in evaluating a service composition by calculating the aggregated values of such properties.

1. Introduction

Telecommunication services and network features are often tightly coupled, separate, and vertically integrated. This vertical approach has an extremely weakening effect on service provider's ability to develop more complex services that could span over heterogeneous telecom networks and IT services [1].

The common vision for implementing services is now the realization of a horizontal service platform, based on shared services and network enablers, which can be easily deployed in a distributed SEE (Service Execution Environment) and that can be used as basic blocks in a service composition which may cover different operators domains. Under such assumptions, the composition of communication services, content-based services, Internet-like services, and messaging services, which may span over different service providers, can affect the quality of service perceived by users. In fact, system administrators working in an operator domain

J. Dong et al. (eds.), *High Assurance Services Computing*,
DOI 10.1007/978-0-387-87658-0_5, © Springer Science+Business Media, LLC 2009

can apply quality enhancements on services running in their own SEE but they cannot access to a third-party SEE hosting services involved in a service composition.

Innovative model engineering techniques, like Model Driven Architecture (MDA) approach [2], tend to be used to abstract commonality between different execution platforms and to facilitate the development of systems that can target different execution environments. The exploitation of these techniques in the context of service engineering and, more specifically, in the telecommunication domain [3] is perceived as an opportunity for exporting on service interface non-functional properties.

A Service Creation Environment (SCE) is then needed to facilitate the composition of existing services and the semi-automatic configuration and deployment of IT-Telecom services [4]. The benefits of service composition stem from the possibility of reusing the effort invested in developing services, thereby enabling faster time-to-market and lower costs in the service development process. Under such assumptions, the SPICE project has designed and implemented an example of SOA in the telecommunication domain [5] in order to fulfill these requirements.

One of the goals of the SPICE platform is to provide high assurance composed services, even if they are made of services running on different application servers, in different domains.

In the following section the architecture of SPICE SEE is described, followed by a description of the SPICE SCE which helps service developer in evaluating the quality of an orchestration of telecom-IT services taking into account non functional properties; the usage of such properties is then discussed in an overview section about SPATEL language [6]; finally the aggregation of both static and dynamic non-functional properties is discussed with an example, before drawing conclusions.

2. SPICE Project

One of the goals of the SPICE Service Creation Environment is to facilitate the composition of existing services, to build new services. The benefits of service composition stem from the possibility of reusing the effort invested in developing services, thereby enabling faster time-to-market and lower costs in the service development process. This leads to direct and indirect benefits to service developers, platform operators and service providers.

The SPICE SCE provides facilities for designers to perform service composition, with a higher degree of automation than is provided in a traditional graphical service designer tool.

SPICE project has developed a SCE and a SEE to respectively compose and execute both IT and telecom services. The SCE allows developers to build their own service and to annotate its SPATEL representation with non-functional properties; moreover SCE allows developers to compose such services in a workflow of SPATEL services, and to get an estimation of the aggregated values of non-functional properties depending on the service composition workflow.

The SPATEL service description is published in a service repository and its functional part is translated to WSDL [19]. In case of SPATEL service compositions a BPEL script is automatically generated by the SCE and then deployed in the Service Execution Environment for orchestrating different web services running on multiple execution platforms. An overview of the main components of the SPICE architecture is sketched in figure 1.

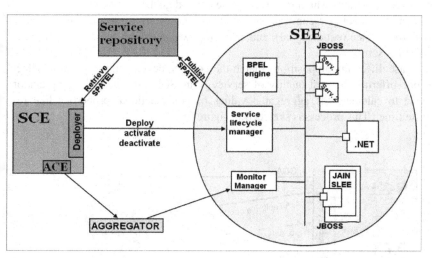

Fig. 1. Main Elements of SPICE Architecture.

The Service Creation Environment (SCE) is used by professional developers for designing arbitrarily complex services by using the SPATEL formalism for high-level design, in combination with general purpose languages for completing the non generated parts of the code of the service. In particular the tool will be used to specify composite services orchestrating other services, which could pre-exist or be developed from scratch.

The SCE provides different pluggable transformers that supports the translation of the SPATEL specification in the interface code for a target execution platform (such as JAIN-SLEE [8], J2EE [9], BPEL [16]). Within the SCE, two components are particularly relevant: the Automatic Service Composition Engine (ACE) and the Deployer.

Deployer is used to package and deploy a SPICE component and/or a SPICE service composition in the target SEE, sending packaged code, WSDL and SPATEL descriptions to the Service Lifecycle Manager which performs the actual service deployment on one of the selected platforms and publish the SPATEL service description on the public service repository.

Service Repository is queried by the SCE to fetch SPATEL descriptions of available services, and these can be used by developer to build a service composition.

For example, the developer specifies in the SCE a service request in terms of its inputs, outputs, preconditions, effects, and some non-functional properties.

This service request is passed to the ACE component which calculates automatically service compositions based on such request: the ACE analyzes SPATEL descriptions of services published in the repository and provides different possible service compositions which may satisfy the desired goal.

Then the developer can evaluate such compositions to see if they actually match the service request (goal), and select one which can be deployed in the SEE as a BPEL script.

In case different compositions match the goal the developer may want to select the one offering the best quality of service: thus SCE can query the Aggregator service to calculate the aggregated values of non-functional properties like response time. This process is sketched in figure 2.

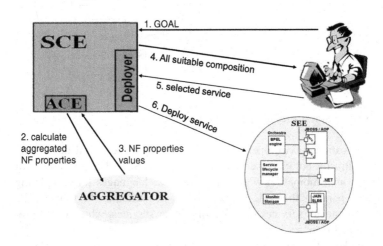

Fig. 2. Service Composition Process.

There has been a lot of interest in defining and working out mechanisms and frameworks for service composition in the industry and the academia [11]. Many approaches use semantic web services, i.e. web services interfaces annotated with semantic tags like WSDL-S [26], or other service description languages [14] [22] are used to more precisely describe information like: provider details, service goal, service parameters' types, service's quality attributes. Annotations follow formal terminologies, which are defined in an ontology, and they are machine-understandable and then usable for being processed by specific tools.

The services can be assembled together by using an automated process based on semantic tags. From this assembly, a "business process", expressing the logic of the calls to "elementary services", is generated. The new composite service is generated from the business process and later deployed. Goal-based approaches intend to provide a composite service from a request expressed in certain format. The request reflects the goals to be reached by the composite service.

For example, Fuji et al. [13] use "semantic graphs" derived from natural language descriptions, while in [28] semantic interfaces are annotated with service goals are used to compose services. A web services composition methodology is achieved by stitching together semantically-annotated web service components in a BPEL flow [27], while a composition of services as a directed graph where nodes refer to web services was presented in [10].

Aggregation of non-functional service properties then becomes a key decision factor for discriminating among a set of suitable service compositions.

In SPICE SCE service compositions are evaluated for their aggregated non-functional properties, selected and ranked; in this case, generation of alternative valid compositions is a process different from aggregation. Moreover, SCE focuses on checking if a service composition matches certain non-functional properties specified in a required service specification and it allows ranking of viable service compositions based on such properties: examples of non-functional properties that can be considered are cost, response time and reliability.

Yu et al. [30] proposed an approach that selects service components that, composed together, have a desired QoS: as input the request is parameterized with a process (e.g. a BPEL process) that identifies service component types rather than running service components.

This approach is also limited to processes that call service components in sequence, without considering choice nodes and loops in a process. Optimal selection of service components is a key issue for creating a service composition [31], but service description must provide more information that can be used to drive the developer during the composition design.

Jaeger et al. [15] proposed a mechanism to determine the overall Quality-of-Service (QoS) of a composition by aggregating the quality attributes of the individual services: they identify abstract composition patterns, which represent basic structural elements of a composition like a sequence, a loop, or a parallel execution and they define aggregation functions for each quality attribute: this theoretical approach is used and partially implemented in this work to calculate aggregate values of some non-functional properties, as described in section 5.

For more details on automatic service composition issues see [13] [23].

In following sections we will see how SPATEL language allows defining and exposing non-functional properties.

3. SPATEL Language

The SPICE project has defined a high-level and executable language for describing composite telecommunication services. This formalism, named SPATEL [6], meaning SPICE Advanced language for Telecommunication services, can essentially, be seen as a customization of the UML language for expressing the definition of service interfaces and service composition logic more suitable for the telecom domain. In contrast with most IT web services, telecom services are generally transactional, asynchronous, stateful and sometimes long-running processes, thus it is important to define constraints on the service interface such as the ordering of operation invocations.

SPATEL can be used both to define a single semantic-annotated service interface and to describe an orchestration of components through state machines which are more suitable for integrating "voice-based" dialogs in a service specification, since state machines are the most used paradigm for expressing the complexity that can be found in human-machine voice conversations.

We should note however that the scope of SPATEL is much broader than the scope of traditional voice services since we have to deal with remote synchronous and asynchronous invocations, parallel threads of execution and it provides means to represent typical voice-based interactions, inheriting from previous research work in the field of voice service modeling [3].

The SPATEL formalism aggregates well-know constructs coming from different sources (VoiceXML [18], ITU-SDL [19], SA-WSDL [21]) in order to provide the needed subset that is needed for a high-level and executable formalism usable in telecom context.

SPATEL formalism has been defined by an EMOF metamodel [25] and it comes with a UML2 profile defining the conventions for using the UML graphical notation, used to build service orchestrations.

The service interface description typically publishes the signature of each operation (its input parameters, result and message types), like in WSDL [19] the well-known standard for web services.

Service developer with SPICE SCE can use such additional information to compose a new service made up of an orchestration of different services, typically running in different service providers' domains.

In SPICE platform each service is described by means of the SPATEL language which allows enriching service interface with semantic annotations and non-functional properties which represents instances of concepts defined in a common ontology defined in the SPICE project [7].

Indeed, without a shared understanding (both of semantics and syntax) between applications, the communication is not feasible, or it has to be obtained with manual integration. In this case an ontology is useful, as it is a formal specification of concepts, axioms and definitions stated in a description logic, that enable computers to understand process its content.

For example, the Ontology Web Language (OWL) [24] describes in XML the concepts and their relationships, with different levels of formality, in a particular domain. By establishing a common vocabulary among services, the ontology files support the sharing and reuse of formally represented knowledge.

An important feature of SPATEL is the ability to annotate the elements of the interface (like the operations and the parameters) with semantics tags and non functional properties to enable better service discovery and automated composition.

Non-functional properties are partitioned on the basis of categories like quality of service (QoS), charging, internationalization, etc... The annotation mechanism is similar to the SAWSDL approach [21], as it relies on pointers to concepts defined in external ontologies.

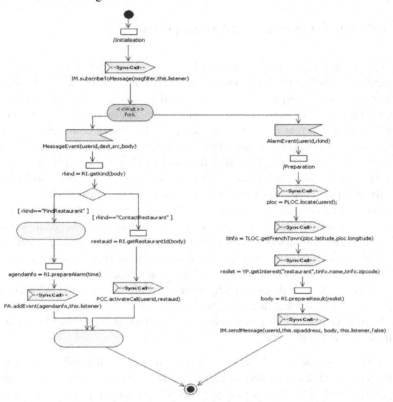

Fig. 3. An example of service composition with SPATEL graphical notation

SPATEL language follows an approach to semantically annotate the different aspects of the service, like types, operations and service goal. The following list contains the different kinds of semantic annotations that are present in SPATEL:

• Annotations on IO parameters of the service.

- Annotations on goals that describe the overall objective of a service or the objective of a single operation exposed by the service.
- Annotations on the effects of a given operation that describe the outcomes of its execution in terms of state achieved by the service or action performed.
- Annotations on the preconditions of a given operation describe the conditions that have to be satisfied in order to allow its execution.
- Annotations on non-functional properties to describe aspects related to the quality of service, charging or resource usage.

In figure 3, an example of SPATEL notation for a composed service is shown, and more details on the graphical notation are described in [6].

4. Ontology for non-functional properties

In commercial communication services a very important aspect is non functional properties or quality attributes of services. They are important to provide and guarantee good usability and a good user experience for the service consumer, and they are important for monitoring and control purposes for the service provider. In SPICE project different categories and attributes have been considered and structured into an ontology of non-functional properties (see figure 4).

In contrast to functional attributes, the number of non-functional attributes can be virtually unlimited, and many research works have already been performed to classify them [12]. A similar initiative to categorize non-functional properties is the Web Services Modeling Ontology (WSMO) that attempts to provide a framework to be used for describing web services and their non-functional properties [29]. The framework offers an outline of the type of non-functional properties that are required: error rate, network quality of service, reliability, robustness, scalability, security, transactions and trust. In SPICE many features and concepts of telecom domain has been described which may partially overlap the WSMO: more details on SPICE ontology are available in [7].

The non-functional categories below are the one considered in SPICE, among all those defined in the ontology:

1. Charging: A function whereby information related to chargeable events is formatted, stored, and transferred, correlated, rated and charging accounts are adjusted accordingly. This is necessary in order to make it possible to determine usage for which the charged party may be billed.
2. QoS properties considered are:

   - Response Time: the time a service operation takes to provide a result whenever it is invoked; average, minimum, and maximum response times are considered.
   - Availability: the percentage of time on which a service is operable and ready to provide its capabilities:

3. Security: Encryption types. Security aspects are usually handled separately in a platform. However, some services provide sensitive information that one does not want to pass unencrypted through the network or to other services. From the service composer viewpoint it is important to evaluate which one of the services in a service orchestration does not encrypt data sent on the network, in order to possibly replace it with another similar service offering such security features.
4. Internationalization: in case of information services (like Yellow Pages) it is important to know in which languages the results can be expressed.

The non-functional properties can be divided into two main groups: static and dynamic properties. For example, charging rates, language support are relatively fixed attributes. Even though the total cost will vary, you know exactly in advanced how it will vary. The values are defined manually, so what you read is what you get. Other attributes like response time will only be an average time provided by the Monitor Manager of the SEE in which the service is deployed.

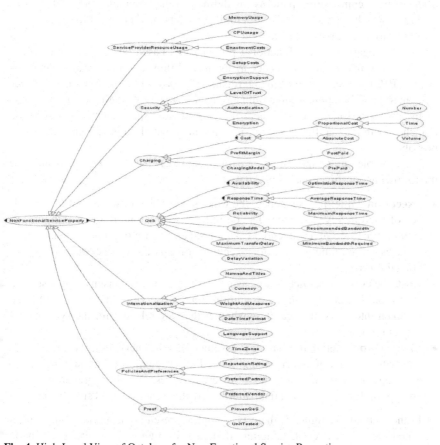

Fig. 4. High-Level View of Ontology for Non-Functional Service Properties

5. Aggregation of Non Functional Properties

The Aggregator defines a pluggable architecture for aggregation of non-functional service properties. Each attribute or attribute category can be addressed in different specific aggregator services which are added to the framework. This allows extensibility of the framework with additional non-functional properties, and enables the reuse of functionality intended to analyze the SPATEL specification which represents the service composition.

The Aggregator assumes that services in a composition do not depend on each other. This assumption states that the result or the execution of one service does not change the quality of other services. Moreover non-functional properties refer to the same definition in the above-mentioned Non-Functional Properties ontology, where their unit of measure is defined along with transformations among different units of measure.

Given a SPATEL representation of a service composition, the Aggregator identifies abstract composition patterns (as defined in the previous work of Jaeger et al. [15]), which represent basic structural elements of a composition, like a sequence, a loop, or a parallel execution.

The aggregation of non-functional properties is based on an algorithm which recognizes composition patterns occurring in workflow and orchestration languages (like BPEL), it applies existing aggregation functions [15], and invokes the specific aggregator components to obtain aggregated values for these patterns.

In case of a decision point where the control flow splits in different separate branches or in the parallel fork case, it is assumed that all branches have the same probability.

For example, three kinds of aggregator components have been implemented for the following non-functional properties:

- **Execution Time**: in a sequence, the time is determined by the sum of the values of each involved service. The definitions for minimum and maximum execution times are in a sequential case the same. In case of parallel execution of services the minimum value for execution time is the largest value of all involved services.
- **Cost**: the cost of a service is a measure for the resources consumed by a service execution. Different from the execution time, all services that were used must be taken into account, regardless whether they are relevant for the synchronizing join or not.
- **Encryption Level**: in this case it is assumed that the encryption level is equivalent with the kind of algorithm and related key's length used for signing or encryption, enumerated in a series of discrete values. For the aggregation of the encryption level in a sequential pattern, only the weakest key is significant.

In the example of figure 5, there is a graph representing a service composition obtained from a SPATEL diagram depicted in figure 3, where each node represents a service and an edge between two nodes represents a temporal sequence in the control flow of the service orchestration. In particular, this figure shows the values of non-functional properties.

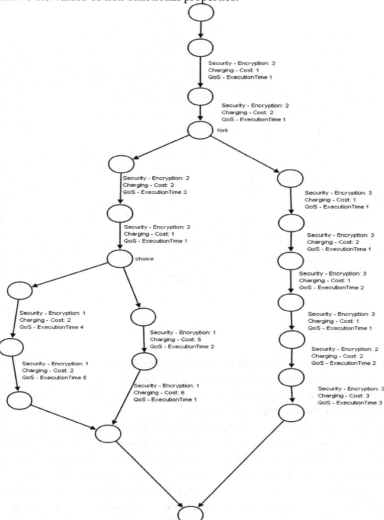

Fig. 5. Initial graph of the service orchestration

The Aggregator can extract this graph from the SPATEL composition and it collapses the nodes in a each sequential path, calculating the aggregated values of the non-functional properties, using the above-mentioned aggregation functions [15]. After a first transformation where all sequential paths are collapsed it is time to collapse parallel nodes in a single one, then the graph is transformed in the one in figure 6; then the algorithm restarts collapsing sequential paths followed by parallel ones. Applying continuously the collapsing of nodes, the graph is reduced to a single node exposing its aggregated non-functional properties.

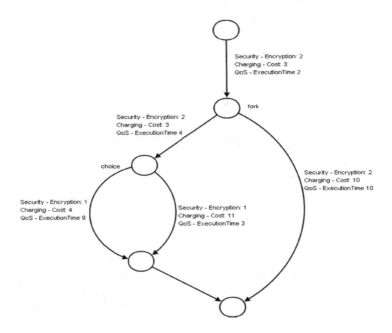

Fig. 6. Service orchestration graph after first aggregation

One of the goals of the SPICE platform is to provide high assurance composed services, even if they are made of services running on different application servers, in different domains, but sharing a common management API to be used by system administrators for monitoring purposes.

The Monitor Manager invokes the management API of each application server in the SPICE SEE, in order to get statistics on response time of each operation of each service deployed in the application server, and it stores these values in its local database. Whenever a system administrator or the Aggregator invoke the Monitor Manager interface, it calculates and returns the requested performance indicators of each service, like values minimum, maximum and average response time. This information can be used by the aggregator which takes information about the non-functional properties of various services and use these values to return an aggregate of non-functional properties' values.

In SPATEL each non-functional property can be set as static or dynamic. If the non-functional property is static, then its value has been set by the service provider before deployment and cannot always be trusted, while if the property is dynamic, it means that its value is calculated at run-time querying the appropriate service in the SEE.

The developer can thus choose a determinate service composition, depending either on static properties (like cost or security level) or on dynamic ones calculated on actual values observed by the Monitor Manager in the SEE.

6. Conclusions

SPICE project has developed a SCE and a SEE to respectively compose and execute both IT and telecom services. The SCE allows developers to build their own service and to annotate its SPATEL representation with non-functional properties; moreover SCE allows developers to compose such services in a workflow of SPATEL services, and to get an estimation of the aggregated values of non-functional properties depending on the service composition workflow.

This chapter described how the SPICE project manages the non-functional service properties at design-time, and how the Aggregator service calculates the overall aggregated non-functional properties of a service composition designed by the SCE developer, relying also on the Monitor manager which provides live values of dynamic non-functional properties such as Response Time.

This kind of evaluation of service composition quality attributes is useful for service developer to carefully select services to be bound in a service composition, which will be deployed and executed as a BPEL orchestration script in the SEE.

Future work is devoted to measure the performance and scalability of this approach on large service repositories and more complex service composition workflow structures.

Acknowledgments

This work has been performed in the framework of the IST project IST-2005-027617 SPICE, which was partly funded by the European Union. Special thanks to all project partners, and in particular to Mariano Belaunde (Orange Labs), Federico Mura, Alessio Bosca (Politecnico di Torino), Mazen Malek Shiaa (NTNU Trondheim), and Anne Marte Hjemas (Telenor).

References

[1] S. Tarkoma, B. Bharat, E. Kovacs, H. van Kranenburg, E. Postmann, R. Seidl, A. Zhdanova, "SPICE: A Service Platform for Future Mobile IMS Services," in Proceedings of IEEE International Symposium on World of Wireless, Mobile and Multimedia Networks (WoWMoM 2007), June 2007, pp: 1-8, ISBN: 978-1-4244-0993-8.
[2] OMG, "Model Driven Architecture". Web link: http://www.omg.org/mda/
[3] M. Belaunde, J.M. Presso, Vision for an industrial application of MDD in the Telecommunications Industry, ECMDA'05 Conference, Springer July 2005.
[4] P. Falcarin, C. Venezia: "Communication Web Services and JAIN-SLEE Integration Challenges". In Journal of Web Services Research (JWSR), Vol. 5(4), IGI-Global, 2008, ISSN 1545-7362.
[5] SPICE (Service Platform for Innovative Communication Environment) project homepage. On-line at http://www.ist-spice.org/
[6] M. Belaunde, P. Falcarin, "Realizing an MDA and SOA marriage for the development of Mobile Services", European Conference On Model Driven Architecture, June 2008, Springer.
[7] C. Villalonga, M. Strohbach, N. Snoeck, M. Sutterer, M. Belaunde, E. Kovacs, A.V. Zhdanova, L.W. Goix, O. Droegehorn, "Mobile Ontology: Towards a Standardized Semantic Model

for the Mobile Domain," in Telecom Service Oriented Architectures Workshop (TSOA-2007), September 2007, to appear on Springer LNCS.

[8] JAIN-SLEE   API   Specification.   Java   Community   Process   website:
http://jcp.org/aboutJava/communityprocess/final/jsr022/index.html

[9] Java 2 Enterprise Edition. http://java.sun.com/javaee/

[10] Zhang, R., Arpinar, I.B., Aleman-Meza, B.: Automatic composition of semantic web services. In IEEE ICWS. (2003), pp 38–41.

[11] M.P. Papazoglou, D. Georgakopoulos, "Service-Oriented Computing," Communications of the ACM, October 2003, Vol. 46, n. 10, pp. 25-28.

[12] J. O'Sullivan, D. Edmond, A.H.M. ter Hofstede, "What's in a service? Towards accurate description of non-functional service properties", Distributed and Parallel Databases, 2002, pp. 117-133, Kluwer ed.

[13] K. Fujii, T. Suda, "Semantics-Based Dynamic Service Composition," IEEE Journal on Selected Areas of Communications, v. 23(12), December 2005, pp. 2361-2372.

[14] Web Ontology Language specification. On-line at http://www.w3.org/2004/OWL/

[15] M.C. Jaeger, G. Rojec-Goldmann, G. Muhl, "QoS Aggregation in Web Service Compositions", IEEE International Conference on e-Technology, e-Commerce and e-Service (EEE'05), 2005, pp. 181-185.

[16] BPEL, Business Process Execution Language for Web Services. On-line at http://www.ibm.com/developerworks/library/specification/ws-bpel/.

[17] OMG, "MOF 2.0 Query/Views and Transformations", http://www.omg.org/spec/QVT/1.0/

[18] W3C/VoiceXML Forum: Voice Extensible Markup Language, www.voicexml.org

[19] W3C, Web Service Definition Language (WSDL), www.w3.org/TR/wsdl

[20] ITU-T, Specification Definition Language (SDL). Web link: www.itu.int/ITU-T

[21] W3C: Semantic Annotations for WSDL and XML Schema, W3C Recommendation, 28 August 2007. Web link www.w3.org/2002/ws/sawsdl/

[22]   OMG,   Uml   Profile   And   Metamodel   for   Services   RFP,
http://www.omg.org/cgibin/doc?soa/06-09-09, September 2009

[23] A. Bosca, G. Valetto, R. Maglione, F. Corno; "Specifying Web Service Compositions on the Basis of Natural Language Requests"; ICSOC'05 3rd International Conference on Service Oriented Computing, Amsterdam, December 2005

[24] Semantic Markup for Web Services (OWL-S), http://www.w3.org/Submission/OWL-S/

[25] OMG, "Meta Object Facility V2.0", http://www.omg.org/spec/MOF/2.0

[26] Web Service Semantics (WSDL-S), www.w3.org/Submission/WSDL-S/

[27] Agarwal, V., Dasgupta, K., Karnik, N., Kumar, A., Kundu, A., Mittal, S., and Srivastava, B. A service creation environment based on end to end composition of Web services. In Proceedings of the 14th international Conference on World Wide Web (2005). ACM Press, New York, NY, 128-137.

[28] Philippe Larvet, "Automatic Orchestration of Web Services Through Semantic Annotations", ICEIS 2007, 9th International Conference on Enterprise Information Systems, June 2007.

[29] Jos de Bruijn, Christoph Bussler, Dieter Fensel, Michael Kifer, Jacek Kopecky, Rubn Lara, Eyal Oren, Axel Polleres, and Michael Stollberg. Web Services Modeling Ontology (WSMO). http://www.wsmo.org/

[30] Yu, T., Kwei-Jay, L.: Service Selection Algorithms for Web-Services with End-to-End QoS Constraints. Information Systems and E-Business Management 3(2): 103-126 (2005)

[31] L. Zeng, B. Benatallah, M. Dumas, J. Kalagnanam, and Q.Z. Sheng. Quality Driven Web Services Composition. In Proceedings of the 12th International Conference on the World Wide Web (WWW), Budapest, Hungary, May 2003. ACM Press.

Chapter 6

High-Assurance Service Systems

Jay Bayne

Milwaukee Institute, 411 E. Wisconsin Ave, Suite 1280, Milwaukee, WI 53092
jbayne@mkei.org

Abstract. High-assurance systems (HAS) are information systems designed and implemented to achieve a degree of *predictable* behavior, with predictability expressed in terms of their *reliability, availability, safety, security* and *timeliness* (RASST) properties. High-assurance *service systems* (HASS) are a special class of HAS providing interactive, network-accessible and dynamically bound *services* to clients typically unknown at design time. *Cyberphysical systems* (CS) are, in turn, a special class of HASS responsible for automation and control services governing a wide range of physical processes. A service, in this context, results from transactional exchanges of information of specified *value* between service providers (servers) and their customers (clients) on behalf of certain application-level objectives. These application-oriented transactions, carried out through discoverable service interface protocols, are governed by *service level agreements* (SLA) expressing performance-related *assurances* that servers agree, *a priori*, to provide to their clients. In dynamically bound service environments, specification of assurances depends on existence of a published set of performance indices and associated measurement processes for RASST and related properties. Consequently, high-assurance service systems require a *performance measurement framework* (PMF) competent to express service-oriented *value propositions* and their RASST dependencies. This chapter introduces a CS PMF, with a focus on three key elements. First, we introduce a *cyberspatial reference model* (CRM) for establishing the identity and location of distributed HASS servers and clients. Second, we define a set of service performance indices to measure RASST properties. Third, we develop an application neutral, yet operational definition of *value* useful in high assurance service systems for defining their respective value propositions.

1. Introduction

The design and implementation of *service systems* represent an important research area within systems science, engineering and enterprise management disciplines [30]. Achieving measurable degrees of assured (predictable) behavior in

J. Dong et al. (eds.), *High Assurance Services Computing*,
DOI 10.1007/978-0-387-87658-0_6, © Springer Science+Business Media, LLC 2009

service systems requires that their performance scale upward with increasing resources and downward when failures occur or capacity saturates—while striving for non-stop operation. Under extreme conditions or catastrophic failures, service systems are expected to stop in a "safe" state, with a reasonable expectation of a subsequent reliable restart.

Cyberphysical systems (CS) are a class of high-assurance service systems responsible for the automation and control of a wide range of physical processes. CS have a long tradition of adhering to RASST requirements, albeit in typically special-purpose and isolated applications. They are *high-consequence systems* due to their responsibility for monitoring and controlling safety-critical infrastructure, including dams, airports, trains, automobiles, commercial buildings, power production and distribution systems, refineries, refrigeration systems, hospitals and weapons systems. The majority of today's CS are legacy systems. They are everywhere and increasingly they interconnect through standardized communications protocols to form ad hoc, loosely coupled *federated systems*. While their individual service levels may be subject to strict assurances (e.g., via specific V&V techniques); their ensemble behaviors are typically unknown and unpredictable, for generally they were not designed for assured levels of interoperation, let alone performance as modern online (interactive and dynamically bound) service-oriented systems[1]. While especially true of legacy systems, even in new distributed systems, management (i.e., HASS administration) remains a significant engineering challenge for emerging software-as-a-service (SaaS) architectures [10, 15, 30].

There are several reasons for this situation. First, contemporary software engineering practices do not in general require coherent models of service system operating environments. Second, there are generally no accepted models of how to administer CS systems, operating alone or in concert. Third, there exist no standardized metrics for continuously monitoring and evaluating service systems, operating individually or as federations. Fourth, there are no general methods dealing with end-to-end timelines in distributed service systems under real-time constraints. Finally, there are no common semantics allowing two or more service systems to articulate their individual *value propositions* in a manner that supports establishment of their mutual *assurances* under dynamic discovery and binding. CS, when interconnected and supporting predictable levels of assured operation, require a common cyberspatial reference model (CRM).

---

[1] Service-oriented architectures (SOA) define application software design patterns appropriate for implementing network-accessible services [10, 15, 30].

2. Cyberspatial Reference Model[2]

The behavior of service systems, independent of their expressed assurance levels, unfolds in *cyberspace*, the environment (reference frame, context or domain) in which human and synthetic actors engage and establish communities of mutual interest (partnerships, federations, alliances, or coalitions). Their interactions are ostensibly for growth and survival, for achieving their stated goals and objectives, and for maintaining dynamic equilibrium (homeostasis) required for sustaining their individual and collective *viability* as sovereign (self-regulating) entities. In cyberspace, service systems create and exchange services deemed valuable by other service systems. They form collaborations (federations, joint ventures or alliances), and often referred to as socio-economic networks or *value webs*. Individual and mutual *value propositions* governing federations establish the high-assurance requirements for individual and collective operation.

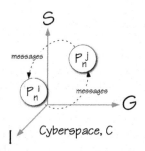

Fig. 1. Interacting Cyberspatial Objects

Entities operating in cyberspace are simultaneously physical (tangible, real) and present in *geospace* (G), informational (logical, virtual) and present in *infospace* (I), and social (organizational, governmental) and present in *sociospace* (S). Within cyberspace, a high-assurance service system creates value through one or more rational agents [33], or *cyberspatial objects* (CO). In a CS environment, *messages* are the means for one CO to exert *forces* on another. Messages flow through infospace to affect decisions at rational sociospatial endpoints that govern the states and behaviors of geophysical processes. In Fig. 1, two CO *processes* operating on behalf of (i.e., subordinate to) CS_n and labeled P_n^i and P_n^j, interact in a region of cyberspace. They affect each other's behavior through sending and responding to messages. Each CO occupies a specific *location* {G,I,S} at a point in time. Each has a unique *identity* and sustains itself by offering services characterized by quantifiable and discoverable value propositions.

---

[2] Some material in this section, without reference to HASS, appeared in the June 2008 issue of the IEEE Transactions on Systems, Man and Cybernetics, Part B (SMCB) under the title *Cyberspatial Mechanics*.

Relationships among cooperating CO are established either statically at design time (a priori) or dynamically at run time (a posteriori), as required. Dynamic binding is accomplished via *trading protocols* [28] through which consumers (clients) *ask* for services and producers (suppliers) respond with *bids*. The consumer subsequently *accepts* a bid that satisfies the *value proposition* underwriting its service request. Following acceptance the producer completes the request by delivering to the client a result satisfying the *ask*. The *value* of the result to the client is defined in the *price[3]* element of the *accept* order. The *marginal value* to the producer is the difference between that *price* and its *cost* of producing a result. Negotiation (i.e., iterative *ask-bid* cycles) may take place prior to an *accept*. In high-assurance systems, trading (binding) protocols must be reliable and transparent (i.e., auditable) and conclude in predictable time within a defined region of cyberspace.

2.1 Service Systems

Describing the behavior of individual service-oriented CO and their HASS containers implies existence of a formal governance process (operations model) and an associated set of operational performance metrics. Comparing behaviors of interacting CO requires that the model and metrics be generalized and scalable, applicable to a potentially wide range of service systems and underlying value propositions. Relative performance (e.g., throughput yield, transaction response time) depends both on structural (organizational) and functional (process) considerations.

Fig. 2 diagrams the internal governance structure of CS_n and its K_n subordinate CO services. This *cybernetics[4]* model was derived from consideration of the structure and function of the human neuroanatomical system. It was introduced by Beer [8] as the *viable systems model* (VSM), mechanizing his theory of *management cybernetics*. Subsequently, this author refined the model and applied it to a broad class of military and manufacturing *enterprise governance systems* (EGS), also called enterprise command and control (EC2) systems [5]. EC2 theory [6] considers a CS a sovereign *enterprise*, governed by one or more rational actors (i.e., its management team or flight crew)[5], organized in a *collaborative* command structure as shown. Governance structures may vary according to regional, eco-

---

[3] Price (cost) may be denominated in currency, energy or mass consumed or in other application-specific figures of merit.

[4] Cybernetics is a systems science of long standing focused on the relation between automation and control in natural and synthetic systems.

[5] Depending on the size and complexity of an enterprise system, one actor (e.g., a pilot) may serve the combined E5, E4 and E3 function or several actors may serve in a team for each individual function.

nomic, political and social norms, but if *viable* (i.e., interactive, sustainable, accountable) they share key operational characteristics [2, 4, 8, 11, 19].

As diagrammed in Fig. 2, CS are composed of potentially many (embedded, encapsulated, subordinate) CO, labeled $EO_n^1...EO_n^k$, each offering through a given business or manufacturing *process* (P_n^k) a specific service. In high-assurance systems, CO (both their platforms and application processes) are typically redundant (either duplicate or triplicate) and distributed to provide failover and fault tolerance protections.

In the face of dynamic and probabilistic demand, achieving a degree of optimal (e.g., cost effective) performance requires that each CS be governed by some form of command structure *accountable* for its behavior. It is customary, logical and intuitive to define governance structures in terms of roles and responsibilities of three primary actors [7, 19, 23, 31], here labeled echelon E5, E4 and E3. E5 (executive) providing decision making at the highest level of authority (accountability), E4 (navigator) providing strategy, analysis and planning, and E3 (operator) attending to tactical execution activities.

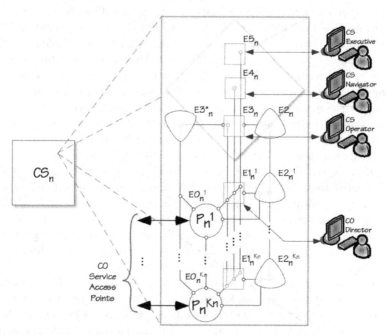

Fig. 2. CS Governance Structure

Agile and adaptive cyberphysical systems are necessarily both proactive and reactive. They maintain their dynamic stability (balance, homeostasis) through *supervisory* controls. As in natural systems, homeostatic control [4, 6, 7, 31] is achieved through two juxtaposed and counter-balancing feedback loops, expressed in Fig. 2 as the *sympathetic* (E3-E1-E2-E3) and *parasympathetic* (E3-E3*-E0-E1-E3) circuits. Furthermore, if autonomous, CO are governed through tactical *regu-*

latory feedback control loops (E0-E2-E1-E0). In a recursive fashion, each E1 actor (CO Director) represents the command function accountable for the next lower level of value production. Consequently, E1 at level n in the management command hierarchy represents E5-E4-E3 at level n-1. In this self-consistent model, command chains may nest to arbitrary levels.

Each $E0^i$ actor (CO production process) encapsulates a specific unit or quantum of value production, described by process P_n^i, $i=1...K_n$. Service-oriented CO are accessible through specific *service access points* (SAP). CO within a CS may be stationary or mobile in each of three cyberspatial dimensions, independently or in unison. If mobile, their velocities and accelerations may also vary in each dimension.

In our construction, cyberspace has nine dimensions. With the inclusion of time, our cyberspace-time model provides cyberspatial objects with 10 degrees of freedom. This definition integrates three historically and semantically distinct coordinate systems. To allow them to form a proper hyperspace *{G,I,S}* supported by a rationalized distance metric, we require a common unit of distance measure.

Our solution makes two key assumptions: 1) in each dimension, a coordinate may be interpreted is an abstract *address object* and 2) the three primary and three subordinate dimensions are orthogonal. At both indexing levels, address objects are 3-tuples: *{G,I,S}={{x,y,z},{g,s,a},{f,p,c}}*. This approach rationalizes addresses by converting each 3-tuple to a standard integer format augmented with domain-specific metadata, the details of which are the subject of a future paper. Each cyberspatial address component (e.g., the infospatial *Service Point* index, "*a*" in *{g,s,a}*) is defined as a 64-bit integer. Consequently, each 3-tuple defines three components of a 192-bit address object on which uniform address arithmetic (supporting intra- and inter-space distance metrics) may be computed.

In the geospatial dimension (e.g., *latitude*, "*x*" in *{x,y,z}*) we have employed indexing relative to traditional geocentric (spherical) coordinates. Alternatively, we could have utilized indexing related to a *digital earth reference model* (DERM) [16] where *{x,y,z}* refers to the location of a hexagonal region defined by a tessellation on the earth's surface. Goals motivating our work include design and implementation of a DERM-compliant CO directory service to be used for identifying and tracking CO and their interdependencies.

Cyberspace is assumed Euclidean (orthogonal) and compact. In our formulation, orthogonality has two complementary and equally important meanings. The first derives from traditional mathematical concepts where orthogonal Euclidean 3-space vectors produce zero dot products. The second is a software design principle resulting from the desire to isolate system behaviors in order to realize compact (small, efficient) functional designs.

From the service software design perspective, orthogonality is one of the most important properties in making complex designs more concise (compact). In a purely orthogonal design, operations have specific and limited consequences; each action (process step), whether implemented with a service or a macro invocation or a language or protocol operation, changes a single object (e.g., a parameter) per invocation without affecting others, thus producing minimal and controlled side effects. There is one and only one way to change a property of whatever object is being controlled.

The cyberspatial position of an object is diagrammed in Fig. 4. The cyberspatial position of CO_i at time t_k is $P_i(t_k) = \{G_i, I_i, S_i\}(t_k)$. The cyberspatial distance between objects CO_i and CO_j is then

$$d_{i,j}^C(t_k) = \sqrt{d_{i,j}^G(t_k)^2 + d_{i,j}^I(t_k)^2 + d_{i,j}^S(t_k)^2}$$

where $d_{i,j}^\chi(t_k)$, for $\chi \in \{G, I, S\}$ are distance metrics for each of the three subordinate dimensions[6].

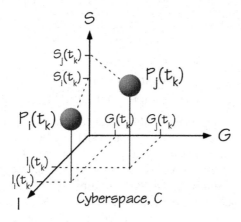

Fig. 3. Cyberspatial Coordinates

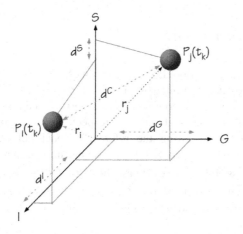

Fig. 4. Relative Cyberspatial Position

---

[6] "$\{...\}$" represents a list or vector of items *and* "$\{...\}(t)$" denotes a list whose elements are functions of time.

2.2 Geospatial Dimension

Geospace provides an earth-centered reference frame for specifying the physical location of an object. $P_i^G(t_k) = \{x_i, y_i, z_i\}(t_k)$ is the *geospatial* location of cyberspatial object CO_i at time t_k. This representation presumes that time is measured uniformly along each axis. We postponse discussion of relativistic effects (e.g., Lorentz transformations) in situations when velocities of geospatial objects *(G_i)* approach vacuum light speed. While this phenomenon is unlikely in geospace and sociospace, it is possible in infospace.

As in standard practice, the geospatial distance between CO_i and CO_j at time t_k is given by

$$d_{i,j}^G(t_k) = \sqrt{d_x(t_k)^2 + d_y(t_k)^2 + d_z(t_k)^2}$$
$$d_x(t_k) = x_i(t_k) - x_j(t_k)$$
$$d_y(t_k) = y_i(t_k) - y_j(t_k)$$
$$d_z(t_k) = z_i(t_k) - z_j(t_k)$$

We note for both practical and historical reasons that geospatial objects also have geo-referenced *service access points* (SAP), referred to as postal addresses and land-line voice and video circuit (aka, *last mile*) addresses. Through these physical addresses real mail, video and voice are sent and received. Increasingly non-tangible service traffic is carried via infospatial circuits in the form of digital voice, video and data (e.g., web content and email). We include postal addresses and analog communications circuits as geospatial addresses since we can map $\{x, y, z\}$ coordinate references to these more traditional forms of physical address.

2.3 Infospatial Dimension

Expanding on work sponsored, in part, by the Air Force Research Laboratory [14], *infospace* provides a framework in which to specify the locations of an object's *service access points*, communications ports on the object through which it interacts with other objects about their respective states, goods and services (value propositions). Following the reference model defned in the Internet Protocol version 6 (IPv6) standard [27], we define a generalized infospatial service port address for service P_i as the 3-tuple $r_i^I = \{g_i, s_i, a_i\}$, where g designates the global network address (nominally 48 bits), s designates the sub-network address (16 bits) and a designates the sub-network's particular service access point (64 bits).

Let $P^I_{i,n}(t_k) = \{g_i, s_i, a_{i,n}\}(t_k)$ be the *infospatial* location of CO_i's n^{th} SAP at time t_k. We define the infospatial distance between access point n on CO_i and access point m on CO_j at time t_k as

$$d^{n,m}_{i,j}(t_k) = \sqrt{d^{n,m}_g(t_k)^2 + d^{n,m}_s(t_k)^2 + d^{n,m}_a(t_k)^2}$$

$$d^{n,m}_g(t_k) = g^n_i(t_k) - g^m_j(t_k)$$

$$d^{n,m}_s(t_k) = s^n_i(t_k) - s^m_j(t_k)$$

$$d^{n,m}_a(t_k) = a^n_i(t_k) - a^m_j(t_k)$$

2.4 Sociospatial Dimension

Sociospace is a framework for specifying the location of an object with respect to its *operational role* within one or more federations. As with the *intra-CS* governance structure of Fig. 2, the *inter-CS* operational structure shown in Fig. 5 is based on an enterprise model developed in [6]. Sociospatial value webs are 3D, with index f designating a specific federation, p designating the enterprise's position along that federation's horizontal production axis and c designating the enterprise's position along the federation's vertical command (accountability) axis. In Fig. 5, $CS_{f,p,c}$ belongs to at least one "root" or "home" federation (i.e., $f=1$). At its creation and until altered, the root context of a CS is that of its parent (superior).

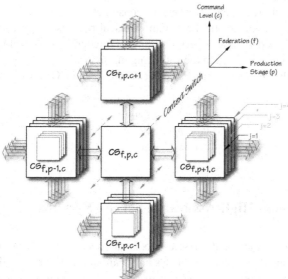

Fig. 5. Sociospatial Service System Structure

Vertically in a given federated service system, $CS_{f,p,c}$ is a subordinate (child) to, and therefore dependent upon (accountable to), a single superior (parent) $CS_{f,p,c+1}$ and is superior to (a parent of) and therefore responsible (accountable) for its subordinates (children) $CS_{f,p,c-1}$. Horizontally, $CS_{f,p,c}$ is a supplier to (producer for) its clients (consumers) $CS_{f,p+1,c}$ and a consumer (client) of its suppliers (producers) $CS_{f,p-1,c}$. The vertical axis defines a federation's chain of authority (command); the horizontal axis defines its logistics (supply) chain. As diagrammed in Fig. 5, each enterprise typically holds membership concurrently in several ($f > 1$) federations, requiring its governance system to maintain situation awareness and sufficient agility to *context switch* among its multiple federations.

Operationally, this technical definition requires the enterprise governance system to treat enterprises and their activities in much the same way multiprogrammed computer operating systems (specifically their kernels) treat running processes. Essentially, each service (CO) is assigned to a *virtual machine* (i.e., particular governance structure) that is allocated by scheduling policy sufficient resources (e.g., CPU, memory, time) to allow its tasks to run to time-bounded completion. Our enterprise governance system (Fig. 2) provides the function of an OS kernel, implementing an *enterprise operating system* (EOS) that maintains integrity among multiple contexts while running the supply and command axis tasks (CO) for each federation in which it is a participant.

$P_i^{S_{n,m}}(t_k) = \{f_i, p_{i,n}, c_{i,m}\}(t_k)$ is the *sociospatial* position of enterprise object CO_i at time t_k. Within any single federation f, a given member typically interacts with multiple concurrent service providers (producers), clients (consumers) and subordinates enterprises. The n and m indices identify the location and role of a particular neighbor, (n) on the producer-consumer axis and (m) on the superior-subordinate axes. For practical and philosophical reasons, as noted in the figure, our model assumes a single superior within each federation. To simplify notation we omit the n and m indices in the following discussion.

We define the sociospatial distance between CO_i and CO_j at time t_k as

$$d_{i,j}^S(t_k) = \sqrt{d_f(t_k)^2 + d_p(t_k)^2 + d_c(t_k)^2}$$
$$d_f(t_k) = f_i(t_k) - f_j(t_k)$$
$$d_p(t_k) = p_i(t_k) - p_j(t_k)$$
$$d_c(t_k) = c_i(t_k) - c_j(t_k)$$

3. Timeliness in High-Assurance Service Systems

Synchronized logical and physical clocks are necessary [21] but not sufficient for guaranteeing that cyberspatial systems can provide services that are, in a measurable sense, *timely* with respect to service-level commitments expected of their federation (sociospatial) partners. Quality clocks do assist in providing accurate timestamps and for supporting high resolution scheduling of local resources, but in collaborative arrangements among distributed agents, group (i.e., end-to-end or transnode) timeliness requires additional facilities.

There is today no generally accepted (let alone, standardized) mechanism to achieve end-to-end timeliness in distributed systems, especially remote method invocations (RMI) allowing two or more distributed CO processes to *rendezvous* in cyberspace-time. There is, however, a significant body of contemporary work addressing the subject [17], including a *thread scheduling* paradigm realized in Real-Time CORBA V1.2 [25] and compliant ACE/TAO [1] open source middleware, the non-distributed Real-Time Specification for Java (RTSJ) [18] and its *distributable thread* (DT) successor introduced in the Distributed Real-Time Specification for Java (DRTSJ) [12].

The paradigm essentially states that when CO_i commits to certain application-level timeliness properties, and subseqeuntly in the course of its execution requires the services of a remote CO_j, it must transmit its expected completion-time requirements (time constraints) along with its service invocation request as part of a distributable thread. In accepting this thread invocation request, CO_j agrees to make *best effort* to adjust its local scheduling policies (e.g., priorities and resource commitments) to meet CO_i's completion time requirements, or to reject the request. CO_j's mechanism for scheduling threads must therefore involve optimality conditions that balance the multitude of typically conflicting completion-time requests. To do so, [D]RTSJ utilizes "pluggable" application-level scheduling policies (e.g., a *utility accrual scheduling* mechanism, as described in [22]).

The DT paradigm depends on 1) the transmission of end-to-end timeliness specifications along with service invocation requests and 2) a means of adhering to these specifications by recipients. These parameterized specifications effectively define an expected application-level quality of service (AQoS) explicitly or implicitly associated with the *service level agreement* (SLA) defined in a CO server's published (discoverable) service profile.

The means adopted for describing completion-time requirements for remote service invocations involves CO_i providing CO_j with a service *deadline* in the form of a specification such as a *time-utility function* (TUF) [20]. A TUF is a parameterized expression describing the value of completing the service request as a function of time, or in the reverse direction, the time value of information returned from the service request. TUF specifications are therefore useful for describing *liveliness properties* of data contained in a message, whether invocation orders or results. Message contents thus take on a *"valid-while"* predicate within a TUF-specified window. This is particularly useful in real-time applications where information quality may deteriorate as a function of time or distance or both.

Completion-time specifications may be described by an infinite number of possible time-value functions. For example, Fig. 6 (a) describes a service request whose completion time value is maximum at t_1 (i.e., "immediately"), deteriorates linearly until t_2, then goes to zero thereafter. Fig. 6 (f) describes a service request where as time progresses the completion time requirements are described by a sequence of increasingly narrower and higher value TUF specifications—

indicative of phased and increasingly critical processes. Fig. 6 (d) represents the simplist to specify and easiest to implement TUF specification—a step function or sequence of step functions.

Let $u(t) = \{tuf\ (t), \{t^{start}, t^{end}\}\}$ be a utility function specification carried along a DT (i.e., within an RMI message payload) specifying completion-time requirements for a given service. $u(t)$ thus defines a specific quantum of service.

$$u(t) = tuf\,(t) \text{ for } t^{start} \le t \le t^{end}$$
$$= 0 \text{ otherwise}$$

Here *tuf(t)* is a piecewise continuously differentiable function in the specified interval. A *deadline* (i.e., *critical* completion-time requirement) is defined as

$$u^{max}(@\,t^{critical}) = Max[tuf\,(t), \{t^{start}, t^{end}\}]$$

In summary, a service is deemed timely (i.e., *real-time*) to the degree it is able to respond to client specified completion-time requirements, requirements carried along distributable threads in the form of time-utility functions. Given the above temporal considerations, we are now in a position to reason about the dynamics of objects whose behaviors unfold in cyberspace-time.

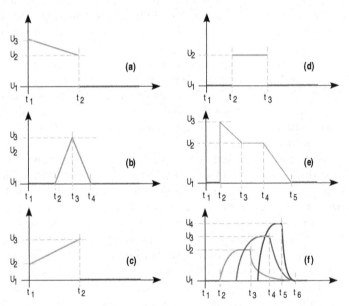

Fig. 6. Time-Utility Functions (TUF)

4. Messages

In addition to the relative motion of cyberspatial objects, we are interested in their communication patterns and, in particular, the forces exerted by information in the form of *messages* flowing among them. The notion of *infospatial force* derives from the *meaning* (semantics) of a message, defined here relative to the capabilities of a recipient and the message's ability to act as *selector* of behavior (goal-directed activity) from among a CO's states of conditional readiness [33]. For cyberphysical systems in particular, messages flow through infospace to affect decisions at rational endpoints in sociospace that are accountable for governing states of geospatial processes.

Let $m_{i,j}(t_k) = \{i, j, n, p, t_k\}$ be a *message* containing a *payload* p with $n \geq 1$ service selectors sent from CO_i to CO_j at time t_k. Timestamp t_k is the time of a "message sent" event in the sender CO_i. The message payload $p = \{\{o_r, q_r, t_r, u_r\}\}$, for $r = 1..n$ contains one or more 4-tuples, each comprising an order o_r, a measure of the *quality* q_r of that order[7], a timestamp t_r identifying when the order was issued and a *completion-time* or *data liveliness* specifications u_r.

o_r is an order (possibly including metadata describing goals, objectives, plans and constraints) that acts as a selector of one of the recipient's available services. The meaning (semantics) of an order is determined by sender and receiver in advance of the message being sent. Typically, a service provider publishes its services and their invocation orders and parameters in its Service Directory.

q_r is an indicator of the quality of an order o_r. Orders and their respective paramters may suffer from a number of quality concerns, including lack of precision, accuracy, pedigree (authenticity), liveliness (age and history) and source (originator and route). These uncertainties, when quantified in a quality indication, provide recipients with a means of invoking *due diligence* or *risk management* activities prior to utilizing information in the order field.

t_r is a timestamp declaring the time at which the order and its associated quality metric were issued. In addition to providing its age, the timestamp establishes partial ordering (sequencing) of message payload elements. t_r is the timestamp of the "message sent" event, the time when a client CO first isued the order to the server CO.

u_r, as previously defined, contains the completion-time specifications (e.g., in the form of a time-utility function) for the invocation request contained in o_r. The timeliness parameters contained in u_r establish the service's expected time-dependent contribution to the requestor's value proposition.

---

[7] We include a quality metric expressly for situations where pedigree, validity, precision or accuracy of orders (selectors) may be in question (e.g., a measurement provided by a sensor in need of calibration or one whose identity has not been verified.)

5. Performance Metrics

A HASS is a sovereign and rational free-market (Keynesian) entity whose sociospatial interactions expect services predicated on assured and quantifiable value propositions. Specific assurances underwrite operating policies that, when properly formed and executed, are sufficient to sustain its existence, establishing and nurturing associated *operational ecosystems* (i.e., *marketplaces*) supporting exchange of goods and services. Achievement of individual and group values requires monitoring of self and group sociospatial, geospatial and infospatial operations by each member. Furthermore, competitiveness in a given ecosystem demands continuous improvement in effectiveness (e.g., energy efficiency, capacity) of value production processes, individually within and collectively among cooperating CS. Such monitoring necessarily requires a set of shared, normalized and domain (federation) neutral assurance metrics—presumably defined and refined by the equivalent of a cyberspatial (i.e., federated) bureau of standards.

We offer the following six assurance indices, described in [6]: three primaries and three secondaries derived from the primaries, for each service offered by a given CO:

Actuality $\alpha_i^S(t)$: a measure of throughput yield (*mps*) actually achieved by

service s in CO_i given its current level of resources

Capability $\chi_i^S(t)$: a measure of throughput yield (*mps*) of service s in CO_i

possible given its current level of resources

Potential $\pi_i^S(t)$: a measure of throughput yield (*mps*) of service s in CO_i

possible given its maximum (design) level of resources

Latency $\lambda_i^S(t) \equiv \chi_i^S(t) / \pi_i^S(t)$: a measure *(%)* of the capacity latent in the

potential of service s in CO_i

Productivity $\gamma_i^S(t) \equiv \alpha_i^S(t) / \chi_i^S(t)$: a measure *(%)* of utilization of the current

capability of service s in CO_i

Performance $\psi_i^S(t) \equiv \alpha_i^S(t) / \pi_i^S(t) = \lambda_i^S(t) * \gamma_i^S(t)$: a measure *(%)* of utilization

of the potential of service s in CO_i

The three primaries satisfy $\alpha_i^s(t) \leq \chi_i^s(t) \leq \pi_i^s(t)$ *mps*.

For an example that ignores scripting and normalizes the design potential of a given service to $\pi = 1$ (100%), suppose a service's current capability is $\chi(t) = .5$ *mps* (50%) and its measured actuality is $\alpha(t) = .35$ *mps* (35%). The result is a productivity index of $\gamma(t) = .35 / .5 = .7$ (70%), a latency index of $\lambda(t) = .5/1 = .5$ (50%) and an overall performance index of $\psi(t) = (.35) / (1.0) = (.7)(.5) = .35$ (35%).

Armed with these six AQoS assurance metrics, we are in a position to discuss various dynamic properties of CO and their services.

6. Service Dynamics

As stated in the introduction, we require each HCO to be viable (i.e., self-sustaining). The viability of a high-assurance server results from its ability to provide one or more services deemed valuable to members of its operational ecosystem. As discussed, we assume each cyberspatial HASS object offers its services through an infospatial *service access point (*aka*, portal)*. A CO may also have "brick and mortar" service portals located in geospace. Services are invoked through messages addressed to service portals, as diagrammed in Fig. 7**Fig. 7.** .

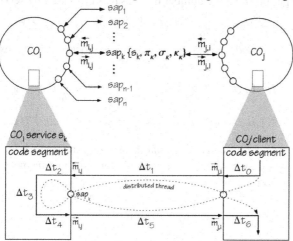

Fig. 7. CO Service Model

Let $\bar{m}_{i,j}^{s}(t)$ and $\vec{m}_{i,j}^{s}(t)$ be messages carrying service orders (demands) from and responses to, respectively, clients CO_j of service s in server CO_i at time t. It follows that $d\bar{m}_{i,j}^{s}(t)/dt$ and $d\vec{m}_{i,j}^{s}(t)/dt$ are the corresponding messaging rates, in messages per second (*mps*), into and out of service s.[8] For lossless channels, $\bar{m}_{i,j}(t) = \vec{m}_{j,i}(t)$ and $\bar{m}_{j,i}(t) = \vec{m}_{i,j}(t)$.

The bidirectional *partial* and *total message volume* of service s in CO_i at time t is the sum of all inbound requests and outbound responses[9], respectively.

---

[8] To simplify the notation without loss of generality, we subsequently drop the subscript "k" distinguishing a particular service s_k .

[9] We do not distinguish between meaningful and meaningless (i.e., spam) messages, since both require some degree of processing. If we did, spam would represent a noise source.

$$\mu_{i,j}^s(t) = \vec{m}_{i,j}^s(t) + \vec{m}_{i,j}^s(t)$$

$$\mu_i^s(t) = \sum_j [\mu_{i,j}^s(t)] = \sum_j [\vec{m}_{i,j}^s(t) + \vec{m}_{i,j}^s(t)]$$

The corresponding *message rates*, in *mps*, through service s in CO_i at time t are, respectively,

$$\dot{\mu}_{i,j}^s(t) = d\mu_{i,j}^s(t)/dt = d\vec{m}_{i,j}^s(t)/dt + d\vec{m}_{i,j}^s(t)/dt$$

$$\dot{\mu}_i^s(t) = d\mu_i^s(t)/dt = \sum_j [d\vec{m}_{i,j}^s(t)/dt + d\vec{m}_{i,j}^s(t)/dt]$$

Symmetry and lossless channels require that[10]

$$d\vec{m}_{i,j}^s(t)/dt = d\vec{m}_{j,i}^s(t)/dt$$

$$d\vec{m}_{i,j}^s(t)/dt = d\vec{m}_{j,i}^s(t)/dt$$

During the period $[t_0, t]$ the number of messages processed by service s is

$$N_i^s[t_0,t] = \int_{t_0}^t \mu_i^s(t)dt = \int_{t_0}^t \sum_j [\vec{m}_{i,j}^s(t) + \vec{m}_{i,j}^s(t)]dt$$

Over the same period, the number of messages processed at the two end-points is

$$N_{i,j}^s[t_0,t] = \int_{t_0}^t \mu_{i,j}^s(t)dt = \int_{t_0}^t \vec{m}_{i,j}^s(t)dt + \int_{t_0}^t d\vec{m}_{i,j}^s(t)dt$$

$$N_{j,i}^s[t_0,t] = \int_{t_0}^t \mu_{j,i}^s(t)dt = \int_{t_0}^t \vec{m}_{j,i}^s(t)dt + \int_{t_0}^t d\vec{m}_{j,i}^s(t)dt$$

We define the *actuality metric* (actual throughput, in *mps*) for service s in CO_i as the message processing (i.e., service completion) rate in *mps* measured at its associated service access point

$$\alpha_i^s(t) = \dot{\mu}_i^s(t)$$

Similarly, the *partial actuality metric* (partial throughput, in *mps*) for services s in CO_i with respect to requests from CO_j is defined as

$$\alpha_{i,j}^s(t) = \dot{\mu}_{i,j}^s(t)$$

Definitions of *capability* and *potential* are somewhat less intuitive. A given cyberspatial *server*[11] (i.e., a *platform* or *host*) may be capable of supporting multiple *services*. That server's resources are assigned to services according to policies concerned with marginal utility, mean service time, server load, criticality of service request (e.g., TUF parameters), hardware platform capacity, availability, return on capital investment, etc.

---

[10] An infospatial form of Kirchhoff's Electrical Current Law

[11] A cyberspatial *server* may be a small embedded or stand-alone computational device, a network of such devices, a business unit, corporate, civil or military agency, etc.

Over its lifetime, a server's capacity may evolve through installation of a progressively larger fraction, within design limits, of its total physical resources (processor, memory, disk, network adapters, personnel, capital, etc) [12]. Services allowed to run on that server will share its current capacity (i.e., its increasing potential), a full hardware complement representing the server's full capacity. If that capacity were assigned to a single service, the service would achieve its full potential (relative to that server, at least). If, on the other hand, the server's full potential were allocated (by some allocation policy) to all executable services, then each would have some measurable capability, but still not achieve its individual full potential on that server.

Let Γ be a HASS server's maximum potential measured in instructions per second (*ips*)[13] when configured with its full complement of hardware resources. Let $\omega\Gamma$ be the server's capability (in *ips*) when operating at a fraction ($0 < \omega \le 1$) of its maximum potential. With reference to the service model depicted in Fig. 7**Fig. 7.** , let $\pi_k(t)$ be the maximum (potential) service rate in messages per second (*mps*) for service s_k at access point sap_k when running alone on the full potential (i.e., dedicated) server. Let κ_k be the number of instructions per message (*ipm*) required by service s_k to react to a given message, with $\bar{\kappa} = 1/n \sum_1^n \kappa_i$ the average number of instructions per message for all n concurrent services. The server is thus capable of an average of $\omega\Gamma / \bar{\kappa}$ messages per second (*mps*).

Let $\sigma_k(t)$ be the fraction of server capacity available to service s_k (by policy) when the server is shared and running with all other services, such that

$$\Sigma_i \sigma_i(t) = 1, \ \ \sigma_i(t) \ge 0 \text{ and } \Sigma_i \sigma(t)_i \pi_i(t) \kappa_i = \omega\Gamma$$

Given that the server's maximum potential Γ is achieved at $\omega = 1$, it follows that service s_k achieves its maximum potential of $\pi_k(t) = \omega\Gamma / \sigma_k(t)\kappa_k$ *mps* when running alone on a dedicated server, with $\omega = \sigma_k(t) = 1$. When running with the other *n-1* services, s_k 's capability is

$$\chi_i^{s_k}(t) = \sigma_i^{s_k}(t)\pi_i^{s_k}(t)$$

$$= \omega\Gamma / \bar{\kappa} - [\sum\nolimits_{j=1}^{j=k-1} \sigma_i^{s_j}(t)\pi_i^{s_j}(t) + \sum\nolimits_{j=k+1}^{j=n} \sigma_i^{s_j}(t)\pi_i^{s_j}(t)]$$

Let $\hat{\pi}(t) = Max(\pi_i(t), i = 1..n)$ be the potential of the service having the greatest capability and $\hat{\pi} = (\pi_i / \pi) \le 1, \forall i$ be the resulting normalized potential of each service.

Then the *normalized capability index* for a service is

---

[12] Equivalently, imagine servers replaced periodically with higher performance servers.

[13] Typically, measures of *ips* are specified in terms of performance against "SPECint," "SPECfp," etc. test suites.

$$\hat{\chi}_i^{S_k}(t) = \sigma_i^{S_k}(t)\hat{\pi}_i^{S_k}(t)$$

$$= \omega\Gamma / \overline{\kappa} - [\sum\nolimits_{j=1}^{j=k-1} \sigma_i^{S_j}(t)\hat{\pi}_i^{S_j}(t) + \sum\nolimits_{j=k+1}^{j=n} \sigma_i^{S_j}(t)\pi_i^{S_j}(t)]$$

Again, for clarity and generality we drop the subscript k.
The *normalized productivity index* for service s is

$$\hat{\alpha}_i^s(t) = \alpha_i^s(t) / \chi_i^s(t) = \hat{\mu}_i^s(t)\Big/ \sigma_i^s(t)\hat{\pi}_i^s(t)$$

The *normalized latency index* for service s is

$$\hat{\lambda}_i^s(t) \equiv \hat{\chi}_i^s(t) / \hat{\pi}_i^s(t) = \sigma_i^s(t)\hat{\pi}_i^s(t)\Big/ \pi_i^s(t) = \sigma_i^s(t)$$

The *normalized performance index* for service s is

$$\hat{\psi}_i^s(t) \equiv \alpha_i^s(t) / \hat{\pi}_i^s(t) = \hat{\mu}_i^s(t)\Big/ \hat{\pi}_i^s(t)$$

By definition, these six performance indices are independent of an object's cyberspatial location. They are applicable, intentionally, to any object (agent process, service) regardless its sociospatial role {*parent, child, producer, consumer* in Fig. 5}. Consequently, the indices provide a scale-free means (along both horizontal production and vertical command axes) of comparing the performance of two or more collaborating (or competing) enterprise objects.

7. HASS Value Propositions

We conclude our introduction of cyberspatial considerations with a discussion of the *value* of a unit or *quantum of service*. Value, introduced in [5], is an intrinsically sociospatial notion, typically associated with the idea that the viability of an autonomous system depends on the degree its *factories* (CO) are profitable— able to produce products and services predicated on marketable *value propositions*. Value propositions are predicates (cost-benefit constraints) governing how factories convert payloads (orders), the raw material in messages, into results that are of utility to clients. Value is in the proverbial "eye of the consumer."

Cleary there are aspects of cost, especially capital assets, which are derived from a CS' geospatial and infospatial structure. These are typically platform or hosting (factory) costs, distinct from the value derived of services running on the platform and costs typically depreciated over very long periods with respect to length of service invocations.

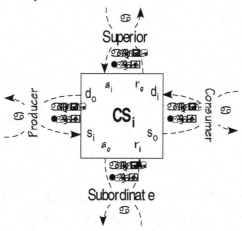

Fig. 8. CS_i Service Interfaces

Within a given federated ecosystem, a high-assurance system offers one or more assured services. Recalling our discussion related to Fig. 5, a CS communicates with neighbors in its ecosystem through service access points. Each CS has at least four, one for each of the four principal operational roles it plays. As shown in Fig. 8, it may operate as 1) a superior to other subordinate CS, 2) a producer (supplier) to other consumer CS, 3) a client (consumer) of other producer CS or 4) a subordinate to other superior CS. A CS typically plays a given role in one federation while concurrently performing a different role in another federation. Notions of assured value are thus partially dependent on the role it is playing at any given time (i.e., its time-dependent *operational context*).

Operational roles are defined through a set of services and associated protocols present at each CS API.

Superior API:

a_i assets in .... *demand orders and accompanying assets issued by a superior to its subordinate CO*

r_o returns out ... *results returned by a subordinate CO to its superior in response to demand orders and asset allocations*

Subordinate API:

a_o assets out ..... demand orders and accompanying assets issued by a CO to its subordinates

r_i returns in ..... results returned by subordinates related to CO demand orders and asset allocations

Consumer API:

d_i demand in .... supply demand orders issued by clients of a CO

s_o *supply out....supplies issued to clients of CO in response to their demand orders*

Producer API:

d_o *demand out..supply orders issued by a CO to its suppliers*

s_i *supply in......supplies issued by producers in response to CO supply orders*

Let $\bar{C}_i^s(o_r,t)$ be the expected cost in server CO_i for execution of order o_r issued at time t,

$$\bar{C}_i^s(o_r,t) = k_s\bar{v}(o_r) + \frac{k_l}{(t^{start}-t)}, \text{ for } t < t^{start}$$

Where k_s is a unitless pricing ($k_s > 1$) or discount ($0 \le k_s \le 1$) strategy and k_l (in dollar-seconds) is a penalty for clients issuing orders with short *lead times* ($\Delta t^{lead} = t^{start} - t$).

Let $\hat{C}_i^s(o_r,t)$ be the cost in the server for achieving the client's maximum utility $\hat{v}(o_r)$ of an order issued at time t.

$$\hat{C}_i^s(o_r,t) \ge \bar{C}_i^s(o_r,t)$$
$$= \bar{C}_i^s(o_r,t)(1 + M_i^s(t))$$

Where $M_i^s(t)$ be the margin (fee) charged by the server for completing an order issued at time t.

$$M_i^s(t) = k_\chi \lambda_i^s(t) + k_v \frac{\tilde{v}(o_r,t) - \bar{v}(o_r)}{\hat{v}(o_r)}$$
$$= k_\chi \frac{\chi_i^s(t)}{\pi_i^s(t)} + k_v \frac{\tilde{v}(o_r,t) - \bar{v}(o_r)}{\hat{v}(o_r)}$$

As previously defined, one or more actionable *orders* are carried within the payload of a *message*, with each order acting as a selector of one of possibly many *behaviors* enabled by a recepient's (server's) state of conditional readiness. The *value* of an order is defined in terms of a sender's (client's) expected benefits from a resulting service invocation. The client is therefore responsible for encoding its assurance requirements (i.e., value proposition) in the TUF parameters accompanying the order.

In our cybernetic model, CS governance (ref. Fig. 9) is implemented through two complementary and concurrent services, one (CO_i^a) dedicated to providing assured governance services to superiors and subordinates along its vertical asset (command) chain, and one (CO_i^p) dedicated to serving consumers and producers along its horizontal production (supply) chain. The performance of CO_i^a is characterized by { $\alpha_i^a(t), \chi_i^a(t), \pi_i^a(t)$ } and CO_i^p by { $\alpha_i^p(t), \chi_i^p(t), \pi_i^p(t)$ }. These CO are necessarily coupled to achieve balance (homeostasis) among competing demands flowing horizontally and vertically through the CS. Their coupling is both direct (CO_i^a to CO_i^p), as diagrammed, and indirect through the CS' *supervisory control* structure (E5-E4-E3-E1).

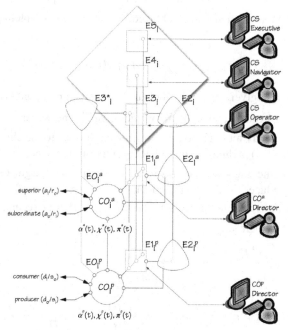

Fig. 9. CS_i Governance Structure

8. HASS Value Metrics

The effectiveness of CS governance is measured by externally and internally visible metrics. Externally (ref. Fig. 8), clients can see the level of service they receive by measuring their partial actuality $\alpha_{i,j}^s(t) = \dot{\mu}_{i,j}^s(t)$. Unless they all get together and compare their partial actualities, they cannot discern CS_i's total actuality $\alpha_i^s(t) = \dot{\mu}_i^s(t)$ nor assess its internal capability, potential, latency, productivity and performance indices unless CS_i chooses to publish its performance indices to its federation affiliates.

We defined $v(o_r, t) = tuf_r(t)$ to be the *value* of an order at time t, as defined by the client's TUF specifications.

Let $\bar{v}(o_r)$ be the mean value (utility) of an order,

$$\bar{v}(o_r) = \frac{1}{(t_r^{end} - t_r^{start})} \int_{t^{start}}^{t^{end}} tuf_r(\tau) d\tau$$

Let $\hat{v}(o_r)$ be the maximum value of an order,

$$\hat{v}(o_r) = Max[tuf_r(t), \{t^{start} \le t \le t^{end}\}]$$

Let $\tilde{v}(o_r, t)$ be the actual value achieved by a server in completing an order at time t.

$$\tilde{v}(o_r, t) = \frac{1}{(t - t_r^{start})} \int_{t^{start}}^{t} tuf_r(\tau)d\tau, \ t^{start} \le t \le t^{end}$$

k_χ is the weight given to maintaining sufficient latent potential (service capacity) to execute new orders and k_v is the weight given to the server's success in realizing the client's maximum utility. In this model, the cost to the client is based on the mean value $\bar{v}(o_r)$, while the marginal incentive in the server is to exceed the mean value. Achieving less than the mean results in the margin being negative and, therefore, reduces the cost to the client.

The client's cost (i.e., the server's *bid* price) $C_j^s(o_r, t)$ for execution of order o_r issued at time t is, therefore,

$$C_j^s(o_r, t) = C_i^s(o_r, t)(1 + M_i^s(t))$$

$$= (k_s \bar{v}(o_r) + \frac{k_l}{t^{start} - t})(1 + M_i^s(t))$$

$$= (k_s \bar{v}(o_r) + \frac{k_l}{t^{start} - t})(1 + k_\chi \frac{\chi_i^s(t)}{\pi_i^s(t)} + k_v \frac{\tilde{v}(o_r, t) - \bar{v}(o_r)}{\hat{v}(o_r)})$$

Above the mean, HASS servers gain additional revenue. Below the mean, clients get a discount. In the case where a server is faced with executing several orders whose maxima are all clustered around the same deadline, the margin calculation provides a strong bias. HASS server CO_i's goal, simply stated, is to maximize the productivity ($\gamma_i^s(t)$) of its assets and its margin ($M_i^s(t)$) while minimizing the cost ($C_i^s(o_r, t)$) of its service.

Fig. 10 summarizes the HASS governance system by showing the supervisory and regulatory control loops (distributed threads) as they implement a service's self-adaptive (autonomic) behavior.

9. Conclusions

Cyberphysical systems (CS) are a class of high assurance service systems (HASS) responsible for the states and behaviors of physical processes operating under federated governance schemes. The performance of such systems requires assurances involving interdependent measures of reliability, availability, safety, security and timeliness. Such assured operation requires specification of HASS operating contexts and metrics capable of describing the "value" of services they provide. This chapter introduces a framework for describing HASS operating contexts, referred to a *cyberspatial reference model* (CRM). Additionally, the chapter introduced a *performance measurement framework* (PMF) comprising a set of time-value metrics.

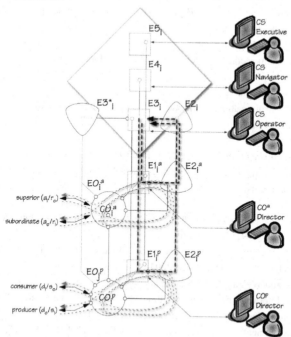

Fig. 10. CS_i Supervisory Control

References

[1] ACE/TAO, http://www.cs.wustl.edu/~schmidt/TAO.html
[2] J. Albus, "Outline for a Theory of Intelligence," IEEE Trans System, Man and Cybernetics, Vol 21, No 3, June 1991
[3] J.S. Anderson and E.D. Jensen, "Distributed Real-Time Specification of Java (DRTSJ)—A Status Report (Digest)," *JTRES'06*, October 11-13, 2006 Paris, France
[4] R. Ashby, *Introduction to Cybernetics*, Chapman Hall, 1957
[5] J.S. Bayne, "A Software Architecture for Control of Value Production in Federated Systems," World Multi-Conference on Systemics, Cybernetics & Informatics, Orlando, July 28th, published in the *Journal of Systemics, Cybernetics & Informatics*, Vol. 1, No. 8, August 2003
[6] J.S. Bayne, *Creating Rational Organizations—Theory of Enterprise Command and Control*, Café Press, September 2006, 260 pages, www.cafepress.com/mcsi
[7] S. Beer, *The Brain of the Firm*, Wiley, 1994
[8] S. Beer, *Decision and Control*, Wiley, 1988

[9]   R.C. Conant, "Laws of Information Which Govern Systems," IEEE Trans of Systems, Man and Cybernetics, Vol 6, No 4, 1976

[10] T. Erl, *Service-Oriented Architecture*, Prentice-Hall, 2005

[11] J. Forrester, *Collected Papers*, Pegasus Communications, 1975 and http://www.systemdynamics.org/

[12] http://jcp.org/en/jsr/detail?id=50

[13] http://uk.encarta.msn.com/encyclopedia_761577951/Homeostasis.html

[14] http://www.infospherics.org

[15] http://www/oasis-open.org

[16] http://www.pyxisinnovation.com/pyxwiki/ index.php?title=Handbook

[17] http://www.real-time.org

[18] http://www.rtsj.org/

[19] E. Jaques, *Requisite Organization*, Cason Hall, 1992

[20] E.E. Jensen, "Utility Functions: A General Scalable Technology for Software Execution Timeliness as a Quality of Service," *Proc. Software Technology Conf.*, Utah State Univ., April 2000

[21] L. Lamport, "Time, Clocks, and the Ordering of Events in a Distributed System," *CACM* Vol. 21 No. 7, July 1978, pp 558-565

[22] P. Li, "Utility Accrual Real-Time Scheduling: Models and Algorithms," *PhD Thesis*, Virginia Polytechnic & State University, 2004

[23] K. Merchant and W. Van der Stede,, *Management Control Systems*, Prentice Hall, 2003

[24] D.L. Mills, "Internet Time Synchronization: the Network Time Protocol," *IEEE Transactions on Communications*, 39, 10 (October 1991), 1482-1493

[25] Object Management Group (OMG), "Real-Time CORBA Specification," V1.2, http://www.omg.org/cgi-bin/doc?formal/05-01-04

[26] RFC1305, NTP Standard, www.ietf.org/rfc/rfc1305.txt

[27] RFC2460, IPv6 Standard, www.ietf.org/rfc/rfc2460.txt

[28] RFC 2801, IOTP Standard, www.ietf.org/rfc/rfc2801.txt

[29] RFC4330, SNTP Standard, www.ietf.org/rfc/rfc4330.txt

[30] J. Spohrer, and D. Riecken, "Special Issue: Services Science," Comm. ACM, July 2006

[31] L. Whitman and B. Huff, "The Living Enterprise Model," Automation and Robotics Research Institute, U Texas at Arlington, 2000

[32] N. Wiener, *Cybernetics*, MIT Press, 1948

[33] M. Wooldridge, *Reasoning About Rational Agents*, MIT Press, 2000

Chapter 7

A Graph Grammar Approach to Behavior Verification of Web Services

Chunying Zhao, Kang Zhang

Department of Computer Science
The University of Texas at Dallas

Abstract Recently, service-oriented architecture (SOA) gains great interest in the software engineering community. SOA allows enterprise applications to be built on loosely-coupled existing services, which are autonomous and platform independent. The ad-hoc property of service-oriented systems challenges the verification and validation of an application's behavior due to the dynamic composition of Web services. This chapter reviews current verification and validation approaches to the composition of Web services, and analyzes techniques for conventional behavior checking that can be migrated to service-oriented systems. It then presents a visual language approach to behavior verification for composite Web services aiming at quality assurance.

1. Introduction

Service-Oriented Architecture (SOA) is a software architecture essentially incorporating a group of loosely-coupled services that communicate with each other through message-exchanging protocols [24]. SOA allows applications to be built using available services on the distributed network independent of underlying implementation platforms. Each service is a unit of work created by a service provider to achieve a certain task for a service consumer/client. Enterprise application developers can take advantage of the available services, and aggregate them for a new e-business application.

Services are composed dynamically, and work collaboratively. Therefore analyzing a service-oriented system becomes challenging due to its nature of loose coupling and dynamic composition. It is even hard to deal with for a high assurance service-oriented system to be deployed in safety-related applications. A high

J. Dong et al. (eds.), *High Assurance Services Computing*,
DOI 10.1007/978-0-387-87658-0_7, © Springer Science+Business Media, LLC 2009

assurance system requires both functional and nonfunctional correctness before its deployment.

There are mainly two categories of sources causing erroneous behaviors of a composite service: errors from individual services, and errors due to the incorrect composition process. As each application is built based on the independently-developed services in a bottom up fashion, the reliability of the service is not guaranteed. In most cases, a service requester chooses a service only based on the service description in the interface. It is possible that the service does not meet its specification. Even if services meet their specifications, they may not meet their service level agreements (SLA). Other sources of erroneous behaviors may come from the composition procedure. Services aggregated in an e-business application may not work coordinately, and thus do not meet their specifications due to information inconsistency. For instance, security is a challenging issue in a composite Web service. A security policy for a service may not be enforced after the service is aggregated into an application. Similarly, even if service compositions meet their specifications, they may not meet their service level agreements. The composition logic may violate certain service protocols.

Conventionally, a feasible solution for a non-SOA based system is to check the behavior of the program and verify if the observed behavior fulfills the expected specifications. It is the same case in a service-oriented system, although the characteristics of SOA differentiate the verification techniques from those for conventional systems.

To verify an application's behavior, researchers have successfully developed many formal modeling and verification techniques in order to eliminate errors as early in the development cycle as possible. Model checking is one of such techniques, and has been widely used to examine software's functional and nonfunctional properties at design level. Model checking techniques can be adapted to verify service-oriented systems [14]. Because the specifications of services are described in standards, such as BPEL4WS and OWL-S, the description languages do not support a formal model checking directly. A mapping from the standard language to a formal model can help to check the correctness of the workflow logic process resulting from service composition. Given a detailed and sound design, however, it is possible that the actual behavior of the system does not faithfully fulfill the specification representing system requirements possibly due to the misunderstanding of design documentations. Therefore, analyzing the actual execution of an application and verifying the observed behavior against the expected behavior can complement the shortcoming of model checking. To capture a real behavior, interaction events, i.e. message exchanges between services, need to be intercepted and analyzed.

This chapter first briefly introduces the concepts of service-oriented architecture and Web services. It then discusses the current issues related to behavior verification, and reviews existing verification and analysis techniques for net-centric service computing. Finally, the chapter presents a graph grammar based approach for verifying the behavior of service-oriented systems.

Essentially, the graph grammar is a rule-based approach which could be used to verify the functional aspect of a system. It casts the behavior verification problem to a visual language parsing problem, i.e. parsing the graphical representation of an actual behavior with user-specified rule-based constraints/properties expressed as a graph grammar. The approach allows developers to check the acceptable sequence of message exchanges between services corresponding to some requirements/specifications. A parsing result indicates whether the observed behavior satisfies its requirements or not.

Using visual language approaches, developers can take advantage of the graphical representation of service behaviors, since graphs have been extensively used for program representations, such as UML diagrams, flowcharts and call graphs, etc. Moreover, it will be more expressive than text-based approaches by visually specifying program properties as a graph grammar and parsing the given graph. Another advantage of the visual languages approach is that graph grammar is adaptive in specifying the composition of components upon user's requirement, which supports the dynamism in services composition.

The graph grammar verification approach is supported by a visual language environment called VEGGIE [2], an integrated graph-grammar induction and parsing system. The system has a friendly interface that allows users to visually display service behaviors in graphs, and define specifications by grammar rules. The parsing function of VEGGIE is built based on a context-sensitive graph grammar formalism, the Spatial Graph Grammar (SGG) [9]. The polynomial time parser of SGG ensures an efficient behavior verification process by taking the user-specified grammar as input, and then automatically parsing the given graph representing a service behavior.

2. Service-Oriented Architecture and Web Service

Service-oriented architecture eases the development of e-business applications. It encompasses a collection of loosely-coupled services. The services are available on the network, and can be aggregated to accomplish a task. The service in a SOA is self-described and independent of IT infrastructures so that application developers can easily create their own applications using the services. In a service-oriented architecture in Fig.1 [24], when a consumer identifies a desirable service, the service consumer will send a request to the service provider via commonly-agreed protocols. Then the service provider responses to the consumer, and provides the service.

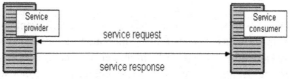

Fig. 1. SOA [24]

Web services defined by W3C [25] represents a promising application for the SOA-based technology. It supports interoperable application-to-application interactions over a network based on a set of XML standards [22][24]. Existing SOA-applications are mostly based on Web services, in which services are communicated via a distributed network. W3C has developed many standards and protocols to describe and coordinate services. The core description and specification languages include WSDL (Web service Description Language) and SOAP [24]. Additional extended specifications released by OASIS include WS-Security and WS-Reliable [26], which are used to secure message exchanges and ensure message reliability between two services.

3. Verification Techniques for Web Service

3.1 Issues in SOA Verification

The functionalities of SOA are logically separated into three levels [22]: service foundation, service composition, and service management and monitoring.

The service foundation is a repository of existing services independent of the underlying infrastructures. The available services across the network are the building blocks for developing e-business applications. Each service fulfills a separate task. Application developers can discover and select services they need for the application. The requester and the provider exchange messages via the network through standard protocols. A service transition generally assumes that the provided service is correct, i.e. the actual characteristics of the services are consistent with the description in the interface. Sometimes the assumption may mislead the application developer who only relies on a service description.

Verifying the properties of a service is the prerequisite of verifying the characteristic of a composite service. The characteristics of each service refer to service properties, either functional or nonfunctional. Functional properties require the service to fulfill a task as expected, while nonfunctional properties include security, real-time and performance issues. At the service foundation level, the service verification should be conducted by services providers. Service requesters also need to check the properties of services with respect to their requirements. To address this, existing traditional computer-based approaches can be migrated to verify services.

Verification of a service is the necessary but not the sufficient condition for the correctness of a SOA-based application. Since a service-oriented system is built on existing services in a bottom-up fashion, services can be aggregated into one composite service. Similarly, composite services can be further aggregated and become another composite service. Issues arise due to the service composition, such as the discovery of desirable services, the compatibility of services, the security policy enforcement, and the automation of the above procedures, etc.

Service composition is the core component of the service-oriented architecture. Automatic discovery of desirable services could aid service composition and verification. Developers have proposed different approaches to modeling Web services to ease service composition [10][11][25], e.g. BPEL and OWL-S. Services themselves shall be adaptive for different requests so as to participate in the composition for more business applications. On the other hand, service discovery algorithms shall have the ability to mine and identify the services they need. In both areas we have witnessed a flourish of publications and real applications in recent years.

To coordinate services in an application, many service interaction protocols have been developed. The coordination and collaboration are called "orchestration" and "choreography". The difference between orchestration and choreograph is that the former, realized via BPEL (Business Process Execution Language for Web service), describes the message-level interactions within a single private business process, while the latter, realized via WS-CDL (Web service Choreograph Description Language), involves the public message exchanges and rules among multiple-process [16]. They both aim at coordinating message-exchanging among multiple-services/processes. Since each existing service is initially developed independently, the data type and requirement may be different, i.e. the message type of each service may be different, security requirements. Therefore, the aggregation of multiple services may cause discrepancy.

3.2 Classification of Verification and Validation Techniques

Developers normally use the term "service conformance" [1] to describe property verification of services in a SOA-based application, i.e. whether the composite services behave properly in the application as expected. The expectation refers to the requirements of the application from the client. A service requester generally chooses a service if the service description (i.e. the specifications about its syntax and behaviors) meets its request, and may assume that the service will not derivate from their specifications under operation. It, however, may not always be the case. The service may not follow its specifications described in the service interface due to incorrect implementation or inconsistency of composition when the service is under operation; then the service requester could be misled by a wrong or malfunctioned service. Such errors may cause unexpected behaviors in the application, and are difficult to detect.

Validating the specification of composite services before deployment in real world applications can help to eliminate early design errors because an implementation based on an incorrect specification could result in a waste of money and time. To address the problem in service-oriented systems, many conventional model checking techniques can be adapted. So far, there have been a lot of work using different techniques to verify the composite Web service behavior [3][4][5][6][7][13][18][19][20]. Currently the research on Web service functional verification can be roughly classified into two categories:

1. Formal method and model checking of business applications;
2. Conformance checking of service behavior using event logs or test cases.

Apart from the verification techniques for functional properties, we classify the verification of services' nonfunctional properties in one category.

3.2.1 Formal Methods and Model Checking

To verify the composite services, researchers have used different formal models, e.g. finite state machine [7], algebra, calculus [6][18][19], Petri nets [13], and various mapping techniques. The major issues addressed in this category include:

- A formal model that can describe a service's syntax and semantics for verification;
- A mapping between the service description language and the formal model.

Foster *et al.* [7] proposed a model-based approach to early design verification. In their work, the specification described via BPEL for composite Web services was represented using UML in the form of message sequence charts corresponding to the workflow scenarios, and then transformed into a finite state process (FSP). The comparison between the FSP representations of design and implementation could be used to detect the difference.

Ferrara [6] developed a design and verification framework for composite Web services using process algebras. The framework translates the BPEL specification into LOTOS, a type of process calculus that was originally used for specifying temporal properties. Basic behaviors and properties, such as data definition and fault handling, are mapped to the process calculus.

Rouached and Godart [18][19] proposed a formal approach to modeling and analyzing the behavior of composite services using event calculus, the principle of which is similar to that of Ferrara [6]. Their work enables developers to detect erroneous behaviors and formally verify service properties. The behavior properties including the invocations of events, effects on state variables, i.e. assignment of values, and conditions on variable's state change, are extracted from the BPEL specifications, and then transformed into event calculus. Then an algebraic specification is built from the event calculus specification. The mapping from BPEL to event calculus enables the formal verification of composite Web service.

3.2.2 Conformance Checking

The second category of work aims at verifying an observed behavior against its expected behavior [1][12][19][20]. The behavior verification of Web services is similar to that of traditional dynamic analysis approaches.

The major issues related to the verification of real behaviors of SOA-based applications include:

- The instrumentation and trace collection techniques.
- The extraction and ordering of events.
- A formal model that can represent the specification language describing services.
- The range of conformance checking, i.e. the interactions related to single (multiple) service(s) or single (multiple) process (es).

Aalst et al. [1][19][20] proposed to check the conformance of service real behavior with respect to service specifications. In their recent work [1][20], the expected behaviors are specified as an abstract BPEL process. The BPEL specifications are then translated into Petri nets so that traditional model checking techniques using Petri nets can be applied to check service conformance. In this approach, SOAP messages enabling the interaction between services in a business application are intercepted and logged. Event messages are extracted from the SOAP messages. Following the transition of the Petri nets, the events in the log can be replayed. Comparing the events that had actually occurred with the events in the Petri nets, missing or extra tokens in the Petri nets provide the clue to the possible errors existed in the service.

Heckel and Mariani [8] developed an automatic service discovery and testing methodology to verify services. A discovery service automatically generates conformance test cases from the service description. A provided service is not allowed to participate in a composition unless it has successfully passed the test, which ensures that the service's implementation is consistent with its description.

3.2.3 Non-functional Checking

Apart from the verification techniques for functional properties, we classify the verification of services' nonfunctional properties in one category. Nonfunctional properties, such as security, real-time, and performance, etc, are also important in service-oriented systems. To address this, the OASIS [26] has released a series of communication protocols, such as WS-Security (Web service Security), WS-Policy, and WS-Reliable, aiming at enforcing security in services interaction and composition. In addition to the standard protocols, there have been techniques [3][4][15][21] addressing different security issues [17], e.g. access control. They enforced security properties in different ways.

Access control is a challenging security issue in composite Web services. Srivatsa et al. [21] developed an access control model and a policy specification language for this model for enforcing access control policies on Web service composition. The model uses the notion of composite roles/principles to abstract properties related to access control, i.e. ordering the sequence of services and entities participating in a transaction of an application. The language is based on pure-past linear temporal logic (PPLTL). The service container is instrumented with a temporally ordered list of entities and services participating in a service invocation. The order can enforce the access policy in that transaction after a service is invoked.

Ono *et al.* [15] developed a method to verify the consistency of security policies using abstraction. Their work aimed at resolving the inconsistency of a service security before and after service composition. Since compositions follow a bottom-up methodology, the security policy with each service may not be properly enforced after the service is aggregated into an application. To address this, the authors translated the service's security policy into a corresponding security qualifier consisting of a security type and a security level. The security qualifier was attached to the service participating in the composition. The set of security qualifiers in an application form a lattice. The security in the application is verified by using an information flow analysis technique on the process flow extracted from the BPEL description.

The development of aspect-oriented programming provides an efficient way to weave security properties represented as aspects into specifications. Charfi and Mezini [3][4] employed the crosscutting concerns of aspect-oriented programming, and defined an aspect-oriented extension to BPEL, named AO4BPEL, for describing service security properties. The successful integration of AOP and SOA paradigms makes the enforcement of nonfunctional concerns on composite Web service applicable and efficient.

To summarize, the existing verification and validation approaches have used different models or logics based on various formalisms to check the correctness of composite services in the business process. A common disadvantage of current methods is that they do not interpret the verification process from a visual perspective. Understanding the verification process without domain knowledge is not easy using existing approaches. Visual languages, however, could help to bridge the gap of complex verification process and human's comprehension.

4. A Graph Grammar Approach to Web Service Verification

This section presents a graph grammar approach to verifying the behavior of Web services [23]. The semi-automatic graph grammar based reverse engineering framework allows developers to specify rule-based constraints or properties as a context-sensitive graph grammar. The graph grammar is adaptive to dynamically bounded services by defining grammatical rules upon different composite services. Then the service behavior represented as a graph is automatically parsed with the specified grammar. We will describe the behavior representation in graph grammar and the approach to verification.

In visual languages, designers have the privilege to use graphical elements, e.g. diagrams, lines and arrows, to represent symbols in the graph grammar definition and parsing. Graph grammar formalism, with a solid theoretical foundation, can be used to describe the structural properties of the desirable service composition, and be used to verify the functional aspect of a system. The behavior verification problem is translated to a visual language parsing problem, i.e. parsing the graphical representation of an actual behavior with user-specified rule-based constraints/properties expressed as a graph grammar. The approach allows developers to check the acceptable sequence of message exchanges between services corresponding to some requirements/specifications. A parsing result indicates whether the observed behavior satisfies its requirements or not.

Using visual language approaches, developers can take advantage of the graphical representation of service behaviors, since graphs have been extensively used for program representations, such as UML diagrams, flowcharts and call graphs, etc. Moreover, it will be more expressive than text-based approaches by visually specifying program properties as a graph grammar and parsing the given graph. Another advantage of using visual languages is that graph grammar can be specified to be adaptive in the composition of components upon user's requirement, which supports the dynamism in services composition.

4.1 Graph Grammar Specifications

We encode service specifications using a context-sensitive grammar formalism, the Spatial Graph Grammar (SGG) [9]. The service verification process is supported by the SGG parsing subsystem of VEGGIE. VEGGIE essentially consists of two parts: visual editors and a parser. The visual editors include a type editor, a grammar editor and a graph editor, which allow developers to specify the syntax and semantics of the behavioral properties using graphical elements. The parsing subsystem can parse the given graph representing the service interaction and generate a parse tree for a valid parsing.

In SGG, the graphical elements in the grammar include nodes and edges. A node is denoted as a rectangle with a name in the center, and has one or more vertices embedded as connecting ports to other nodes. Edges connecting nodes could be directed or undirected according to the user's definitions. Edges connect nodes via vertices to maintain the syntactic connections between the nodes. Fig.2 (b) is a typical node in SGG, where a node E is represented as a rectangle and has two embedded vertices D and N. Following this format, developers can draw both terminal and non-terminal symbols. Attributes, e.g. names and types, can be annotated in a node. In general, nodes can represent modules of any granularity in a program. In this chapter, nodes represent events; and edges are used to connect events denoting the method invocations within one service or message communications between services.

Each grammar consists of a set of graph rewriting rules also called *productions*. A production has a *left graph* and a *right graph*. The context-sensitivity allows the left graph of each production to have more than one node. Also, to guarantee the termination condition, the left graph always has less number of nodes or edges than that of the right graph. We use productions to represent the message exchanges corresponding to a behavior specification. For instance, Fig.3 (b) is a graph grammar production. Its left graph is a new non-terminal node, and its right graph represents the call graph in Fig.3 (a). The composition of service into "meta" service could be represented recursively by the LHS and RHS of the productions. A subgraph representing the composition of several services (i.e. each service is a node in the subgraph) could be the RHS of a production, and its LHS could be a single node representing a composite service recursively.

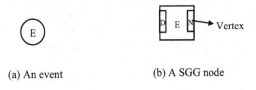

(a) An event   (b) A SGG node

Fig. 2. Node representation

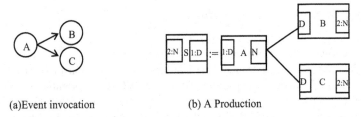

(a)Event invocation   (b) A Production

Fig. 3. Production representation

VEGGIE provides a visual interface for the user to define grammars. The graph grammars are used to specify all the acceptable method invocations or messages exchange patterns. Prohibited method invocations can also be specified with negative productions. Each production is associated with the predefined semantics using *action code*, i.e. a piece of Java code executed when the right graph of the production is applied. Applying a production to a given application graph can be called as an *L-application* or *R-application*. A visual language, defined by a graph grammar, can be derived using *L-applications* from an initial null graph, usually represented by a special symbol λ. On the other hand, *R-applications* are used to verify the membership of a graph, i.e. grammar parsing. If a given application graph, typically called a *host graph*, is eventually transformed into λ, the parsing process is successful and the graph is considered to represent the type of design with the structural properties specified by the graph grammar. A parsing process when applied to behavior verification can check both the syntax and semantics of the given service. The integer annotated within a vertex servers as a marker to preserve the context, i.e. the connections with the surrounding elements in the parsed graph during subgraph replacement.

The verification process via graph grammar parsing is shown in Fig.4. The observed behavior is represented as a call graph to be parsed in the verification system. The specifications in the BPEL and properties for the service behavior are translated into productions and semantic actions to be performed when the productions are applied.

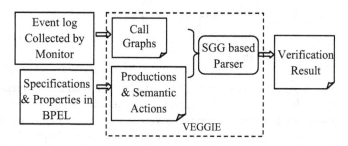

Fig. 4. Architecture of the verification system

More formally, a host graph is a tuple $G = <N, V, E, L, s, t, \mathfrak{f} >$:

- N is the set of nodes.
- V is the set of vertices in N.
- E is the set of edges.
- L is the set of labels of the nodes, vertices and edges.
- $s: E \rightarrow V$ and $t: E \rightarrow V$ are two functions that specify the source and target points of an edge, respectively.
- $\mathfrak{f}: E \cup V \cup N \rightarrow L$ is a function assigning labels to nodes, vertices and edges.

The context-sensitive grammar representing service behavioral properties is defined as a tuple $G = <T, N, E, P>$:

- P is a finite set of productions specifying the behavior properties, e.g. the acceptable sequence of event invocations satisfying a certain constraint.
- T is a finite set of terminal nodes in P, representing the events occurring in the scenario.
- N is a finite set of non-terminal nodes in P.
- E is a finite set of edges in P, connecting the senders and receivers of messages.

We can perform two types of behavior verification: (1) verifying the acceptable call/message sequences in a scenario; (2) detecting illegal behaviors or security related activities. Suppose in a application, service A does not have the authority to exchange message with service C, but can only indirectly exchange message with

C via service B. Fig.5 describes such a scenario, in which the solid lines depict the correct scenario while the dotted line illustrates an illegal scenario. Both the correct and the illegal behaviors can be verified using predefined constraints. Likewise, other types of behaviors such as a missing connection in a causal link or a cycled causal link can also be identified.

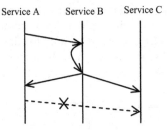

Fig. 5. An example message-exchange scenario

Fig.5 shows a legal scenario depicted in solid lines and an illegal scenario depicted in dotted lines. The legal scenario serves as the acceptable calling sequences/message exchanging we intend to verify, and the illegal scenario is the call sequence/message exchanging not allowed in the service behavior.

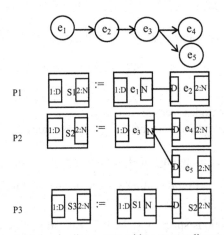

(a) A legal call sequence with corresponding productions

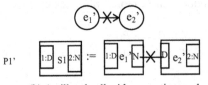

(b) An illegal call with a negative production

Fig. 6. Example productions

Fig.6 (a) shows the corresponding productions (P1, P2 and P3) for the legal behavior. Users can use this set of productions as a specification to automatically
parse the given services' call graph, i.e. the interaction graph. If the parser produces a valid result, the service is proven to behave as expected. Otherwise, the
service does not satisfy the specification defined by the grammar. Fig.6 (b) shows
an illegal behavior with its production P1'. A valid parsing result for such a negative production indicates that the service violates certain constraints.

4.2 Interface of VEGGIE

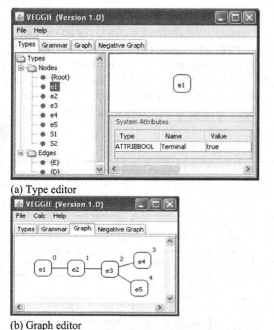

(a) Type editor

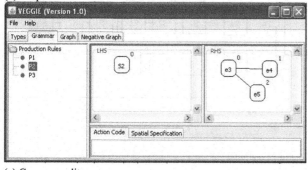

(b) Graph editor

(c) Grammar editor

Fig. 7. The User-Interface of VEGG

Fig.7 shows the interface of VEGGIE, including the type editor (Fig.7 (a)), the graph editor (Fig.7 (b)) and the grammar editor (Fig.7 (c)). It illustrates the visual appearance of productions in Fig.6 (a). The type editor displays the properties of events that occurred in the service behavior. The grammar editor is used for defining graph grammar productions corresponding to an expected behavior or other nonfunctional requirements, e.g. security. The graph editor can import and display the extracted behavior from execution logs corresponding to the interaction between services.

4.3 An Example

Fig.8 (a) depicts the process flow of a simplified abstract scenario for an example order service [1]. Fig.8 (b) lists the corresponding graph grammar representing the expected behavior of the scenario. The terminal nodes in the productions can be message/method invocations. The graph grammar specifies the sequence of events, and forms a hierarchical relationship between the system states. A valid parsing of the grammar indicates that the observed behavior meets the requirements.

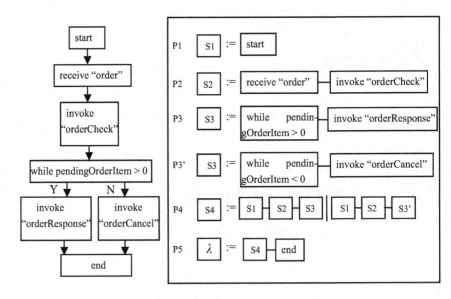

(a) An abstract view of an order process   (b) Productions

Fig. 8. An order process and its graph grammar

5. Conclusions

Service-oriented architecture is characterized by dynamical composition of services available over the network. This chapter has reviewed the state-of-art of verification techniques and discussed related issues in service-oriented systems for quality assurance. Existing work in the literature on Web service verification generally adapts the conventionally formal verification and security checking approaches, and applies them in the context of Web services.

To improve the previous methods on the visual aspects, we have presented a graph grammar based approach for verifying behavioral properties of Web services using a visual language and parsing technique. The acceptable or prohibited unsafe interactions between services can be represented as a graph grammar, which is used to automatically parse and verify the observed service behavior. The graph grammar could be partially generated by VEGGIE's grammar induction subsystem, and be further modified by users if needed.

Our future work will focus on combining the developer's domain knowledge with the graph grammar syntax so that productions automatically induced by the induction subsystem of VEGGIE could represent service specifications without human's intervention. The graph grammar approach may also be improved to support the verification of other non-functional properties of high assurance systems. One possible way to achieve this is to take advantage of semantic actions included in productions by defining various constraints of events performed in the parsing procedure to define the constraints of events. Aspect-oriented programming could also be integrated into the framework to specify nonfunctional properties.

Reference

[1]   W.M. van der Aalst, M. Dumas, C. Ouyang, A. Rozinat, and E. Verbeek, "Conformance Checking of Service Behavior", *ACM Transactions on Internet Technology*, Vol. 8, No. 3, Article 13, 2008, pp. 13:1-13:30.

[2]   K. Ates, J.P. Kukluk, L.B. Holder, D.J. Cook, K. Zhang, "Graph Grammar Induction on Structural Data for Visual Programming", *Proc. 18th IEEE International Conference on Tools with Artificial Intelligence(ICTAI/06)*, Washington D.C. USA, 13-15 November 2006, pp. 232-242.

[3]   A. Charfi and M. Mezini, "Aspect-Oriented Web Service Composition with AO4BPEL", *Proc. 2nd IEEE Europe Conference on Web Services(ECOWS'04)*, Erfurt, Germany, 27-30 September 2004, pp. 168-182.

[4]   A. Charfi and M. Mezini, "Using Aspects for Security Engineering of Web Services Compositions", *Proc. 2005 IEEE International Conference on Web Services (ICWS'05)*, Orlando, Florida, USA, 11-15 July 2005, pp. 59-66.

[5]   W. De Pauw, M. Lei, E. Pring, L. Villard, M. Arnold, and J.F. Morar, "Web Service Navigator: Visualizing the Execution of Web Services", *IBM System Journal*, Vol. 44, No. 4, 2005, pp. 821-845.

[6]   A. Ferrara, "Web Service: A Process Algebra Approach", *Proc. 2nd International Confer-ence on Service Oriented Computing (ICSOC'04)*, New York City, NY, USA, 15-18 No-vember 2004, pp. 242-251.

[7]   H. Foster, S. Uchitel, J. Magee, and J. Kramer, "Model-based Verification of Web Service Composition", *Proc. 18th IEEE International Conference on Automated Software Engi-neering (ASE'03)*, Montreal, Canada, 6-10 October 2003, pp. 152-163.

[8]   R. Heckel and L. Mariani, "Automatic Conformance Testing of Web Services", *Proc. 8th International Conference on Fundamental Approaches to Software Engineering (FASE'05)*, Edinburgh, Scotland, 2-10 April 2005, pp. 34-48.

[9]   J. Kong, K. Zhang, and X. Q. Zeng, "Spatial Graph Grammars for Graphical User Inter-faces", *ACM Transactions on Computer-Human Interaction*, Vol.13, No.2, 2006, pp. 268-307.

[10]   M. Koshkina and F. van Breugel, "Modeling and Verification of Web Service Orchestra-tion by Means of the Concurrent Workbench", *ACM SIGSOFT Software Engineering Note*, Vol. 29, No. 5, 2004, pp. 1-10.

[11]   Z. Liu, A. Ranganathan, and A. Riabov, "Modeling Web Services Using Semantic Graph Transformation to Aid Automatic Composition", *Proc. 2007 IEEE International Confer-ence on Web Services (ICWS'07)*, Salt Lake City, Utah, USA, 9-13 July 2007, pp. 78-85.

[12]   K. Mahbub and G. Spanoudakis, "Run-time Monitoring of Requirements for System Composed of Web-Services: Initial Implementation and Evaluation Experience", *Proc. 2005 IEEE International Conference on Web Services (ICWS'05)*, Orlando, Florida, USA, 11-15 July 2005, pp. 257-265.

[13]   A. Martens, "Analysis and Re-Engineering of Web Services", *Enterprise Information Sys-tem VI*, Springer Press, 2006, pp. 169-176.

[14]   S. Nakajima, "Verification of Web Service Flows with Model-Checking Techniques", *Proc. 1st International Symposium on Cyber World: Theories and Practice*, Tokyo, Japan, 6-8 November 2002, pp. 378-385.

[15]   K. Ono, Y. Nakamura, and T. Tateishi, "Verifying the Consistency of Security Policies by Abstracting into Security Types", *Proc. 2007 IEEE International Conference on Web Ser-vices (ICWS'07)*, Salt Lake City, Utah, USA, 9-13 July 2007, pp. 497-504.

[16]   M.P. Papazoqlou, P. Traverso, S. Dustdar, and F. Leymann, "Service-Oriented Computing: State of the Art and Research Challenges", *IEEE Computer*, Vol. 40, No.11, 2007, pp. 38-45.

[17]   C.K. Patrick, C.K. Fung, "Web Services Security and Privacy", *Proc. of 2007 IEEE Inter-national Conference on Web Services (ICWS'07)*, Salt Lake City, Utah, USA, 9-13 July 2007, pp. xxxii-xxxiii.

[18]   M. Rouached and C. Godart, "Requirement-Driven Verification of WSBPEL Process", *Proc. 2007 IEEE International Conference on Web Services (ICWS'07)*, Salt Lake City, Utah, USA, 9-13 July 2007, pp. 354-363.

[19]   M. Rouached, W. Gaaloul, W.M.P. van der Aalst, S. Bhiri, and C. Godart, "Web Service Mining and Verification of Properties: An Approach Based on Event Calculus", *Proc. 2006 International Conference on Cooperative Information Systems (CoopIS'06)*, LNCS 4275 Springer, Montpellier, France, October 29 - November 3, 2006, pp. 408-425.

[20]   A. Rozinat and W.M. P. van der Aalst, "Conformance Checking of Process based on Mon-itoring Real Behavior", *Information Systems*, Vol. 22, No. 1, 2008, pp. 64-95.

[21]   M. Srivatsa, A. Iyengar, T. Mikalsen, I. Rouvellow, and J. Yin, "An Access Control Sys-tem for Web Service Compositions", *Proc. 2007 IEEE International Conference on Web Services (ICWS'07)*, Salt Lake City, Utah, USA, 9-13 July 2007, pp. 1-8.

[22]   V. Terziyan and O. Komonenko, "Semantic Web Enabled Web Services: State-Of-Art and Industrial Challenges", *Proc. 1st IEEE Europe Conference on Web Services (ECOWS'04)*, LNCS 2853, Erfurt, Germany, September 23-24, 2003, pp. 183-197.

[23]   C. Zhao and K. Zhang, "A Grammar-Based Reverse Engineering Framework for Behavior Verification", Accepted in *Proc. of 11th IEEE High Assurance Systems Engineering Sym-posium (HASE'08)*, Nanjing, China, 3-5 December 2008.

[24] http://www.service-architecture.com/web-services/articles/service-oriented_architecture_soa_definition.html
[25] http://www.w3.org/Submission/OWL-S/
[26] http://www.oasis-open.org/home/index.php

Chapter 8

A Formal Framework for Developing High Assurance Event Driven Service-Oriented Systems

Manuel Peralta[*], **Supratik Mukhpadhyay**[*], and **Ramesh Bharadwaj**[**]

[*1]Utah State University, Logan, UT 84322-4205, USA

{m.peralta, supratik.mukhopadhyay}@usu.edu

[**]Naval Research Laboratory, Washington DC 20375-5337, USA

ramesh@itd.nrl.navy.mil

Abstract We present a formal framework for developing distributed service-oriented systems in an event-driven secure synchronous programming environment. More precisely, our framework is built on the top of a synchronous programming language called SOL (Secure Operations Language) that has (i) capabilities of handling service invocations asynchronously, (ii) strong typing to ensure enforcement of information flow and security policies, and (iii) the ability to deal with failures of components. Applications written in our framework can be verified using formal static checking techniques like theorem proving. The framework runs on top of the SINS (Secure Infrastructure for Networked Systems) infrastructure developed by at the Naval Research Laboratory.

1. Introduction

Service-oriented architectures (SOAs) (Newcomer 2002) are becoming more and more common as platforms for implementing large scale distributed applications. In an SOA, applications are built by combining services, which are platform independent components running on different hosts of a network. SOAs are now being deployed in mission-critical applications in domains that include space, health-

---

[1] Supported in part by the National Science Foundation under grant number CCF-0702600. Any opinions, findings, conclusions or recommendations expressed in this material are those of the author and do not necessarily reflect the views of the National Science Foundation or United States Government

J. Dong et al. (eds.), *High Assurance Services Computing*,
DOI 10.1007/978-0-387-87658-0_8, © Springer Science+Business Media, LLC 2009

care, electronic commerce, and military. Client requests are met by on-demand discovery of a set of suitable services which, when appropriately composed, will satisfy the client's service requirements. Delivery of services to clients is governed by *service level agreements* (SLAs) which additionally specify the *quality of service* (QoS) that the service provider needs to guarantee and the appropriate penalties for their violation. QoS constraints that a service provider guarantees may include security, timeliness, and availability. Such guarantees are difficult to satisfy when services are spatially distributed over a network which is subject to active attacks, network congestion, and link delays. Such attacks and failures pose a formidable challenge in delivering services that meet the SLAs.

In this chapter, we present a distributed service-oriented asynchronous framework in an event-driven (Luckham 2005) formal synchronous programming (Benveniste, Caspi et al. 2003) environment (a' la' LUSTRE (Halbwachs 1993), SCR (Bharadwaj and Heitmeyer 1999), and Esterel (Berry and Gonthier 1992)). More precisely, we present a model-driven approach (OMG) based on a synchronous programming language SOL (Secure Operations Language) that has capabilities of handling service invocations asynchronously, provides strong typing to ensure enforcement of information flow and security policies, and has the ability to deal with failures of components. Our approach allows rapid development and deployment of *formally verified* service-oriented systems that provide guarantees that clients' requirements will be met and SLAs will be respected.

The inspiration behind our approach are the Kahn synchronous process networks (Kahn 1974) developed by Kahn in the 1970's. Like the "computing stations" in (Kahn 1974), workflows in our framework are ``synchronous" continuous functions that are triggered by events in the environment. However, unlike the "computing stations" which are as expressive as Turing machines, workflows, in our framework, correspond to (finite) state-machines. In the synchronous programming paradigm, the programmer is provided with an abstraction that respects the synchrony hypothesis, i.e., one may assume that an external event is processed completely by the system *before* the arrival of the next event. One might wonder how a synchronous programming paradigm can be effective for dealing with widely distributed systems where there is inherent asynchrony. The answer may seem surprising to some, but perfectly reasonable to others: We have shown elsewhere (Bharadwaj and S.Mukhopadhyay 2008) that under certain sufficient conditions (which are preserved in our case) the synchronous semantics of a SOL application are preserved when it is deployed on an asynchronous, distributed infrastructure. The individual modules follow a "publish-subscribe" pattern of interaction while asynchronous service invocations are provided using continuation-passing (Appel 1992). The design of SOL was heavily influenced by the design of SAL (the SCR Abstract Language), a specification language based on the SCR Formal Model (Heitmeyer, Jeffords et al. 1996). Applications written in our framework can be verified using formal static checking techniques like theorem proving. We provide a static type system to ensure respectively (1) static type soundness, and (2) to prevent runtime errors in the presence of third party (possibly COTS) component services that may undergo reconfigurations at runtime due to network faults or malicious attacks. The framework runs on the top of the SINS (Secure Infrastructure for Networked Systems) (Bharadwaj 2002) infrastructure developed at the Naval Research Laboratory. SINS is built on the top of the Spread toolkit (Amir and Stanton 1998) which provides a high performance virtual synchrony messaging service that is resilient to network faults. A typical SINS system comprises SINS Virtual Machines (SVMs), running on multiple disparate hosts, each of which is responsible for managing a set of modules on that host. SVMs on a host communicate with SVMs on other hosts using the secure group communication infrastructure of Spread. SINS provides the required degree of trust for the modules, in addition to ensuring compliance of modules with a set of requirements, including security policies.

The rest of the chapter is organized as follows. Section 2 presents related work. Section 3 provides a brief description of the SOL language along with several illuminating examples. Section 4 provides a brief description of the SINS platform. A static type system enforcing secure information flow in SOL programs is presented in Section 5. Section 6 describes our experiences in developing high-assurance service-oriented systems using our framework. Section 7 provides some concluding remarks.

2. Related Work

Service-based systems (some times identified with web services even though the scope of service-based systems is much broader) have traditionally adopted document-oriented SOAP-based (Newcomer 2002) messaging for communicating XML data across a network. SOAP, by default, is bound to the HTTP (Birman 2005) transport layer. SOAP over HTTP provides a basic one-way synchronous communication framework on the top of which other protocols like request/response type RPC (Birman 2005) can be implemented. The protocol adopted by a particular application needs to be supported by the underlying runtime infrastructure. SOAP does not support interaction patterns like request/callback, publish/subscribe or asynchronous store and forward messaging. The definition of SOAP can be extended to provide such interaction patterns; such extensions require providing new semantics to an existing system.

In contrast, our framework is based on the synchronous programming language SOL. In SOL, the message passing between modules (henceforth we will use the term agent for module instances) is based on a (push) publish-subscribe. A module listens to those "controlled variables" of another module that it "subscribes to" by including them as its "monitored variables". A module receives the values of its monitored variables as input and computes a function whose output can change the values of its controlled variables. Service invocations (both synchronous and asynchronous) needed to compute the function are dealt uniformly using continuation passing. SOL agents run on the SINS platform which is built on the top of the Spread toolkit that provides guaranteed message delivery and resilience to network faults. Dynamic reconfiguration the system in response to failures can be obtained using a "hierarchical plumbing" as in (Yau, Mukhopadhyay et al. 2005). The event-driven publish-subscribe-based interaction between the individual modules make SOL ideal for programming service-based systems that are deployed in networks involving sensors and other physical devices having complex dynamical behavior.

In (Talpin, Guernic et al. 2003), the authors use a synchronous framework for globally asynchronous designs. However, their framework is more suited to a hardware design environment rather than a large scale distributed computing one. The nesC (Gay, Levis et al. 2003) programming language at U.C. Berkeley has been designed for programming networked embedded systems. It supports asynchronous calls to components using events to signify the completion of a call. In the polyphonic C# (N. Benton 2005) programming language, asynchronous method calls are supported using queues. A set of methods at the server end defines a "chord". A method call is delayed until all methods in the corresponding chord are invoked. The asynchronous service invocation framework in our approach is reminiscent of the "programming with futures" paradigm adopted in languages like E (http://www.erights.org), even though E adheres to the capability-based computing paradigm rather than synchronous programming.

The communicating concurrent processes, the dominant paradigm for distributed application development, have remained unchallenged for almost 40 years. Not only is this model difficult to use for the average developer, but in addition it fails as a paradigm for designing applications that must satisfy critical requirements such as real-time guarantees (Lee 2005). Therefore, applications developed using conventional programming models are vulnerable to deadlocks, livelocks, starvation, and synchronization errors. Moreover, such applications are vulnerable to catastrophic failures in the event of hardware or network malfunctions. Here we present an alternative approach. We embed an asynchronous framework in an event-driven synchronous programming environment (like LUSTRE (Halbwachs 1993), SIGNAL, SCR (Bharadwaj and Heitmeyer 1999), and Esterel (Berry and Gonthier 1992)). As opposed to other synchronous programming languages like ESTEREL, LUSTRE and SIGNAL, SOL is a synchronous programming language for distributed applications. Compared to Rapide and other event triggered architectures (Luckham 2005), (Chandy 2004), our framework is service-oriented. We guarantee that the distributed asynchronous implementation faithfully refines the synchronous specification. Also we can deal with asynchronous service invocations using a continuation passing approach. The SOL language integrated with formal verification tools ensures the development of applications free from errors like deadlock, starvation, etc.

We presented a preliminary version of our work at COMPSAC 2008 (Bharadwaj 2008). The current chapter extends (Bharadwaj 2008) by providing continuation-passing-based semantics of asynchronous service invocation, program transformations for handling failures, and a static type system for the SOL language for enforcing secure flow of information.

3. SOL: The Secure Operations Language

A *module* is the unit of specification in SOL and comprises of type definitions, flow control rules, unit declarations, unit conversion rules, variable declarations, service declarations, assumptions and guarantees, and definitions. A module in SOL may include one or more *attributes*. The attribute `deterministic` declares the module as being free of nondeterminism (which is checked by the SOL compiler). Attribute `reactive` declares that the module will not cause a state change or invoke a method unless its (visible) environment initiates an event by changing state or invoking a method (service); moreover, the module's response to an environmental event will be immediate; i.e., in the next immediate step. The attribute `continuation` declares that the module will serve as a continuation for some (external) service invocation. Each (asynchronous) external service invocation is managed by a continuation module that receives the response for the invocation and informs the module invoking the service about it. An *agent* is a module instance. In the sequel, we will use the terms module and agent interchangeably.

The definition of a SOL module comprises a sequence of sections, all of them optional, each beginning with one or more keywords. Built in data types as well as user-defined types as well as enumerated types can be defined in the type definitions section.

Besides, this section allows the user to declare "secrecy" types (e.g., secret, classified, unclassified etc.) in order to enforce information flow policies and prevent unwanted downgrading of sensitive information from "secret" variables to "public" variables. The flow control rules section provides rules that govern the downgrading/flow of information between variables of different "secrecy" types (e.g., the rule unclassified => classified, signifies that a variable of type unclassified can be assigned to a variable of type classified, i.e., information flow from an unclassified to a classified variable is allowed). The flow control rules can be used to compute the secrecy types of expressions from those of its constituent variables. If not specified in the flow control section, information flow between variables/expressions with different secrecy types is allowed only in the presence of explicit coercion provided by the programmer. These policies are enforced statically by a type system. The unit declaration section declares units for the physical quantities that the module monitors and manipulates (e.g., lb, kg, centigrade etc.). This section provides conversion (coercion) rules between the different units (e.g., kg=2.2 lb). Units of expressions can be computed from the units of their constituent subexpressions. The variable declaration section for reactive/deterministic modules is subdivided into five subsections (see Section 5 for details of how these types and units are managed). The continuation variable declaration subsection defines continuation variables that will be used for service invocations. There will be one continuation variable for each service invocation in a module. The type "continuation" before a variable designates it as a continuation variable (e.g., continuation cont;). Corresponding to each node in a distributed system, there will be a continuation module handling the service invocation associated with all agents on that node; they transfer the results of service invocations to invoking agents through continuation variables. The other four subsections declare the "monitored" variables in the environment that an agent monitors, the "controlled" variables in the environment that the agent controls, "service" variables that only external service invocations can update, and "internal" variables introduced to make the description of the agent concise. The monitored variables section can include failure variables that are boolean variables indicating the failure of other modules (e.g., the declaration `failure boolean I;` declares a boolean variable `I` that will become true if a module named `I` in the environment fails; see Section 3.4 for details). A variable declaration can specify the unit (declared in the unit declaration section) of the physical quantity that it is supposed to assume values for (e.g., int weight unit lb;). Assignment of a variable/expression with a unit U to a variable with unit V is allowed only if it is specified in the unit conversion rules section. In that case, the value of the variable/expression is converted to the unit V using the corresponding conversion rule before being assigned to a variable with unit V . The declaration of a monitored variable can be optionally accompanied by failure handling information that may specify it being substituted in all computations by another monitored variable in case the module publishing it fails (e.g., the declaration `integer x on I y` specifies that the monitored variable `y` should replace the variable `x` if the failure variable `I` corresponding to the module named `I` in the environment is true). The service declarations section declares the methods that are invoked within a module along with the services providing them. It also describes for each method the preconditions that are to be met before invoking the method as well as the post conditions that the return value(s) from the method is/are supposed to respect. The preconditions and postconditions consist of conjunctions of arithmetic constraints as well as type expressions. A type expression is a set of atomic type judgments of the form x :: T where x is a variable and T is a type. These conditions are enforced dynamically under a runtime environment.

The `assumptions` section includes assumptions upon which correct operation of the agent depends. Execution aborts when any of these assumptions are violated by the environment resulting in the failure variable corresponding to that agent to be set to true. The required safety properties of the agent are specified in the `guarantees` section. Variable definitions, provided as functions or more generally relations in the `definitions` section, specify values of internal and controlled variables. A SOL module specifies the required relation between *monitored variables*, variables in the environment that the agent monitors, and *controlled variables*, variables in the environment that the agent controls. Additional internal variables are often introduced to make the description of the agent concise. In this chapter, we often distinguish between monitored variables, i.e., variables whose values are specified by the environment, and *dependent variables*, i.e., variables whose values are computed by a SOL module using the values of the monitored variables as well as those returned by the external service invocations. Dependent variables of a SOL module include the controlled variables, service variables, and internal variables.

3.1 Events

SOL borrows from SCR the notion of *events* (Heitmeyer, Jeffords et al. 1996). Informally, an SCR event denotes a change of state, i.e., an event is said to occur when a state variable changes value. SCR systems are event-driven and the SCR model includes a special notation for denoting them. The following are the notations for events that can trigger reactive/deterministic modules. The notation @T(c) denotes the event "condition c became true", @F(c) denotes "condition c became false", @Comp(cont) denotes that "the result of the service invocation associated with the continuation variable cont is available", and @C(x) the event "the value of expression x has changed". These constructs are explained below. In the sequel, PREV(x) denotes the value of expression x in the *previous state*.

$$@T(c) \stackrel{\text{def}}{=} \sim PREV(c) \wedge c$$

$$@F(c) \stackrel{\text{def}}{=} PREV(c) \wedge \sim c$$

$$@C(c) \stackrel{\text{def}}{=} PREV(c) \neq c$$

Events may be triggered predicated upon a condition by including a "when" clause. Informally, the expression following the keyword when is "aged" (i.e., evaluated in the *previous* state) and the event occurs only when this expression has valuated to *true*. Formally, a *conditioned event*, defined as

$$@T(c) \ when \ d \stackrel{\text{def}}{=} \sim PREV(c) \wedge c \wedge PREV(d)$$

denotes the event "condition c became true when condition d was true in the previous state". Conditioned events involving the @F and @C constructs are defined along similar lines. The event @Comp(cont) is triggered by the environment in which the agent is running and is received as an event by the agent whenever the result of a service invocation is received by the continuation module associated with the module. We will define the event @Comp in terms of associated continuation modules in Section 3.5.

Each controlled and internal variable of a module has one and only one *definition* which determines when and how the variable gets updated. All definitions of a module m implicitly specify a *dependency relation*. Note that variable a may depend on the **previous** values of other variables (including itself) which has no effect on the dependency relation. A *dependency graph* may be inferred from the dependency relation in a standard way. It is required that the dependency graph of each module is acyclic.

Intuitively, the execution of a SOL program proceeds as a sequence of *steps*, each initiated by an event (known as the *triggering event*). Each step of a SOL module comprises a set of variable updates and service invocations that are consistent with the dependency relation D_m of that module. Computation of each step of a module proceeds as follows: the module or its environment nondeterministically initiates a triggering event; each module in the system *responds* to this event by updating all its dependent (i.e., internal, service, and controlled) variables. In the programmer's view all updates and service invocations of the system are assumed to be synchronous (similar to the Synchrony Hypothesis of languages such as Esterel, LUSTRE, etc.) – it is assumed that the response to a triggering event is completed in one step, i.e., all updates to dependent variables and all method calls are performed by the modules of the system before the next triggering event. Moreover, all updates are performed in an order that is consistent with the partial order imposed by the dependency graph.

3.2 An Automated Therapeutic Drug Monitoring System in SOL

In this subsection, we present a (part of a) skeleton in SOL of a distributed automated therapeutic drug monitoring system in a hospital. We will use this as a running example later in this chapter. A scenario of the operation of the system is depicted in Figure 1. A sensor (can be a nurse sitting at a terminal) at a patient's bed in the hospital monitors the patient's vital data (e.g., saturation, heartbeat, blood pressure etc.). As soon as the vital data indicate that the patient's condition is critical, the sensor reports the vital data to the central hospital server along with a report on the patient's condition (critical). The central hospital server contacts the patient's doctor (e.g., by sending a message to her palm pilot) with the patient's vital data and the report (critical) from the sensor. The doctor can look up a drug appropriate for the patient's condition and invoke a service provided by the pharmaceutical company (producing the drug),with the vital data of the patient, that computes the correct dosage corresponding to the patient's current state. Further, if the patient's saturation is below a certain threshold, the doctor can order her to be put on oxygen. The doctor communicates her response (dosage, oxygen) to the central hospital server which in turn communicates it to the nurse (patient sensor and actuator) that attends the patient by administering the required dosage of the drug or by putting her on oxygen. The patient sensor (or the nurse) reports to the hospital service whenever the state of the patient changes (e.g., turns from critical to noncritical) which in turn reports to the doctor for appropriate action. Due to space limitations, we show here only the SOL module running on the doctor's palm pilot in Figure 2. The complete therapeutic drug monitoring system consists of SOL modules for the "doctor", the "hospital server", and the "nurse/patient sensor and actuator". The modules translate directly into Java and run unmodified on the SINS middleware.

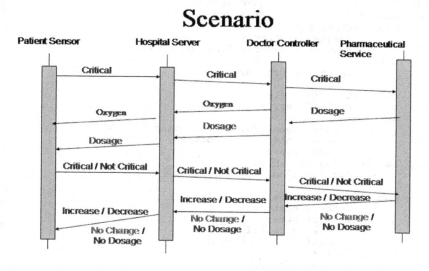

Fig. 1. Automated therapeutic drug monitoring scenario

The `doctor` module is implemented as a deterministic reactive module. We identify four monitored variables – `heartrate`, `pressure` (unit lb/sqinch), `saturation` and `patient condition` corresponding to the vital data heart rate, blood pressure and saturation of the patient as well as the condition of the patient (critical or noncritical) that the module obtains from the hospital server. We also identify a service variable `c dosage` (unit mg) that is defined by invoking the pharmaceutical service, a continuation variable `cont` that is passed as a continuation while invoking the service, and two controlled variables `output dosage` (unit cc) and `oxygen` that correspond respectively to the dosage and the decision whether to put the patient on oxygen sent back to the hospital server. The hospital server listens to these two controlled variables (among others). We also identify a service `pharmserv:compute dosage` that provides the compute dosage method exported by the pharmaceutical company named (and addressed) `pharmserv`. It is invoked with the vital data of the patient as arguments and with the variable `cont` being passed as a continuation. The service invocation is used to obtain the required dosage of the patient and defines the service variable `c dosage`. The preconditions for invoking the service provided in the services section specify that the types of all the three formal parameters x, y and z should be Integer while the postcondition always holds true. The return value from the service invocation should be of type dosage. The unit conversion rules section defines a cc to be equal to 0.887 times an mg so that the value of the variable c dosage is to be multiplied by 0.887 (by the runtime environment) before being assigned to the controlled variable output dosage.

The module doctor responds to a triggering event4 by updating its dependent variables in compliance with the dependency (partial) order.

```
deterministic reactive module doctor {
    type definitions
            dosage = Integer;
            condition={critical,not_critical};
    units
            lb_per_sqinch, mg, cc;

    unit conversion rules
            cc=0.887 mg;
    services
            dosage pharmserv:compute_dosage(x,y,z),
            pre= x::Integer, y::Integer, z:: Integer
            -- post=true;
    continuation variables
            continuation cont;

    monitored variables
            Integer heartrate;
            Integer pressure unit lb_per_sqinch;
            Integer saturation;
            condition patient_cond;
    service variables
            dosage c_dosage unit mg;

    controlled variables
            dosage output_dosage unit cc;
            Boolean oxygen;
    Definitions
    // definitions of controlled and service variables
            c_dosage = initially null then
                    if{
                        [] @C(patient_cond) && @C(heartrate)
                                             && @C(pressure)
                        -> pharmserv:
                        com-
            pute_dosage(heartrate,pressure,saturation
                        ^cont;
                    }// service invocation
    output_dosage= initially null then
                    if{
                        [] @Comp(cont)-> c_dosage;
                    } //update of controlled variable
    oxygen= initially false then
                    if{
                        [] @T(saturation<65) -> true;
                        [] @T(saturation>90) -> false;
                    }

}
```

Fig. 2. Doctor Module in SOL

3.3 SOL Definitions

The definitions section is at the heart of a SOL module. This section determines how each internal, service, and controlled variable of the module is updated in response to events (i.e., state changes) generated either internally or by the module's environment. A variable definition is of the form x = initially init then expr (where expr is an expression), and requires the initial value of x to equal expression init; the value of x in each subsequent state is determined in terms of the values of variables in that state *as well as the previous state* (specified using operator PREV or by a when clause). A *conditional expression*, consisting of a sequence of branches "[ ] guard→ expression", is introduced by the keyword "if" and enclosed in braces ("{" and "}"). A guard is a boolean expression. The informal semantics of the conditional expression if { []g_1 → $expr_1$ []g_2 → $expr_2$. is defined along the lines of Dijkstra's *guarded commands* (Dijkstra 1976) – in a given state, its value is equivalent to expression $expr_i$ whose associated guard g_i is true. If more than one guard is true, the expression is nondeterministic. It is an error if none of the guards evaluates to true, and execution aborts setting the failure variable corresponding to that module to true. The conditional expression may optionally have an otherwise clause with the obvious meaning.

3.4 Failure Handling

Benign failures in the environment are handled by program transformations incorporated in the SOL compiler that automatically transform a SOL module based on the failure handling information provided in the monitored variable declaration section. Given the declaration failure Boolean I in the monitored variable section of a failure variable signifying the (benign) failure of a module I in the environment and the declaration Integer x on I y of a monitored variable x (y is also a monitored variable), the SOL compiler transforms each definition z=initially null then expr, where z is a dependent variable and expr is an expression in which x occurs, to

```
z= initially null then
        if{
                [] I -> expr[y/x];
        }
```

where expr[y/x] is the expression obtained by replacing each occurrence of the variable x by the variable y.

3.5 Service Invocation

We consider two modalities in the SOL language: service invocation expressions
and ordinary expressions. A service variable is defined by a definition in terms of
a service invocation expression. A service invocation expression is of the form
`A:B(varlist)^cont` where the identifier `A` is the name/URL of the service,
`B` is the name of the method invoked, `varlist` is the list of variables passed as
formal arguments to the method, and `cont` is the passed continuation variable. In
this case, the service variable depends on the variables in `varlist`. For each service invocation in a module, a distinct continuation variable is used. Internally,
each service invocation is handled by a continuation module that uses the continuation variable to transfer the value to the invoking module. Corresponding to each
node in a distributed system is a continuation module that handles the service invocations for all modules running on that node. A continuation module has the
same structure as the reactive/deterministic ones except that it can have an additional subsection in the variable declaration section: *channel variables*. Channel
variables receive completion signals from external services. In addition, it can
have another section called *triggers* that lists actions in the environment that the
module can trigger. Actions in the trigger section can be defined in the same way
as variables. The variable `Chan` below is a channel variable that receives a completion signal from an external service. A continuation module for a node in a distributed system is generated automatically by the SOL compiler from the SOL definitions of the modules running on the node and is kept away from the view of the
programmer. For example, the continuation module handling the service invocation in Figure 2, is given below (for simplicity of understanding we only show a
part of the continuation module).

```
continuation module Handler{
        channel variables
        String Chan;

        triggers
                Boolean @Comp(cont);

        definitions
                @Comp(cont) =
                        if{
                                []@C(Chan)-> true;
                        }
}
```

When the agent `doctor` defining the service variable `c dosage` is executed,
the agent environment invokes the service by sending it a message. The preparation of this message involves marshaling the arguments as well as the continuation, which includes information about the channel `Chan` on which the completion of the service invocation is to be signaled. Once the service signals the
completion on `Chan`, the guard `@C(Chan)` in the continuation module handling
the service invocation becomes true. The variable `@Comp(cont)` in the envi-

ronment gets set to true. In module `doctor`, this in turn sets the value of the service variable `c dosage` to the value received as the response from the service. The triggering of the event `@Comp(cont)` in the `doctor` module results in the controlled variable `output dosage` being assigned the value of `c dosage` which at that point is the value returned as a response to the service invocation. Note that the invocation of the service can be *asynchronous*, i.e., the response from the service may not arrive instantaneously. The `@Comp(cont)` variable above is a monad (Wadler 1994) that represents incomplete service execution. Computations that do not depend on the response received from the service invocation (i.e., definitions of dependent variables that do not depend on the service variable receiving the response from the service invocation) are not blocked waiting for the response from the service. For example, in Figure 2, the decision whether to put the patient on oxygen can be made without waiting for the pharmaceutical service to return the required dosage. Hence the definition of the variable `oxygen` can be executed while waiting for the response from the pharmaceutical service, if one of the events `@T(saturation<65)` or `@T(saturation>90)` is triggered. Computations dependent on the result of the service invocation must be guarded by the monad `@Comp(cont)`, where `cont` is the variable passed as continuation in the service invocation, so that they wait until the result of the service invocation is available (signaled by the triggering of the `@Comp(cont)` event).

3.6 Assumptions and Guarantees

The assumptions of a module, which are typically assumptions about the environment of the subsystem being defined, are included in the `assumptions` section. It is up to the user to make sure that the set of assumptions is not inconsistent. Users specify the module invariants in the `guarantees` section, which are automatically verified by a theorem prover such as Salsa (Bharadwaj and Sims 2000).

4. SINS

SOL agents execute on a distributed run-time infrastructure called SINS. A typical SINS implementation comprises one or more SINS Virtual Machines (SVMs), each of which is responsible for a set of agents on a given host. SVMs on disparate hosts communicate peer-to-peer using the Agent Control Protocol (ACP) (Tressler 2002) for exchanging agent and control information. An ancillary protocol, termed the Module Transfer Protocol (MTP) manages all aspects of code distribution including digital signatures, authentication, and code integrity. Agents are allowed access to local resources of each host in compliance with locally enforced security policies. An inductive theorem prover is used to statically verify compliance of an agent with certain local security policies. Other safety properties and security requirements are enforced by observer agents (termed "security agents") that monitor the execution of application-specific agents and take remedial action when a violation is detected.

5. A Static Type System for Enforcing Information Flow Policies in SOL

In this section, we present a static type system that enforces the information flow policies ensuring safe downgrading of information.

Let **S** denote a typing environment, **x** range over the variables of a module, **expr** over the set of expressions in the module, **t** over the set of types defined in the type definitions section of the module, and u over the set of units defined in the unit declaration section of the module. A typing environment **S** is defined as

$$S ::= \varnothing \mid S \cup \{ x \rightarrow t \text{ unit } u \}$$

where $x \rightarrow t$ **unit** u denotes that **x** is of type **t** and unit **u**. Here the unit qualifier is optional. Let us define $S(x) = t$ if $x \rightarrow t$ **unit** $u \in S$, or $x \rightarrow t \in S$ and $S_{unit}(x) = u$ if $x \rightarrow t$ **unit** $u \in S$. We will write S |- d if the definition **d** is well-typed under the typing environment **S**. We will write **expr** :: **t** to denote that the expression **expr** has type **t** and **expr#u** to denote that expression **expr** has unit **u**. The significant typing rules for the static type system for SOL are given in Figure 3. The judgments **[type]** and **[unit]** are obvious. The judgment **[expr]** infers the secrecy type of an expression from those of its subexpressions (**op** is a binary operator/relation symbol). If under the typing environment **S**, the secrecy types of the expressions **expr₁** and **expr₂** are t and t' respectively, and $t \Rightarrow t'$ is a flow conversion rule (i.e., belongs to *FlowRules*), then the secrecy type of the expression **expr₁ op expr₂** is **t'**. Informally, the rule states that, if binary operation/relation is applied on expressions, one of which is classified and the other unclassified, then the secrecy type of the result is still classified. In the judgment **[if]**, **if(expr, expr₁, expr₂)** denotes the if expression if [ ]expr -> expr₁ otherwise -> expr₂. The judgment **[expru]** states that if under the typing environment **S**, the expressions **expr₁** and **expr₂** have units **u** and **v** respectively, then a binary operation can be applied on the expressions if there exists a conversion rule from the unit **u** to the unit **v** (or vice versa) declared in the unit conversion rules section of the module (here **e(v)** is an expression containing **v**). In case **u** is defined in terms of **v**, the unit of the resultant expression will be **v**. The judgments **[odeft]** and **[odefu]** provide the type and unit checking rules for definition. We explain **[odeft]**; **[odefu]** is similar. Intuitively the rule **[odeft]** states that the value of an unclassified expression can be assigned to a variable declared as classified. More formally, under the typing environment **S**, the value of an expression of type **t''** can be assigned to a variable of type **t** only if it is permitted by a rule in the flow conversion section. Finally, the judgments **[onecast]** states that an assignment of an expression of type **t″** to a variable of type **t** is allowed if explicitly coerced by the programmer. A module **m** typechecks if every definition in the module type checks relative to the declarations, flow rules, and unit conversion rules. A module **m** is secure if it typechecks.

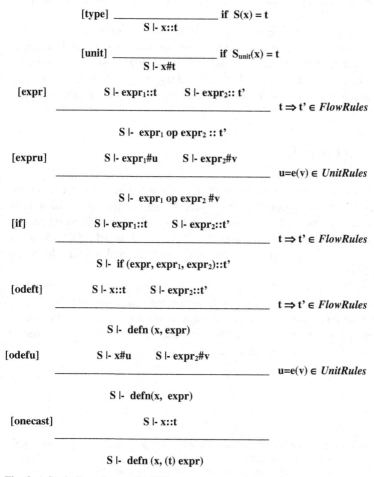

[type] _____ **if** $S(x) = t$
$$S \vdash x::t$$

[unit] _____ **if** $S_{unit}(x) = t$
$$S \vdash x\#t$$

[expr] $S \vdash expr_1::t$ $S \vdash expr_2:: t'$
_____ $t \Rightarrow t' \in FlowRules$
$$S \vdash expr_1\ op\ expr_2 :: t'$$

[expru] $S \vdash expr_1\#u$ $S \vdash expr_2\#v$
_____ $u = e(v) \in UnitRules$
$$S \vdash expr_1\ op\ expr_2\ \#v$$

[if] $S \vdash expr_1::t$ $S \vdash expr_2::t'$
_____ $t \Rightarrow t' \in FlowRules$
$$S \vdash if\ (expr, expr_1, expr_2)::t'$$

[odeft] $S \vdash x::t$ $S \vdash expr_2::t'$
_____ $t \Rightarrow t' \in FlowRules$
$$S \vdash defn\ (x, expr)$$

[odefu] $S \vdash x\#u$ $S \vdash expr_2\#v$
_____ $u = e(v) \in UnitRules$
$$S \vdash defn(x, expr)$$

[onecast] $S \vdash x::t$
_____
$$S \vdash defn\ (x, (t)\ expr)$$

Fig. 3. A Static Type System for SOL

6. Experiences

Our approach has been used for developing significantly large mission-critical service-oriented applications. These include a torpedo tube control protocol

(TTCP) at the Naval Research Laboratory, an automated therapeutic monitoring system (a simplified version of which was presented above, a sensor network-based distributed system for soil and water management, and a distributed control system for intelligent management of an electric power grid. Graduate students as well as professional programmers were involved in these projects. The applications written in SOL were first verified using theorem provers for functional correctness before submitting to the SOL compiler for type checking and compilation.

One of the facts that we observed was the reluctance of professional programmers in using SOL due to its unusual syntax (compared to C++, Java). In order to gain industrial acceptance, we are currently trying to embed SOL as a domain-specific extension of Java. The resulting embedding (called SOLJ) (Bharadwaj 2007) has a Java-like syntax, with extensions that can again be compiled to Java.

7. Concluding Remarks

SOL is based on ideas introduced in the Software Cost Reduction (SCR) (Heitmeyer, Jeffords et al. 1996) project of the Naval Research Laboratory which dates back to the late seventies. The design of SOL was directly influenced by the sound software engineering principles in the design of SAL (the SCR Abstract Language), a specification language based on the SCR Formal Model (Heninger, Parnas et al. 1978).

The goal of SINS is to provide an infrastructure for deploying and protecting time- and mission-critical applications on a distributed computing platform, especially in a hostile computing environment, such as the Internet. The criterion on which this technology should be judged is that critical information is conveyed to principals in a manner that is secure, safe, timely, and reliable.

References

[1] Amir, Y. and J. Stanton (1998). The Spread Wide Area Group Communication System. Baltimore, MD, The Johns Hopkins University.
[2] Appel, A. W. (1992). Compiling with Continuations, Cambridge University Press.
[3] Benveniste, A., P. Caspi, et al. (2003). "The synchronous languages 12 years later." Proceedings of the IEEE 91(1): 64-83.
[4] Berry, G. and G. Gonthier (1992). "The Esterel synchronous programming language: Design, semantics, implementation." Sci. of Computer Prog. 19.
[5] Bharadwaj, R. (2002). "Verifiable Middleware for Secure Agent Interoperability." Proc1 Second Goddard IEEE Workshop on Formal Approaches to Agent-Based Systems (FAABS II).
[6] Bharadwaj, R. and C. Heitmeyer (1999). "Model Checking Complete Requirements Specifications using abstraction." Automated Softw. Engg. 6(1).

[7] Bharadwaj, R., S. Mukhopadhyay (2007). SOLj: A Domain-Specific Language (DSL) for Secure Service-based Systems. IEEE International Workshop on Future Trends in Distributed Computing Systems. Sedona, AZ, IEEE Computer Society: 173--180.

[8] Bharadwaj, R., S. Mukhopadhyay (2008). A Formal Approach for Developing High-Assurance Event-driven Service-Oriented Systems. COMPSAC 2004, Turku, Finland, IEEE Computer Society.

[9] Bharadwaj, R. and S.Mukhopadhyay (2008). From synchrony to SINS, Utah State University.

[10] Bharadwaj, R. and S. Sims (2000). "Salsa: Combining Constraint Solvers with BDDs for Automatic Invariant Checking." Proc. 6th International Conference on Tools and Algorithms for the Construction and Analysis of Systems (TACAS'2000), ETAPS 2000.

[11] Birman, K. P. (2005). Reliable Distributed Systems, Springer.

[12] Chandy, K. M. (2004). Event Servers for Crisis Management. HIPC.

[13] Dijkstra, E. W. (1976). A Discipline of Programming, Prentice-Hall.

[14] Gay, D., P. Levis, et al. (2003). The nesC language: A holistic approach to networked embedded systems. PLDI: 1-11.

[15] Halbwachs, N. (1993). "Delay Analysis in Synchronous Programs." the International Conference on Computer-Aided-Verification 697: 333-346.

[16] Halbwachs, N. (1993). Delay Analysis in Synchronous Programs. the International Conference on Computer-Aided-Verification, Springer-Verlag. 697: 333-346.

[17] Heitmeyer, C. L., R. D. Jeffords, et al. (1996). "Automated Consistency Checking of Requirements Specifications." ACM Transactions on Software Engineering and Methodology 5(3): 231-261.

[18] Kahn, G. (1974). The Semantics of a Simple Language for Parallel Programming. IFIP Congress.

[19] Lee, E. A. (2005). "Absolutely Positively on Time: What Would It Take?" Computer 38(7): 85-87.

[20] Luckham, D. (2005). The Power of Events, Addison Wesley.

[21] N. Benton, L. C., and C. Fournet (2005). "Modern Concurrency Abstractions for C#." ACM TOPLAS 26(5): 769--804.

[22] Newcomer, E. (2002). Understanding Web Services, Addison Wesley.

[23] OMG. Retrieved 31st October, 2008, from http://www.omg.org/mda/.

[24] Talpin, J.-P., P. L. Guernic, et al. (2003). Polychrony for Formal Refinement-Checking in a System-Level Design Methodology. ACSD: 9-19.

[25] Tressler, E. (2002). Inter-Agent Protocol for Distributed SOL Processing. Washington, DC, Naval Research Laboratory.

[26] Wadler, P. (1994). "Monads and Composable Continuations." Lisp and Symbolic Computation 7(1): 39-56.

[27] Yau, S. S., S. Mukhopadhyay, et al. (2005). Specification, Analysis, and Implementation of Architectural Patterns for Dependable Software Systems. IEEE WORDS.

Chapter 9

Towards A Dependable Software Paradigm for Service-Oriented Computing

Xiaoxing Ma[12], S.C. Cheung[2], Chun Cao[1], Feng Xu[1], Jian Lu[1]

[1]State Key Laboratory for Novel Software Technology, Nanjing University, Nanjing, China.
E-mail: {xxm, caochun, xf, lj}@nju.edu.cn

[2]Department of Computer Science and Engineering, Hong Kong University of Science and Technology, Kowloon, Hong Kong. Email: {csxxm, scc}@cse.ust.hk

Abstract: Service-Oriented Computing (SOC) is an emerging computational paradigm that achieves business goals through dynamic service integration over the Internet. It provides interesting features such as flexible service coordination, dynamic system evolution, and service access control. While these features increase the power and flexibility of computation, they brings along new challenges. This chapter reviews the various challenges of supporting SOC and discusses the issues of addressing them using adaptive service coordination architecture. The architecture is motivated by the principle of solving complex problems through concern separation. For example, our architecture separates the concerns of (a) coordination logic from service entities, (b) service evolution from service interaction, and (c) user-centric trust management from dependability analysis. The concern separation is achieved by four artifacts: a service coordination and evolution model, environment-driven self-adaptation support, a coordination-aware access control mechanism and a trust management framework. The architecture provides a flexible infrastructure by which SOC can be seamlessly supported.

1. Introduction

Service-Oriented Computing (SOC) advocates the unanimous use of services, in particular, for applications spanning across multiple geographical locations or organizational boundaries. Services encapsulate business capabilities and are accessible through network in a platform-independent way. Services are used as fundamental elements in an SOC application. SOC is a promising approach to resource sharing and business integration over the Internet. Despite its vagueness and hypes, the major challenges of SOC arise from its fundamental change of how information systems are constructed and used. The change triggers us to migrate from an information web to a *software web*. Like the information web, the

J. Dong et al. (eds.), *High Assurance Services Computing*,
DOI 10.1007/978-0-387-87658-0_9, © Springer Science+Business Media, LLC 2009

strength of software web comes from the tremendous amount and variety of resources over the Internet, and more importantly the network effects of the interconnection of these resources. Unlike the information web which is mainly presented for human browsing, the software web facilitates the dynamic federation of independent services to solve specific application problems effectively and dependably, much in the same line as Open Resource Coalition [36] and Internetware [21]. SOC brings forth a new software paradigm with challenges different from its traditional counterparts.

Software systems often run under some *environment* where necessary resources and services are provided. Conventional software systems based on standalone computers, local area networks, or intranets are typically developed on the assumption of invariant environment resources such as available CPUs, memories, underlying system calls, network bandwidth, and functionalities provided by other software systems. Such assumption can no longer be made by SOC systems that rely on dynamic service integration over the Internet. SOC systems themselves are often published as services, and serving users with changing requirements. As a consequence, SOC systems are expected to be *dynamically adaptive*, i.e., they should be able to change their structure and behavior at runtime to cope with changing environment and requirements. For example, they need to switch to an alternative service when the primary one is unavailable or not preferred anymore. They may also integrate new services to provide users with additional features. In other words, they must be capable to reconfigure themselves to adapt to changes in their environments and requirements.

Dependability of SOC systems therefore requires attentions different from those of conventional systems. While the dependability of conventional software systems is derived from their precise specification and stable implementation, the dependability of SOC systems relies on their resilience to the change of environment/requirement and their capability of dynamic system adaptation, or even self-adaptation [37]. As defined by Avizienis et al. [2], dependability refers to *"the ability to deliver service that can justifiably be trusted"*, or *"the ability of a system to avoid service failure that are more severe than is acceptable"*. It is generally understood as a global concept that encompasses system attributes including reliability, availability, safety, integrity, security, timeliness, etc. The open and dynamic nature of the Internet environment and the changing requirement makes it impractical and unnecessary to give a precise and complete specification that conventional verification and validation are based on. As a consequence, the dependability of SOC applications in such an environment is generally not in a *hard* sense but in a *soft* sense. That is to say, rather than pursuing the absolute high-assurance such as those of life-critical systems, the temporary derivation from normal behavior is allowed for a SOC system but a degree of confidence that the system would sustain *sufficient* level of service quality will achieved by a combination of a priori validation and dynamic monitoring and adaptation [36]. What complicates things even further is that services used in the Internet environment are *autonomous*, which means not only that they are developed, deployed and managed independently, but also that they have their own interests and behavior rationales. To build a trustable system out of such autonomous services, extra mechanism beyond conventional verification and validation must be provided to ensure the trustworthiness of the system.

These distinguishing features require a set of new software models and enabling techniques that would make SOC a new software paradigm. As a step towards this new paradigm, this chapter presents a coordination model for the construction of dynamically adaptive service oriented systems based on the concept of built-in runtime software architecture [23]. Under this model each service of a service-oriented system is situated in and coordinated by an active architectural context, which mediates the interactions among the services. The architectural context is explicitly implemented using a distributed shared object, on which dynamic adaptation behaviors are specified. With an intrinsic reflective computation [24] mechanism the adaptation behavior specified at the architectural level can be automatically carried out. Moreover, an architecture for self-adaptive service oriented applications is also introduced. To close the loop of control for self-adaptation, the architecture bridges the gaps between environment, system and application goals with an ontology-based approach.

In addition to the adaptive coordination model, an access control model is proposed for services to carry out the fine-grained access control rules which are in accord with the coordination logic, i.e., software architecture in our approach, so that the coordination can proceed successfully while the services are secured. At the same time, the services can still keep their autonomy discretionarily with a new decentralized authorization mechanism.

Even further, to address the complex trust issues of services and the independent subjects behind them in the open Internet environment, three classes of trust relationships are first identified, and a trust management framework is then designed to help the understanding and assurance of the trustworthiness of SOC applications.

By explicitly addressing the issues that were hidden and entangled in conventional software paradigms, the proposed model facilitates the decoupling of coordination logic from service entities, of system evolution from service interaction and of user-centric trust management from the artificial-based dependability analysis, in addition to the well-known decoupling of service providers from service consumers. This further separation of concerns is useful to the management of complexity of the development of dependable service-oriented system under the Internet environment.

This chapter identifies the imminent challenges of SOC, and presents our framework to address these challenges in a major national research project. Since the project is still at its early stage, some of the ideas have not been fully articulated. Yet, the framework should provide a useful stepping stone to help develop effective solutions to address the SOC challenges. This chapter is outlined as follows. Section 2 presents the background, motivation and overview of our framework. Sections 3 and 4 describe an adaptive coordination model and a self-adaptive architecture, respectively. Section 5 gives an account of a coordination-aware access control mechanism, which is followed by a trust management framework in Section 6. Section 7 concludes this chapter.

2. Motivation and approach

Service oriented computing is attracting much attention from both academy and industry. But there is little consensus on how it should be like as a software engineering paradigm, despite of the increasing number of WS-* standards and proposals. In this section, we limit our discussion to the new challenges that SOC brings to Web Services. A comprehensive survey on the current status and research challenges of SOC can be found in existing literature, e.g. in [31].

2.1 Web Services and new challenges

Papazoglou and Georgakopoulos [30] divide SOC tasks into three layers. The bottom layer consists of basic service operations and their description. The middle layer (a.k.a. *composition layer*) concerns about service composition, which involves issues such as service coordination, conformance ensuring and QoS considerations. The upper layer (a.k.a. *management layer*) manages service-oriented applications based on specified business goals and rules, such as measuring, monitoring and dynamic (re)configuration. Let us review the major challenges of each layer and the inadequacy of existing solutions.

At the bottom layer, Web Services provide an adequate solution. Web Services define a common interaction protocol and a description language for services in terms of SOAP and WSDL. This enables service providers and consumers to interact using their own favorite platforms and programming languages. UDDI further allows service providers and consumers to advertise and look up their services dynamically through a public registry. Though widely accepted, Web Services defines no guidelines at the application level on how a service-oriented system can be constructed.

At the composition layer, the limitation becomes apparent. Under the paradigm of SOC, web services are subject to composition rather than direct human interaction. Milanovic and Malek [28] describe four essential requirements for Web Service composition.

- *service connectivity,* which means there must be some mechanism to glue up the services by directing messages between services' ports;
- *non-functional properties,* which can be addressed explicitly;
- *composition correctness,* which requires verification of some critical properties of the composite;

- *composition scalability*, which means the mechanism should scale with the number of service involved.

There are two additional requirements for the support of a full fledge service composition over the Internet:

- *programmable coordination* mechanism should be provided to federate autonomous services to satisfy particular demands, in a flexible but disciplined way. This requirement can be viewed as an enhancement to service connectivity. Beyond providing the communication channel between services and adapting their interfaces, the mechanism should also support the explicit management of the interaction between the services, according to the application logic.

- *dynamic adaptation* should be supported to make the system survival from ever-evolving environment and user requirement. There are three classes of adaptations. First, particular services used in the system would be dynamically discovered, bound, used and replaced. Second, the architectural configuration of the system would be changed at runtime. Third, there may be some situations beyond the expectation of the system developers, and ideally the system should *evolve online* to include in new knowledge and capability to cope with the new situations.

The central task of this layer is to find a flexible composition model that matches these requirements. Service orchestration and choreograph languages such as BPEL and WSCDL have been proposed to composite web services. BPEL is essentially a process oriented approach to service programming, which implements business processes by invoke other services. Besides its limitations on support for non-functional properties and correctness verification [28], its orchestration viewpoint does not suit for coordination need, since they just treat other services as subordinates like procedures in structured programming and objects in OO programming. This viewpoint also makes the dynamic adaptation very difficult -- although dynamic service binding can be used, the architectural reconfiguration is hardly supported because there is no explicit architecture. WSCDL-style service choreograph does concentrate on service coordination, but they are essentially specification and generally not directly executable.

OWL-S [26] provides an ontology to facilitate automatic discovering, invocation, composition, and monitoring of Web services. While theoretically this approach is interesting the efficient of the logic reasoning would be a problem because the amount and variety of services. Other approaches such as the Service Component Architecture of IBM address mainly the interoperability between Web Services, but rarely the problem of service composition.

At the management layer, more work is needed for service oriented systems. There is already some work addressing the management web services such as IBM's WS-Manageability and OASIS's WSDM. A related survey can be found in [32]. They refine existing network management and distributed system management framework with standard Web Services interfaces. At the same time, they use the framework to management web service resources. However, they focus more on services than service oriented systems. For example, to serve the business goal better in the open and dynamic environment, the problem of dynamic (self-) adaption must be considered seriously [31]. In addition, to ensure the dependability of service-oriented systems, the trust relationships among related subjects must be identified, evaluated and managed. While these issues involve many non-technical business factors, technical facilities are needed to manage the mappings between these factors to the structure and behavior of service-oriented systems.

2.2 Paradigmatic considerations

Web services may be built on top of multiple programming models, such as Visual Basic, Java and C#. Under these models, a remote service is treated as a remote object. Recent programming environments often provide useful facilities to encapsulate objects into web services and generate proxy objects for web services. However, conventional software paradigms such as structured programming, object-oriented programming and component-based paradigms cater mainly for standalone systems and LAN/intranet environments, which are originally designed for collaboration within a small community as compared with the Internet. Conventional paradigms are inadequate for SOC in the following ways.

1. They emphasize on computation rather than coordination [29] (the coordination logic is often hidden in the computation logic) while the latter is often the central task of service-oriented application systems.
2. They are originally designed for stable structures while service-oriented systems embrace dynamic evolution.
3. They assume full control and tight coupling of building blocks of a system while services can be highly autonomous in service-oriented applications.

Efforts have been made to standardize various kinds of issues involved in the development of dependable service oriented applications, such as reliability, transactions, security, trust, management, to name a few. But the lack of a suitable coherent programming model makes them more an application of conventional techniques for the web services in an ad hoc way than a systematic approach for a new dependable paradigm for SOC.

2.3 A coordination-centric approach

We propose a coordination-centric approach to SOC, as shown in Fig. 1. A programming model based on the concept of built-in runtime software architecture [23] is adopted for explicit description and manipulation of coordination logic.

Based on this coordination model, a set of techniques are proposed to help the constitution of a dependable software paradigm for SOC.

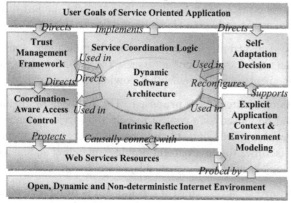

Fig. 1. A Coordination-centric approach to SOC.

Software architecture as a service coordination model. Software architecture, which *"involves the description of elements from which systems are built, interactions among those elements, patterns that guide their composition, and constraints on these patterns"* [38], provides the following benefits in modeling service coordination.

- *Explicit and programmable coordination.* Software architecture treats connectors as first class programming concepts. This allows connectors to be reconfigured dynamically to reflect coordination changes.
- *Support for non-functional properties.* One of the motivating benefits of software architecture is its support for the early analysis of system properties, esp. non-functional ones.
- *Verifiable correctness.* There are various formal models and verification tools proposed to help the ensuring of architectural correctness.
- *Dynamic adaptation.* Software architecture embodies essential information that should be held by the implementation to support and regulate future adaptation and evolution [1, 14].

In our approach, runtime software architecture models are used as the kernel of the coordination logic, and they are also used to provide up-to-date information for related facilities including adaptation decision, access control, trustworthy analysis, etc.

An intrinsic reflection mechanism is designed to support the implementation and the dynamic adaptation of software architecture. Software architecture must be faithfully implemented to take effect. Different from traditional approaches where software architecture is just used as abstract specifications and become implicit in implementation, we explicitly keep it at runtime. Unlike most runtime software architecture approaches [8, 14] where the consistency between architecture and system is maintained extrinsically, we propose an intrinsic mechanism of building the architecture using the object-oriented computing model. The intrinsic mechanism facilitates the seamless support of both planned and unplanned dynamic architectural reconfigurations.

To enhance the dependability of service oriented applications constructed using this coordination model, three important issues, viz. self-adaptation, access control and trust management are addressed with following techniques.

A self-adaptation architecture is proposed. The architecture supports *automatic* adaptation based on closed-loop control to help the service oriented system survive from the evolving environment and changing user requirements. It also includes explicit facilities for environment probing, modeling and management, and as well an ontology based reasoning and adaptation driven mechanism.

A coordination-aware access control mechanism is designed. While traditional access control strategy always makes conservative decisions to ensure protection, the explicit coordination model provides valuable information to allow maxim flexibility of the participation in coordination but without compromising of the autonomy and security of the services.

A trust management framework is proposed. Under the SOC paradigm, services are generally developed, deployed, tested, and used by different parties with different interests while traditional dependability analysis and assurance often implicitly assume unconditional trust relationship between these parties. Trust management is an effective approach to dealing with the complexity. With the information provided by the explicit coordination model, the trust management framework can be used to enhance the dependability of SOC systems in the selection of candidate services, evaluating the trustworthiness of systems, and directing the access control strategies.

2.4 A running example

Throughout the rest of this chapter, a hypothetic SOC system, which is a value-adding web service based on existing web services, will be used as an illustrative example. Suppose the business of the system is to provide a comprehensive ticket booking service for travelers. The system would help the travelers to plan and manage their trips and delegate all physical transportation to other existing services such as airlines, trains, coach buses, etc.

Although very simple, such a SOC system would involve a serial of technical issues, among which we will address:

1. How to construct the system flexibly so that it can be dynamically adapted when necessary? And how to let the system adapt itself with little or even no human interaction?

2. How to protect the autonomous services from being abused while they are contributing themselves to the system? How such protection mechanisms can fit in the dynamic scenario of the system?

3. How to help the users to justify their confidence on the service and dealing with the complex trustworthy issues between the users, service providers?

3. Dynamic adaptive coordination model

As discussed, software architecture is used as the central abstraction of our coordination model. There are two difficulties to overcome in this approach. First, the architecture specification must be mapped into implementation to make the coordination logic executable. Second, the dynamic architecture specified at the architectural level must be carried out smoothly at the implementation level.

A considerable amount of research efforts have been made to bridge the gap between architecture specification and implementation [27], but software architectures were mainly treated as design specifications rather than materialized and operational/functional entities in the final running systems. Although software architecture specifications can help the development and management of dynamic system adaptations [17, 19, 8], as the upper part of Fig. 1 shows, maintaining the consistency between a software architecture specification and the working system implementation can be tedious.

To further ease the understanding, expressing and realization of dynamic adaptation at implementation level, the software architecture should be directly implemented at this level. Encoding the architecture specification into a data structure is not enough – it requires continual synchronization with the system's current configuration. But if this synchronization was carried out by an external party, each service must publish special handlers that allow the external party to control synchronization and monitor the relevant internal state. The provision of such handlers also leads to complex security and privacy issues. As such, our reified software architecture adopts an *intrinsic* mechanism [24].

3.1 Intrinsic approach

An intrinsic mechanism should fully integrate service coordination into the programming model. As discussed above, the coordination mechanism of the object-oriented programming model (in the form "target.method(...)") is inadequate for SOC over the Internet. During the process of determining the target object the system coordination structure is gradually consolidated with a loss of organizational and architectural information. Let us illustrate this using an example where a company evolves its management structure. Suppose that all employees of Bill's company report to Bill initially. This can be realized by having a link going from each employee object to the Bill object. Bill is therefore the "**target**" of the link. Now, the company has recruited a new manager, Tom, to offload Bill's work. To reflect the change, the "**target**" should then be redirected to Tom. But in the original architecture decision the person who is responsible for hearing report is neither Bill nor Tom, not even the boss role or the project manager role, but the *current* role in charge of project development according to the *current* organization or architecture of the company. In the two scenarios, the reference is eventually bound to a specific value and the underlying architecture information is lost.

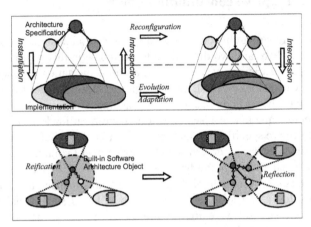

Fig. 2. Software architecture reification.

With these considerations, a dynamic software architecture-based programming model (illustrated by the lower part of Fig. 2) is proposed in [23], which features:

- *Built-in runtime software architecture object* The software architecture concerns are separated from interacting component objects, and expressed explicitly as a first class object in the final implementation. The cross-component references are dynamically interpreted according to this architecture object. In other words, the references are "functions" over the current software architecture configuration. In this way the change of the architecture object will immediately affects the interaction between the components. Naturally anticipated dynamic reconfigurations are implemented as the behavior of the architecture object.

- *Unanticipated dynamic reconfiguration support* Once the software architecture is reified as an object, inheritance and typing mechanisms of object oriented programming model can be applied to architectural evolutions of the system. In addition to the planned reconfiguration just mentioned, some unanticipated reconfiguration can be implemented as new behavior of an architecture object whose class inherits the original's. With the help of dynamic class loading and object instantiation, the system's architecture object can be polymorphically replaced with the new one, and then the new reconfiguration behavior eventually carried out.

- *Distributed shared object implementation* The above discussion assumes a centralized architecture object, which is convenient for the developer to express the coordination logic. However, the underlying implementation in the open network environment must be distributed flexibly. We adopt a distributed shared object mechanism: the dynamic architecture object is co-implemented with a group of coordinated sub-objects located at every node involved. Each sub-object provides a logically unified architectural context for the local component.

3.2 The programming model

A *service* in our model is an instance of a service type with a network access address. A *service type* consists of four components:

1. Provided interfaces. Functionalities provided by the service. They are typically WSDL portTypes in Web Services platform.
2. Required interfaces. Functionalities that are required for current service to work properly. Explicit specification of required interfaces facilitates the direct modeling of value-adding/composite services. It also brings symmetry to service composition.
3. Protocol. Temporal constrains on the operations in the interfaces.
4. QoS specifications. The service can guarantee what level of service quality provided certain QoS of the services on which it depends is ensured.

Then a SOC *application* system is a closed service. A *closed service* is a service with no required interface or each of its required interfaces is either statically bounded to a closed service or subject to dynamically binding.

At the programming level, a service-oriented application consists of following elements:

- *Component objects.* A component delegates business functionality to natively implemented functionalities[1] or other web service(s). It serves via its provided interfaces in condition that it is served via its required interfaces. Note that a component object is not a service but a broker between the service and the architecture context of the application. This additional layer of indirection provides room for compensation of architectural mismatch [13] and facilitates dynamic replacing of services.
- *Connector objects.* Connectors focus on non-functional aspects such as communication, security, reliability, logging, etc. Connectors are implemented as

---

[1] A purist would also require that native implemented functionalities should also be encapsulated as web services.

interceptors syntactically transparent to the components and do not affect the business logic of the application.

- *Architecture Object.* The architecture object implements the application's structural organization and related behavior constraints. It is this object through which the components are finally connected together. It is also the locus where dynamic adaptation capabilities are realized.
- *Mappings.* Component objects must be mapped to the component roles in the architecture object to get the necessary architectural context. Each required interface is fulfilled indirectly by a provided interface or interfaces (a multiplexer connector may be employed) of other components under the management of the architecture object. In practice the mapping can be defined with a graphical tool. Syntactical type checking and even behavioral compliance checking can be included here.

The behavior of an architecture object is defined by its class. Architecture classes reify the concept of software architecture styles. All architecture classes must inherit from a system class RTArchitecture directly or indirectly. RTArchitecture provides some basic functions for the development of specific architecture class, including: 1) basic architecture topology, which is merely a canonical programming-level representation of software architecture specification in ACME [15]; 2) redirection of the cross-component reference according to current architecture topology; 3) supports for the distributed implementation of the architecture object. Here some consistency assurance mechanisms from basic synchronization to two-phase commit protocol are needed. 4) basic reconfiguration activities, including addition/deletion of component roles and links between them, replacement of the component for a role.

An architecture class library can be provided by the development environment to support the reuse of common architectural styles. Developers derive their own architecture class from an existing class to best fit their application on hand.

For example, suppose our value-adding ticket-booking system is to be constructed with a locally implemented value-adding service and a set of transportation services discovered from the Internet. The value-adding service provides comprehensive tick-booking service via its provided interface, and requires transportation services via its required interface. These services are coordinated with a simple Master/Slave architecture. The value-adding service will be use in the Master component object, and the transportation services will be used in Slaves.

A class of simple Master/Slave style can be readily declared as follows:

```
public class MSArch extends RTArchitecture implements ISlave, IMaster {
    //methods declared in ISlave
    //for slaves to pull jobs from the master
    public Object invokeOnMaster(Method m, Object[] params)
        throws Exception{...};
    //methods declared in IMaster -- omitted
    ... ...
    //implementations for dynamic reconfiguration
```

```
public void addSlave(SLAVE T){...};
public void removeSlave(SLAVE T){...};
... ...
//Constructors
public MSArch(ArchConfig ac){...};
... ...
}
```

The architecture class provides each of its players with an interface. The mapping tool will generate dynamic proxies with the method defined in this interface to fulfill the required interfaces of the associated component object. In this example a weakly typed method invokeOnMaster is provided to redirect calls from slaves to master to the proper component mapped to the master. Here we assume the slaves pull jobs from the master. If the master needs to push jobs to slaves, then invokeOnSlaves should be defined for IMaster. A multiplexer connector should also be used to resolve the mismatching during the mapping process.

For our example, an architecture object will be instantiated from the MSArch class with concrete architectural configuration. The required interface of the value-adding service will be finally fulfilled by the provided interfaces of the transportation services, with the broking and managing of the component objects and the architecture object.

3.3 Support for dynamic reconfigurations

It is natural to implement dynamic reconfigurations as the behavior of the architecture object. In our example, more transportation services could be discovered at runtime and need to be included in to make the service of the system more comprehensive. Uncompetitive transportation services also should be dropped out. Thus the Master/Slave architecture should support the online insertion and removal of Slaves. Since the object defines the architecture, dynamic reconfigurations are treated as the object's behavior. They are implemented as modification methods of the class. In MSArch, insertion and removal of Slaves are defined with methods addSlave() and removeSlave(). The implementation of these methods is mainly changing the topology with the facilities provided in RTArchitecture. Remember the object implementation can be physically distributed, thus it often has to use the two-phase commitment support to ensure atomicity.

There could be some reconfiguration requirements gradually discovered after the system was put into operation. Common solutions for these unanticipated reconfigurations require a system restart. However, the stop of service could bring a high cost in some circumstance, esp. when there were valuable data not persistently stored. Our approach also provides a reasonable support for unanticipated dynamic reconfigurations. A new subclass of the original architecture class shall be defined to implement new reconfiguration behavior. For our example, suppose that with more and more transportation service included in and the increasing popularity of our comprehensive ticket-booking service, the Master itself would be overloaded, which falls into a situation beyond the anticipation of the original system architect. Now the architecture should be evolved to a new style of Extend Master/Slave which also supports multiple Masters to share the workload. Therefore a new architecture class EMSArch is defined, in which new Masters can be added, and related interactions are adjusted accordingly:

```
public class EMSArch extends MSArch implements IEMaster
{
    //New reconfiguration behavior
    public void addMaster(MASTER M){...};
    public void removeMaster(MASTER M){...};

    //Redefined behavior. Some load balancing can be implemented here.
    public Object invokeOnMaster(Method m, Object[] params)
        throws Exception{...};

    //methods in IEMaster to support coordination among masters -- omitted
    ......
}
```

Prior to reconfiguration, a new architecture object is instantiated from the class EMSArch. This new object is programmed to enact the semantics of the new architecture, and can be used to replace the original architecture object. After the new architecture object is initialized with the same state as the original architecture object, required reconfigurations (i.e. insertion of new Masers) are then carried out.

Note that, while the upgrading of architecture object is transparent to existing component objects (and thus the services they use), it can be visible to the *new* services added in henceforward. This means, gradually, with more and more new services added in and old services dropped out, the agreement between the application and the services can be upgraded. This is an approach to implement online co-evolution.

We have developed a prototype system to support the programming model. The kernel of the system is to build and maintain a distributed shared architecture object according to the architecture class and the architecture configuration specified by developers with a graphical editing framework. The system will use the architecture object to build the active coordination context for each services involved. Architecture configuration and reconfiguration are given in a formalism based on graph grammars. With a Graph Transformation tool, the reconfiguration behavior of the architecture object is checked at runtime to ensure the architectural integrity. Details about the supporting system can be found in [23, 22]. Further work on behavior compatibility checking and QoS assurance are currently undergoing.

4. Self-adaptive architecture

The above coordination model allows the SOC application system to be adapted at runtime. But to make it *self*-adaptive to the changing environment and user requirements, additional facilities dealing with environment probing and user goal interpreting must be included, and finally an architecture based on closed-loop control with feed backs should be built.

From a software developer's viewpoint, one of the fundamental difficulties is to reconcile users' goals, environment assumptions, and implementation limits. The users' goals are in the problem domain while the implementation is in the solution domain. The data about the environment by themselves cannot be understood and used to drive the system adaptation -- they must be interpreted with the knowledge from the problem domain to be meaningful. In conventional software development process, the users' goals and environment assumptions are transformed gradually down to the implementation with various decomposition and refinement techniques, which is not applicable because the three parts are to be reconciled simultaneously at runtime.

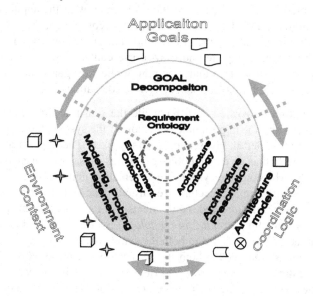

Fig. 3. A self-adaptive architecture

Reconciliation is achieved in our approach through three tiers of interactions, as depicted in Fig. 3. At the base tier (outermost in Fig. 3), just like any distributed software systems, the application system makes use of the service resources in the environment and acts upon the environment to do its current business. At the middle tier, the environment context is explicitly handled with corresponding facilities and expressed as structured data; the basic system is reified as a built-in runtime software architecture object to provide an abstract architecture view; and the user goals are decomposed into tractable sub-goals. Finally at the top tier (innermost in Fig. 3), based on the semantic framework defined by application goals and domain knowledge, the runtime software architecture model interacts with the environment context model in a unified ontology space, which is driven by a set of adaptation rules or manual directions. The architecture covers three major parts:

Environment handling facilities To reconcile the differences between the scattered environmental data and the abstract user requirements at runtime, an explicit handling of the environment issues is needed, which consists of the following three tiers. First, the primitive environmental data are probed and processed so that related attributes of environment elements are measured. The effects of the system are also reflected in these attributes and they will be used as feedbacks. Second, the probed data are filtered and managed as the context of the system, and events of interest of context changes are raised. Third, a context model is built with an ontology that provides the conceptualization of a common understanding of the domain. With this formal model of the environment context, the context information is uniformly stored and well-managed, and some high-level processing such as conflict resolving, context fusion and reasoning are carried out to enhance its consistency, integrity and usability. At the same time, with the application goals and domain knowledge that are also ontologically represented, the context information is readily interpreted in the problem domain of the application. With these facilities, a consistent, complete and easy-to-use context representation (*context ontology*) and its interpretation under current application goals can be achieved, which provides a basis for the decision of system adaptations.

Open coordination subsystem To reconcile the semantic differences between user requirements and the target implementation of the system, the adaptive coordination model presented in last section is firstly used. The abstract architectural specification is reified as an explicit object, which is causally connected to the real system. Thereby, the concrete system implementation and the abstract specification in terms of software architecture are virtually connected. However, the gap between software architecture and requirements still remains. For this purpose, an ontological representation (*architecture ontology*) is further developed to describe software architecture with respect to both the static configuration and the dynamic evolution processes, and declare both its description and prescription. This ontological representation is more problem-oriented, while what it describes essentially coincides with what the runtime architecture object reflects, and the evolution described with ontology can delegate the runtime architecture object to put into execution.

Here software architecture is used as an artifact to reconcile the problem domain and the solution domain. Also, it facilitates the abstract descriptions of system status and behaviors needed in the specification of adapting policies.

Goal-driven adaptation logic With the above facilities, the description of both a coordinated service oriented system and its environment is brought to an abstract level closer to the problem domain. To complete the loop of self-adaptation, a semantic framework is needed to express the adaptation logic, which specifies what should be done on the executing system under what conditions of the environment and the system itself to keep a goal satisfied. In addition to the above environment ontology and architecture ontology, a *requirement ontology* is also adopted as the conceptualization of the domain knowledge and application goals. The requirement ontology resembles some ideas of the goal-oriented requirement engineering [18], which expresses user requirements in the form of a Goal Refinement Tree. As there can still be conceptual and semantic gap between the three ontologies, a set of *transformation ontologies*, which are somewhat like ontology mappings, is further developed to glue them up. These ontologies constitute an ontology space, which become the juncture of the three major part of a self-adaptive system.

In implementation, OWL/RDF is used as the ontology language in our approach. Ontology tuple instances are stored in a shared space. A collection of reasoning engines is deployed upon the space and turns it into a blackboard system. The engines include standard OWL Description Logic reasoning engines, customizable rule-based adaptation engines and interfaces for direct user manipulations.

With such a mechanism, the closed loop of control with feedbacks works as follows: The system's running would have affects on the environment. Related low-level information is probed from environment, and then interpreted according to application domain knowledge. Triggering events are raised when the interpreted information indicates some application goals are missed or to be missed. Adaptation rules are evaluated and some operations over the system architecture are derived. Eventually, the operation is carried out by the runtime architecture object and the system is adapted on the fly. It's the responsibility of adaptation rule designer to ensure the stability, accuracy, settling time of the control suitable for the application. More research is definitely necessary to fit these concepts and associated techniques from control theory in software intensive systems. Some work and references can be found in [8].

With respect to the extensibility, the mechanism also facilitates the online introduction of new domain knowledge, adaptation rules and reasoning engines into the ontology space. Moreover, the cognizance of the environment and new reconfiguration behaviors can also be injected by the expansion in ontology.

Let us exemplify the approach with our ticket booking system. Suppose one of its goals is to keep responsive. This goal is refined as that the average response time for a transaction should less than, say, five seconds. This information can be expressed in GORE style as:

Name: Goal_Responsiveness
Des.: Response time is less than 5s
Def.: $\forall sys : TicketingSys, av\_resp : Number.\ responseTime(sys, av\_resp) \rightarrow lessThan(av\_resp, 5)$

The goal is specified in the requirement ontology. Following is the corresponding OWL specification.

```
<owl:Class rdf:ID="TicketingSystem">
  <rdfs:subClassOf rdf:resource="#Goal"/>
  <rdfs:subClassOf>
    <owl:Restriction>
      <rearon:lessThan rdf:datatype="http://www.w3.
org/2001/XMLSchema#int">5</rearon:lessThan>
      <owl:onProperty>
        <owl:DatatypeProperty rdf:ID="responseTime"/>
      </owl:onProperty>
    </owl:Restriction>
  </rdfs:subClassOf>
</owl:Class>
```

From now on less formal but more readable forms instead of XML codes will be used to present contents of ontologies.

Ontological representation of architecture style consists of three parts – *Architecture Description Ontology* (ADO), *Architecture Manipulation Ontology* (AMO) and *Architecture Control Ontology* (ACO). ADO imitates ACME by defining common concepts such as component, connector, configuration, system, role, etc., as well the relationship between them. For specific architecture style such as Master-Slave, refined concepts such as master component, slave component, multiplexer connector, etc. are defined. AMO declares reconfiguration operations on the architecture. For the Master-Slave style there are insertion and removal of slaves, binding/unbinding of services to/from the components. For the Extended Master-Slave style, there are also operations of insertion and removal of masters. ACO specifies the rationale of the architecture and its reconfiguration. It takes the form of "under what condition what operations are to be invoked to get what consequence". For our example, there would be ACO specifications such as

```
Condition: ¬satisfied(System.performance) ∧ fullCapacity(Master)
Operation: UpgradeToEMS, addMaster
Consequence: ¬fullCapacity(Master)
```

Here satisfied and fullCapacity are style-specific predicates. In implementation these predicates can be coded as static methods of the architecture class discussed in Section 3.

Putting all pieces together, the adaptation process works like this: first of all, user experienced delay and network latency are probed and reported in the context ontology regularly. With some ontology transformation, OnlineTicketSystem.responseTime in the requirement ontology is then computed out. Once it violates   the   restriction   of   the   goal,   a ¬satisfied(TicketingSystem.responseTime) event is raised. With another ontology   transformation,   the   event   is   translated   to   ¬satisfied(System.performance) in ACO. Finally according to the rules in ACO, the actions UpgradeToEMS and addMaster defined in AMO is invoked. These actions are implemented by the architecture object as discussed in Section 3. Contrasting to hard-coded decision components for autonomic behavior, this mechanism enables autonomy knowledge learned after system put into operation to be naturally added in at runtime. Together with the unanticipated architecture reconfigurations discussed earlier, it provides a reasonable support for online evolution of service oriented systems.

Some preliminary implementation and experimentation of the ideas discussed above have been carried out with positive initial results. More details are described in [21].

5. Coordination-aware service access control

5.1 Motivation and challenges

Services must be shielded from illegal accesses or abuses to avoid the leakage of the sensitive information/computing resources that they encapsulate. New challenges arise when applying exercise access control to real-life service-oriented computing systems [10, 4, 3]. The overall access control for SOC is to secure the autonomous services while they are in coordination with others to achieve a specific application goal over the Internet. The heuristic rule is to make service accesses as restrictive as possible; only those accesses that are necessary to the success of the coordination are approved. To realize the heuristic rule, the access control at service levels should consider the following features: 1) The interacting services are autonomous entities rather than simple objects like files; 2) The service access actions are being carried out in the context of the coordination and their mutual relationships are established within that context; 3) The open and dynamic nature of the Internet complicates the relations between services.

In a conventional access control model, entities issuing the access requests are called *subjects* while those being accessed are *objects*. Therefore, the fundamental models take the picture of a unidirectional relation from a subject to an object [35]. Reasonably, "what the subject can do" is the basis for the access control decisions. However, with autonomous services interacting with each other in some context of coordination, both of the service requestors and service providers have their own points of interests. They contribute simultaneously to the execution of the coordination. Besides the authorization status of the service requestors, the way that a service serves also functions on the decision that access control system produces. That is to say, from the perspective of access control, both "what the subject can do" and "how the service serves" affect the decisions explicitly. Therefore, the access control model for SOC should depict the bidirectional relation between the autonomous services and their requestors. The conventional requestor-restricting style of doing control against one party should be in a new style of harmonizing the both, which is considered a novel *symmetrical* view over the access control for SOC paradigm.

Protecting services in the coordinating applications requires circumscribing the accessing actions (i.e., service interactions) within the context of the coordination. In this way, only those accesses necessary to the success of the coordination application are considered legal. Therefore, the access control should take the coordination context into account. Whether the two parties of one instance of service interaction are *harmonizable*, i.e. whether the interaction should be approved depends on the logic of the coordination. Beyond the trust relationships between the different entities which are conventionally the basis for the access decision making, the access control should additionally be aware of the runtime status of the coordinating system. The access control system needs to construct some projection from the coordination logic to the access control rules for the services participating in the coordination, and by this means, binds access control with coordination tightly to realize a coordination-aware access control system.

Lastly, for the SOC paradigm, the open, dynamic and non-deterministic environment affects more than the programming model and the supporting techniques. On the whole, such an environment impacts the access control for systems running within it in two aspects. First, the dynamism of the environment leads to the varying in the entities, which causes the predefined trust relationship and the access control decisions to change. Second, the openness makes it almost impossible for individual entities to have a complete knowledge about the entire environment and thus baffle the access controller when no enough information is in hand to produce a right decision. Consequently, in addition to the fundamental view upon the access control for autonomous services as well as the coordination context to be considered, the access control system to be built for the SOC paradigm needs to be adaptive to changes and have mechanisms to figure out those locally unsolvable.

5.2 Access control for service computing

To meet the challenges discussed above, a set of work on the access control for the service-oriented computing systems is proposed.

A base access control model is proposed for the description of the symmetrical relation between the autonomous services and their requestors as well as the enforcement of the corresponding access control rules for service protection. In the current work of our own, the classic widespread-adopted RBAC [12] model, which defines the access rules in terms of user authorization, is adapted. To capture the service autonomy and depict the symmetrical interacting scene, as we have argued above, a notion of service role is incorporated into RBAC to denote additionally the serving status of the services while the original RBAC has only the notion of user role for the essentially unilateral authorization status of the users (subjects). The resulting model is called SRBAC. By this extension, a service requestor's authorization can be computed with a function which enumerates the all the services with a service role that is *harmonizable* with his user role when those roles are all activated in user-side sessions and service-side ones respectively.

The SRBAC model facilitates the expressing of the relationships between interacting services in coordination respecting the access control for them. The access controller now can make decisions from both parties of the interactions by checking the requestor's and the service's status synthetically. Thus, It is left to the coordination context to specify whether the statuses of both sides are harmonizable, which exactly makes the procedure of access control *coordination-aware*. The point of enacting the specifications to secure services in coordination is to generate access rules from the coordination logic cautiously without making any illegal accesses possible nor failing the executing of coordination potentially. Following this idea, an approach of projecting the coordination logic, which is the software architecture information in our manner of coordination, onto access control rules is attempted. The component-connector view of architecture is translated into a symmetrical service-coordination view of access control, which are a set of generated rules under a coordination-level authorization model. By such a translation, how a service (usually an abstract service as the logical and physical are decoupled, as discussed in the previous section) is participating in the coordination is described from the in perspective of access control within the coordination-scope. And with that, the relationship between two interacting services, and further whether that interaction is necessary with respect to the coordination can be further deduced for the final access control decisions. By locally enforcing the coordination-scope rules, access control systems for individual services can identify and approve the necessary interaction with respect to the coordinating application, which ensures that the participating services are contributing exactly to the success of the application and thus the security policy for the service-oriented computing applications is correctly enforced.

As the coordination-scope rules in accord with the coordination logic actually present the security concerns of the application, the respect for autonomy of the services is embodied by offering the discretion for services to take it or not. A service connection mechanism is thus proposed for services to denote its policy of taking other service's access rules as its own, which mean anyone that can be proven a legal service requestor of that other service will be allowed to access the original service too. So by establishing a service connection from itself to an abstract one defined in the coordination domain, the local service stats its participation in the coordination and acceptance of the coordination-scope rules, which can be freely revoked on seceding from that coordination. This mechanism also generally serves as a technique of the decentralized access control and be a complement to conventional solutions, such as RT [20]. The symmetry view over access control requires spontaneously an additional delegating mechanism in terms of the services being protected besides the requestors to be the controlled in those traditional schemes. The proposed concept of service connection realizes explicitly to state one service's dependency on another respecting the serving policy. Such a mechanism gives a direct and convenient way to declare the delegation while the conventional approach needs to translate it into connections between service requestors in terms of authorization.

The left requirement of dynamic access control is considered at both the base level as well as the coordination level. As for the base level, some conventional dynamic access control techniques [16, 42] are introduced onto SRBAC model with enhancements. Concretely, the original predefined relations bridging the services and their requestors in SRBAC, through the notion service roles as well as user roles, are applied activating conditions. More expressive than the existing work about the dynamic access control techniques, the one on SRBAC takes advantages of the base model where the services are assigned with a role too to capture the serving status. The dynamic changes in the service side have directly effects upon the access control thereout. Besides varying in the raw access control rules, the argued dynamism in coordination is also seriously considered in the design of the expressing of coordination-scope access rules, with which the service-service relationship is denoted as a conjunction that spans all the involved sub-relationships. As such, a circumstance that happens during the coordination and affects the system security would result in the changes in access rules. For example, system security can be affected by component replacing, architecture adjusting or any variation in trust relationship among the participators. With the coordination logic and the access rules fully synchronized, the dynamism in coordination is reflected in the access control system on the fly.

5.3 Access control for the ticketing system

Let us revisit the example of our ticket booking system. We show how the access rules are developed as the coordinating system are built up and how those rules are enforced at the administration domains of participating services.

As discussed earlier, a Master-Slave architecture is firstly selected, from which the ticketing system is about to be built up. According to the architecture, the system consists of three components, i.e. one master and two slaves. Concerning the access control problem here, the end users of the system are also included. The connectors in the architecture tell about how the components interact, that is, users can call the master component and the master component further request services from the slaves. The relation of *invokes* thus defines the access rules in the scope of the architecture. For this illustrative example, the ticketing system needs a value-adder to be the master, two transporters to be slaves and some members as end users. So with respect to the access control, the logical design process for the system specifies "what kind of services can be coordinated as a component in the architecture". This is done by defining the rules in the logical-system scope, which includes engineering roles for the service candidates, namely Value-adder, Transporter and Member, as the service qualification as well as declaring the relation of *fulfilling*. When the ticket booking system is going to be instantiated and put into production, the practical services are bound. For the qualified services to be incorporated into the system, the physical-system-scope rules are specified by *entitling* the services with corresponding roles. See Figure 4.

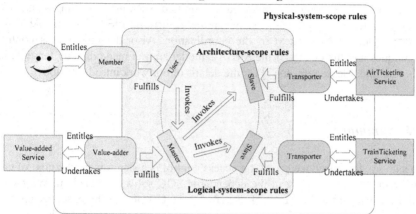

Fig. 4. Coordination-level Authorization

Three relations *Entitles, Fulfills, Invokes* are specified to govern the entities at the scopes of architecture, logical-system and physical-system respectively. For example, as the system *entitles* Value-addedService as a Value-adder which *fulfills* a Master, and AirTicketTingService is *entitled* with a role of Transporter that *fulfills* a Slave, the former service can invokes the latter one because the Master can *invoke* the Slave in the architecture. Such a design enables the access rules be dynamically synchronized with the system. Any changes in the system architecture (components or connectors), the logical design (qualification declaration for system components) or the physical status (service binding) can directly affects the access rules and, finally, the access control decisions.

The above finishes the development and management of the access rules at the side of the coordinating system. On the other side of the service administration, the service provider should take explicit actions to join the coordination and accept the access policy defined at the coordination system, as the autonomy should be totally reserved. The service connection works here as a delegation mechanism. For an AirTicktingService from SuperAirline to take part in the coordination, which means any requestor can access its AirTicktingService as long as it is authorized with the Transporter role by the administration domain of the coordinating system of TicketingSystem:

$$TicketingSystem.Transporter \Leftarrow SuperAirline.AirTicketingService$$

Let us retrospect doing access control for the service coordination again. When SuperAirline is about to contribute his AirTicketingService service to the TicketingSystem, it establishes a service connection as shown above. When a request that has no local policy to grant (or deny) arrives, it consults the TicketingSystem for the decision. TicketingSystem checks according to the rules generated from the system state to see whether the requestor plays a role in the coordination which does has the right to access AirTicketingService. If a positive answer is returned,

SuperAirline grants the request. Please be noted that the work for coordination-aware access control is quite simplified in this example to make it easier to understand. And some techniques involved are omitted, such as implanting some session identification into the requests when the Value-addedService calls AirTicketingService in the context of the coordination. Also, dynamic access control techniques and the details of the SRBAC model are not made directly tangible in this example. Please refer to [7] for the details of our work introduced above.

5.4 Summary

To sum up, the introduced work on access control is a step toward the goal of ensuring the service security in the dependable SOC software paradigm. We try to build an efficient access control system for SOC from the base access control modeling to the coordination-scope access control enforcing. To meet the peculiar protection requirements in coordinating the autonomous services in an open, dynamic and non-deterministic environment of Internet, a symmetrical view over the access control leads to the adapting, enriching and innovating on the conventional access control models, techniques and mechanisms. With the base model, its advanced enhancements and lastly the coordination-aware techniques integrated, it finally shapes a technical framework of the coordination-aware access control approach. And this work attests to a preliminarily technical scheme to feasibly bridging the gap between the software system itself and the assurance of its dependability that we keep pursuing.

6. Trust management for SOC

The dependability of service-oriented application systems involves much more issues than of traditional systems because they work in a truly decentralized environment. Even worse is that generally the information available is incomplete and inaccurate, which make it very difficult, if possible, to evaluate the services and system objectively and accurately in the same way as used before.

Firstly, the relationships among the principals involved in the development and operation of service oriented systems are very complicated. Traditionally, users specify requirements and developers build system accordingly. There is a straight forward one-to-one but tightly coupled trust relationship between them. And this trust is ensured by reliable means of verification and validation. Similar simple trust relationships exist between developers of different parts of the system and between developers at different development stages. The software quality control and assurance in this situation is thus well-defined, mainly concerning about how well software is designed (quality of design), and how well the software conforms to that design (quality of conformance) [33]. But in the situation of SOC, in order to provide the flexibility required by the open environment, system users, developers and service providers are greatly decoupled, and new principles such as service integrators, brokers, are introduced in. The relationships among them appear in a many-to-many manner, and may change all the time. In addition, these relationships are not subject to any centralized management. This complexity, dynamism and autonomy make conventional methods on software dependable analysis not directly applicable anymore.

Furthermore, with independent interests, preferences and knowledge, different principles involved in a service oriented system may have difference view of the system, and thus different view of its dependability. This lack of consensus also makes the traditional approach, where developers play a leading role in system construction and dependability assurance, and dependability is mainly measured by a common set of objective metrics, not appropriate. Instead, a user-centric assessment of the dependability must be adopted, with more subjective and personalized metrics.

Take the scenario of our ticket booking service for example. A user, Tom, is going to use our service. But how can he be *confident* that our service will satisfy his needs? Obviously, testing and inspection are not generally feasible here. Simple answers would be that he *trusts* the principal (i.e. the company) behind the service, or indirectly he trusts the recommendation of some independent assessment agency. But what if Tom wants to justify this trust with considerations that in fact other unfamiliar transportation services are used, and, his personal preference can be different from others, e.g., he prefers train to airplane and hates to be delayed?

With these considerations, a trust management framework is proposed for SOC. The framework explicitly distinguishes three kinds of trust related relationships, and helps to assess them in a personalized and subjective way.

Classification of trust relationships As shown in the bottom of Fig. 5, there are three different kinds of direct relationships in SOC.

- *Trust relationships between principals.* It describes whether or to what extent a principle trusts another principle. For instance, the user Tom trusts an independent service assessment agency as a recommender.
- *Confidence relationships between principals and services.* It describes how confident a principal is about a service would satisfy his purpose. For instance, the company needs to be confident about the service before publish it.
- *Dependence relationships between services.* It describes how a service is affected by other services under certain coordination logic. For instance, the dependability of our ticket booking service would depend on other transportation services, and also our architecture would provide certain degree of fault-tolerance if multiple transportation services of each kind are used.

Indirect relationships can be described with combinations of these three kinds of relationships. For example Tom's confidence about an unfamiliar service may come from his trust to a recommender and the recommender's confidence about the service.

The dependence relationships between services are generally objective, and are often subject to V&V methods, such as architecture-based software reliability [40, 34] prediction. But the former two kinds of relationships are less tractable, and are often implicitly assumed in conventional software development. Fortunately, there are some trust management [6, 5] models originally designed for the authorization across different security domains, which can help us to solve the similar problems in the dependability assessment of SOC systems.

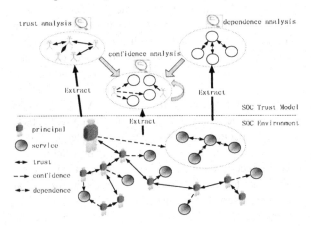

Fig. 5. Trust management framework.

As shown in the upper part of Fig 5, the goal of our dependability assessment is to derive the confidence relationship between principals and services. But generally this relationship is co-determined by many other relationships of the three kinds.

Evaluation of trust between principals A fundamental different character of the Internet from traditional computing environment is the independency of principals. The risks of incorporating undependable resources, e.g. low quality services provided by unprofessional even malicious providers, false information from dishonest recommenders, must be reduced as much as possible. How to determine the trustworthiness of principals is critical to assess a service since its dependability is computed on the basis of information provided by them. A trustworthiness evaluation model is proposed in [39], which can be used to evaluate trust relationships among principals dynamically based on direct subjective interaction experiences and indirect experiences with recommendations. It provides a general approach to the quantification of trust with a feed-back process that converges as the experience accumulating. It also reflects the evolution of trust relationships and is immune to non-systematic misleading recommendations.

Assessment of confidence of principals on services The problem of deciding the confidence of a principle on a service is twofold. First, the principle may have no priori knowledge or experience on the service. It is necessary to use the recommendations of other principles. Second, while traditionally a common set of criteria with objective metrics are often used in the dependability analysis, SOC system users often have their customized criteria with subjective metrics. Thus the recommended information, even from a trusted principle, is not fully reliable because it may be under a different set of criteria. We address this problem as follows. An ontology-based framework is designed to describe and differentiate customized evaluation criteria. Trust recommendation information can be collected through user's social network with trust credential chains. Then the information is synthesized with considerations of recommenders' trustworthiness and the semantic distance between the evaluation criteria.

Analysis of dependence relationships between services A (composite) service is commonly built on top of other services. The dependability of the composite service depends on dependability of participating services and the coordination logic among the services. While conventional reliability analysis techniques can be used, there are still two additional issues to address. First, existing methods usually require thorough analysis and are thus time consuming, which may not be acceptable for the quick construction and online evolution of service-oriented systems. Second, there is a need to find critical service whose dependability is most important to the dependability of the whole system. Addressing these issues, an architecture-based approach is developed. With the explicit architectural information provided by the coordination model, the approach efficiently computes the dependence values between the composite service and the participating services. The confidence on the composite service can be improved effectively by replace the highly depended services with better ones. More details of this approach can be found in [41].

7. Conclusion

Service oriented computing is widely recognized for its great potential. But currently, SOC is still at its early stage. Its maturity depends on the mutual prompting between economical and technical innovations. Economically there must be viable business models so that there could be a large number and variety of services, which is the prerequisite of senseful SOC. Technically, systematic software engineering methods, techniques and supporting platforms are need to meet unprecedented challenges including:

• Full fledge self-adaptation support that enable services and service oriented systems to survive under the open, dynamic and non-deterministic environment of the Internet.

- Self-management of services and service oriented systems, which helps to minimize human interactions in administrating the tremendous amount of service.
- Understandable and practical QoS assurance for complex service-oriented system in the open and dynamic environment.

In this chapter, we have presented our view on how to build a dependable service-oriented system that dynamically adapts to the changing environment and user requirement, and introduced our efforts on the adaptive service coordination model, the self-adaptive system architecture, the coordination-aware access control mechanism and the trust management framework, as a step towards a dependable software paradigm for SOC.

The approach to self-adaptation taken in this chapter requires a system, which coordinates a set of services with a logically centralized control, to explicitly maintain a model of itself and the goals to achieve. The system shall assess its own behavior and reconfigure itself to adapt to the evolving environment and requirements. Another approach is *self-organization*, which is often inspired by some biological and social system, relies on the *emergent* behavior resulted from local interactions of a large number of components under simple rules. Self-organizing systems are truly decentralized and do not have explicit representations of the system properties or goals [9]. Although some cases exists [25], software engineering based on self-organization is far from viable because it is generally very difficult to infer global system properties from the properties of the components.

Acknowledgement

The work is supported by the NSFC grant under no. 60736015, 60721002, 60603034, the 973 Program of China under no. 2009CB320702 and the 863 Program of China under no. 2007AA01Z178.

References

[1] Aldrich J (2003) *Using Types to Enforce Architectural Structure*. PhD thesis, University of Washington, August 2003.
[2] Avizienis A, Laprie JC, Randell B, Landwehr C (2004) Basic concepts and taxonomy of dependable and secure computing. *IEEE Transactions on Dependable and Secure Computing*. 1(1):11-32
[3] Bhatti R, Bertino E, Ghafoor A (2005) A Trust-based Context-Aware Access Control Model for Web Services. *International Distributed and Parallel Databases Journal* 18(1): 83-105
[4] Bhatti R, Joshi JBD, Bertino E, Ghafoor A (2004) XML-based RBAC Policy Specification for Secure Web-Services. *IEEE Computer* 37(4):41-49
[5] Blaze M, Feigenbaum J, Lacy J (1996) Decentralized trust management. In: *Proc. 17th Symposium on Security and Privacy*. 164-173

[6] Blaze M, Feighenbaum J, Keromytis, AD (1999) Keynote: trust management for public-key infrastructures. In: Christianson B, Crispo B, William S, et al., eds. *Cambridge 1998 Security Protocols International Workshop.* Berlin: Springer-Verglag, 59-63

[7] Cao C (2007) On Access Control in Service Computing. PhD thesis, Nanjing University, 2007.

[8] Cheng SW (2008) *Rainbow: Cost-effective software architecture-based self-adaptation.* Ph.D. thesis. School of Computer Science, Carnegie Mellon University, Pittsburgh, PA.

[9] Cheng BHC, de Lemos R, Giese H, et al. (2008) Software engineering for self-adaptive systems: A research road map. In: Dagstuhl Seminar Proceedings 08031.

[10] Sirer EG, Wang K (2002) An access control language for web services. In: *Proceedings of the Seventh ACM Symposium on Access Control Models and Technologies* ACM, New York, NY, 23-30. doi:10.1145/507711.507715

[11] Ferguson DF, Stockton ML (2005) Service-oriented architecture: Programming model and product architecture. *IBM SYSTEMS JOURNAL* 44(4):753-780

[12] Ferraiolo DF, Sandhu R, Gavrila S, Kuhn DR, Chandramouli R. (2001) Proposed NIST standard for role-based access control. *ACM Trans. Inf. Syst. Secur.* 4(3): 224-274

[13] Garlan D, Allen R, Ockerbloom J (1995) Architectural mismatch or why it's hard to build systems out of existing parts. In: *Proceedings of the 17th international Conference on Software Engineering* 179-185.

[14] Garlan D, Cheng SW, Huang AC, Schmerl B, Steenkiste P. (2004) Rainbow: Architecture-based self-adaptation with reusable infrastructure. *Computer*, 37(10):46–54

[15] Garlan D, Monroe RT, Wile D (2000) Acme: Architectural description of component-based systems. In: Leavens GT, Sitaraman M, eds. *Foundations of Component-Based Systems*, Cambridge University Press. 47–68

[16] Hulsebosch RJ, Salden AH, Bargh MS, Ebben PW, Reitsma J (2005) Context sensitive access control. In: *Proceedings of the Tenth ACM Symposium on Access Control Models and Technologies* (Stockholm, Sweden, June 01 - 03, 2005). SACMAT '05. ACM, New York, NY, 111-119

[17] Krammer J, Magee J (1998) Analysing dynamic change in distributed software architectures. *IEE Proceedings-Software*, 145(5):146-154

[18] Lamsweerde AV. (2000) Goal-oriented requirements engineering: a guided tour. In: *Proceedings of the 5th IEEE International Symposium on Requirements Engineering*. Toronto: IEEE Computer Society, 249—262

[19] Le Metayer D (1998) Describing software architecture styles using graph grammars. *IEEE Transactions on Software Engineering* 24(7):521–533

[20] Li N, Mitchell JC, Winsborough WH (2002) Design of a Role-Based Trust-Management Framework. In: *Proceedings of the 2002 IEEE Symposium on Security and Privacy* (May 12 - 15, 2002). SP. IEEE Computer Society, Washington, DC, 114.

[21] Lu J, Ma X, Tao X, Cao C, Huang Y, Yu P (2008) On environment-driven software model for Internetware, *Science in China, Series F: Information Science*, 51(6):683-721

[22] Ma X, Cao C, Yu P, Zhou Y (2008). A supporting environment based on graph grammar for dynamic software architectures. *Journal of Software*, 19(8):1881–1892.

[23] Ma X, Zhou Y, Pan J, Yu P, Lu J (2007) Constructing Self-Adaptive Systems with Polymorphic Software Architecture. In: *Proceedings of the 19th International Conference on Software Engineering and Knowledge Engineering* 2-8

[24] Maes P (1987) Concepts and experiments in computational reflection. SIGPLAN Not. 22(12):147-155

[25] Mamei M, Menezes R, Tolksdorf R, and Zambonelli F (2006) Case studies for self-organization in computer science. *Journal of Systems Architecture* 52(2):440-460

[26] Martin D, Paolucci M, McIlraith S, et al. (2005) Bringing Semantics to Web Services: The OWL-S Approach. In: Cardoso J, Sheth A eds. SWSWPC 2004. LNCS 3387:26 – 42

[27] Medvidovic N, Taylor RN (2000) A classification and comparison framework for software architecture description languages. *IEEE Transaction on Software Engineering*, 26(1):70–93

[28] Milanovic N, Malek M (2004) Current solutions for Web Service composition. *IEEE Internet Computing*. November/December 2004:51-59

[29] Papadopoulos GA, Arbab F (1998) Coordination Models and Languages, *Advances in Computers* 46:330-401

[30] Papazoglou MP, Georgakopoulos D (2003) Service-oriented computing: Introduction. *Commun. ACM* 46(10):24-28. doi:10.1145/944217.944233

[31] Papazoglou MP, Traverso P, Dustdar S, Leymann F, Krämer BJ (2006) Service-Oriented Computing: A Research Roadmap. In: *Service Oriented Computing*, Dagstuhl Seminar Proceedings.

[32] Papazoglou MP, van den Heuvel WJ (2005) Web services management: a survey. *IEEE Internet Computing* 9(6):58 – 64

[33] Pressman S (2005) *Software Engineering: A Practitioner's Approach*. Sixth Edition. McGraw-Hill Education

[34] Reussner R, Schmidt H, Poernomo I (2003) Reliability prediction for component-based software architectures, *Journal of Systems and Software* 66(3):241-252

[35] Samarati P, de Vimercati SC (2001) Access Control: Policies, Models, and Mechanisms. In: Focardi R, Gorrieri R eds. *Revised Versions of Lectures Given During the IFIP WG 1.7 international School on Foundations of Security Analysis and Design on Foundations of Security Analysis and Design: Tutorial Lectures* Lecture Notes In Computer Science, vol. 2171. Springer-Verlag, London. 137-196

[36] Shaw M (2000) Sufficient correctness and homeostasis in open resource coalitions: How much can you trust your software system. In: *Proceedings of the Fourth International Software Architecture Workshop*, IEEE Computer Society, 2000. 46~50.

[37] Shaw M (2002) Self-Healing": Softening Precision to Avoid Brittleness. Position paper for Workshop on Self-Healing Systems.

[38] Shaw M, Garlan D (1996) *Software Architecture: Perspective on an emerging discipline*. Prentice Hall.

[39] Wang Y, Lu J, Xu F, Zhang L. (2006) A trust measurement and evolution model for Internetwares. *Journal of Software* 17(4):682-690 (in Chinese with English abstract).

[40] Wang W, Wu Y, Chen M (1999) An architecture-based software reliability model. In: *Proc. Of Pacific Rim International Symp. On Dependable Computing*

[41] Xu F, Pan J and Lu W. (2008) A Trust-based Approach to Estimating the Confidence of the Software System in Open Environments. Technical Report. Institute of Computer Software, Nanjing University

[42] Zhang G, Parashar M (2003) Dynamic Context-aware Access Control for Grid Applications. In: *Proceedings of the 4th international Workshop on Grid Computing* IEEE Computer Society, Washington, DC.

Chapter 10

Developing Dependable Systems by Maximizing Component Diversity

Jeff Tian[1], Suku Nair, LiGuo Huang, Nasser Alaeddine and Michael F. Siok

Southern Methodist University, Dallas, Texas, USA

Abstract   In this chapter, we maximize component diversity as a means to achieve the goal of system dependability. Component diversity is examined from four different perspectives: 1) environmental perspective that emphasizes a component's strengths and weaknesses under diverse operational environments, 2) target perspective that examines different dependability attributes, such as reliability, safety, security, fault tolerance, and resiliency, for a component, 3) internal perspective that focuses on internal characteristics that can be linked logically or empirically to external dependability attributes, and 4) value-based perspective that focuses on a stakeholder's value assessment of different dependability attributes. Based on this examination, we develop an evaluation framework that quantifies component diversity into a matrix, and use a mathematical optimization technique called data envelopment analysis (DEA) to select the optimal set of components to ensure system dependability. Illustrative examples are included to demonstrate the viability of our approach.

1. Introduction

The concept of software quality is generally associated with good user experience characterized by the absence of observable problems and satisfaction of user expectations, which can also be related to some internal characteristics of the software product and its development process (Pfleeger et al., 2002; Tian, 2005). A quantitative measure of quality meaningful to both the users and the developers is product reliability, which is defined as the probability of failure-free operations for

---

[1] For correspondence, contact Dr. Jeff Tian, Computer Science & Engineering Dept., Southern Methodist University, Dallas, Texas 75275, USA. Phone: +1-214-768-2861; fax: +1-214-768-3085; e-mail: tian@engr.smu.edu.

J. Dong et al. (eds.), *High Assurance Services Computing*,
DOI 10.1007/978-0-387-87658-0_10, © Springer Science+Business Media, LLC 2009

a specific time period or input set under a specific environment (Musa, 1998; Thayer et al., 1978). Dependability is a broader concept that encompasses reliability, availability, safety, security, etc. as its attributes (Avizienis et al., 2004; Basili et al., 2004; Laprie, 1992)

Most modern software systems and software-intensive systems, including service-oriented systems, are made up of many components or services. Several factors contribute to overall system dependability, including the dependability of individual components or services, their collective strengths and weaknesses, the overall system architecture that may either be static or dynamically composed, the application environment that may be dynamically evolving and subject to external disturbances and/or threats, interactions within and beyond system boundary, etc. It has been recognized that diversity is a critical asset for a system to be dependable and fault tolerant (Gashi et al., 2007; Lyu and Avizienis, 1992).

In this chapter, we develop a generalized framework where diversity can be evaluated and maximized for general component-based systems. In doing so, we focus on the diversity of individual components in terms of their evaluated dependability attributes under diverse operational conditions. We also map internal assessments of these components to external dependability attributes by assessing their linkage empirically or logically. For a specific set of stakeholders, their values and preferences can also be used to assess the relative importance and trade-off among dependability attributes. With this evaluation framework in hand, we also develop an overall methodology that maximizes system diversity using a mathematical optimization technique called DEA (data envelopment analysis). By doing so, we hope to achieve our goal of ensuring system dependability via diversity maximization that combines collective strengths of individual components while avoid, complement, or tolerate individual flaws or weaknesses.

In subsequent sections, we first review basic concepts of dependability and its context in Section 2. We then present our framework for environment characterization in Section 3, followed by direct evaluation of component dependability and diversity maximization in Section 4. We focus on internal attributes as contributors to dependability and develop an approach to evaluate such internal contributors directly or map them to external dependability attributes in Section 5. Stakeholder's value perspective on dependability and trade-off among dependability attributes is described in Section 6. Finally, we provide a summary and discuss future work in Section 7.

2. Basic Concepts and Context

The International Federation for Information Processing Working Group 10.4 (IFIP WG10.4, see www.dependability.org) defines dependability as "the trustworthiness of a computing system which allows reliance to be justifiably placed on the services it delivers". It further states that dependability includes as special cases such attributes as reliability, availability, safety, and security. Others have also included additional attributes, such as integrity and maintainability as attributes for dependability, and availability, confidentiality, and integrity as attributes for security (Avizienis et al., 2004). The concepts of failures and faults play a very important role in identifying, characterizing, and analyzing the threats to dependability, with their standard definitions (IEEE, 1990) given below:

- *Failure*: The inability of a system or component to perform its required functions within specified performance requirements. It is an observable behavioral deviation from the user requirement or product specification.
- *Fault*: An incorrect step, process, or data definition in a computer program, which can cause certain failures.

In the literature, an additional term *error* is used to denote either a deviation of the system's total state as an intermediary between internal faults and external failures (Avizienis et al., 2004; Laprie, 1992) or as a missing or incorrect human action that causes the injection of faults (IEEE, 1990; Tian, 2005). Since there is a general agreement of the definitions of faults and failures, and most means to achieve dependability can be adequately characterized by related activities targeted at faults and/or failures, such as fault prevention, fault tolerance, fault removal, failure containment, and failure impact reduction, we focus on failures and faults only in this chapter while leaving out errors to avoid possible confusion.

As stated earlier, this chapter focuses on component diversity and its positive impact on overall system dependability. Therefore, we will focus on failures caused by individual and collective components, and faults that can be traced to those components, either as faults at individual components, or inconsistency (and by extension, lack of diversity) faults across multiple components. Explicitly excluded in this chapter are component integration issues that form another major category of root causes of system failures (Mili et al., 2007; Yacoub et al., 2004).

Different stakeholders will focus on different dependability attributes and different levels of expectations, which requires that dependability being captured in a specific context (Basili et al., 2004). The events that lead to dependability issues can be identified and characterized, specific failure types, scope, and impact can be characterized and analyzed with the help of some concrete measures defined on observation data, and reactions, such as impact mitigation, recovery, and occurrence reduction, can be guided by measurable goals. For example, reliability is defined for a specific environment (Musa, 1998; Thayer et al., 1978). Similarly, security can be captured by observable, verifiable attributes related to the context rather than their hypothesized causes in terms of vulnerabilities, counter measures and mitigation measures (Mili et al., 2007). Therefore, the context characterization would include event characterization and failure characterization that can be used to characterize observable system behavior and unexpected deviations. In this chapter, we use the operational profiles commonly used to guide usage based statistical testing as a concrete and quantitative way for event characterization, as described in Section 3. Failure characterization can be handled directly with dependability attribute assessment because different types of failures can be mapped to problems associated with different dependability attributes by their failure type, scope, and impact, as we will elaborate in Section 4.

3. Operational Profiles to Capture Environmental Diversity

The information related to usage scenarios, patterns, and related usage frequencies by target customers and users of a system can be collected, analyzed and organized into some models, commonly referred to as operational profiles (OPs). An OP is a quantitative characterization of the way a software system is or will be used in field (Musa, 1993; Tian, 2005). Environmental diversity of a software component can be captured by the OPs it has been or will be subjected to. By doing so, we can avoid the negative consequences, such as reduced system reliability (Weyuker, 1998), of improper reuse due to different OPs.

3.1 Operational profiles

There are two commonly used types of OPs: Musa's flat OP (Musa, 1993), a list of disjoint set of operations and their associated probabilities of occurrence, and Markov OP (Mills, 1972; Whittaker and Thomason, 1994), a finite state machine (FSM) with probabilistic, history-independent state transitions.

Figure 1 gives an example Musa OP for the web site www.seas.smu.edu, listing the number of requests for different types of files by web users and the related probabilities (Tian and Ma, 2006). This particular OP can also be viewed as a specialized access report, where individual web pages are grouped by file types to form individual service units in ranking order.

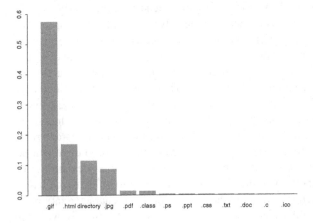

Fig. 1. An operational profile (OP) of requested file types for the SMU/SEAS web site

Figure 2 (left) is a sample Markov OP (Tian and Ma, 2006), with probabilistic state transitions. For large systems, a collection of Markov chains might be used as the system OP, organized into a hierarchical framework called unified Markov models (UMMs) (Kallepalli and Tian, 2001). Various sub-operations may be associated with each individual state in the top-level Markov chain, and could be modeled by more detailed Markov chains, such as the one in Figure 2 (right) for expanded state E. Recognizing the heterogeneous nature of many systems and their components, functions, and behavior, we extended our UMMs to include other possible usage models in a hierarchical structure (Tian and Ma, 2006).

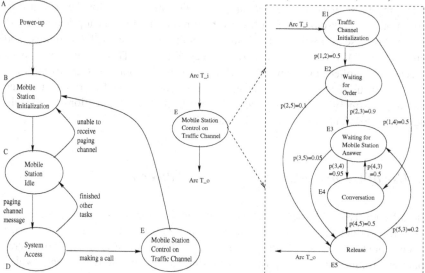

Fig. 2. An example Markov chain (left) and the expanded Markov chain for state E (right)

3.2 Operational profile construction

There are three generic methods for information gathering and OP construction, in decreasing accuracy: actual *measurement* of usage at customer installations, *survey* of target customers, and usage estimation based on *expert opinions*. Fortunately, the availability of existing system logs or traces offers us the opportunity to collect usage information for OP construction without incurring much additional cost (Tian and Ma, 2006). TAR (*top-access report*) and CPR (*call-pair report*) can be extracted from such system logs or traces and serve as the basis for our OP construction. TAR lists frequently used top-level operations and associated probabilities. CPR lists call-pairs (transition from one individual state to another) and the associated frequencies. For new systems or applications, similar information about the "intended" customer usage can be obtained by surveying potential customers or from experts.

For Musa OP, there are two standard procedures for OP construction. The first one follows a stepwise refinement to construct a series of increasingly detailed profiles: customer profile, user profile, operational mode profile, functional profile, and operational profile (Musa, 1993). The second one identifies operation initiators, chooses tabular or graphical representation, comes up with operations list, measures occurrence frequencies, and obtains occurrence probabilities (Musa, 1998). For Markov OP, we can follow the standard procedure for constructing the underlying FSM first, and then obtain probability information for the state transitions. For our hierarchical OP, TAR can be directly used as our top level flat OP. We can traverse through CPR for strong connections among TAR entries, and construct an UMM for each of these connected groups. This strategy have been successfully applied, including: flat OP for cartridge support software from Lockheed-Martin used by fighter pilot and support personnel, and hierarchical usage modeling for mobile communications and for web-based applications (Kallepalli and Tian, 2001; Tian, 2005; Tian and Ma, 2006).

3.3 Use of OP to capture environmental diversity

The different types of operational environments a component has been subjected to during product development and in prior operations can be used to characterize the environmental diversity for this component. There are several types of operational environments: static, transient, recurrent, and dynamic environments, which may affect our choice of appropriate OPs to capture environmental diversity.

In a *static* environment, each operation has a fixed probability of being invoked, and the overall operational sequence can be specified similarly. These probabilities are time invariant. For this type of environment, a single OP, typically in the form of a Musa OP, would be sufficient for our component and system dependability evaluation. However, because each component may only provide a limited number of functions or services, this system level OP may need to be customized or projected to the operations list for a specific component.

A *transient* environment can be specified by a single Markov OP or a single set of UMMs, with one or more sources and one or more sinks. One starts from a source state, goes through a sequence of states with pre-determined probabilities, and will eventually end up in a sink state. Many non-recurrent executions or services consisting of multiple stages would be suitable for modeling using such transient Markov chains.

A *recurrent* environment is one with recurrent or perpetual state transitions, which can also be specified by a single Markov OP or a single set of UMMs. As an important subset of recurrent environment, in a *stationary* environment, an equilibrium can be reached in a Markov chain (Karlin and Taylor, 1975), with the probability of leaving a system state balanced by the probability of entering the state from other states collectively. The stationary probability π_i for being in state i can be obtained by solving the following set of equations:

$$\pi_j = \sum_i \pi_i p_{ij}, \qquad \pi_i \geq 0, \quad \text{and} \quad \sum_i \pi_i = 1,$$

where p_{ij} is the transition probability from state i to state j. The stationary probability π_i indicates the relative frequency of visits to a specific state i after the Markov chain reaches this equilibrium. In this case, the stationary behavior of the system can be reduced to a distribution similar to those used in Musa OPs. Another important subclass of recurrent Markov chains is *periodic* chains, where instead of converging to a unique set of values for { π_i }, the values might be varying with a fixed periodicity to form a periodic chain.

A truly *dynamic* environment would not only involve system state changes but also probability changes, coupled with many possible unanticipated changes or disturbances, which may also include dynamically created or destroyed system states. In this case, a single Markov OP or a single set of UMMs will not be adequate to model the environmental diversity. Instead, some mega-models or mega-chains are called for. However, a practical solution to diversity assessment would favor solutions based on proven models. Therefore, we use a sequence of snapshots to model the environmental diversity for this situation while balancing the needs for accurate characterization of system changes with the overhead of handling large numbers of snapshots. Each snapshot will be a Musa OP, a Markov OP, or a set of UMMs.

For each OP, we can perform a specific dependability evaluation for each component under this specific environmental context. The evaluation results would reflect the component dependability as well as environmental diversity of the specific components. If a single OP is defined for a system, a single set of dependability evaluation results can be obtained for each candidate component and compared to others for component selection and system dependability maximization. For a dynamic environment, OP-dependability pairs will be used as input to evaluate component diversity to maximize overall system dependability. These topics will be discussed next.

4. Assessing Dependability Attributes and Maximizing Diversity

Once the environmental context is defined for a component, we can then proceed with direct assessment of the different attributes of dependability for a given component. This assessment will yield results that can be further analyzed to maximize overall system diversity and dependability using a mathematical optimization technique called data envelopment analysis (DEA).

4.1 Identifying dependability attributes

As stated in Section 2, dependability attributes may include reliability, availability, safety, security, integrity, maintainability, confidentiality, fault tolerance, resilience, etc. In addition, different stakeholders will focus on different attributes and different levels of expectations. The dependability issues can be identified and characterized by analyzing the system events and failures. Since our operational profiles (OPs) described in the previous section will be used as a concrete and quantitative way for event characterization, we now turn to failure characterization and the related dependability assessment for individual dependability attributes.

The identification of dependability issues and related failures will be carried out with direct involvement of customers, users, or domain experts. This effort will yield a list of dependability attributes that would be meaningful to specific customers under a specific market environment. For example, for web-based applications, reliability, usability, and security were identified as the primary quality attributes, and availability, scalability, maintainability, and time to market were identified as additional important quality attributes (Offutt, 2002). Among these attributes, the majority can also be identified as relevant dependability attributes for this context, including reliability, security, availability, and maintainability.

4.2 Assessing individual dependability attributes

Once such dependability attributes are identified, they can be measured or evaluated based on system logs, execution traces, or other data sources recorded or measured during normal operational use or during product development and testing. Since dependability needs to reflect the context of customer usage, usage-based statistical testing guided by the operational profiles would be assumed if we are evaluating dependability using data from software development and testing (Musa, 1998; Tian, 2005). For example, product *reliability* can be directly measured for in-field operations and summarized in the measure MTBF (mean-time-between-failures). During OP-guided software testing, the failure observations over time or over different input states can be fitted to time-domain software reliability growth models (SRGMs), input-domain reliability models (IDRMs), or tree-based reliability models (TBRMs) to obtain such measures as failure rate or intensity, expected number of cumulative failures, MTBF, etc. (Musa, 1998; Thayer et al., 1978; Tian, 2005).

Similarly, other dependability attributes can be measured and obtained accordingly. For example, MTTR, or mean-time-to-repair, can be a summary measure of maintainability; and availability can be defined and measured by MTBF/(MTBF+MTTR). For some dependability attributes, such as safety and security, a direct quantification may be difficult. However, at least some rating in terms of levels using an ordinal scale is possible. As a general rule, all these individual dependability attributes can be assessed by analyzing the corresponding failures and their corresponding scope and impact. Therefore, for each component under each OP, this step would yield a dependability vector whose individual elements are the corresponding values of assessment results for specific dependability attributes. For both component diversity evaluation and its extension to service diversity evaluation, this vector would represent independent interests of services or desirable properties for components. This vector is directly analyzed using DEA below. In the case conflicting interests or desirable characteristics exist, a value assessment based on stakeholders' interests, priorities, and trade-offs can be performed, as we will present in Section 6.

4.3 Diversity maximization via DEA (data envelopment analysis)

Data Envelopment Analysis (DEA) is a non-parametric analysis method used to establish a multivariate frontier in a dataset, a best practice frontier. It uses linear programming techniques to measure the efficiency of Decision Making Units (DMUs) using a comparison of a weighted sum of process outputs to a weighted sum of inputs (Charnes et al., 1994), which is supported by software tools including Pioneer II used in the example below (Barr, 2004). Recently, it has been applied to evaluate technical efficiency and performance for software projects (Herrero and Salmeron, 2005; Siok, 2008).

The DEA method requires the use of a production efficiency model, as illustrated in Figure 3. This is a conceptual model of the production system that identifies the inputs to and outputs from the software production process under study. Process inputs, those items needed to effect the design and development of the software, are identified on the left side of the model. Process outputs, the results or products produced as a result of executing the software process, are listed on the right. When executed, the DEA model will attempt to minimize inputs and maximize outputs. So, model inputs and outputs were selected such that these are desirable consequences for these model variables.

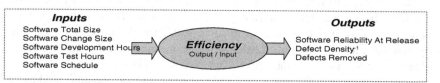

Fig. 3. DEA and Production Efficiency Model

Figure 4 is an illustrative example using only two output variables, component reliability captured by the measure MTBF and component security ratings for individual components A, B, C, D, and E. In this case, we would like to maximize both reliability and security, but without a specified tradeoff between the two. DEA would yield components A, C, and E on the efficiency frontier, and the other components B, and D not on the frontier. As we can see, B is dominated by C, i.e., C is better than B in both reliability and security. On the other hand, D is dominated by a linear combination of C and E, although C and E individually would not dominate D. So, in this example, components A, C, and E would receive the maximal score of 1, and will be provided as premier choices for system composition to maximize system dependability.

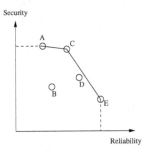

Fig. 4. DEA analysis of two dependability attributes reliability and security

4.4 A comprehensive DEA example

Thirty-nine completed avionics software development projects were studied earlier (Siok, 2008) and thirteen of them are included in the following DEA example. All software is implemented as embedded, real-time scheduled operations with hard and soft real-time tasks as well as some background processing. The metrics used in the DEA example include three inputs and two outputs. The inputs include 1) the change size that counts the effective lines of code changed from the previous version of software, 2) total labor measured in labor-hours spent in all development activities, and 3) software schedule measured in actual calendar months used to develop and release the software. All of the software projects in this study developed new software products derived from previous versions of the same, therefore change size is more meaningful than total size. The outputs include 1) total defects discovered during peer reviews, walkthroughs, inspections and testing activities, and 2) software reliability metric mean-time-to-failure (MTTF) at release computed by fitting the defects data to some SRGMs.

   Figure 5 illustrates the results when running the 3-input, 2-output production efficiency DEA model on the 13 project dataset. Software Project Identifier (ID) (i.e., the DMU number) and efficiency score are provided. The software projects with a score of 1 (i.e., DMUs 13, 15, 22 and 34) were best at minimizing Total Labor, Software Schedule, and Change Size Code in favor of maximizing Software Reliability at Release (measured as MTTF) and total defect removed during product development. These projects are on the best practice frontier for this dataset. The other projects were not efficient in comparison. All these projects can also be sorted in rank order in tabular form.

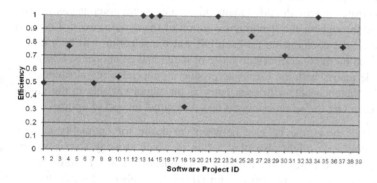

DEA Software Project Efficiency
-- CI Projects, AR-I-V Model --

Fig. 5. CI Projects DEA Efficiency

4.5 Other considerations for diversity maximization

In the above application of DEA, diversity is maximized due to the underlying assumption that each attribute constitutes an output variable, who's values are to be maximized in coordination with other input and output variables. To enhance the preference for diverse components, we could also introduce an explicit diversity attribute, which can be independently evaluated. For example, a baseline can be defined ahead of time, and each component's diversity score can be assessed with respect to this baseline. Let b_i be the baseline score for dependability attribute i, then a component c with corresponding dependability attribute scores $\{c_i\}$ can then be calculated as $\sum_i(|c_i - b_i|)$. Alternatively, $\{b_i\}$ can be calculated from the moving average of the current components that have already been selected or evaluated.

For an environment that can be modeled by a single OP or a single set of Markov chains, DEA as described above can be directly used to maximize component diversity and the DEA score can be consulted as a primary input for component choice decisions. However, as stated in Section 3, a dynamic environment might require us to use a series of OPs as snapshots in a sequence to capture the environmental context. There are essentially two ways we can extend the above DEA analysis approach for this environment:

- If dynamic substitution and re-assembly of components is supported in the composite system, we can then treat each snapshot OP separately and make the

optimal choices locally. This would resemble re-evaluation of all the components for their dependability attributes for each OP, and then making a series of
selections of the optimal components for system composition for that specific
OP to achieve optimal diversity.

- If the composite system should remain stable, i.e., same components chosen
  will be used throughout the dynamic evolution of the system, we still need to
  re-evaluate all the components for each OP, but the selection will be a global
  decision based on the overall performance of individual components. Essentially, the whole matrix with the Cartesian product of dependability attributes and
  OPs will be flattened out, with each entry as an output variable in the global
  DEA. For each OP, the selection might be sub-optimal instead of optimal.

In practical applications, the balance between the desire for optimality and reduced re-assembly cost might also play a role in which strategy above will be
used, or using a mixed strategy that combines elements of the two. In addition, the
computationally intensive optimization with DEA should also be taken into consideration, particularly for runtime evaluation of candidate components or services
before dynamic binding. Simplified models with simpler production efficiency
functions using fewer input/output variables or approximate solutions should be
considered to achieve a balance between desired accuracy, reduced overhead, and
timeliness of decisions.

5. Diversity: Internal Perspective

Under many circumstances, direct measurement and assessment of component dependability outlined above might not be available, feasible, or cost-effective. For
example, during the development process, we do not have a finished system or its
components yet. Sometimes, tight performance constraints or environmental sensi-
tivity due to the critical or confidential nature of the application might also prevent
the direct in-field measurement of component dependability. Under such circumstances, indirect assessment via internal contributors is needed.

5.1 Internal diversity as contributors to system dependability

As described in Section 4, direct dependability assessment typically takes the form
of analyzing failures and their corresponding type, scope, and impact. Since there
is a general causal relationship between faults and failures, indirect system dependability assessment can be carried out by assessing the faults and their characteristics. In fact, the assumption of fault diversity has been the cornerstone for software
fault tolerance, particularly in the generic technique called N-Version Programming (NVP) (Lyu, 1995). By ensuring fault diversity, not every version or every

component fail on the same input under the same operational environment, thus resulting in improved system dependability.

Researchers have work on increasing the product and process diversity in the hope of improved fault tolerance. For example, the use of independent teams, diverse specification and implementation methods, and management controls produces diversity of faults for improved reliability and dependability (Lyu, 1995; Lyu and Avizienis, 1992). As a concrete example, execution diversity, design diversity, data diversity, and configuration diversity have been shown to greatly improve fault tolerance of database management system constructed using several commercial-off-the-shelf SQL database servers (Gashi et al., 2007). When security is concerned, the fault concept needs to be expanded to include general vulnerabilities, and security-based testing is critical to ensure that counter measures and mitigation measures can address those vulnerabilities (Mili et al., 2007).

On the other hand, software faults can be caused by many factors, some more controllable than others. Much of the research in software measurement and quality improvement has focused on establishing the predictive relationship between software faults and various measures of software products and processes (Basili and Perricone, 1984; Fenton and Pfleeger, 1996). For example, much of the work on software complexity strives to establish the positive correlation between fault count or fault density and complexity. Much of the software quality improvement research has focused on identifying high risk or fault-prone areas for focused and cost-effective remedial actions (Munson and Khoshgoftaar, 1992; Tian, 2005).

Based on the above discussion, we next develop two generic ways to analyze internal diversity in our overall framework:

- *Fault-failure mapping for dependability diversity assessment*: When fault information is available, a straightforward fault-failure mapping can be employed to map the faults into failures under a specific environment characterized by our operational profile. Thereafter, the same evaluation technique based on failure analysis and dependability maximization using DEA on individual dependability attributes described in Section 4 can be applied.

- *Internal diversity assessment*: When fault information is unavailable, we can consider using various other software measurement data to perform an indirect assessment of component and system diversity and dependability.

One requirement of this approach, as with all internal assessment, is the availability of such internal information as internal faults and other internal measurement data. This requirement might limit the use of such assessments, particularly for service computing where services are independently developed, deployed, and maintained without allowing us to access internal characteristics.

5.2 Analysis of internal diversity and fault diversity

In the indirect dependability diversity assessment via internal diversity analysis, measurement data could include component internal characteristics, such as size, complexity, etc., as well as process, people, technology, and other characteristics. These measurement data are usually more readily available during product development and composition. We can use such measures and related diversity scores instead of component dependability scores as input data matrix for use with our diversity maximization using DEA described in Section 4. Notice here there are some complications involved because some of the measurement are simply nominal or categorical instead of ordinal or quantitative, such as the labeling of different processes, design methodologies, and implementation technologies used. A diversity score comparing them to some baseline, either a static baseline or a running average type of baseline need to be defined before DEA can be applied. On the other hand, software product metrics, such as size and complexity, are quantitative, and can be used directly as input to DEA.

One drawback of this indirect diversity maximization is the generally weak and sometimes complicated empirical relationship between such diversity and system dependability. Therefore, if fault data are available, we should try our best to map them to failures, and then use direct diversity assessment and maximization technique described in Section 4. Even if this mapping is not possible for lack of operational profile or other alternative contextual information that substantiates the causal relationship between faults and failures, direct fault diversity maximization is still preferred to internal diversity maximization above. In this case, some fault classification and analysis scheme, such as orthogonal defect classification and its recent development (Chillarege et al., 1992; Ma and Tian, 2007), can be used to provide input data to be directly analyzed by DEA. Again, we might involve some categorical information such as fault type. A fault diversity scoring scheme similar to that for internal diversity needs to be developed for this purpose.

5.3 Fault-failure mapping for dependability diversity assessment

Many defect-tracking tools and associated defect repository are used in industry during product development and maintenance to help track and manage defects in an effective way. If we evaluate their potential impact based on defect severity and likely usage scenarios, it would give us corresponding failure data, which can then be evaluated for dependability as we described in Section 4. Besides the raw defect data, the operational profile and the defect priority list need to be constructed to help us assess fault exposure and severity.

This mapping was applied to a deployed web application product "A", an online ordering application from the telecommunications industry that processes a couple of million requests a day (Alaeddine and Tian, 2007). It consists of hundreds of thousands of lines of code and utilizes IIS 6.0 (Microsoft Internet Information Server) and was developed using Microsoft technologies such as ASP, VB scripts, and C++. It provides a wide range of services, including: browse available telecom services, view accounts information, submit inquiries, order new services, change existing services, view order status, and request repair. The web anomalies are divided into categories based on the severity, and weights assigned to each of these categories by domain expert in Table 1.The list below details the individual steps involved in this fault-failure mapping procedure:

Table 1. Anomaly priority list

Impact	Description	Weight
Showstopper	Prevents the completion of a central requirements	100%
High	Affects a central requirement and there is a workaround	70%
Medium	Affects non-central requirement and there is no workaround	50%
Low	Affects non-central requirement for which there is a workaround	20%
Exception	Affects non-conformity to a standard	5%

1. Classify the faults that are extracted from anomaly repository and find the top classes of faults. Figure 6 shows the Pareto chart for these anomaly classes. The top three categories represent 76.50% of the total defects.
2. Based on the data from web access logs, find the number of hits per server per day and calculate the total number of transactions. For product "A", the number of hits was 235,142 per server per day with an estimated 40 hits per transaction on average. Therefore, the number of transactions per day per server is 235142/40 = 5880.

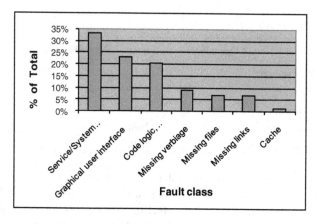

Fig. 6. Pareto chart for fault classes

3. Use the defined operational profile and the number of transactions calculated above to determine the number of transactions processed every day for each operation using the following formulas:

Number of Operational Transactions (operation)
= Total Transactions * Operational probability (operation)

The operational profile is given by the operation probability column for each operation in Table 2 based on customer usage data for "A". We then calculated the number of transactions for each operation in Table 2.

Table 2. Operational profile and number of operational transactions

Operation	Operation Probability	# of Operational Transactions
New order	0.1	588
Change order	0.35	2058
Move order	0.1	588
Order Status	0.45	2646

4. Use the defined priority list with the data from steps 1 and 3 to calculate the failure frequency of the faults' impact per each operation within the operational profile using following formula:

Failure frequency (operation, priority)
= # Operational Transactions (operation) * priority list _weight (priority)

Table 3 shows the failure view of the order status for product "A". This means any order status showstopper produces 2646 failures per day per server for product "A". Similar tables can be calculated for other operations to build the complete failure view of the anomalies.

Table 3. Failure view of order status

Application Operation	Impact	# Operational Transactions	Failure Frequency
Order status	Showstopper	2646	2646
Order status	High	2646	1852
Order status	Medium	2646	1323
Order status	Low	2646	529
Order status	Exception	2646	132

These steps map individual faults into potential failure instances, effectively providing an assessment of fault exposure under this usage environment defined by the operational profile. We also found that defect data repository and web server log recorded failures have insignificant overlap, leading to our decision to use both for effective reliability improvement. When we prioritized the testing by focusing on risk areas, we first fixed faults based on the given priority queue rank, so we could achieve better cost-efficiency in reliability improvement. By fixing the top 6.8% faults, the total failures were reduced by about 57%. The corresponding reliability improved from 0.9356 to 0.9723. Similarly, related failure characterization and analysis described in Section 4 can be carried out for evaluating other dependability attributes. Therefore, this fault-failure mapping allows us to evaluate component dependability and to use the evaluation results as input to maximized component diversity for overall system dependability maximization.

6. Diversity: Value Perspective

Direct measurement and assessment of system/software dependability might not capture what project success-critical stakeholders truly care about. The universal one-size-fits-all software dependability metrics are unachievable in most project situations. Value dependencies vary significantly by stakeholders and situations, making statements such as "Your system has a software reliability rating of 0.613" usually meaningless. Occasionally, a very stable organization can develop and manage to an organization-specific software reliability metric whose change from 0.604 to 0.613 or from 0.621 to 0.613 will be highly meaningful. But in most situations, stakeholder and situation differences make such single software dependability metrics infeasible.

6.1 Stakeholder value dependencies on dependability attributes

Mapping dependability attributes to value-based perspective becomes more meaningful to target success-critical stakeholders. Table 4 provides a top-level summary of the relative strengths of dependency on information system dependability attributes, for classes of information system stakeholders exhibiting different patterns of strengths of dependency (Huang, 2006). Its initial portions were obtained from empirical analysis of different classes of information system stakeholders' primary concerns during win-win requirements negotiations. The dependency ratings refer only to <u>direct</u> dependencies. For example, system developers, acquirers, and administrators are concerned with safety or security only to the extent that a system's information suppliers, users, and dependents are concerned with them. And information suppliers and system dependents are only concerned with reliability and availability to the extent that these help provide their direct concerns with security and safety. Value-based dependability analysis explicitly considers cost and schedule as dependability attributes.

Table 4. Information system top-level stakeholder value dependencies on dependability attributes

Dependability Attributes	Info. Supplier	System Dependents	Info. Brokers	Info. Consumers Mission – Critical	Info. Consumers Mission – Un-critical	System Controllers	Developers	Maintainers	Administrators	Acquirers
Protection										
Safety		**		**		**				
Security	*	**	**	**		**				
Privacy	**		**	*	*					
Robustness										
Reliability		*	*	**		**			*	*
Availability		*	*	**		**			*	*
Survivability		*	*	**		**			*	*
Quality of Service										
Performance		**	**	*		**			*	*
Accuracy& Consistency	**		**	**	*	**			*	
Usability	*		*	**	**	**			*	
Evolvability			*	**	*	*		**	*	**
Interoperability			**						*	**
Correctness							*			**
Cost							*			**
Schedule			*	**	*	*	**			**
Reusability								**	*	*

** Critical　　　　*** Significant**　　　　**( ) Insignificant or indirect**

6.2 Quantitative model for value-based dependability ROI analysis

The Value-Based Software Dependability ROI analysis model (Boehm et al. 2004; Huang, 2006) integrates the cost estimating relationships (CER's) from the Constructive Cost Model COCOMO II (Boehm et al., 2000); the software quality attribute estimating relationships (QER's) from the Constructive Quality Model COQUALMO (Steese et al., 2002); and the value estimating relationships (VER's) supplied by the system's stakeholders.

A typical value-versus-availability relationship can appear as a production function as shown in Figure 7. Below a certain level of investment, the gains in availability don't avoid bankruptcy like Ashton-Tate DBase-4. Beyond this level, there is a high returns segment, but at some point, incremental gains in availability don't affect users' frustration levels, resulting in a diminishing-returns segment.

The initial availability VERs involve simple relationships such as the operational cost savings per delivered defect avoided, or the loss in sales per percent of the system downtime, shown as the linear approximation of a particular segment of production function in Figure 7. Many organizations providing e-services also use such relationships to measure loss of revenue due to system downtime. For example, on the higher side, Intel estimates its loss of revenue as $275K ($US) for every hour of order processing-system downtime; other companies estimate $167K (Cisco), $83K (Dell), $27K (Amazon), $8K (E*Trade), and $3K (Ebay).

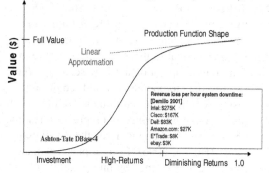

Fig. 7. Typical value estimating relationships (VERs) of availability

Based on such value-based quantitative model, dependability ROI analysis can be performed for different types of software systems. Figure 8 compares the availability ROI analysis results of two different types of software systems: the normal business Sierra Mountainbikes Order Processing System and mission-critical NASA Planetary Rover (Huang, 2006). The trend of the Order Processing System is in a dashed line and that of the Planetary Rover is in a solid line. Thus we see that different mission situations lead to different diminishing returns points for the business application, whose ROI goes negative in going from a High to a Very High RELY rating; and for the planetary rover application, whose positive ROI is sustained through Very High, but not through Extra High.

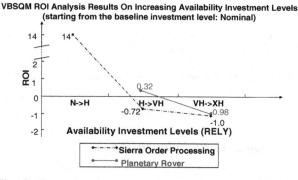

Fig. 8. Comparing the availability ROI analysis results of Sierra Mountainbikes Order Processing System and NASA Planetary Rover

Dependability ROI analysis can also be performed on different operational scenarios within the same software system. Multiple stakeholder negotiation of NASA/USC Inspector Scrover (ISCR) system goals involves a mix of collaborative win-win option exploration with prototyping and analysis of candidate options. Here, the value-based quantitative dependability model can be used to help the stakeholders determine how much availability is enough for the three primary classes of ISCR scenarios. For instance, there are 15 KSLOC of software for mission-critical scenarios such as *Target Sensing* and *Target Rendezvous*. Its cost per instruction of a Nominal COCOMO II Required Reliability level is $6.24/LOC (at graduate-student labor rates), leading to a nominal cost of $93.6K. A failure in the mission-critical software is likely to cause complete contamination and replacement of the robot and the lab, with an impact equal to the $2.5M of an entire lab. A failure and loss of availability of the online-operational ISCR scenarios (i.e., display continuous video images and sensor data to operator) would require repair and rerun of the mission, possibly losing $200K of lab equipment. A failure of post-mission data analysis would require debugging, fixing, and regression testing the software, typically costing about $14K. Figure 9 summarizes the Availability ROI analysis results for the ISCR system (Huang, 2006). From a pure calculated ROI standpoint, one could achieve some potential savings by interpolating to find the availability-requirement levels at which the ROI goes from positive to negative, but it is best to be conservative in a safety-related situation. Or one can identify desired and acceptable availability levels to create a tradeoff space for balancing availability with other dependability attributes.

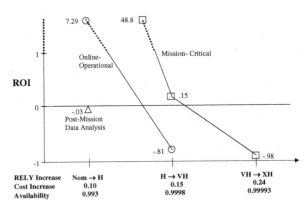

Fig. 9. Summary of VBSQM ROI analysis of ISCR Increment 3 availability goals

6.3 Tradeoff analysis among dependability attributes

Stakeholder value dependencies on software dependability attributes are often in conflict and require negotiated solutions. Furthermore, multi-criterion decision solutions are complicated by tradeoff relations among dependability attributes. Many dependability attributes reinforce each other. An unreliable system will not be very secure; a poorly-performing system will not be very usable. On the other hand, many conflicts arise in trying to satisfy multiple quality criteria. Complex security defenses slow down performance and hamper usability. Fault tolerance solutions spread information around and complicate security defenses, along with adding performance overhead. Tightly-coupled performance optimizations complicate the achievement of evolvability and reusability, as well as aspects of security and fault tolerance. All of the above add to project costs and schedules. These tradeoff relations complicate the ability to find solutions that satisfy a combination of dependability attribute levels.

Figure 10 presents the COCOMO II tradeoff analysis of three dependability attributes "cost, schedule, and reliability" for a software project with 100 KSLOC. It clearly shows the "cost, schedule, quality: pick any two" effect (Huang and Boehm, 2005). For example, suppose that the project wants a High RELY level (10K-hours MTBF) and a 20-month delivery schedule within a budget of $5.5M. Unfortunately, a High RELY level and a 20-month schedule require a budget of $7.33M. For a cost of $5.5M, the project can get a High RELY level and a delivery schedule of 23.5 months, or a 20-month delivery schedule but a Low RELY level. The three circles in Figure 10 represent the three resulting "pick any two" points. On the other hand, the project can apply the Schedule-Cost-Quality as Independent Variable (SCQAIV) strategy to determine a "pick all three" solution (Boehm et al., 2002). This is done by prioritizing the product features and determining what quantity of top-priority features can be developed as an Initial Operational Capability (IOC) satisfying the desired schedule, cost, and MTBF goals. Using the COCOMO II Most Likely and Pessimistic estimates, this can be done with 50% confidence for a 90-KSLOC IOC or 90% confidence for a 77-KSLOC IOC.

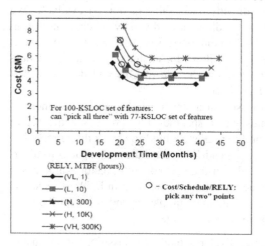

Fig. 10. COCOMO II Cost/SCED/RELY tradeoff analysis (100-KSLOC Project)

7. Conclusions and Future Work

In this chapter, we developed a generalized and comprehensive framework where component diversity can be evaluated for general component-based systems and system dependability can be maximized. We then employed a mathematical optimization technique called data envelopment analysis (DEA) to select the optimal set of components that maximizes component diversity based on their individual dependability and diversity evaluation results. Illustrative examples were included to demonstrate the viability of our approach. Component diversity is examined and maximized from four different perspectives:

- *Environmental perspective* that emphasizes a component's strengths and weaknesses under different operational environments. We examined different types of operational environments, ranging from static, transient, recurrent, to dynamic environments and used different types of operational profiles (OPs) ranging from Musa's flat OPs, Markov OPs, Unified Markov Models, and their combination in a time series to capture this environmental diversity and provide the operational context for dependability evaluation.
- *Target perspective* that examines different dependability attributes, such as reliability, safety, security, fault tolerance, and resiliency, for a component under a specific OP. We developed an evaluation framework based on analysis of failure type, scope and impact, which quantifies component dependability attributes into a vector for a specific OP or a matrix for a set of OPs representing snapshots of a dynamically changing environment. We then employed DEA to select the optimal set of components to ensure system dependability by maximizing component dependability diversity.
- *Internal perspective* that focuses on internal contributors to dependability when component dependability is not directly measurable or not yet available. We developed two generic methods to handle internal diversity: 1) direct use of internal diversity evaluation results for component selection using DEA, and 2) mapping of internal faults to external failures for related dependability evaluation and diversity maximization through the use of OPs and domain expert judgment about fault exposure and impact.
- *Value-based perspective* that focuses on a stakeholder's value assessment of different dependability attributes under specific OPs. For a specific set of stakeholders, their values and preferences were used to assess the relative importance and trade-off among the dependability attributes. Compared to diversity maximization via DEA directly on the dependability vector, value-based perspective customizes the production efficiency function in DEA to a specific stakeholder's quantified preferences among multiple dependability attributes so that an optimal choice of components can be made.

The first three of the above perspectives resemble the classification of quality in use, external and internal metrics of software product quality defined in ISO/IEC standard 9126 (ISO, 2001). Our perspectives were customized for dependability attributes and their evaluation and analysis for components and systems, with an emphasis on the overall environment and addition of stakeholder's value perspective.

As with any quantitative analysis, such as our use of DEA on component dependability vectors, noise in the data can lead to inaccuracies of analysis results and sometimes wrong conclusions. However, our multi-perspective framework would make this less of a problem due to the intrinsic diversity due to the different measurement data and analyses performed for those different perspectives.

We plan to carry our future work to address other important issues for system dependability maximization and experimental validation of our approach. Other factors contribute to overall composite system dependability, including overall system architecture, dynamic system composition and evolution, interactions within and beyond system boundary, etc., will be examined. We will explore the integration of our multi-dimensional approach with existing work on compositional approaches that assess system reliability, performance, and other dependability attributes based on that of individual components, system architecture, and dynamic interactions (Wu et al., 2003; Yacoub et al., 2004). For experimental evaluation and validation of our approach, we plan to construct a testbed under the guidance of our OPs to focus on likely problems and system behavior under injected or simulated problems. In addition, injection of unanticipated (and unlikely) problems and system behavior will be handled by systematic application of diverse ideas such as program mutation, exception handling, and boundary extensions. When integrated with our work on diversity maximization, all these will lead to improved dependability of composite systems used in a wide variety of application domains.

Acknowledgments

The work reported in this chapter was supported in part by NSF Grant IIP-0733937. We thank the anonymous reviewers for their constructive comments.

References

[1] Avizienis, A. A., Laprie, J.-C., Randell, B., and Landwehr, C. (2004). Basic concepts and taxonomy of dependable and secure computing. *IEEE Trans. on Dependable and Secure Computing*, 1(1):11–33.

[2] Barr, R. (2004). DEA software tools and technology: A state-of-the-art survey. In Cooper, W., Seiford, L. M., and Zhu, J., editors, *Handbook on Data Envelopment Analysis*, pages 539–566. Kluwer Academic Publishers, Boston, MA.

[3] Basili, V. R., Donzelli, P., and Asgari, S. (2004). A unified model of dependability: Capturing dependability in context. *IEEE Software*, 21(6):19–25.

[4] Basili, V. R. and Perricone, B. T. (1984). Software errors and complexity: An empirical investigation. *Communications of the ACM*, 27(1):42–52.

[5] Boehm B., Port D., Huang L., and Brown A.W. (2002). Using the Spiral Model and MBASE to Generate New Acquisition Process Models: SAIV, CAIV, and SCQAIV. *CrossTalk*, January, pp. 20-25.

[6] Boehm B., Abts C., Brown A.W., Chulani S., Clark B., Horowitz E., Madachy R., Riefer D., and Steece B. (2000). *Software Cost Estimation with COCOMO II*, Prentice Hall.

[7] Boehm B., Huang L., Jain A., Madachy R. (2004) "The ROI of software dependability: The iDAVE model", *IEEE Software*, vol. 21, no. 3, pp. 54-61.

[8] Charnes, A., Cooper, W. W., Lewin, A. Y., and Seiford, L. M., editors (1994). *Data Envelopment Analysis: Theory, Methodology, and Applications*. Kluwer Academic Publishers, Boston, MA.

[9] Chillarege, R., Bhandari, I., Chaar, J., Halliday, M., Moebus, D., Ray, B., and Wong, M.-Y. (1992). Orthogonal defect classification — a concept for in-process measurements. *IEEE Trans. on Software Engineering*, 18(11):943–956.

[10] Fenton, N. and Pfleeger, S. L. (1996). *Software Metrics: A Rigorous and Practical Approach, 2nd Edition*. PWS Publishing, Boston, MA.

[11] Gashi, I., Popov, P., and Strigini, L. (2007). Fault tolerance via diversity for off-the-shelf products: A study with SQL database servers. *IEEE Trans. on Dependable and Secure Computing*, 4(4):280–294.

[12] Herrero, I. and Salmeron, J. L. (2005). Using the DEA methodology to rank software technical efficiency. *Communications of the ACM*, 48(1):101–105.

[13] Huang L. (2006). "Software Quality Analysis: A Value-Based Approach". *Ph.D. Dissertation*. Proquest.

[14] Huang L. and Boehm B. (2005). Determining How Much Software Assurance Is Enough? A Value-Based Approach. In *Proceedings of 4th International Symposium on Empirical Software Engineering (ISESE)*.

[15] IEEE (1990). IEEE Standard Glossary of Software Engineering Terminology. STD 610.12-1990.

[16] ISO (2001). *ISO/IEC 9126-1:2001 Software Engineering - Product Quality - Part 1: Quality Model*. ISO.

[17] Kallepalli, C. and Tian, J. (2001). Measuring and modeling usage and reliability for statistical web testing. *IEEE Trans. on Software Engineering*, 27(11):1023–1036.

[18] Karlin, S. and Taylor, H. M. (1975). *A First Course in Stochastic Processes, 2nd Ed.* Academic Press, New York.

[19] Laprie, J.-C., editor (1992). Dependability: Basic Concepts and Terminlogy, Depaendable Computing and Fault Tolerance. Springer-Verlag, New York.

[20] Lyu, M. R., editor (1995). *Software Fault Tolerance*. John Wiley & Sons, Inc., New York.

[21] Lyu, M. R. and Avizienis, A. A. (1992). Assuring design diversity in N-version software: A design paradigm for N-version programming. In Meyer, J. F. and Schlichting, R. D., editors, *Dependable Computing for Critical Applications 2*. Springer-Verlag, New York.

[22] Ma, L. and Tian, J. (2007). Web error classification and analysis for reliability improvement. *Journal of Systems and Software*, 80(6):795–804.

[23] Mili, A., Vinokurov, A., Jilani, L.L., Sheldon, F.T. and Ayed, R.B. (2007). Towards an Engineering Discipline of Computational Security. In *Proceedings of 40th Annual Hawaii International Conference on System Sciences (HICSS 2007)*.

[24] Mills, H. D. (1972). On the statistical validation of computer programs. Technical Report 72-6015, IBM Federal Syst. Div.

[25] Munson, J. C. and Khoshgoftaar, T. M. (1992). The detection of fault-prone programs. *IEEE Trans. on Software Engineering*, 18(5):423–433.

[26] Musa, J. D. (1993). Operational profiles in software reliability engineering. *IEEE Software*, 10(2):14–32.

[27] Musa, J. D. (1998). *Software Reliability Engineering*. McGraw-Hill, New York.

[28] Offutt, J. (2002). Quality attributes of web applications. *IEEE Software*, 19(2):25–32.

[29] Pfleeger, S. L., Hatton, L., and Howell, C. C. (2002). *Solid Software*. Prentice Hall, Upper Saddle River, New Jersey.

[30] Siok, M. F. (2008). *Empirical Study of Software Productivity and Quality*. D.E. Praxis, Southern Methodist University, Dallas, Texas, U.S.A.

[31] Steese B., Chulani S., Boehm B. (2002). Determining Software Quality Using COQUALMO. *Case Studies in Reliability and Maintenance*, W. Blischke and D. Murthy, eds., Jon Wiley & Sons.

[32] Thayer, R., Lipow, M., and Nelson, E. (1978). *Software Reliability*. North-Holland, New York.

[33] Tian, J. (2005). Software Quality Engineering: Testing, Quality Assurance, and Quantifiable Improvement. John Wiley & Sons, Inc. and IEEE CS Press, Hoboken, New Jersey.

[34] Tian, J. and Ma, L. (2006). Web testing for reliability improvement. In Zelkowitz, M. V., editor, *Advances in Computers, Vol.67*, pages 177–224. Academic Press, San Diego, CA.

[35] Weyuker, E. J. (1998). Testing component-based software: A cautionary tale. *IEEE Software*, 15(5):54–59.

[36] Whittaker, J. A. and Thomason, M. G. (1994). A Markov chain model for statistical software testing. *IEEE Trans. on Software Engineering*, 20(10):812–824.

[37] Wu, X., McMullan, D. and Woodside, M. (2003). Component Based Performance Prediction. In *Proceedings of the 6th ICSE Workshop on Component-Based Software Engineering: Automated Reasoning and Prediction (CBSE6)*, Portland, Oregon.

[38] Yacoub, S., Cukic, B., and Ammar, H. (2004). A scenario-based reliability analysis approach for component-based software. *IEEE Trans. on Reliability*, 54(4):465--480.

Chapter 11

High Assurance BPEL Process Models

Mark Robinson, Hui Shen, Jianwei Niu

Department of Computer Science, University of Texas at San Antonio

One UTSA circle, San Antonio, Texas, 78249

Abstract. An increasing number of software applications and business processes are relying upon the use of web services to achieve their requirements. This is due in part to the use of standardized composition languages like the Business Process Execution Language (BPEL). BPEL allows the process designer to compose a procedural workflow from an arbitrary number of available web services and supplemental "programming-like" activities (e.g., assigning values to variables). Such composition languages naturally bring concerns of reliability, consistency, and durability, let alone safety and security. Thus, there is a need for formal specification and analysis of BPEL compositions for high assurance satisfaction. We propose the use of Unified Modeling Language (UML) sequence diagrams as a means for analysis of BPEL process consistency and demonstrate our technique with two examples.

1. Introduction

Today, web services play an important role in service-oriented computing, as the web is an inarguably ubiquitous medium. Web services provide domain-specific functionality to client and server applications alike, with the interface to those services exposed over the web. There are many web services currently available and incorporating a web service into an application is simple, although the integration may impose a reasonable learning curve. Creating a web service is also simple, with many different development platforms already equipped to produce web services.

Web services offer numerous advantages to both the web service consumer and the web service provider. The use of web services affects the software engineering process in many advantageous ways. Some of these advantages are:

J. Dong et al. (eds.), *High Assurance Services Computing*,
DOI 10.1007/978-0-387-87658-0_11, © Springer Science+Business Media, LLC 2009

- Fast and cheap to deploy – while these advantages are not unique to web services, it is worth stating that reductions in time-to-market and cost-to-market are real benefits from utilizing web service technology. Web service providers specialize in their domains and realize economies of scale by making their services affordable to web service consumers. Additionally, the use of the Internet as a communication medium reduces cost.
- Reusability – one can easily reuse the same web services in new applications, no matter which development language is being used (e.g., PHP, JSP, .NET). The only requirement is that the development language provides support for accessing web services.
- Accessibility – many different platforms and devices may utilize the functionality of web services, including mobile devices. Client-side applications, ad-hoc queries, and web sites/applications may all access the same web service (see Figure 1). The web service provider may also freely control how the service is accessed and how a service consumer is charged for its use. This allows for a variety of governance and payment options for the web service, more easily allowing it to fit the budgetary constraints of the service consumer.
- Centralized method of discovery – web service providers can register their web services with online registries that provide descriptions of the web services provide. A description may also include pricing for the use of the service and a link to the interface specifications required to communicate with the web service (e.g., WSDL document).
- Maintainability – the provider of the web service is responsible for maintaining, securing, and updating the web service and its data. The web service consumer bears none of the labor for these tasks, although it is normal for the web service provider to pass on some of the cost for maintenance to the web service consumers.
- Value-added content – integration of services that provide proprietary functionality and/or data may increase the value of the web service consumer's product, particularly if the consumer is acting as a service broker.
- Loose coupling – the consumer of the web service does not care how the provider of the service implements the service, provided its functionality is known, consistent, and reliable. Future changes to the service or switching web service providers will not necessitate changes to the consumer's application as long as those changes do not affect the service interface.

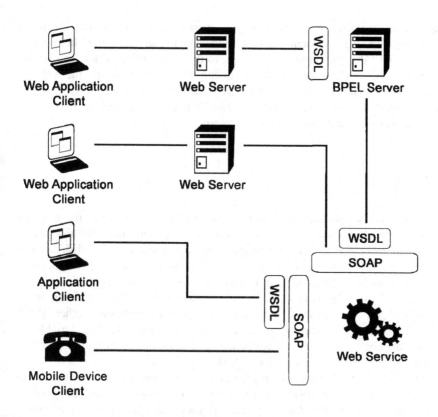

Fig. 1. Various devices and platforms accessing the same web service.

Integrating web services into a software project can be a frightening notion, as the developer might begin to consider some of the negative possibilities of such integration: loss of service, price gouging, data security and privacy, etc. But, these concerns have always existed in component-based software engineering. Trust and long, solid track records can help ease fears of integration disaster. But if those are in short supply, contracts and service level agreements can be tailored to suit both parties' concerns and project requirements. Web service providers and consumers should also consider Business Interruption and Errors and Omissions insurance to protect each party in the areas where a contract does not.

A web service is essentially a program that is located on a web server and has its interface exposed to the outside world using Internet protocols (of which the normal "web" comprises just a few). The web service interface is constructed in a standardized fashion using a technology like the Simple Object Access Protocol (SOAP). A web service performs a very specific function, or set of functions. The functions typically suit a single domain, e.g., a product catalog. Expected function input and output has to be provided to potential consumers in order for the potential consumers to know how to address the interface. This can be accomplished using web service directories, developer documentation, or Web Service Definition Language (WSDL) documents. A WSDL document is an Extensible Markup Language (XML) description of the interface to the web service. Many web service client technologies can use the WSDL document directly to utilize the web service. WSDL documents simplify the interface aspect of using web services. Using technologies like SOAP or WSDL, the task of integrating a web service into an application (e.g., a web site) is straightforward.

1.1 BPEL

There is a further abstraction of web service technology known as the Business Process Execution Language (BPEL). BPEL is a scripting language that allows compositions of web services and programming operations to accomplish business process goals. Web services may be composed into sequential and/or concurrent process flows. A BPEL process in turn is accessed as a web service via a WSDL interface. Thus, a BPEL process essentially becomes a broker, providing an arrangement, or orchestration, of other web services (including other BPEL processes). The programmability of BPEL includes operations like variable assignment, loop and conditional constructs, and fault and event handling. BPEL processes, like WSDL, are specified in XML.

BPEL possesses its own nomenclature for composition and components. A single unit of workflow processing is referred to as an activity (e.g., assigning values to variables, invoking a web service, etc.) Web services calls are known as invocations. Data are passed to and from web services through messages. Web services that are part of a BPEL process are thought of as partners and the references describing the accessibility of web services are referred to as partner links. The context of a service within a BPEL process is described as a partner role, which is actually just a semantic label for an endpoint reference, describing where a web service is located and how to access it. Activities that may be accomplished in parallel are encapsulated within a flow construct.

Several tools and models currently exist to abstract and simplify the implementation of BPEL. These tools significantly aid and accelerate process implementation and modeling is necessary to verify process consistency. However, the process developer must still possess a fundamental understanding of BPEL, its terminology, and its limitations. This is especially important if one wishes to implement high assurance BPEL processes.

BPEL addresses the high assurance concern of availability in two ways. Firstly, BPEL allows the dynamic changing of endpoint location (i.e., the location of web services to be invoked). This allows a BPEL process to use an alternate web service in the event that a previous one cannot be located or does not respond in a timely fashion. BPEL's second method of addressing availability is a byproduct of its nature as an internet-accessible service. Load balancers can be implemented to balance web service requests for high-demand web services among many different servers providing the requested service.

Security is not an inherent part of BPEL. In order to implement a secure BPEL process, the process must be built on top of other rugged security mechanisms. Transport-level security may be achieved using the Secure Socket Layer (SSL), a widely used point-to-point security mechanism. To better protect integrity and confidentiality, message-level security mechanisms should also be employed. Web Services Security (WS-Security) is such a security mechanism that packages authentication information into each message to strengthen trust between web service consumers, BPEL processes, and remote web services.

1.2 Motivation

While BPEL is a useful and powerful scripting language for creating compositions of web services, its support for high assurance service-oriented computing is lacking. Some of BPEL's problems that complicate high assurance satisfaction are:

1. BPEL has a unique nomenclature that straddles the line between programmer and business process specialist. Fully understanding all of BPEL's terminology, capabilities, quirks, and deficiencies carries a significant learning curve for most people.
2. BPEL's power comes from its ability to compose complex orchestrations of an arbitrary number of web services into business process solutions. However, BPEL's powerful scripting ability also makes it quite easy for a process to succumb to logical errors and design inconsistencies.
3. BPEL is currently an evolving de-facto standard for web service composition. Processes created with BPEL today may not be compatible with the BPEL of tomorrow or they may not easily be able to exploit the latest advancements in BPEL and web service technology. There is also the distinct possibility that a different and incompatible web service composition language will replace BPEL in the future.

UML sequence diagrams model time-ordered interactions between entities. Interactions represent events and can express data traveling between entities. The entities may represent humans and/or non-human processes. We propose that UML sequence diagrams can suitably model BPEL processes and provide a remedy to these glaring problems. We demonstrate our proposal using two examples of BPEL processes that we have implemented.

2. Related Work

In addition to the business computing industry, BPEL and web services in general have drawn a fair amount of interest from the research community. This is due in part to the distributed processing benefit web services bring to computing. But the interest in web services is also due to the fact that web service technology is in its early infancy and there is considerable room for research and improvement.

O'Brien et al. discuss several quality attribute requirements that should be strongly considered when designing a software architecture that involves web services [1]. These attributes are interoperability, performance, security, reliability, availability, modifiability, testability, usability, and scalability. They also highlight the importance of acquiring suitable service level agreements to guarantee adequate satisfaction of these requirements from third party service providers. Kontogiannis et al. [2] identify three areas of challenges for adoption of service-oriented systems: business, engineering, and operations. They also reveal an underlying set of "cross-cutting" concerns that these areas share and propose a Service Strategy to address these concerns. Sarna-Starosta et al. [3] propose a means of achieving safe service-oriented architectures through the specification of service requirements using declarative contracts. Monitoring and enforcement of these contractual obligations are handled through the use of hierarchical containers and middleware.

Zheng et al. [4] propose a type of finite state machine, called Web Service Automata (WSA), to formally model web services, such as BPEL. They state that using WSA, they are able to model and analyze most of BPEL's features, including control flow and data flow. Their proposal includes a mapping from WSA to the input languages of the NuSMV and SPIN model checkers. Zheng et al. [5] use the WSA mapping to generate test cases in the NuSMV and SPIN model checkers. State, transition, and du-path test coverage criteria are expressed in Linear Temporal Logic and Computation Tree Logic. The logical constructs are used to generate counterexamples, which then provide test cases. These test cases are used to verify a BPEL process' control and data conformance and WSDL interface conformance.

In [6], Ye et al. address inter-process inconsistency through the public visibility of atomicity specifications. They adapt the atomicity sphere to allow a service to provide publicly the necessary details of "compensability and retriability" while keeping its proprietary details private. Their technique for constructing the atomicity-equivalent public views from its privately held process information involves the use of a process algebra, which they describe and prove mathematically.

Based on Service Oriented Architecture (SOA), the Bus model is a kind of service model to integrate heterogeneous services. Li et al. [7] develop a formal model for services, which has three levels: the programs model, the agents model, and the services model. The bus system is constructed from the parallel composition of the formal models. To exchange information, the service interacts with the bus space instead of the other services, so concurrency is described by the global space of the bus system.

Chu et al. [8] design an e-business system using an architecture-centric design. They combine Semantic Web technology and e-business modeling to construct and semantically describe a service-oriented e-business model. The architecture-centric system design follows a "divide-and-conquer" method of decomposing the goal and defining and validating the architecture. The semantics definition helps discover registered services automatically and automated verification of system reconfiguration. In this way, the business goal can be mapped into services.

Dun et al. [9] model BPEL processes as ServiceNets, a special class of Petri net. Their approach constructs a formal model through a transformation into an S-Logic representation using an enriched form of reduction rules. They are able to analyze correctness and detect errors of the BPEL process from the ServiceNet's "throughness". Laneve et al. [10] propose a web transaction calculus, webπ, which assists in the verification of the compensable property for web service technologies that utilize web transactions as their fundamental unit of work. A compensable web service is one that facilitates the undoing of work should the web service fail to complete successfully. webπ is an extension to π-calculus. Web service languages are translated into webπ where their transactional protocols may be analyzed.

Foster et al. describe and implement a model-based approach for verification of web service compositions [11][12]. Their tool translates UML sequence diagram scenarios describing web service compositions into Finite State Process (FSP) algebra. The FSP algebra is then used for equivalence trace verifications of the compositions. Their tool also directly translates BPEL4WS into FSP algebra. In [13], Foster et al. discuss a model-based approach using finite state machines to represent web service compositions. They semantically describe the web service processes to verify compatibility between the processes and that the composition satisfies the overall system specification. In [14], Foster et al. present a detailed procedure for translating web service compositions expressed in BPEL4WS into Finite State Process (FSP) notation. They describe BPEL4WS constructs in terms of FSP semantics and analyze the mapping of specific activities using Labelled Transition Systems.

Akkiraju et al. [15] propose a framework for supporting web service compositions that provides functions such as security, access control, business partner discovery and selection, service level agreement monitoring, and logging. They believe that their framework fills in several of the inherent high assurance gaps of web service composition languages. Fu et al. [16] construct a Web Service Analysis Tool (WSAT) for analysis and verification of web service compositions. Their tool creates an automata-based intermediate representation of the composition. Control flow in the intermediate representation is restricted by the use of "synchronizability" conditions and Linear Temporal Logic and the SPIN model checker are then used to verify the composition and check its properties. Nakajima et al. [17] investigate the modeling of the Web Services Flow Language (WSFL) and the benefit of model checking the web service compositions for reliability. They conclude that their model checking experiments successfully detect faulty flow descriptions and can be expanded to accommodate alternative semantics.

3. BPEL Process Examples

We present two examples that are drawn from one of our largest reservoirs of real business experience: insurance quoting and tracking. These examples are not meant to demonstrate elegant or solid BPEL process design. Both examples include simple errors. We use these examples to illustrate how our approach to BPEL modeling and analysis using UML sequence diagrams reveals problems of inconsistency and design errors.

3.1 Example 1

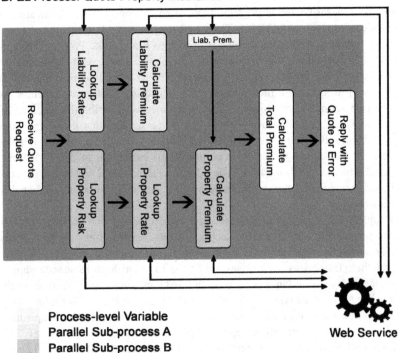

Fig. 2. The first example BPEL process for quoting insurance.

The first example of a BPEL process is an insurance quote processing and response system. The overall process design involves obtaining a quote for property and liability insurance (see Figure 2). The two different types of premium can be calculated independently using a Flow activity. There are several steps involved before a final quote can be determined (if at all) and returned to the BPEL service consumer. The BPEL process responsible for quoting property insurance proceeds through each step of the quoting process, calling other web services (located on either itself or remote servers). This example demonstrates an inconsistency error resulting from a mistake in implementation that creates a dependency between two concurrent sequences of activity in a BPEL flow activity.

The process steps of the first example are:

1. The first step of the example receives the request for the quote along with any data required for quoting (input requirements are specified within the WSDL document for the BPEL web service).
2. The second step of the process forks into two separate and concurrently executing sub-processes. Sub-process A requests a liability rate from the remote web service. Sub-process B requests property risk information from the remote web service.
3. Sub-process A requests liability premium to be calculated. The resulting liability premium is stored in a process variable. The Sub-process B requests a property rate from the remote web service.
4. Sub-process B requests property premium to be calculated, passing the previously calculated liability premium to determine if a discount modifier is necessary.
5. The process waits for both sub-processes to complete before requesting the remote web service to add the premium data and apply additional taxes and fees.
6. Lastly, the BPEL process replies to the calling service consumer, providing the resulting quote. If a fault occurs at any point during the BPEL process, the BPEL process replies to the calling service consumer with error information.

Below is simplified BPEL code for the first example, beginning with the flow activity, splitting the process into concurrent sub-processes:

```
<flow>
<sequence>
<invoke partnerLink="QuotePartner"
        operation="getLiabilityRate"
        inputVariable="propertyType"
        outputVariable="liabilityRate" />
<assign>
    <copy>
      <from variable="liabilityRate" />
      <to variable="liabilityPremiumInput" part="rate" />
    </copy>
```

```
          <copy>
            <from variable="insuredValue" />
            <to variable="liabilityPremiumInput" part="insuredValue" />
          </copy>
      </assign>
      <invoke partnerLink="QuotePartner"
            operation="calculateLiabilityPremium"
            inputVariable="liabilityPremiumInput"
            outputVariable="liabilityPremium" />
  </sequence>
  <sequence>
  <invoke partnerLink="QuotePartner"
            operation="getPropertyRisk"
            inputVariable="zipCode"
            outputVariable="propertyRisk" />
  <invoke partnerLink="QuotePartner"
            operation="getPropertyRate"
            inputVariable="propertyRisk"
            outputVariable="propertyRate" />
  <assign>
          <copy>
            <from variable="propertyRate" />
            <to variable="propertyPremiumInput" part="rate" />
          </copy>
          <copy>
            <from variable="insuredValue" />
            <to variable="propertyPremiumInput" part="insuredValue" />
          </copy>
          <copy>
            <from variable="liabilityPremium" />
            <to variable="propertyPremiumInput" part="liabilityPremium" />
          </copy>
      </assign>
      <invoke partnerLink="QuotePartner"
            operation="calculatePropertyPremium"
            inputVariable="propertyPremiumInput"
            outputVariable="propertyPremium" />
  </sequence>
  </flow>
  <assign>
          <copy>
            <from variable="propertyPremium" />
            <to variable="totalPremiumInput" part="propertyPremium" />
          </copy>
```

```
        <copy>
            <from variable="liabilityPremium" />
            <to variable="totalPremiumInput" part="liabilityPremium" />
        </copy>
    </assign>
    <invoke partnerLink="QuotePartner"
            operation="calculateTotalPremium"
            inputVariable="totalPremiumInput"
            outputVariable="quoteWithTaxes" />
    <reply partnerLink="RequestorPartner"
            variable="quoteWithTaxes"
    </reply>
```

3.2 Example 2

Our second BPEL process example also involves an insurance quote processing and response system (see Figure 3). When the process receives a request for a quote, it attempts to calculate premium based on parameters provided in the request. If the premium calculation succeeds, then a quote is emailed to the requestor and a quote request notification is emailed to the company's agents so that the agents may contact the requestor if the requestor fails to submit an application for insurance within a certain timeframe.

BPEL Process: Simple Quote Request

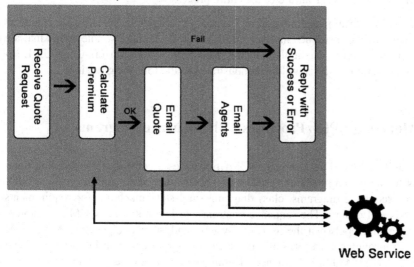

Fig. 3. The second example BPEL process for quoting insurance.

If an error occurs during the process execution, it is still important that email be dispatched to both the requestor and the agents. The requestor should receive a nicely formatted apology from the quoting system, along with alternate methods of contacting the insurance agency directly for a quote. Additionally, the agents need to know how to contact the requestor to try to assist them with the quoting process. Thus, the requirements for the second example state that the process should always email the requestor and the agents, regardless of the outcome of the process. Figure 3 clearly demonstrates that if the Calculate Premium activity fails then this requirement will not be satisfied. The second example serves to illustrate a discrepancy between the software requirements and the design and/or implementation of the software. We will show in the following section that our verification method can detect this discrepancy.

The process steps of the second example are:

1. The first step of the example receives the request for an insurance quote along with any data required for quoting (input requirements are specified within the WSDL document for the BPEL web service).
2. The BPEL process attempts to calculate premium based on the received parameters.
3. If the premium calculation invocation fails, the BPEL process replies to the requestor with an error and a "Sorry for the inconvenience" message. If the premium calculation succeeds, a quote is emailed to the requestor.
4. Company agents are notified of the request for a quote, along with the calculated premium. Our requirements dictate that this step should always occur, but our implementation fails to completely satisfy this requirement.
5. Lastly, the BPEL process replies to the calling service consumer with an indication of success or failure of the entire process.

These two examples are based on our real experience in the software engineering realm of the insurance industry. Both examples include simple errors that are typical of rushed or incomplete design. Detection of these errors using UML sequence diagram analysis will be demonstrated in the following sections.

4. Modeling BPEL Processes with Sequence Diagrams

The Unified Modeling Language (UML) provides a collection of modeling notations for describing different aspects of a software system, such as use-case diagrams, sequence diagrams, class diagrams, and state machines for requirements analysis and design. The sequence diagram is a key notation of UML to capture the interaction between the user, the system, and other components. A sequence diagram provides a scenario of one use case diagram using an intuitive graphical representation. Multiple sequence diagrams can be combined together to provide the design of system. We model BPEL processes with sequence diagrams which will ease efforts in utilizing BPEL and enable them to detect hidden errors.

BPEL has structured activities that provide the execution order in a collection of activities. For example: the flow activity in BPEL represents concurrency and synchronization of multiple activities; pick represents nondeterministic choice from multiple activities, and so on. UML 2 provides some structured control constructs, such as combined fragments and interaction use, to express concurrent message exchange.

A sequence diagram has two dimensions, the vertical dimension represents time and the horizontal dimension represents objects participating in the sequence diagram [18]. In a sequence diagram, the vertical dash lines represent participants, called lifelines. The name of each lifeline is shown in the rectangle on the top of each dash line. The horizontal lines between lifelines represent messages passing between participants. The intersection points between lifelines and messages are called occurrence specifications [19].

Combined fragments, introduced in UML 2, represent different types of control flow. A combined fragment is composed by one interaction operator and one or more interaction operands. In Figure 4, the interaction operator "par" represents a parallel combined fragment, which has at least two interaction operands. In a parallel combined fragment, the occurrence specifications in the same operand keep their order but the occurrence specifications in different operands may execute in any order [19]. The negative combined fragment with the interaction operator "neg" has one interaction operand and it is not enclosed in other sequence diagrams. All the possible traces generated by this fragment are invalid traces [19]. The interaction operator "assert" represents the combined fragment as a mandatory behavior at that point in the sequence diagram. If the execution reaches the beginning of the assertion fragment, then the assertion fragment must execute. All other continuations result in invalid traces [18].

With these features, a UML sequence diagram can represent most BPEL structured activities, e.g., BPEL consumer, BPEL process, and web service are presented as lifelines, flow can be shown by a parallel combined fragment, and pick can be shown by an alternative combined fragment. Table 1 shows the mapping from BPEL constructs to UML sequence diagrams.

Modeling BPEL with sequence diagrams enables the building of tools to detect potential errors of system design. The number of errors needs to be minimized at the design level as this greatly helps to simplify the work of implementation and verification.

Table 1. Mapping from BPEL to UML sequence diagram constructs.

BPEL Activity	Activity Description	UML Sequence Diagram Construct	Construct Description
receive	wait for an incoming message to arrive	receive a message	the message can be synchronous or asynchronous
reply	send a message in response to previously received message	send a reply message	the message is synchronous
invoke	call a one-way or request/response operation (e.g., another web service)	send a call message	the message can be synchronous or asynchronous
assign	modify the value(s) of one or more variables	a reply message contains attribute assignments as arguments	the message is synchronous
throw	create a fault	send a fault message to the fault handler actor	fault handler actor is represented as a lifeline
exit	immediately end the BPEL process	combined fragment--break	the condition of the operand is true
wait	pause for a period of time or until a specified time	the timer actor sets a period of time	when a period of time elapses, a timeout message is generated
empty	do nothing (i.e., a no-op)	the timer actor sets one cycle	the actor generates a timeout message
sequence	perform enclosed activities in sequential order	combined fragment--weak sequencing	the messages execute sequentially
if	perform an activity based on condition satisfaction	combined fragment--alternatives or option	the conditions of all operands are mutually exclusive in alternatives
while	perform the enclosed activity as long as the condition is true	combined fragment--loop	the condition in BPEL is mapped to the condition of loop, minint=0, maxint=infinite
repeatUntil	perform the enclosed activity until the condition is true	combined fragment--loop	the negation of condition in BPEL is mapped to the condition of loop, minint=1, maxint=infinite
forEach	perform the enclosed activity a specified number of times	combined fragment--loop	condition=true, minint=0, maxint=N+1
pick	wait for one of many possible messages to arrive or a timeout	combined fragment--alternatives	at most one operand is chosen
flow	perform the enclosed activities concurrently	combined fragment--parallel	the messages in different operands are interleaved

5. BPEL Inconsistency Analysis

Different BPEL scenarios are based on different views, but they may be relevant to each other and conflicts that are called inconsistencies may exist among them. These inconsistencies can be detected by comparing multiple sequence diagrams with pre-defined inconsistency rules. Once detected, software engineers can fix the system design to remove the conflicts to make the software system consistent. To demonstrate detection of inconsistency in our examples, we provide two sample inconsistency rules.

Inconsistency Rule 1: detecting inconsistency between valid traces and invalid traces. Valid traces are generated from sequence diagrams with no negative combined fragments. Sequence diagrams with negative combined fragments generate invalid traces. An inconsistency exists when a valid trace associates directly with an invalid trace for predetermined properties of the software.

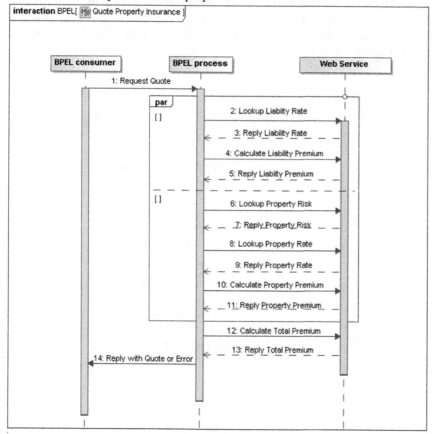

Fig. 4. BPEL Process: Quote Property Insurance.

Inconsistency Rule 2: detecting inconsistency between sequence diagrams with assertion combined fragments and other sequence diagrams. If any trace in a sequence diagram exists without the assertion and conflicts with a trace containing the assertion, then there is an inconsistency.

5.1 Analysis of Example 1

Figure 4 is a sequence diagram representing our first example of a BPEL process for quoting property insurance. When the BPEL process receives a quote request from a consumer, the process forks into two interleaving sub-processes and a task from either sub-process can be chosen to execute. One sub-process is for liability premium and the other is for determining a property rate. The interleaving relation of sub-processes is shown with a parallel combined fragment in the sequence diagram. The tasks in the same operand in Figure 4 keep their order, but tasks in different operands can be executed in any combination of orders. In this way, one sequence diagram can represent multiple execution traces.

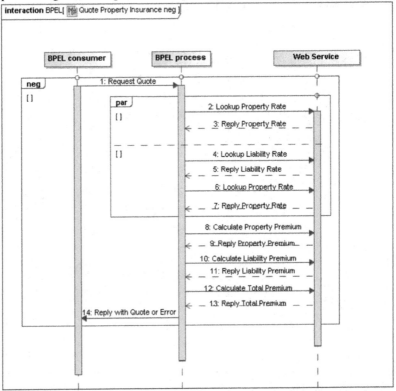

Fig. 5. One constraint in Quote Property Insurance.

This begs the question: are all of these execution traces valid? Is there a dependency among tasks from different sub-processes?

Assume that a software requirement states that the Calculate Property Premium task needs the value of Liability Premium in order to determine a discount modifier. It is easy to find the dependency that the Calculate Property Premium task should not happen before the Calculate Liability Premium task. Figure 5 shows this constraint in a sequence diagram with a negative combined fragment. Negative combined fragments define that all possible execution traces inside are invalid. A negative combined fragment tells a software engineer that the execution traces within the fragment should not happen in the software system. In Figure 5, the tasks inside the parallel fragment are still interleaving to each other, but the Calculate Property Premium task happens before the Calculate Liability Premium task. The negative fragments demonstrate that all the executions traces cannot happen. Comparing Figures 4 and 5, we detect an inconsistency and the design of system in Figure 4 will not provide a reliable implementation. Therefore, the design should be modified and the process re-verified with sequence diagram modeling.

5.2 Analysis of Example 2

Figure 6 is a sequence diagram of our second example BPEL process: Simple Quote Request. When a service consumer sends a request for an insurance quote to the Simple Quote Request BPEL process, the process invokes an external web service to calculate premium and the external web service replies with the resulting premium. The reply may be a success message (the resulting premium) or a failure message (with a specific error). After the BPEL process receives the reply message from the external web service, the process must email a quote to the consumer and inform the company agents of the request for a quote. Finally, the BPEL process replies to the BPEL consumer with a success or error message.

Software engineers may provide an execution trace of the system in Figure 7. In this execution trace, the BPEL process invokes the calculate premium operation from the external web service and receives a failure response. The BPEL process replies with a failure message to the BPEL consumer. The assertion fragment in Figure 6 is skipped. The assertion fragment in Figure 6 defines that after the BPEL process receives a reply from the external web service after calculating premium, only the Email Quote activity can happen. Instead, the reply from the BPEL process to the BPEL consumer happens in Figure 7. An inconsistency is therefore detected between the two sequence diagrams.

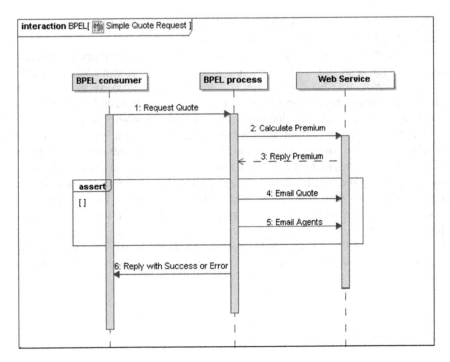

Fig. 6. BPEL Process: Simple Quote Request

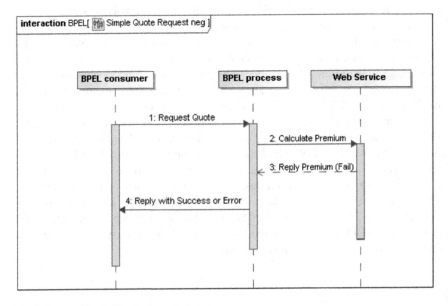

Fig. 7. One conflict in Simple Quote Request.

5.3 Evaluation

Our analysis technique has only two manual steps for discovery of inconsistencies. The first step is to create an initial sequence diagram in MagicDraw that models a BPEL process. The second step is the selection of inconsistency rules to use in trace generation. Once these steps are performed, traces are generated automatically, the inconsistency rules are applied, and the analyst is presented with a list of inconsistency warnings. The analyst must then examine each warning in the report and determine if the warning necessitates a design change.

By generating a negative combined fragment, our analysis method exposed an inconsistency in the implementation of our first example. The presence of traces within a negative combined fragment provides the software engineer with immediate knowledge of inconsistencies within the BPEL process. For our second example, we generated a valid execution trace for the BPEL process that did not include a required assertion combined fragment. This demonstrates a second type of inconsistency where the requirements of the BPEL process are not met (the activities of emailing the quote and agents)

Our inconsistency analysis approach with sequence diagrams facilitates rapid and thorough detection of inconsistencies within BPEL processes. Our approach may also be easily extended to accommodate other web service composition languages. Sequence diagrams are very intuitive, promote swift analysis, and inconsistencies between them (as traces) tend to be visually prominent. Additionally, there are currently many tools available to easily assist one in the generation of sequence diagrams.

6. Conclusions

Currently, BPEL is in a nascent state. It is a technology that straddles the line between software development and business process specification. As a result, BPEL contains some of the arcane expression of a programming language mixed with business-oriented terminology and process logic. BPEL is certainly a powerful abstraction language that can render compositions of distinct web services to solve business problems. These compositions can then be exposed as their own web services, which may be used by themselves in web service consumer applications or other BPEL processes. However, BPEL nomenclature carries a significant overhead for its initiates. Also, BPEL is not structured well to easily detect neither logical errors nor inconsistencies. Lastly, as an evolving de-facto standard for web service composition, what works for BPEL today may not work tomorrow.

For these reasons, we feel that BPEL implementation should be accomplished using abstracted design tools to simplify construction and ease the learning curve of BPEL's nomenclature. This will accelerate implementation and help reduce er-

rors. We have shown that modeling techniques such as our UML sequence diagram analysis approach can rapidly and automatically facilitate discovery of
BPEL design flaws of inconsistency. Sequence diagrams are very intuitive and
show temporal-based execution naturally. But tools and models do not obviate the
need for the process designer to fully understand the fundamentals, quirks, and
shortcomings of BPEL and web services. Such understanding is crucial in order to
construct BPEL processes that hope to satisfy the different aspects of high assurance service-oriented computing.

6.1 Future Work

We feel that UML sequence diagrams hold some promise of a straightforward,
well-adopted, and useful means of verifying consistency and reliability in BPEL
processes. There is, of course, more investigation needed in this area. We also
want to experiment with the use of UML sequence diagrams as a high-level BPEL
process composition tool, generating BPEL code underneath the sequence diagrams.

The integration of web services within a software development project is an
important consideration for software engineers. Web services may save time and
money in implementation, simplify maintenance challenges, and enrich the overall
specifications of the software. Currently, software engineers and workflow spe-
cialists must peruse registries of available web services and manually determine
the suitability of each available web service in terms of functionality, cost, and interface specifications. There has been some research in semantically describing
and automatically identifying web services within compositions and their initial
results are promising. If web services can provide information regarding their specifications and context in a formal and standardized fashion, then the suitability of
web services for a given software project could be determined automatically. This
would allow engineers to simply "point" to a set of web service registries and receive a suitability report of all appropriate web services. The suitability report
could then be automatically matched to the software project's own set of specifications to determine which implementation gaps could be satisfied by which web
services.

State machines synthesized from our sequence diagrams may be adapted to
provide BPEL process design. Whittle and Schumann [20] presented an algorithm
for synthesizing state machines from multiple UML 1 sequence diagrams, which
do not support structured control constructs. Uchitel et al. [21] provide a method
to synthesize behavior models from multiple message sequence charts. Message
sequence charts are similar to UML sequence diagrams. We may be able to synthesize state machine behavior models from UML 2 sequence diagrams such that
we will be able to perform some formal analysis, like model checking.

References

[1] O'Brien L, Merson P, Bass L (2007) Quality Attributes for Service-Oriented Architectures. International Workshop on Systems Development in SOA Environments

[2] Kontogiannis K, Lewis GA, Smith DB et al (2007) The Landscape of Service-Oriented Systems: A Research Perspective. International Workshop on Systems Development in SOA Environments

[3] Sarna-Starosta B, Stirewalt REK, Dillon LK (2007) Contracts and Middleware for Safe SOA Applications. International Workshop on Systems Development in SOA Environments

[4] Zheng Y, Krause P (2007) Automata Semantics and Analysis of BPEL. Digital EcoSystems and Technologies Conference 147-152

[5] Zheng Y, Zhou J, Krause P (2007) A Model Checking based Test Case Generation Framework for Web Services. Fourth International Conference on Information Technology 715-722

[6] Ye C, Cheung SC, Chan WK (2006) Publishing and composition of atomicity-equivalent services for B2B collaboration. Proceedings of the 28th international Conference on Software Engineering 351-360

[7] Li Q, Zhu H, He J (2008) Towards the Service Composition Through Buses. High Assurance Systems Engineering Symposium 441-444

[8] Chu W, Qian D (2008) Architecture Centric System Design for Supporting Reconfiguration of Service Oriented Systems. High Assurance Systems Engineering Symposium 414-423

[9] Dun H, Xu H, Wang L (2008) Transformation of BPEL Processes to Petri Nets. Theoretical Aspects of Software Engineering 166-173

[10] Laneve C, Zavattaro G (2005) Foundations of web transactions. Proceedings of Foundations of Software Science and Computation Structures 282-298

[11] Foster H, Uchitel S, Magee J et al (2006) LTSA-WS: A Tool for Model-Based Verification of Web Service Compositions and Choreography. International Conference on Software Engineering 771-774

[12] Foster H, Uchitel S, Magee J et al (2006) Model-based Verification of Web Service Compositions. 18th IEEE International Conference on Automated Software Engineering

[13] Foster H, Uchitel S, Magee J et al (2004) Compatibility Verification for Web Service Choreography. 3rd IEEE International Conference on Web Services

[14] Foster H (2003) Mapping BPEL4WS to FSP, Technical Report. Imperial College

[15] Akkiraju R, Flaxer D, Chang H et al (2001) A Framework for Facilitating Dynamic e-Business Via Web Services. OOPSLA 2001 - Workshop on Object-Oriented Web Services

[16] Fu X, Bultan T, Su J (2004) WSAT: A tool for Formal Analysis of Web Services. 16th International Conference on Computer Aided Verification

[17] Nakajima S (2002) Model-Checking Verification for Reliable Web Service. Workshop on Object-Oriented Web Services

[18] Rumbaugh J, Jacobon I, Booch G (2004) The Unified Modeling Laguage Reference Manual Second Edition. Addison-Wesley, United States

[19] Object Management Group (2007) Unified Modeling Language: Super-structure v2.1.2.

[20] Whittle J, Schumann J (2000) Generating statechart designs from scenarios. International Conference on Software Engineering 314-323

[21] Uchitel S, Kramer J, Maggee J (2003) Synthesis of behavioral models from scenarios. IEEE Transactions on Software Engineering 99-115

[22] Arlow J, Neustadt I (2008) UML 2 and the Unified Process, Second Edition. Addison-Wesley, United States

[23] OASIS (2007) Web Services Business Process Execution Language Version 2.0.

Chapter 12

Specifying Enterprise Web-Oriented Architecture

Longji Tang, Yajing Zhao, Jing Dong

Department of Computer Science, the University of Texas at Dallas

Richardson, TX 75083, USA

{ltang, yxz045100, jdong}@utdallas.edu

Abstract. The Web-Oriented Architecture (WOA) is a new software architectural style that extends Service-Oriented Architecture (SOA) style to the Web. The WOA is originally created by many new web applications and sites, such as social websites and personal publish websites. The EWOA is expected to be a part of next generation of Enterprise Service-Oriented Architecture (ESOA) for enterprise. In this chapter, we specify the Enterprise WOA (EWOA) both structurally and behaviorally based on the generic model of ESOA. We analyze the software quality attributes of EWOA as well as the relationship between EWOA and ESOA. We also discuss how EWOA meets the enterprise requirements for high-assurance service computing.

1 Introduction

With successful application of Web 2.0 [19] by a lot of new web applications and websites, such as Google AdSense, Wikipedia, blogging, and the emergence of many new web technologies, such as RESTful web services, AJAX, RSS, JSON, Rudy and Mashup, the Web-Oriented Architecture (WOA) is gaining great attention from both industry and research community. The traditional SOA [7] is an overall umbrella concept and style for how to create the web services with WS-* style, SOAP protocol and WSDL language. The ESOA is an integration style of SOA for enterprise. However, the web, HTTP protocol and web browsers do not directly support the SOAP and WSDL specification, and the design and implementation of traditional SOA and ESOA requires complex tools and frameworks because of its complexity. The WOA is really a push back on the complexity of the traditional WS-* style SOA. It is an alternative style for web-centric web services. Fig. 1 shows how the SOA core with reach WOA [14]. The traditional SOA is service-centric instead of web-centric, thus can be applied to web-centric and

J. Dong et al. (eds.), *High Assurance Services Computing*,
DOI 10.1007/978-0-387-87658-0_12, © Springer Science+Business Media, LLC 2009

desktop applications. However the traditional SOA style does not take advantages of web simplicity for web-centric web services. That is why it is not widely adopted for web-centric applications. The question is "Can WOA meet enterprise and co-exist with traditional SOA?" The answer is "yes". Many software vendors, such as IBM, Oracle, and SUN, push WOA and Web 2.0 very hard for enterprise.

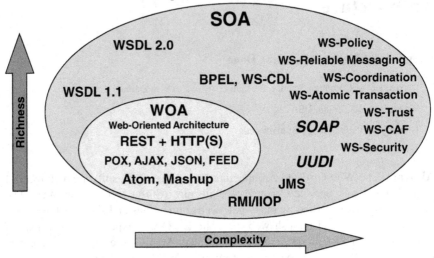

Fig. 1. SOA Core with Reach – WOA

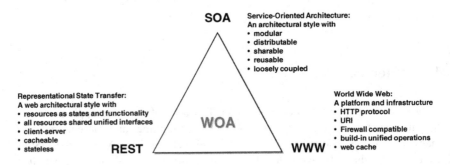

Fig. 2. Triangle of Web-Oriented Architecture

In this chapter, we call the WOA for a web-oriented enterprise as EWOA. WOA as sub-style of SOA and a new way to build service-oriented applications on the web has not been well-defined. To introduce it, we use the definition from Cartner's Nick Gall [11]:

> "WOA is an architectural style that is a sub-style of SOA based on the architecture of the WWW with the following additional constraints: globally linked, decentralized, and uniform intermediary processing of application state via self-describing messages."

Nick Gall also gives an interesting mathematical formula for defining WOA as

$$WOA = SOA + WWW + REST \tag{1.1}$$

The mathematical formula can be depicted by the WOA triangle shown in Fig. 2.

In the WOA triangle, the SOA is the parent architectural style of WOA which is built on many SOA principals, such as statelessness and loosely coupled-ness. The WWW and REST is the base of WOA. The WWW is the platform and infrastructure of WOA. It is a mature global network based on HTTP protocol. The REST (Representational State Transfer) [9] is the foundation of WOA architectural style. It is a simple web architectural style which is developed as "an abstract model of the Web architecture to guide our redesign and definition of the Hypertext Transfer Protocol and Uniform Resource Identifiers"[10]. The model can be formally defined as the following 4-tuples

$$REST = < Elements, Principals, Constraints, Quality > \tag{1.2}$$

where

$$Elements = \{REST\ Data,\ REST\ Connectors,\ REST\ Components\} \tag{1.3}$$

$$Principals = \{Application\ states\ and\ functionality\ as\ resources,\ Representation\ of\ a\ resource,\ Stateless,\ Layered,\ Cacheable\} \tag{1.4}$$

$$Constraints = \{Web\ Platform,\ HTTP\ Protocol,\ URI\ Addressing,\ Client\text{-}Server,\ Uniform\ HTTP\ Interfaces\} \tag{1.5}$$

$$Quality = \{Performance,\ Scalability,\ Simplicity,\ ...\} \tag{1.6}$$

The rest of this chapter is organized as follows. In Section 2, we introduce an algebraic model of EWOA based on the generic model of ESOA we defined in [25]. Section 3 presents the realization of the EWOA model. Section 4 discusses the relationship between EWOA and ESOA. The last two sections cover related work and future research.

2 Specifying EWOA

We have defined the Enterprise Service-Oriented Architecture (ESOA) as the sets of architectural elements, environment, principals and processes in [25]. In this chapter, we define EWOA as the sub-style of ESOA. Thus, EWOA is also defined as the sets of web-based architectural elements, environments, principals and processes based on [9] and [19]:

$$EWOA= \langle S_R, C_R, D_R, S_R I, S_R M, S_R P, S_R Q \rangle, \tag{2.1}$$

In which

$$S_R = \{ s_R \mid s_R \text{ is a RESTful web service.} \}, \tag{2.2}$$

$$C_R = \{ c_R \mid c_R \text{ is a web client.} \}, \tag{2.3}$$

$$D_R = \{ d_R \mid d_R \text{ is a WOA data element.} \}, \tag{2.4}$$

$$S_R I = \{ w_R \mid w_R \text{ is a WOA platform} \}, \tag{2.5}$$

$$S_R M = \{ m_R \mid m_R \text{ is a WOA management.} \}, \tag{2.6}$$

$$S_R P = \{ p_R \mid p_R \text{ is a WOA process.} \}, \tag{2.7}$$

$$S_R Q = \{ q_R \mid q_R \text{ is a WOA quality attribute.} \}, \tag{2.8}$$

Although formula (2.1) has the same algebraic form as the definition of ESOA in [25], the algebraic model (2.2) to (2.8) is more concrete. We define EWOA (2.1) as sub-style of ESOA. We discuss the relationship between EWOA and ESOA in Section 4. In the following subsections, we specify set (2.2) through set (2.8) formally and informally.

2.1 RESTful Web Services

The RESTful web services (RWS) is the key elements of EWOA. Like a generic service model we defined in [25], formally, we can define a RWS s_R as the following 5-tuple:

$$s_R = (I_R, M_R, R_R, l_R, Q_R), \tag{2.9}$$

where

$$I_R = \{ i_R \mid i_R \text{ is a HTTP interface} \}, \tag{2.10}$$

$$M_R = \{ s_R \mid s_R \text{ is a RWS state} \}, \tag{2.11}$$

$$R_R = \{ r_R \mid r_R \text{ is a web resource} \}, \tag{2.12}$$

$$l_R = \{u_R \mid u_R \text{ is a URI.}\}, \tag{2.13}$$

$$Q_R = \{q_R \mid q_R \text{ is a service quality attribute}\}, \tag{2.14}$$

Formula (2.10) indicates the RESTful web services has uniform interfaces which are HTTP GET, POST, PUT, DELETE, HEAD, OPTIONS, TRACE and CONNECT based on HTTP 1.1. For most enterprise web applications, the first four interfaces cover almost every operation as shown in Table 1.

Table 1. Uniform Service Interfaces

HTTP Interface	Semantics in RESTful Web Services
GET	Retrieve information from resource
POST	Add new information
	Show its relation to old information
PUT	Update information
DELETE	Discard information

Formula (2.11) shows that a RWS has a set of states maintained as part of the content transferred from client to server and then back to client, which include

- Application state, which is the information for the server to understand how to process the request. The authorization and authentication information are examples of application states.
- Resource state, which is the representation of the values of the properties of a resource.

Formula (2.12) indicates a RWS serves a set of resources which are application states and functionalities of the RWS. Formula (2.13) tells us a RWS can be described by a set of URIs each of which is a single string including the service address and the specification of the resource. For example, a service for browsing all books URI looks like

http://www.amazon.com/books

Formula (2.14) is a set of RWS service quality attributes which include performance, scalability, simplicity, etc. The detail analysis of them is presented in Section 5.

Algebraic Characteristics of Set (2.1): For any resource $r \in R_R$, there exists one or many URI in l_R for the resource. If resources r_1 and $r_2 \in R_R$, then only one statement will be true: $r_1 \neq r_2$ or $r_1 \equiv r_2$. It shows that the same resources or the same URIs have the same behavior or result to the client. Therefore a non-POST RWS is idempotent.

We propose an abstract algebraic model (2.1) of RESTful web services. Fig. 3 presents the relationship between sets in (2.1) and structural and behavioral models of RWS. The relationship between set (2.10) through set (2.13) can be summarized as follows:

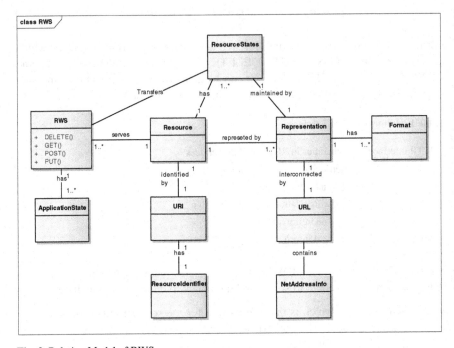

Fig. 3. Relation Model of RWS

- A RWS, with application states, serves resource through processing request and transfers resource states from one to another in term of response.
- A resource, which is a conceptual entity, can be represented by many representations which are concrete manifestation of the resource.
- A resource has one unique URI and many resource states. Each state is maintained by the resource representation.
- An URI has the resource identifier.
- A resource representation can be located by an URL with network address and other information which includes the protocol (http or https), hostname, path and extra information for describing how to get the representation of a resource.
- A resource representation can be represented by multiple formats, such as XML, HTML, and JSON.

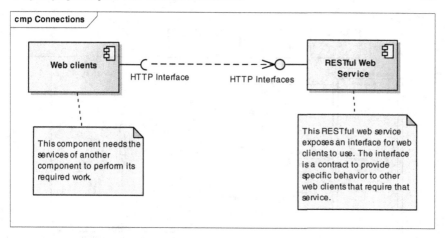

Fig. 4. Connection Model of RWS

Fig. 4 shows the RWS' connectional models. We leave the discussion of RWS' behavior model in the next section.

2.2 RESTful Web Service Consumers

According to the connection model of RWS in Fig. 4, any web client can be the consumer of RESTful web services. For each $c_R \in C_R$, it has the following behaviors:

- Connect to web services by HTTP protocol
- Send RESTful requests through RESTful interfaces
- Consume RESTful web services in WWW browsers or any web application.

There are two interaction models, which describe how web clients consume RESTful web services:

- Synchronous interaction model

  The Java JDK HttpURLConnection[13], Apache's HttpClient [2] and Microsoft's WebHttpBinding of WCF [8] all provide the client model for accessing RESTful web services synchronously. The model is based on HTTP request and reply model. The sequence diagram in Fig. 5 depicts the model.

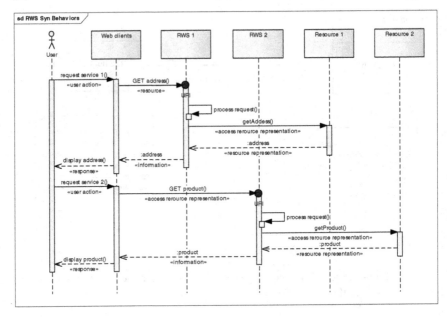

Fig. 5. Synchronous Interaction Model.

The UML 2.1 sequence diagram depicts two RESTful web services RWS 1 and RWS 2 which serve two user requests: GET address and GET product for a shopping page on the web. To best describe the behaviors of RESTful web services, we create a RESTful profile with the following stereotypes:

– <<user action>>
– <<resource>>
– <<access resource representation>>
– <<resource representation>>
– <<information>>
– <<response>>

which are helpful at describing the interaction behavior between service consumers and RWS. They are also used in the UML sequence diagram of describing the following asynchronous interaction model

• Asynchronous interaction model

The EWOA uses HTTP which is a synchronous request/response protocol. The question is whether the EWOA can support asynchronous interaction for long-running processes. In fact, there exist some standard asynchronous interaction patterns supported by HTTP, which are independent from RESTful web services approach. The patterns are listed in Table 2.

Table 2. Standard Asynchronous Interaction Patterns

Asynchronous Patterns	Description
Reliable one-way messaging (Fire-and-forget)	Service consumer does not wait for response
Polling	Service consumer periodically polls the request status
Callback	Service provider calls consumer back when service is done

In EWOA, the web clients can interact with RWS asynchronously by using AJAX which is a set of technologies including the asynchronous JavaScript and XML [19]. The UML sequence diagram in Fig. 6 shows such model.

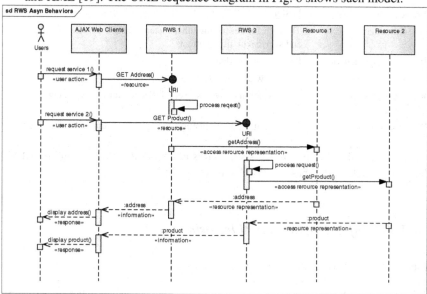

Fig. 6. Asynchronous Interaction Model

The sequence diagram shows that the user can submit two service requests to two RWS in almost parallel to update web page blocks and without going to web server and refreshing the page for each request. We will provide a detail analysis on AJAX in our future work.

2.3 WOA Data Elements

As a RESTful architectural style, the D_R in the model (2.1) plays an important role for understanding, specifying and designing WOA systems. The D_R is a finite set which consists of certain abstract data types supported by the style. They can be informally defined in Table 3.

Table 3. WOA Data Elements

Data Elements	Specification
Resource	The intended conceptual target of a hypertext reference [9], such as an online address book and a shop invoice
Resource metadata	The data for specifying a resource, such as a source link
Resource identifier	URI and URL
Representation	The current or intended state of a resource, such as HTTP document, XML document, and JPEG image
Representation metadata	The data for describing the representation, such as Media type, last-modified time
Service specification	WSDL 2.0 RESTful web service specification
WOA metadata	The data for describing other metadata, such as message integrity and service quality contracts
WOA Management data	Security policy data
WOA process data	Workflow description
Web configuration data	Configuration of Web servers, DNS, Server Proxy, Gateway, Cache
Web container data	Configuration of application server web container, such as weblogic web container

In Table 3, the first five rows, such as Resource and Representation, are REST data [10] which are the base of WOA data elements.

2.4 WOA Infrastructure and Platform

Table 4. Role and Functionality of Infrastructural Components

Infrastructural Components	Example	Role and functionality
Web servers	Apache HTTP server, and IIS	HTTP communication, service request and response processing, HTTP security, Cookie, session management
Proxy servers	SUN' SQUID	HTTP server routing, RESTful web service routing
DNS	Round Robin DNS	URI addressing
Gateway	CGI	RESTful web service provider
Web Containers	java web container	RESTful web service provider
Server connectors	Libwww, JDK, NSAPI, .NET, DNS lookup, Tunnel (such as SOCKS, SSL)	Make connection between client and server
Cache service or servers	Browser cache, JCache, Akamai Cache Network	Store short-life data for improving performance

Unlike traditional ESOA, EWOA is built on existing web infrastructure in the enterprise. The $S_R I$ in (2.1) can be defined as a set of servers and services:

$S_R I$ ={Web servers, Proxy servers, Gateway, DNS, Server connectors, Cache servers, Web containers of application servers}   (2.15)

For small and some medium enterprises, the WOA infrastructure is a subset of $S_R I$. For example, they may not have application servers, even Proxy servers. Formula (2.15) describes the major components in a generic EWOA infrastructure. The role and functionality of each infrastructural component are defined in Table 4.

2.5 WOA Management

The EWOA is the WOA for enterprise, so it also includes WOA management $S_R M$ which is a set of web application system management tools and services for managing RESTful services. The $S_R M$ includes

- RESTful web services registry
- Firewalls for network security management, such as Perimeter firewall, NAT firewall, XML firewall
- Filters for request and response management, such as Java HTTP filter
- Security services for application security management, such as authentication, authorization, REST parameter analysis and XML threat analysis
- Logging services for error and exception management
- Agents and Monitors for performance management

We will discuss the importance of WOA management for high-assurance RESTful web service computing in Section 3

2.6 WOA Processes

Traditional web service architectures are designed to accommodate simple point-to-point interactions – there is no concept of a logical flow or series of steps from one service to another. In an enterprise, the business often requires software system to have the capacity to process complicated business processes, such as workflow, transaction, online order and shipping. Supporting services composition (orchestration and choreography) is fundamental to the web services vision. Therefore the service processes is one of core elements in ESOA [25]. As we know, there are two specifications, BPEL and WS-CDL, handling the different approaches of orchestration and choreography of SOAP-based web services in traditional WS-* style ESOA for various complicated business process management. Although there is no corresponding standard for EWOA processes, RESTful web services composition, such as client-side or server-side Mashup, has been practicing at Web. iGoogle is a good example. The Web is the most complicated global enterprise business platform. To meet the increasing requests for handling complicated web business processing and services interactions, many software industry vendors and researchers are working on specification and tools for WOA processes of both RESTful orchestration and choreography. The Bits is a minimalist choreography language for Web [6]. The Bite runtime architecture is implemented by IBM Project Zero [15]. An approach to RESTful process choreography based on the Asynchronous Services Access Protocol (ASAP) is proposed in [16]. There are several approaches to RESTful process orchestration [2][21]. A common idea is to extend BPEL for RESTful web services orchestration. Fig. 7 depicts how to extend BPEL for two RESTful web services s_R^1 and s_R^2 orchestration.

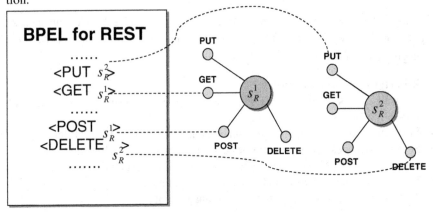

Fig. 7. RESTful Web Services Orchestration by Extended BPEL

2.7 WOA Quality Attributes

The quality attribute requirements drive high assurance software architecture design [3]. They also drive the ESOA and EWOA system design for high assurance. In this section, we define a set of quality attributes as architectural properties of EWOA style. The REST and the Web are two bases of WOA. The quality attributes of both WEB and REST are discussed in [9]. We list the major parts in Table 5.

Table 5. Quality Attributes of WEB and REST Style

Quality Attributes	Description for WEB and REST
Performance	Network performance which is one of infrastructure performance which can be improved by interaction style
Efficiency	REST is cacheable. Using cache can improve application performance and network efficiency
Scalability	WEB is internet-scale
	Using proxy style can increase web scalability
Simplicity	REST is very simple style by client-server for separating concerns
Security	HTPS, SSL, firewalls provide basic WEB infrastructure security. REST does not address application security.
	Firewall visibility increases security, but visibility may reduce payload level security.
Evolvability	WEB is easy to evolve. REST style can improve web architecture evolvability.
Extensibility	REST supports the gradual and fragmented deployment of changes within an already deployed architecture
Reusability	The components defined by REST are reusable
	REST style use uniform HTTP interfaces
	Sharable proxy and cache style all increase reusability
Reliability	REST style can help reliability by avoiding single failure point, enabling redundancy, using monitoring, or reducing scope of failure to a recoverable action.
Visibility	"Within REST, intermediary components can actively transform the content of messages because the messages are self-descriptive and their semantics are visible to intermediaries."
Modifiability	REST style also improves system modifiability through supporting evolvability, customizability, configurability and reusability.
Customizability	It is induced by remote evaluation and code-on-demand style
Configurability	WEB Servers and other mediators, such as proxy are configurable.

Table 5 describes the basic quality attributes of the WOA style. For the EWOA which is enterprise-level WOA style, we have to address additional non-functional requirements to some of quality attributes, such as security, reliability, manageability, governance. We define high-assurance EWOA style which can address further enterprise non-functional requirements.

3. High-Assurance EWOA

To achieve high-assurance SOA in the enterprises, specifically at defense, financial industry and mission critical business systems, the traditional ESOA style addresses the enterprise architectural non-functional requirements or quality attributes through the WS-* standards [7] and governance framework. They are presented in our previous work as a set of SOA managements [25] which can be governed by QoS rules and policies. Therefore the system based on traditional ESOA-style is very complicated in general. The WOA is a lightweight approach to SOA at Web, so it greatly reduces the complexities of SOA with its two fundaments: REST style and mature Web infrastructure. Because of its simplicity nature, EWOA does not need WS-* like complicated governance and management. However, to meet enterprise requirements for high-assurance service computing, such as web transaction, e-Business of inter-organizations and inter-business partners, dynamic web information system integration, EWOA needs RESTful governance. The SOA governance includes design time governance and runtime governance. In this chapter, we focus on specifying the EWOA-style runtime governance that is what we have defined WOA management in Section 2. In our specification, the RESTful lightweight governance may include

- RESTful services registry/repository
- RESTful security management
- RESTful application controller, such as a java servlet

We propose the high assurance RESTful information system architecture as shown in Fig. 8 based on the EWOA style we have specified.

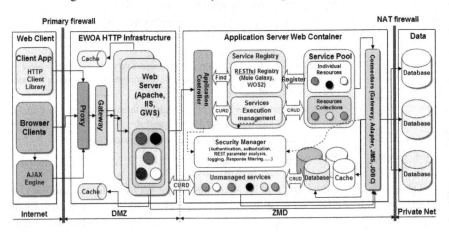

Fig. 8. High-Assurance RESTful Information System Architecture

The RESTful architecture consists of the following parts:

- A set of web clients which include any client application by using HTTP client library and any web site with or without AJAX.
- An EWOA HTTP infrastructure which includes a set of web servers and services, such as web servers - Apache, IIS and GWS, and services - proxy, gateway, web cache. The EWOA infrastructure also includes a set of data source connectors, such as Adapters, JMS and JDBC.

- A set of RESTful services which can be severed by two kinds of resources - individual resources by GET, PUT and DELETE interfaces and resource collections by GET and POST interfaces. We define two kinds of RESTful web servers:

  - Managed RWS which is registered by the service registry
  - Unmanaged RWS which is for getting public data only.

  The RWS can be deployed in either the web server extension, such as secure cgi-bin, or web containers, such as weblogic and Tomcat.

- The EWOA management consists of an Application Controller, a Security Manager and a Service Registry which includes a repository storing description of RWS and policy as well as configuration data, and server and application monitors. The controller can also act as an RWS orchestration engine.

Due to the simplicity nature of the RWS and the architectural properties of REST style, we point out in Table 5, EWOA style system is of higher performance and simplicity compared to traditional WS-* SOAP style ESOA system. However the security of RESTful applications for enterprise should be taken into consideration to achieve high-assurance service computing. As we know, the RWS only support four interfaces GET, POST, PUT and DELETE. Let us define three sets of operations:

- $A = \{a \mid a \text{ is an idempotent and safe operation}\}$
- $B = \{b \mid b \text{ is an idempotent and unsafe operation}\}$
- $C = \{c \mid c \text{ is a non} - \text{idempotent and unsafe operation}\}$

Then we have the following security relationship:
$$GET \in A, \ PUT, DELETE \in B, \ POST \in C$$
and
$$A \subset B, \ C \subset O - B$$
Fig. 9 depicts the relationship and exposes the security concerns.

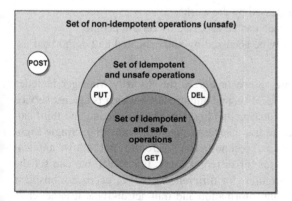

Fig. 9. Venn Diagram of RESTful operations.

Except GET, all other operations are unsafe. Even GET has some security vulnerabilities, such as QueryString attack and XML/JSON out attack. Unlike SOAP, at the message level, RESTful services are using plain text html for request and POX or JSON for response, therefore they do not provide payload-level security for routing RESTful request to multiple different servers, such as proxy, gateway, web servers and web containers. Table 6 shows a security and QoS comparison between REST message and SOAP message.

Table 6. Comparison of REST and SOAP Messages

Message	REST POST	SOAP POST
Header	There is no QoS defined in header	Can specify QoS in header
Body	Payload in plain text (HTML or XML), which is visible to cross all traveling servers	Payload inside SOAP Envelope, which is visible only for the end application.
Envelope	There is no Envelope for payload	There is SOAP envelope for payload
Example	POST/HTTP/1.1 Host: http://www.amazon.com Book: RESTful Web Service Credit Card: Visa Number: 123456789 Expire: 11-01-20-12	POST/HTTP/1.1 Host: http://www.amazon.com Contenttype: application/soap-xml Charset=uft-8 <env:Envelope xmlns:env=" http://www.w3.org/2003/05/ soap-envelope"> <env:Header> <!--Header information here--> </env:Header> <env:Body> <!--Body or "Payload" here, a Fault if error happened --> </env:Body> </env:Envelope>

From the example in Table 6, the customer's credit card information is in the insecure REST payload. Nevertheless it can be protected by SOAP envelope at the payload level. In general, the data of any enterprise can be categorized as

- Public data which can be accessed by the world
- Internal confidential data which can be accessed by certain people
- Business data which can only be accessed by authenticated and authorized users.

In our proposed architecture shown in Fig. 8, the Security Manager includes authentication which is against identity, and authorization which is against service policy, URI analysis, response filtering and logging. For the second and third category of data, we always need to use a security manager with SSO (Single Sign-On) and ACL (Access Control List) technologies, where the ACL allows application to set the data access control for different users. For RWS, we can set the permission to use different operations for different users. For accessing business critical data, such as user account information and transaction data, it is better to use SOAP style web services. However, the RESTful approach has bigger performance and simplicity advantages than WS-* SOAP approach for accessing the public data, specifically by getting them by GET. The unmanaged RWS can serve this kind of data in a very cheap way. In the next section, we discuss the relationship between EWOA and ESOA. Moreover a hybrid approach is proposed.

4. Relationships between EWOA and ESOA

We have defined a generic model of ESOA in [25]. The RESTful-based EWOA and traditional WS-* based ESOA are two sub styles of the model in [25]. Roger Smith has compared SOA and WOA styles in [23]. He points that "SOA and WOA work at different levels of abstraction. SOA is a system-level architectural style that tries to implement new business capabilities so that they can be consumed by many applications. WOA is an interface-level architectural style that focuses on the means by which these service capabilities are exposed to consumers." Based on our specification and model, ESOA is a SOA style for enterprise integration, thus it is a system-level abstraction. The EWOA is a WOA style for enterprise at the web presentation tier. The EWOA style is a design guideline for (1) constructing and consuming RESTful web services for web-based applications and (2) producing the web applications to consume the services created by ESOA. Based on (2), the EWOA is just an interface-level abstraction. The EWOA will become a style of system-level abstraction at web. The traditional ESOA also provides the way for building applications of consuming the services, which are SOAP-based service clients. Both EWOA style and traditional ESOA style have their advantages and disadvantages. Pautasso and his colleagues made a detail comparison between RESTful and WS-* web services in [4]. The EWOA may be good enough for small and some middle enterprises, such as social web-based companies, the eServices of small to middle business. Some middle and most large enterprises have already adopted traditional ESOA. There are existing SOAP based web services and SOA infrastructure. Moreover complicated business process and high-security transaction require WS-* based ESOA approach. However, there are many services computing in the enterprises, such as enterprise Mashup, customer help system, which can be done by EWOA approach in very simple and cheaper way. Therefore the hybrid approach with both RESTful-based EWOA and WS-* based ESOA is the best architectural decision. Amazon web service architecture is a good example of adopting hybrid approach [1]. Fig. 10 depicts a hybrid approach of ESOA-style information system architecture we have proposed in this chapter.

From our proposal, you can see that all RESTful web services are only allowed to access the data outside the enterprise private network where critical business data are normally stored. The hybrid approach to ESOA-style system is a better architectural tradeoff between

- complexity and simplicity
- security and performance

- higher assurance and cost QoS and lower assurance and cost QoS

More detailed study about the tradeoff of architectural attributes of WS-* style and RESTful style will be done in the future.

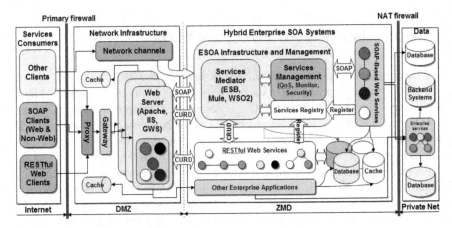

Fig. 10. Hybrid Enterprise SOA System Architecture

5. Related Work

The WOA vs. SOA and REST vs. SOAP have been debating in recent years. The RESTful web services and new WOA style are getting more and more attention from the research community and software industry. The foundation of the RESTful services is the REST principles and style innovated in [9]. The importance of REST style is uncovered by new web application development, such as web 2.0, WOA. However there are few works on specifying the WOA and EWOA. Some approaches, such as the RESTful Web Services [20], specify the RESTful approach as Resource-Oriented Architecture (ROA). Gall defines WOA in [11]. There are some discussions about the REST and SOAP debates, such as [18,26]. Roger, Smith gives an analysis of new way of web development, which is the bottom-up WOA in [23]. Pautasso and his colleagues makes a detailed comparison for architectural decision on the RESTful web services vs. "Big" WS-* based web services in [4]. Many software vendors specify WOA from their products prospective, such as Amazon web services [1], Mule Galaxy [17], Microsoft WCF as well as BizeTalk server [8], SUN's Java API JAX-WS for REST as well as GlassFish application server [24] and IBM sMash and Zero Project [15]. In [25], we have proposed a generic algebraic model of ESOA that can be used for specifying RESTful style SOA.

6. Conclusions and Future Work

The research work of EWOA in this chapter is based on research and practices of RESTful web services, and a new architectural style WOA and the generic model of ESOA we have proposed in [25]. As we defined, the EWOA style consists of a set of design principals based on REST [9] and Web 2.0 [19] and a set of architectural elements of infrastructure, management, process and a set of software quality attributes. Compared with traditional WS-* ESOA style with top-down development approach, complicated infrastructure-centric design and heavyweight QoS governance, EWOA is a web-based architectural style with bottom-up development approach, simple web data (hypertext) centric design and lightweight QoS governance. Although EWOA is an alternative to the ESOA in some enterprise and some systems in enterprise, the governance, quality of services, security and manageability are equally important. In this chapter, we analyze the security and manageability issues of EWOA and proposed two approaches in Fig. 9 – pure RESTful system architecture with RESTful QoS governance and in Fig. 11 – a hybrid approach with both REST and SOAP for enterprise. Since the EWOA is a new paradigm for service computing, many research opportunities are challenging software researchers. Future research work may include

• Formalism of WOA and EWOA style
• UML profile for RESTful modeling
• RESTful workflow and process
• RESTful design patterns
• Software quality tradeoff of both ESOA and EWOA

With further research and practices, WOA and EWOA will become more mature and more powerful.

References

1. Amazon Web Services, http://aws.amazon.com/about-aws/
2. Apache ODE RESTful BPEL, http://ode.apache.org/restful-bpel-part-i.html
3. L. O'Brien, L. Bass and P. Merson, "Quality Attributes and Service-Oriented Architectures", Technical Note, CMU/SEI-2005-TN-014.
4. P., Cesare; Zimmermann, Olaf; Leymann, Frank (2008-04), "RESTful Web Services vs. Big Web Services: Making the Right Architectural Decision", 17th International World Wide Web Conference (WWW2008) (Beijing, China).
5. L. Clarkin and J. Holmes, Enterprise Mashups, The Architecture Journal, 13 (2007)
6. F. Curbera, M. Duftler, R. Khalaf and D. Lovell, Bite: Wrokflow Composition for the Web, International Conference on Services Oriented Computing (2007), LNCS 4749, pp. 94-106, 2007
7. T. Erl, Service-Oriented Architecture, Prentice Hall, 2005

8. D. F. Ferguson, Dennis Pilarinos and John Shewchuk, The Internet Service Bus, The Architecture Journal, 13 (2007)

9. R. T. Fielding, "Architectural Styles and the Design of Network-based Software Architectures", PhD thesis, University of California, Irvine, 2000

10. R. T. Fielding, R. N. Taylor (2002-05), "Principled Design of the Modern Web Architecture", *ACM Transactions on Internet Technology (TOIT)* (New York: Association for Computing Machinery) **2** (2): 115–150

11. Nick   Gall,   Why   WOA   vs.   SOA   Doesn't   Matter?   (2008)   at http://www.itbusinessedge.com/item/?ci=47620&sr=1

12. M. T. Gamble and R. Gamble, Monoliths to Mashup: Increasing Opportunistic Assets, 25(6):71-79, 2008 IEEE Software

13. M. D. Henson, SOA Using Java Web Services, Prentice Hall, 2007

14. D.   Hinchcliffe,   The   SOA   with   reach: Web-Oriented   Architecture,   2006   at http://blogs.zdnet.com/Hinchcliffe/?p=27

15. IBM sMash, http://www.ibm.com/developerworks/ibm/library/i-zero1/

16. M. zur Muehlen, J. V. Nickerson and K. D. Swenson, Developing web services choreography standards – the case REST vs. SOAP, Decision Support Systems 40 (2005) 9-29

17. Mule Galaxy at http://mule.mulesource.org/display/MULE/Home

18. P. Prescod, Roots of the REST/SOAP Debate, Extreme Markup Languages, (2002)

19. Tim O'Reilly, What Is Web 2.0, (2005, Retrieved on 2006) O'Reilly Network.

20. L. Richardson and Sam Ruby, "RESTful Web Services", O'Reilly, 2007

21. D. Rosenberg, Web-Oriented architecture and the rise of pragmatic SOA, blog (2008) at http://news.cnet.com/8301-13846_3-10031651-62.html

22. F. Rosenberg, F. J. Duftler, and R. Khalaf, Composing RESTful Services and Collaborative Workflows, 12(5):24-31,2008 IEEE Internet Computing

23. R. Smith, Smart Web App Development, (2008) InformationWeek

24. SUN GlassFish, http://www.sun.com/software/products/glassfishv3_prelude/

25. L. Tang, J. Dong and T. Peng, A Generic Model of Enterprise Service-Oriented Architecture, 4th IEEE International Symposium on Service-Oriented System Engineering (2008)

26. S. Vinoski, REST Eye for SOA Guy, 11(1):82-84, 2007 IEEE Internet Computing

Chapter 13

Designing an SOA for P2P On-Demand Video Delivery

Zhenghua Fu[1], Jun-Jang Jeng[1], Hui Lei[1], and Chao Liang[2]

[1]IBM T.J.Watson Research Center, Hawthorne, New York 10532, USA

[2]Polytechnic Institute of NYU, Brooklyn, New York 11201, USA

Abstract. Compared with the traditional client/server streaming model, peer-assisted video streaming has been shown to provide better scalability with lower infrastructure cost. In this chapter, we describe how peer-assisted video streaming can be implemented through real-time service oriented architecture. This chapter presents an overall design of the Peer-Assisted ContenT Service (PACTS). We discuss the motivation, principles and service oriented architecture of PACTS modules and specify the workflow among them. By organizing elements of traditional video streaming and peer to peer computing into loosely-coupled composable middleware services and distributing them among participating entities, PACTS enables high-quality low-cost video streaming at a large scale and in real time. We illustrate the challenges and our approaches in designing distributed and highly efficient algorithms. In particular, the algorithms for performing peering-selection and incentive-driven pre-fetching are studied in detail. These designs are extensively evaluated by packet-level simulations which are beyond the scope of this paper. We show that our implementation of PACTS effectively offload server's bandwidth demand without sacrificing the service quality. This benefit is further verified in dynamic settings with system churns.

1. Introduction

The Media and Entertainment industry has been undergoing significant innovations during recent years. One of the fastest growing areas is Internet Video On-Demand (VoD). YouTube, for example, has about 20 million views a day with a total viewing time of over 10,000 years to date [1]. Other popular providers include MSN Video, Yahoo Video, NBC, ABC, Hulu, etc which all receive extremely high volume of traffic because of their On-Demand video streaming services. Currently, none of the above providers charges a subscription fee. The contents are provided free of charge, sometimes with periodic commercials and

J. Dong et al. (eds.), *High Assurance Services Computing*,
DOI 10.1007/978-0-387-87658-0_13, © Springer Science+Business Media, LLC 2009

advertisements. The providers buy bandwidth from Internet Service Providers (ISP) or Content Distribution Networks Providers (CDN) at about 0.1 to 1.0 cents per video minutes [2], assuming the videos are encoded in low quality (200-400 Kbps). At these rates, it is estimated that YouTube pays over 1 million dollars a month in bandwidth costs.

Because of the high bandwidth cost, few VoD providers are significantly profitable today. Furthermore, as the user population grows and video quality increases, the bandwidth cost is expected to grow exponentially. This makes the VoD service even less profitable, if not impossible to deploy at all. In order to reduce the server load, the bandwidth resources at the user side could be exploited. Table 1 shows bandwidth distribution of users having requested MSN video from April to December, 2006 [2]. According to the table, significant bandwidth resources are available at the user side. For example, more than 60% users have upload bandwidth of 768 Kbps, sufficient for delivering a medium quality video to other users. This suggests the use of peer-to-peer data transfer technologies. Existing peer-to-peer file sharing system, such as BitTorrent [3] or Kazza, provides poor service quality for video. First of all, it requires the user to download the whole file before playback. Secondly, the content may be of low quality, corrupted or even malicious. The low cost but low quality model of P2P file sharing can not be directly applied to the current VoD streaming service.

Table 1. Download and Upload bandwidth distribution (kbps) of Internet VoD users.

	Modem	ISDN	DSL1	DSL2	Cable	Ethernet
download	64	256	768	1500	3000	>3000
upload	64	256	768	384	768/384	768
Share (%)	2.8	4.3	14.3	23.3	18.0	37.3

Service oriented architectures have been proposed for peer-to-peer operation model [7][8][9][10]. Ref. [7] describes a SOA framework for decentralized peer-to-peer web service. Java Agent Development Framework (JADE) was proposed in [8] as a service component and program API for peer-to-peer file sharing using the JAVA programming language. Refs. [9] and [10] propose service models for content search in peer-to-peer networks using Distributed Hash Table (DHT) based algorithms. However, none of these works address the issues of the quality of service in real-time video streaming and the related service composition.

There are several challenges in designing a service oriented VoD streaming system using the peer-to-peer operation model. First of all, a service model needs to be established to allow user requests to be collectively fulfilled by the server and peers with quality of service constraints. This includes SLA specification, real-time service composition and scheduling that fit into the requirements of peer-assisted operations. Second, to satisfy streaming requests, service providers need to quickly find and identify peers, if they exist, that have the required content and bandwidth in a large network of users. Finally, with peers contributing bandwidth, group dynamics, such as user joins/leaves, have direct impact on service quality. Fast and efficient recovery from disconnections, failures or attacks becomes an important part of the overall system design. In this chapter, we propose a peer-to-peer architecture called Peer Assisted Content Delivery Service (PACTS). The goal is to reduce the high bandwidth utilization at VoD servers by leveraging the upload capability at the user side while maintaining the quality of streaming service. In particular, we made the following contributions.

Scalable SOA Design We propose extensions of both server and client side architectures to leverage peer-to-peer streaming scalable to a large number of concurrent sessions. Typically, VoD streaming servers, such as YouTube, service a large amount of concurrent download sessions. In order to avoid service bottleneck at the server, we push the details of peer-to-peer work flows, including resource discovery and scheduling, to the client side. This also provides backward compatibility and allows the server to service both clients with and without peer-to-peer extensions.

Real-time Vertical Service Composition PACTS represents a service model for real-time video streaming from multiple service providers to an end user. In the context of peer-to-peer streaming, an end user gets partial feeds from multiple peers streaming at different rates. The end user performs service composition periodically to orchestrate the rate allocation among multiple providers. This real-time vertical composition is a new model for the application of peer assisted multimedia streaming.

Incentive-driven SLA As an integrated part of the SOA model, we propose a simple way for SLA specification. We analytically show a specification that provides QoS differentiation based on end users' contribution factors. In addition, given a server bandwidth budget, the SLA specification is able to maximize the bandwidth utilization by providing highest video quality to end users.

Peer-to-Peer Implementations There are several challenges in actually implementing PACTS in a large scale distributed and dynamic environment. The goal is to use existing off-the-shelf media software package for achieving low cost high quality on-demand video streaming. On the control plane, we propose algorithm for peering selection to construct an overlay that leads to highly efficient resource utilization. On the data plane, we propose an incentive-driven data forwarding and scheduling algorithm to address the heterogeneous bandwidth distribution among neighboring peers.

The rest of the chapter is organized as follows. Section 3 describes the system architecture of both servers and end users. Section 4 proposes a service model for peer assisted video streaming from multiple service providers to an end user. Section 5 presents an analytically model for SLA specification. Section 6 discusses the challenges in PACTS implementation and proposed two algorithms for achieving resource efficiency. Section 7 concludes the chapter.

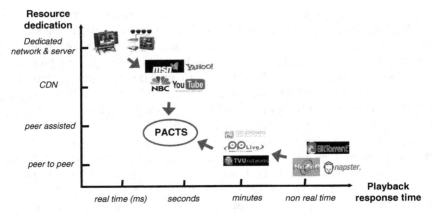

Fig. 1. Taxonomy of Internet video delivery technologies and applications

2. Related Work

Peer-to-peer file sharing applications such as BitTorrent [3], Kazaa, utilize user upload bandwidth for scalable, low cost content distribution. Figure 1 illustrates the taxonomy of Internet video delivery technologies and applications. Each category has different server bandwidth requirements ranging from high (dedicated network and server) to minimal (peer to peer) as shown on the vertical axis. In return, they provide different levels of video streaming quality, measured by playback response time ranging from real-time to non real-time as shown on the horizontal axis. Hard real-time applications such as video conferencing have strict delay constrains in the order of milliseconds. Dedicated network and server infrastructure are usually established for high bandwidth requirement. At the lower right end of Figure 1, peer-to-peer file sharing applications such as BitTorrent [3] require no server bandwidth. Video contents are divided into chunks; peers exchange missing chunks using their upload bandwidth until the entire file is received. As a consequence, continuous playback during downloading is usually not possible due to the fact that chunks may arrive out-of-order. Users must wait until the entire file is downloaded.

Moving away from hard real-time applications, VoD services such as You-Tube, MSN Videos use CDN [4] technology to distribute replicas of same content to servers all accross the Internet. User requests are serviced by the closest server in terms of network distance. CDN can achieve playback latency in the order of seconds. However, as the rapid increase in both user population and video bit rate, the server bandwidth becomes a bottleneck.

Recently, PPLive [5] and CoolStreaming [6] broadcast live TV program to a large amount of users over the Internet using peer-to-peer technologies. In Cool-Streaming [6], the server divides the live feed into chunks to be individually pulled by users. Missing chunks are provided by neighbors using their upload bandwidth. Compared with P2P file sharing, they allow users to playback the downloaded contents with delay in order of minutes, without incurring significantly more server bandwidth resources. In this chapter, we propose PACTS, a real-time service oriented architecture that provides comparable service quality with traditional CDN based approach but significantly reduces bandwidth utilization at the server by leveraging peer assistance.

3. System Architecture

We describe the system architecture of PACTS in two parts, the server side and client side. The architecture extends the traditional client-server VoD service model to include both client-server and peer-to-peer operations.

3.1 Design Goals

A key design principle of PACTS is to keep the server side architecture and service model as simple as possible by *pushing the complexity to the client side*. Practical VoD server must handle large amount of users concurrently. For example, YouTube has about 230 views per second on average [2]; during peak time or flash crowd, the number could be much bigger [13]. Maintaining per-session state information for dynamic service composition at server side reduces the scalability of the service model. In PACTS, the client-server operations are stateless; peer assistance such as content search, bandwidth contribution and QoS adaptation are dynamically composed by client side service modules. Another advantage of such architecture is information accuracy. It allows the end user to locally measure its current QoS and make resource scheduling decisions based on this real-time information. Our real-time service oriented architecture has following benefits compared to the existing P2P system designs such as [6].

Transparency to users The service modules provide atomic functions that hide the implementation details from the user. For example, applications that broadcast a live session have different search requirements and behavior from applications that provides VoD. However, the directory service module provides interface that makes the implementation transparent to users such as the download control service (Figure 3). This flexibility allows for the same architecture to be used for different applications with minimum change.

Adaptivity A central capability of PACTS architecture is the adaptivity to dynamics in peer-to-peer network. This includes proactive service quality measurement, service re-composition and failure recovery in real-time. The server also adjusts the SLA with end users according to the measurements of bandwidth utilization and peer contribution to all downloads meets minimum QoS and users contributing more bandwidth are rewarded with higher QoS.

Extensibility The PACTS architecture and service model can be extended to support different video streaming applications such as VoD, live broadcasting or video conferencing. It is also backward compatible with traditional client-server model and accepts requests from end users both with and without peer assistance capability. This is important for incremental software deployment in practice.

3.2 Server Side Architecture

The architecture of the server side is presented in Figure 2. The design maintains the backward compatibility with the traditional client-server architecture. Most of the back-end service modules such as content manager and billing can be reused. Main peer-to-peer functionalities are handled by the two new service modules, the Resource Manager at the back end and the P2P Content Directory Service at the front end. The Resource Manager determines the QoS level at which an incoming user request should be serviced based on parameters such as server bandwidth utilization and the user's contribution level.

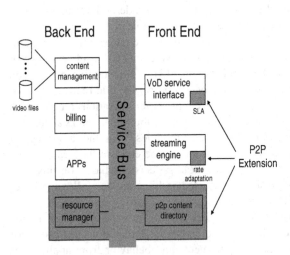

Fig. 2. VoD server architecture with extensions for peer assistance capabilities.

The P2P Content Directory maintains a top level mapping between titles of video and addresses of potential feeders. Once kicked off from the server, the search is propagated among peer nodes until either the demand is satisfied or a maximum search distance has reached. Simple extensions are added to the front-end modules. We need a capability to communicate SLA at the service interface module. Rate adaptation capability [14] is also needed at the streaming engine to respond to the dynamic service composition at the user side. This can be easily implemented since in today's RTP streaming engine, such as [12], sophisticated adaptation algorithms have already been built in.

3.3 Peer Side Architecture Design

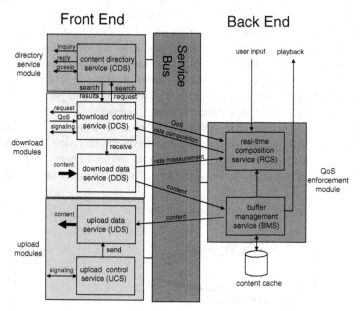

Fig. 3. Peer side architecture

Comparing to the traditional client/server model where the client needs only to receive stream feeds from the server, PACTS client implements key service modules enabling peer-to-peer resource discovery and scheduling. Figure 3 presents software architecture of a PACTS peer node. The front end consists of search service modules, download and upload service modules, implementation interfaces for signaling and data exchange with other peer nodes via network sockets. Back end consists of modules for service composition and cache management. They expose the interfaces to end users for initiating the download service and to periodically retrieve the downloaded content from cache for playback.

 User selects a desired video and initiates a request to RCS for downloading the chosen video. RCS composes the service with server being the only contributor and forwards the requests to the DCS. DCS first starts a search of the video in peer nodes by invoking the local CDS service and wait for the reply. Meanwhile, DCS sends a request to the server and starts the DDS for receiving the feed. As the peers are coming in, RCS is periodically invoked to re-compute the rate composition among all service contributors.

4. The Service Model

Figure 4 provides an overview of the client-server operation. User initiates a request to the server specifying the video she wants to download. The request also includes the user's previous contribution level for other peers. Based on this information, the server responds with a QoS level she is entitled to be serviced, a set of peers that has previously downloaded the same video, and a unique identification number for the video. Meanwhile, the server starts to feed the stream using the rate according to the decided QoS. Upon receiving the peer set, the user initiates a search for potential contributors for the requested video. We noted that the operation is stateless; once the search is initiated, matching peers contact the original node directly. As the contributors arrive, the receiving node composes a new rate allocation and moves the load from the server to peers. Upon receiving the recompose message, the server and peers adjust the feeding rate accordingly.

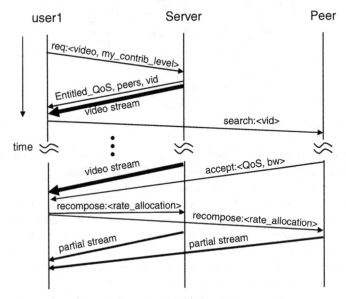

Fig. 4. Client-Server Interactions for Dynamic Service Composition

5. SLA Specifications

In order to encourage users to contribute their upload bandwidth, PACTS provides differentiated QoS to users based on their contributions to other peers. Service Level Agreement (SLA) maps contribution measures onto the QoS level subject to constraints on server resources and optimization goals. In this section, we describe the metrics that are used to differentiate the QoS, the method for measuring user's contribution and an SLA model.

5.1 Metrics Definitions

5.1.1 QoS Metrics

We define the following QoS metrics used in SLA model.

Video Quality Using a layered encoder, a video can be compressed into several sub-streams consisting of one base layer stream and several enhanced layer streams which progressively improve visual quality of the video presentation. The better the video quality, the more layers are needed and hence a higher bandwidth will be consumed. We denote the layers for user j as l_j, $l_j = 0,1,2,...,K-1$, where layer 0 is the base layer guaranteed for all end users and K is the highest layer. The corresponding streaming rate is denoted as $R_0,...,R_{K-1}$.

Playback Quality Due to peer dynamics or network congestion, the download rate may fluctuate causing jitters at playback. In such situations, RCS at the end user re-composes a rate allocation to move the load from lagging peer to the leading peer. If not enough leading peers are available, RCS decreases the video quality by removing the current highest layer. To improve the playback quality, end user could recruit a few more contributing peers for faster failure recovery. Maximum number of contributing peers allowed is a metric controlling the playback quality.

Advertisement and Premium Content Optionally, service provider could offer less advertisement or access to premium content to end users having a much higher contribution factor. The contribution factor is defined in the following.

5.1.2 Contribution Metrics

PACTS measures an end user j's contribution factor, η_j, as the ratio between bandwidth contribution and consumption. A factor of 0 means the end user does not contribute any bandwidth; a factor of 1 means the end user uploads as much as he downloads.

5.2 A Model for SLA

In this section, we derive a formulation to show how to differentiate QoS based on end users' contribution factors to achieve system level goals. Specifically, we seek for a mapping between user j's contribution factor to the video quality to be serviced at the rate of r_j, subject to the constraints of server bandwidth limitation.

We start from the case when all peers have contribution factor $\eta_j = 0$. This case corresponds to the traditional client-server service model where client does not contribute any bandwidth. R_0 should be guaranteed even without peer assistance. Therefore, $R_0 = b_s / \lambda$, where λ is the request arrival rate measured at the server and b_s is the server bandwidth budget.

In general, if end user j's contribution factor is η_j, he is entitled to receive video at rate r_j. A simple mapping from η_j to r_j is given in (1).

$$r_j = R(0) + \eta_j \cdot (R_{K-1} - R_0) \tag{1}$$

To select a video layer l_j based on r_j, we have

$$l_j = \arg \max_l \{ R_l \le r_j \} \quad l=0,1,...,K\text{-}1 \tag{2}$$

According to Equation (1), the server provides a better QoS for users with a higher contribution factor. From a capacity planning's perspective, such QoS differentiation incurs a risk for bandwidth overload at the server which in turn degrades the overall QoS. To enforce QoS strategy given in Equation (1), we need to derive R_{K-1}, the rate upper bound, subject to the limitation of server bandwidth b_s.

Proposition 1 According to the service model given in (1), given server bandwidth limitation b_s and average user contribution factor $\bar{\eta}$, R_{K-1} is bounded by the following.

$$R_{K-1} \le R_0 \cdot \frac{2 - \bar{\eta}}{1 - \bar{\eta}} \tag{3}$$

where $R_0 = b_s / \lambda$. We note that both $\bar{\eta}$ and λ can be estimated at the server. In particular, to estimate $\bar{\eta}$, server records each user's contribution factor at request time and maintains a running average or linear prediction.

First of all, we require that the total bandwidth available at the system should be greater or equal to the demand. This translates to the following inequality.

$$b_s + \sum_j \lambda_j r_j \eta_j \geq \sum_j \lambda_j r_j \tag{4}$$

where λ_j is the request arrival rate at end user j. Replace r_j with (1), and (4) becomes

$$b_s \geq R_0 \cdot (\lambda - 2\sum_j \lambda_j \eta_j + \sum_j \lambda_j \eta_j^2) + R_{K-1}(\sum_j \lambda_j \eta_j - \sum_j \lambda_j \eta_j^2) \tag{5}$$

Here we assume that λ_j and r_j are two i.i.d. random variables, i.e., users' request rates are statistically independent with their contribution factors. At system steady state,

$$\sum_j \lambda_j \eta_j \to \lambda\overline{\eta}$$

$$\sum_j \lambda_j \eta_j^2 \to \lambda\overline{\eta}^2 \tag{6}$$

Combining (5) and (6), and noting that $R_0 = b_s / \lambda$, we can derive equation (3).

5.3 Discussion

In this section we described a SLA specification that differentiates download rate, i.e., the playback quality, according to a peer's contribution. The goal is to reduce server bandwidth cost by encouraging peers to contribute their bandwidth.

In this service oriented model, every peer is both a consumer and provider; it utilizes services from peers and is motivated to serve other peers in need. The model can be generalized to a wider context in large scale peer to peer settings as illustrated in Figure 5.

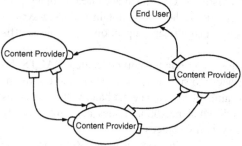

Fig. 5. A general peer-to-peer service model where nodes can be both content providers and consumers

In the following, we present design and implementation of the above SOA model in context of On-demand Internet Video Streaming.

6. PACTS Design and Implementation

In this section, we present the system implementation of PACTS. We use existing video streaming technologies, such as MPEG-4 codec implemented in popular products like IBM Video Charger [12], Microsoft Media Player [15] or Quick-Time [16]. Our goal is to propose a turn-key solution integrating off-the-shelf software into a peer-to-peer system that provides large scale high quality video streaming service with low bandwidth cost for the content provider.

6.1 Design Rationale

Although scalable encoding has been added into current H.264 standard [17], most consumer side players can not decode layered video streams. Given this constraint, we slightly modified the previous SLA specification. Specifically, videos are encoded in only one layer. Based on peer's contribution factor, SLA selects a downloading rate instead of a target quality (layer) for it to be serviced at. The more a peer contributes, the faster it can download.

Note that this is not the only possible implementation; other incentive alternatives, such as adaptations in advertisement frequencies, premium content availability or even monetary rewards are also possible. The principle is to differentiate service quality based on contribution with minimum quality guarantee. In this chapter, we focus on the study of such incentive-driven SLA specifications within the framework of real-time peer-to-peer SOA model and its behavior in large scale on-demand video streaming system. Specifically, PACTS system design and implementation address following fundamental challenges:

- *Peering Selection.* Among a set of existing peers, how does a newly joined peer pick a subset to form its neighborhood and how to maintain it during system churn. As we will show later, this has a significant impact on the resource efficiency.
- *Service Composition.* Once the neighboring relationship is decided, PACTS decomposes the content delivery service into sub-services to be carried out by individual neighbors. With the constraints of heterogeneous bandwidth capacities and content availability at each individual neighbor, nodes need to carefully coordinate to efficiently utilize the system resources.
- *Incentive-driven SLA.* Providing incentive in asynchronous VoD system is challenging. The asymmetric data flows between peers with different playback

progress make direct reciprocity incentive mechanism, such as tit-for-tat of BitTorrent [3], infeasible. Furthermore, unlike BitTorrent, real-time playback is needed in VoD system. Therefore, chunks in a large file can not be downloaded in arbitrary order; they must be downloaded before the playback time in order for on-line streaming.

In the following, we will first show how the proposed real-time peer-to-peer service model helps to reduce the server cost, which is addressed in Section 6.3. Furthermore, we quantitatively study the benefits of the incentive-driven SLA in various dynamic settings in Section 6.4.

6.2 System Model

A key design issue of P2P VoD systems is to minimize the server bandwidth cost by efficiently utilizing peers' upload bandwidth. P2P VoD systems have two unique features: the playback progresses on peers are asynchronous; peers can download content beyond its current playback range. In addition, to cope with bandwidth variations and peer-churn, a peer normally buffers a certain amount of video beyond its playback progress.

Notations: To model a typical P2P VoD system, we introduce the following notations for peer i in the system:

- *Playback progress pi*: the current playback position of peer i, indexed by the sequence number of the video chunk being played.
- *Buffering progress bi*: the sequence number of the first missing chunk beyond current playback position *pi*.
- *Buffering level* τ_i : the number of continuous buffered chunks beyond the current playback progress point. By definition, $\tau_i = bi - pi$.
- *Playback buffering threshold Wrd*: the number of buffered chunks necessary for smoothing playback. We call the sliding window *[pi, pi+Wrd]* peer i's continuous playback range.
- *Contribution level* η_i : the number of chunks that peer i has uploaded to other peers since it joins the system.

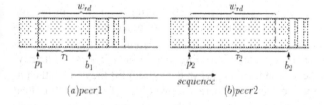

(a)peer1 (b)peer2

Fig. 6. Peer buffer status

Figure 6 illustrates two different peer buffer statuses. On Peer 1, the buffer level τ_1 is lower than the playback buffering threshold Wrd. It is downloading the missing chunks in the continuous playback range. We call peer 1 is in the normal playback mode. On peer 2, the buffer level τ_2 is higher than the playback buffering threshold Wrd. Peer 2 is downloading chunks outside of the playback range. We call peer 2 is in the *pre-fetch* mode.

6.3 Peering Selection

PACTS connects peers if their buffering points are close enough. In stead of picking neighbors randomly, a node picks its peers with approximate bi values. We term this peering strategy as Buffering Progress Based (**BPB**). As we will show in the following, the problem with random peering is its poor resource efficiency. In fact, as a peer node's buffering point progresses, it finds less and less suppliers from which it can download content from – earlier-joined peers may have left and newly-joined peers cannot supply needed content. BPB groups peers according to arrival time within in certain threshold.

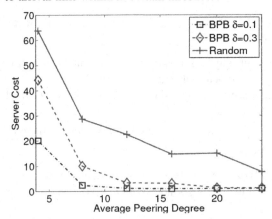

Fig. 7. Server Cost Savings in peer assisted VoD system with various peering strategies

We use simulation to demonstrate the benefits of server bandwidth cost savings using P2P model. In particular, we compare BPB peering with random peering strategy. Towards this goal, we generate an instance of a peer-assisted video-on-demand system using a discrete simulation. During the simulated session with duration $T=100$, peers arrive at the system according to a Poisson process with arrival rate equals to 2 peers per second. Peers stay in the system till they finish the entire video viewing. The video rate is r. There are two types of peers with upload bandwidth $1.5r$ and $0.5r$ respectively. The normalized average peer upload bandwidth around 1.2.

With random peering, upon arrival, a peer randomly picks k peers already in the system as its neighbors. With BPB peering, peers are ordered in an increasing order of their arrival times. A peer who arrived at the system with rank i will randomly pick k neighbors from peers with arrival ranks in the range of $[i - \delta *N, i]$ given total N online peers. By changing δ, we manipulate the playback progress closeness of neighbors in the constructed BPB graph. We then compare the server cost under BPR and random peering strategies under five snapshots of the system. For each snapshot, we calculated the minimum required contribution from the server as the server cost plotted at Y-axis at Figure 7.

The results shown at Figure 7 indicate that with limited peering degree, BPR-peering can significantly reduce the server cost compared with random peering. For example, in the case where each node finds no more than 7 neighbors, a server is able to support 200 concurrent users with bandwidth of only 2 times of the individual content streaming rate. That's about 100 times savings compared with traditional client/server service model. In addition, we observe the tremendous cost savings from BPB peering compared with random peering strategy.

6.3.1 BPB Implementation

The key to BPB peering is to find peers with close buffering progresses. To facilitate BPB peering, the tracker sorts the list of active peers according to their arrival times. When a new peer joins in, the tracker records its arrival time and appends it to the end of peer list. Then the tracker will return the new peer with an initial peer list consisting of a number of random peers at the end of the list. Those peers will be the suppliers for the new peer. When there is no pre-fetching, buffering on peers advances roughly at the same pace, namely the playback rate. Peers who arrive close in time will remain close in buffering progress. During the session, when a peer needs to connect to new neighbors, either due to neighbor departures or unsatisfactory peering connections, it can contact the tracker for additional peers. The tracker can quickly search through the sorted list to find peers with close buffering progress for the requesting peer. In addition, due to BPB peering, a peer's neighbors' neighbors should also have close buffering progresses with the peer. Without going to the tracker, a peer can find new "close" neighbors in the neighbor lists returned by its neighbors.

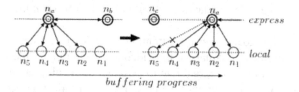

Fig. 8. Dynamic BPB peering

With pre-fetching, buffering on peers advance at different rates. A peer joins the system later can possibly download video faster than his neighbors who arrived earlier and gain larger buffering progress. Once this happens, the download rate of the peer will be slowed down due to the lack of enough suppliers. The peer should then trigger dynamic BPB peering to find more suppliers satisfying the BPB peering criterion.

Figure 8 shows a simplified example of dynamic BPB peering. Towards the goal of downloading the whole video, node na runs on the "express track" with larger download speed, while its neighbors runs on the "local track" with smaller download speed. As time evolves, it catches up with the buffering progress of its neighbors. To maintain its download rate, it connects with n1 with larger buffering progress and disconnects from peer n5 with the smallest buffering progress.

To facilitate this dynamic BPB peering, a centralized solution is to have the tracker keep track of peers' buffering progresses and help peers to find new neighbors with close buffering progresses. Peers need to periodically report their current buffering progresses to the tracker. And the tracker also needs to constantly resort the peer list. This will incur large signaling and processing overhead on the tracker and peers. On the other hand, peers constantly exchange their buffering progresses with their neighbors. Due to dynamic BPB buffering, there is a good chance that a peer, even doing fast pre-fetching, can find peers ahead of him by searching through the neighbor lists returned by its neighbors. Then instead of requesting from the tracker, peers can request complementary peer lists from neighbors and pick appropriate peers with close buffering progress to connect.

6.4 SLA for Incentive-Driven Pre-fetching

To coordinate the asynchronous demands of peers and maintain system-wide Quality of Experience (QoE), we propose an *Adaptive Taxation* scheme to regulate the pre-fetching on heterogeneous peers. Original taxation scheme [17] is applied to provide incentive in live streaming system. The bandwidth can be regarded as peer's wealth. Resource-rich peers contribute more bandwidth to the system, and subsidize for the resource-poor peers. The tax regulated redistribution of peer wealth helps improve the social welfare and then reduce server cost.

However, in [17], the tax ratio is fixed and the *demogrant rate* (i.e., the minimum rate a peer receives even if it does not contribute anything) is adaptive. This has the drawback of not being able to guarantee the minimum QoS when the demogrant rate becomes too low.

In order to meet the design goal of ensuring minimum service level (i.e. each peer is at least offered a service rate equals to the video playback rate) while enforcing incentives, PACTS fix the demogrant rate to be equal to the playback rate and adaptively adjusts the tax ratio. Suppose we pose a taxation ratio t on peers.

Then one peer with contribution level η_i and lifetime T_i, could get the average download rate r_i to accumulate expected buffer level

$$\bar{\tau}_i = (r_i - r)T_i = \frac{\eta_i}{t}$$

To make the aggregate tax revenue $\sum r_i$ and budget expenditure $\sum \eta_i / T_i$ balanced, the taxation ratio t needs to be adaptive to the system wide resource availability. To decide the ratio, we have

$$t = \sum \eta_i / \sum \tau_i$$

Within the framework proposed in Section 5, SLA module of PACTS VoD server maintains an adaptive tax ratio t based on the current measurement of system resource. In a resource rich system, peers accumulate different amount of buffering levels proportional to their contributions and the system tax rate t which is given by the PACTS SLA module at the backend. In a resource deficit system where average upload bandwidth is limited, i.e. $\bar{u} < r$, peers bandwidth along are not enough to sustain minimum service quality. In this case server bandwidth is needed to meet the SLA requirements.

7. Performance Evaluation

We use simulations to evaluate the performance of PACTS. In particular, we quantitatively study the benefits of the proposed peering and pre-fetching strategies. Throughout this section we use the term *bpbp_np* and *ranp_np* to refer to the BPB-peering and random peering strategies without incentive based pre-fetching respectively. *bpbp_inc* refers to our incentive-driven pre-fetching strategy with the combination of the BPB-peering. For comparison purpose, a random peering strategy with non-incentive-driven pre-fetching, denoted by *ranp_wp*, is also developed and measured in our simulations.

7.1 Simulation Setup

We developed a packet-level event-driven simulator in C++ to study the performance. Our simulator adopts the infrastructure of the simulator engine of [18] simulating the end-to-end latency in terms of real-world latency measurement results. Two 4-CPU servers are applied to accelerate the simulations.

We follow the common assumption that the *download* bandwidth of each peer is large enough and is not a limiting factor in the system. The video's playback rate is set to be 400kbps with each chunk being 5K bytes. We distinguish three types of DSL users with upload bandwidth being 1Mbps, 384kbps and 128kbps respectively. By varying the distributions of these types we obtain different *normalized* average bandwidth (w.r.t. the playback rate), as shown in Table 2. In the simulation, we use a single video with 30mins length. One single simulation round lasts for 90mins to get a better view of the system behavior. We believe that the video length and the simulation duration are already long enough to demonstrate the features of different strategies.

Table 2. Normalized peer average bandwidth and the corresponding fraction of DSL connection types.

ρ	Fraction of Peers (1M, 384K, 128K)	ρ	Fraction of Peers (1M, 384K, 128K)
0.90	0.15, 0.39, 0.46	1.40	0.34, 0.52, 0.14
1.00	0.20, 0.40, 0.40	1.50	0.43, 0.38, 0.19
1.12	0.23, 0.46, 0.31	1.60	0.49, 0.36, 0.15
1.20	0.25, 0.53, 0.22	1.70	0.54, 0.32, 0.14
1.30	0.30, 0.50, 0.20	1.80	0.60, 0.30, 0.10

Peers arrive to the system according to a Poisson process with arriving rate $\lambda_i =$ 1/4 per second. The system population is approximately 500 after the startup phase. The default number of neighbors for each peer is 15. The size of the playback buffering threshold and pre-fetching window are both 4 seconds. Peers broadcast buffer-map messages every 0.5 second and the token number information is piggybacked within the message. The server bandwidth cost consists of two parts, due to the complementary pull from peer for missing chunks and request scheduled from peers who receive the tokens from server respectively. The number of tokens sent out periodically from server corresponds to 1Mbps. To make the comparison fair, we generate the peer arrivals and upload bandwidth configuration beforehand and use the same setting to compare different strategies.

7.2 Simulation Results

We first show the effectiveness of the proposed SOA model by measuring the server bandwidth saving in PACTS. We then further study the results on different pre-fetching schemes to illustrate the benefits of our incentive-driven SLA model.

7.2.1 Server Cost Savings

The server bandwidth saving is the most important performance metric. In the following, we present a detailed study based our simulations.

We begin by showing an evolution of server cost during one simulation session. Figure 9(a) shows the instant aggregate user demand and the peer bandwidth when the normalized average peer bandwidth (ρ) equals to 1.3. There are no peers in the system at the beginning. The first peer finished playback and leave the system at 1, 800 second. The time period *[0, 1800]* is the system startup phase. Fig. 9(b) presents the instant server cost under the different strategies. We can observe that the server cost of random peering strategies increase almost linearly at the startup phase as the number of peer increases, then the curves oscillate closely with the instant peer average bandwidth.

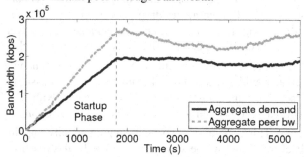

(a) Demand vs. available resource

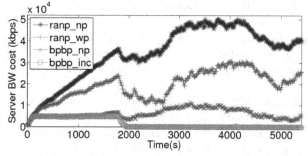

(b) Instant server cost

Fig. 9. Server cost under different peering strategies

However, for BPB-peering strategies, it is interesting to observe that the server cost increases in a short period and maintains almost constant at the startup phase. Peers join the system early have limited data to share with each other. The server has to stream data to them directly. When more peers get into the system, peers start to download data from each other. When the startup phase is over, the server's bandwidth utilization drops nearly to zero in *bpbp_inc* strategy. Later simulation results show that a certain amount of peers which have evolved into seeds take the place of the server.

Figure 9(b) shows that when ρ = 1.3, the random-peering without pre-fetching strategy (*ranp_np*) can save at least around 75% server bandwidth comparing to the traditional client/server service model where no peer assistance is available. The saving can be improved to 85% with pre-fetching. Using BPB-peering, the *bpbp_np* can enhance the saving further to around 95%. Moreover, our simulation shows that *bpbp_inc* can stabilize the server bandwidth utilization to a very low level after the startup phase.

7.2.2 Impacts of Peering and Incentive Strategies

We further examine the server cost savings with different normalized peer average bandwidth. Fig. 10(a) shows the average server cost after the first 50 mins. As the system resource increases, the cost of all strategies drops. *bpbp_np* and *bpbp_inc* both achieve most bandwidth saving. In particular, *bpbp_inc* achieves zero server bandwidth cost when $\rho > 1.2$. The BPB-peering effectively improves the scheduling efficiency, resulting in more server bandwidth saving. Pre-fetching enables peers to download future content with extra bandwidth, thus reduces the possibility of data pull from the server in the future. The *ranp_wp* strategy with pre-fetching can also work without server when ρ = 1.8. When ρ =0.9, *bpbp_np* slightly outperforms *bpbp_inc*. This is because the pre-fetching potentially impairs some peers' normal playback when the whole system is in a bandwidth resource deficit status. This disadvantage can be conquered in PACTS by giving more preference to neighbors who haven't fill up the playback window during the scheduling.

Although *bpbp_np* and *bpbp_inc* perform closely in terms of server bandwidth saving, pre-fetching of *bpbp_inc* produces seeds in the system. Fig. 10(c) illustrates the number of seeds during the simulation with normalized bandwidth equal to 1.5.

It is very impressive that using bpbp_inc, the seed number can even reach nearly 40% of all peers. On the other hand, the ineffectiveness of random peering leads to less number of seeds in *ranp_wp*. The existence of seeds makes the system resource allocation more flexible and thus more robust to peer dynamics. In fact, seeds can completely take the place of the server.

Peers only exchange the interested area information, which is efficient to keep the overhead low. Fig.10(b) shows the control traffic throughput compared with data traffic. The overhead contributes less than 5% percentage for all cases. As the resource increases, the exchange between peers become more effective with large enough bandwidth, which leads to less control overhead in return. The same phenomena can be observed between random peeing and BPB-peering strategies, because the latter is more effective than the former.

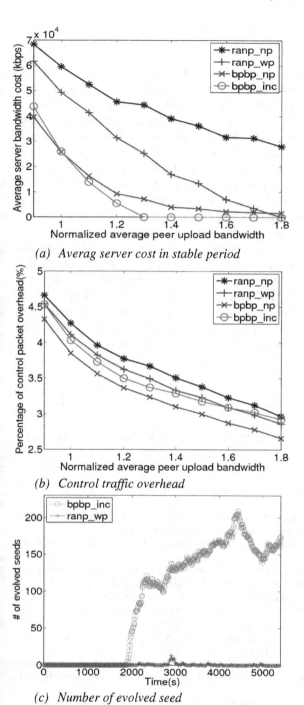

(a) *Averag server cost in stable period*

(b) *Control traffic overhead*

(c) *Number of evolved seed*

Fig. 10. Performance with various normalized peer bandwidth distribution

8. Conclusion

In this chapter, we proposed a service oriented architecture for peer assisted VoD streaming system. In particular, we presented the architecture design for both server side and client side service modules. Our design leverages the benefits of a service oriented approach such as agility, ease of configuration and ability to adapt to change. Based on this design, we outlined a service model that performs real-time composition for peer assisted video streaming. Finally, we proposed a model for SLA specification. The SLA differentiates QoS to end users based their bandwidth contributions to the system. Following this SLA model, we analytically derived minimum and maximum QoS level given a bandwidth budget at the server side. The SLA computation is simple to implement; the system parameters used in the computation can be easily observed and maintained by the server.

We further described an implementation of the proposed SOA model, the PACTS. We presented the design rationales of PACTS followed by the detailed algorithms in peering strategy and incentive-driven pre-fetching. The design is being extensively evaluated by packet-level simulations, which will be presented in another paper shortly. As the future work, we will show that PACTS effectively offload server's bandwidth demand without sacrificing the service quality. This benefit is further verified in dynamic settings with system churns.

References

[1] L. Gomes, "Will All of Us Get Our 15 Minutes On a YouTube Video?" *Wall Street Journal*, Aug. 30, 2006
[2] C. Huang, J.Li and K.W.Ross, "Can Internet Video-On-Demand be Profitable?" *In Proceedings of SIGCOM* 2007
[3] B. Cohen, "Incentives Build Robustness in BitTorrent", *In Proceedings of 1st Workshop on Economics of Peer-to-Peer Systems*, 2003
[4] K.L.Johnson, J.F.Carr, M.S.Day and M.F.Kaashoek, "The Measured Performance of Content Distribution Networks", *Computer Communication Journal*, Elsevier, 2001
[5] T.Silverston, O. Fourmaux, "Measuring P2P IPTV Systems", *In Proceedings of NOSSDAV*, 2007
[6] X.Zhang, J.Liu, B.Li and T.S.P.Yum, "Coolstreaming/DONet: A Data-Driven Overlay Network for Efficient Live Media Streaming", *In Proceedings of IEEE INFOCOM*, 2005
[7] R.Mondejar, P.Garcia, A.F.G.Skarmeta, "Towards a Decentralized p2pWeb Service Oriented Architecture", *In Proceedings of National Community Policing Conference – Community Policing: Leading the Way to a Safer Nation*, 2006, Washiongton, D.C.
[8] F.Bellifemine, G.Caire, A.Poggi, G.Rimassa, "JADE, A White Paper", *Technical Report*, Telecom Italia Lab, exp – Volume 3 – n.3 – September 2003
[9] A.Cherenak, M.Cai, M.Frank, "A Peer-to-Peer Replica Location Service Based on A Distributed Hash Table", *In Proceedings of ACM/IEEE Conference on Supercomputing (SC2004)*, 2004
[10] C.Schmidt, M.Parashar, "A Peer-to-Peer Approach to Web Service Discovery", *In Proceedings of ACM Conference on World Wide Web*, 2004

[11] M.Hefeeda, A.Habib, D.Xu, B.Bhargava, B.Botev, "CollectCast: A peer-to-peer Service for Media Streaming", *in Multimedia Systems Journal*, 2005 - Springer

[12] "IBM Video Charger", October 2005, http://www.306.ibm.com/software/data/videocharger

[13] X.Hei, C.Liang, J.Liang, Y.Liu, K.W.Ross, "A Measurement Study of a Large-Scale P2P IPTV System", *IEEE Transaction on Multimedia*, 2007

[14] C. Venkatramani, P. Westerink O. Verscheure, P. Frossard "Securing Media for Adaptive Streaming", ACM Multimedia, 2003.

[15] "Microsoft Media Player", *www.microsoft.com*

[16] "QuickTime Player", *www.apple.com*

[17] Y.hua Chu, J.Chuang and H.Zhang, "A case for taxation in peer-to-peer streaming broadcast", in *Proceedings of ACM SIGCOMM* workshop on Practice and theory of incentives in networked systems, 2004

[18] M.Zhang, Q.Zhang, L.Sun and S.Yang, "Understand-ing the power of pull-based streaming protocol: can we do better?" *IEEE Journal on Selected Areas in Communications*, 2007.

[19] Z.Fu, C.Wu, J.J.Jeng, H.Lei, "PACTS: A Service Oriented Architecture for Real-Time Peer-Assisted Content Delivery Service", *In First IEEE International Workshop On Real-Time Service-Oriented Architecture and Applications (RTSOAA)* 2008, Finland.

Chapter 14

A Coverage Relationship Model for Test Case Selection and Ranking for Multi-version Software

Wei-Tek Tsai, Xinyu Zhou, Raymond A. Paul[†], Yinong Chen, Xiaoying Bai*

Computer Science & Engineering Department, Arizona State University, USA

{wtsai, xinyu.zhou, bnxiao, yinong}@asu.edu

†Department of Defense, Washington, DC, USA

†Raymond.Paul@osd.mil

*Department of Computer Science and Engineering, Tsinghua University, China

*baixy@tsinghua.edu.cn

Abstract. Testing a group of software artifacts that implement the same specification is time consuming, especially when the test case repository is large. In the meantime, some of test cases may cover the same aspects in the software under test, and thus it is not necessary to apply all the test cases. This paper proposes a Model-based Adaptive Test (MAT) case selection and ranking technique to eliminate redundant test cases, and rank the test cases according to their potency and coverage. This technique can be applied in various domains where multiple versions of an application are available for testing, such as web service group testing, n-version applications, regression testing, and specification-based application testing. MAT is a statistical model based on earlier testing results, and the model can accurately determine the next sets of test cases to minimize the testing effort. It can be applied to testing of multi-versioned web services, and the results shows that MAT can reduce testing effort while still maintain the effectiveness of testing.

1 Introduction

Service-Oriented Architecture (SOA) and Web services have received significant attention recently. SOA is used in the web 2.0 [25], which facilitates colla-

J. Dong et al. (eds.), *High Assurance Services Computing*,
DOI 10.1007/978-0-387-87658-0_14, © Springer Science+Business Media, LLC 2009

borative sharing and communication for all participants. One reason that prevents services from being widely used, particular those services developed by third parties, is whether these services are reliable enough to be trusted in mission-critical applications.

As reported in CBDi Forum (http://searchwebservices.techtarget.com/) in 2002: "Web services are not yet widely used because of reliability concern. The concern is 'Will the service work correctly every time when I need it?' As yet few are thinking about the issues of testing and certification. We suggest that testing and certification of Web services is not business as usual and that new solutions are needed to provide assurance that services can really be trusted."

While the security issues of services are still a concern, many standards, such as WS-Security, WS-Secure Conversation, WS-Privacy, WS-Trust, XACML and SAML, have been studied and published, which have produced the level of security that customers are confident with. For example, people are now doing their communication, banking, and shopping through Internet and services. However, despite progress in SOA, service verification and testing techniques are not mature enough to support dependable and trustworthy computing. The current web service and SOA research is largely focused on the protocols, functionality, transactions, ontology, composition, semantic web, and interoperability. Little research has been done on dependability and trustworthiness of services developed by different service providers.

In the SOA development, application builders can search and discover services from service brokers, and use services provided by different services providers. Who is responsible for the overall dependability of a system that consists of many services developed by different service providers? At what layers should reliability and security mechanisms be deployed? These are new challenges. To address these new problems, efforts from all the involved parties are necessary, including policy makers such as government agencies that may propose reliability criteria, standard making consortiums to establish the means to evaluate those criteria, industries such as service providers and brokers to follow the agreed criteria, service consumers to use only those certificated services, and research institutions to provide technology for reliability modeling and evaluation.

Current web services are based on UDDI or ebXML server that provides directory and brokerage services similar to the telephone yellow book. A service broker is not responsible for the quality of services it refers to. Thus, the trustworthiness of service presents a concern for users. Traditional dependability techniques such as correctness proof, fault-tolerant computing, model checking, testing, and evaluation, can be used to improve the trustworthiness of individual service. However, these techniques need to be redesigned to handle the dynamic applications composed of service at runtime.

Verification can be enforced through the entire SOA development lifecycle [15], including modeling phase, development phase, composition phase, deployment phase, and even at runtime. A traditional approach to verify an SOA application via the IV&V (Independent Verification and Validation) is to have all the service code available, and let an independent team to test each code, and then test the application exhaustively using all the combinations of services. In this way, a SOA application can be composed without dynamic testing, because all the combinations have been tested earlier. However, this approach can be too expensive to implement, because the number of services available as well as their combinations can be huge. Another serious issue of this approach is that service providers may not be willing to share the source code, and thus making this approach infeasible.

2 Testing Techniques in SOA Lifecycles

A number of studies have been done to address the testing problems of SOA applications. In [6], Canfora and Di Penta presented the opportunities and challenges in SOA testing. In [2], various SOA verification and testing techniques are presented including monitoring, reliability modeling and analysis.

Testing and evaluation is part of software lifecycle, as well as in each step of the lifecycle. SOA lifecycle includes modeling and design, development, registration and publication, deployment, and operation and maintenance. Various testing techniques have been developed in each step of the lifecycle.

2.1 Testing in Modeling and Design phase

In [28], Zheng et al proposed a model checking based test case generation framework to test whether the implementation of web services conforms to its BPEL and WSDL models. The SPIN and NuSMV model checkers are used as the test generation engine, to achieve state, transition and du-path coverage criteria for BPEL models.

In [15], Narayanan and McIlraith proposed a Petri Net (PN) based web service simulation, verification and validation. In their approach, web services are modeled by DAML-S, then translated to PN. Based on the Petri Net model of the web service, many existing Petri Net techniques can be applied to simulate, verify and validate the web service. Specifically, linear algebraic techniques can verify the properties of the web service; Coverability graph analysis, model checking and reduction techniques can analyze the dynamic behavior of the Petri Net; Simulation and Markov-chain analysis can evaluate the performance of the web service. The verification on the Petri Net can check the reachability, liveness and deadlocks of the web service.

2.2 Testing in Assemble/Composition Phase

In [14], Milanovic and Malek reviewed and compared existing approaches to service composition, including BPEL, OWL-S, Web Components, Algebraic Process, Petri Nets, Model checking and Finite State Machines. In [13], Koehler and Srivastava discussed and compared two approaches to service composition: an industry solution which uses WSDL and BPEL4WS, and a semantic web solution which uses RDF/DAML-S and Golog/Planning.

In [10], Garcia-Fanjul et al used SPIN model checker to automatically generate test suites for composite Web service specified in BPEL. In their approach, BPEL specification is first transformed into a PROMELA model, and then test case are generated and selected to provide transition coverage.

2.3 Testing in Registration Phase

After service is tested and deployed by the service provider, it should be tested again by other parties before its registration on the service registry.

In [3], Bertolino et al. presented a framework which extends the UDDI registry role and supports the validation of services before registration. The testing approach, which is called audition, is based on a Protocol State Machine (PSM) which is a behavior diagram of the UML 2.0. PSM is a state machine with the preconditions and post-conditions specified along with each state.

In [11], Heckel and Mariani proposed that services should be tested by automatic testing agents called "discovery services" before their registration. The "discovery services" uses Graph Transformation (GT) rules to test the compatibility between clients and services. The discovery service can automatically generates conformance test cases based on the service description and its GT rules, then execute the test cases on the Web Service.

In [29], Zhu proposed a service oriented testing framework which involves various parties in the testing of WS applications. When registering a service, a kind of auxiliary service called "testing services" should also be registered with the "functional service". The testing service can be provided by the same vendor or by a third party. One functional service can correspond to multiple testing services to perform various testing tasks. Ontology can be used to describe, publish and register testing services.

2.4 Testing in Deployment Phase

In [27], a TTCN-3 based stress testing approach was proposed. The tests stored on the server side are in the form of Abstract Test Suite (ATS), which is a language and platform-independent format. The ATS test cases are publishable and discoverable. The TTCN-3 compiler can convert the ATS test cases into various language-dependent formats, such as test in java, test in c#, test in Perl and so on. In [16], Nevedrov introduced a performance testing tool JMeter to check the performance of SOA applications.

2.5 Testing in Runtime Phase

The Web Services Policy Framework (WS-Policy) [22], developed by BEA, IBM, Microsoft, and SAP, provides a general-purpose model and corresponding syntax to describe and communicate the policies of a Web Service. WS-Policy defines a base set of constructs that can be used and extended by other Web Services specifications to describe a broad range of service requirements, preferences, and capabilities. WS-Policy provides a flexible and extensible grammar for expressing the capabilities, requirements, and general characteristics of entities in an XML Web Services-based system. WS-Policy defines a framework and a model for the expression of these properties as policies.

In [19], Robinson proposed a monitoring framework called ReqMon that supports formalization of high-level goals and requirements. ReqMon also supports the automation of monitor generation, deployment, and optimization. ReqMon is composed of five components: event capture, analyzer, repository, presenter and reactor. The event capture component receives runtime events and put the events into the event streams. The analyzer is used to update the status of monitors. The repository is a database for storing the events and monitor histories. The monitors are implemented by model checking, SQL queries and Event Condition Action (ECA) rules.

3 Objectives

3.1 Requirement for Verification Framework

An open verification framework is beneficial for SOA: It provides an experimental testbed for researchers; it also provides the updated data necessary for various service research projects such as service performance and reliability assessments. In the open testing framework, the service repository, test case database, and ranking data are open, i.e., the public can use them and can contribute to them too. The verification models and tools, including testing and verification mechanisms, test case generation methods, reliability and ranking models, are all public, extendable and replaceable.

In addition, the open verification framework should be able to rank services, test cases, test case generation algorithms, and reliability models.

One requirement for web service testing is rapidly testing multiple versions of services of the same specifications. The atomic and composite services can be specified in WSDL, OWL-S, and BPEL. Based on the specifications, test cases can be generated by test case generation techniques. The SOA verification techniques include testing, model checking, simulation, policy enforcement, and other mechanisms such as completeness and consistency. This paper focuses on the testing aspects, in particular, how to test services efficiently.

3.2 Testing Services Adaptively

Statistics has been shown to be promising for software testing. Whittaker proposed a statistical software testing model and applied Markov chain to that model [23]. Statistical testing follows black-box testing with two extensions: the input sequence must be stochastically generated and the test history must be analyzed from a statistical point of view. The statistical testing model can be modeled as a Markov chain and a testing Markov chain. The usage Markov chain is used to model the state diagram of the software, while the testing Markov chain is used to collect the testing profiles. Software cybernetics [5] leverages controlled Markov chain (CMC) technique for software testing. The software under test serves as a controlled object and the software testing strategy serves as the controller and optimizer. In this way the software and the testing strategy forms a CMC, and control theory of Markov chains can be used to tackle software testing. However, CMC is currently limited to those software testing processes that can be modeled as Markov chains.

This chapter proposes a Model-based Adaptive Testing (MAT) for multi-versioned software based a model called Coverage Relationship Model (CRM). The CRM can be used to select and rank test cases, and can identify and eliminate those duplicate test cases or those test cases that cover the same aspects. The MAT also can be used to rank the test cases according to their potency in an adaptive manner. In this way, software can be efficiently tested using the most potent test cases and without minimized duplication effort. Furthermore, as more data will be collected, the model can automatically re-rank test cases based on the new testing results.

The proposed technique can be applied to various domains where multiple versions of applications are available such as:

- N-version programming [6]: N-version programming is used to fault-tolerance approach to ensure the reliability of systems. In an N-version programming model, multiple versions of system are used to implement the same function, and versions can be used as software recovery blocks as backup.
- Regression Testing: In a system development lifecycle, multiple versions of software will be developed, and in modern software development processes such as agile process, a new version of software can be created on a daily basis. Furthermore, in the Web. 2.0 paradigm [25], not only a new version will be created on a hourly basis, but also end users will be involved as co-developers while using the delivered products. Thus, during the entire development processes, numerous versions of software will be available.
- Standard-based testing: Standard-based applications are the systems that implement the functionality and interfaces specified in a published standard. For example, OASIS [17] and W3C [24] have published numerous standards, and vendors may develop their own software to implement those standards, and thus standard making organization often need to publish test cases to ensure that they meet the standard requirements. .
- Web Service Testing. Group Testing technique was originally developed for blood testing [9], and later for to software regression testing and web service testing [12][1]. Group testing can be used when detecting faults in multiple versions of the same specification.
- The chapter is organized as follows. Section two introduces the CRM and the algorithm of constructing the CRM. Section three optimizes the full CRM into a Simplified CRM (S-CRM) and then analyzes the implications of various coverage probabilities in the S-CRM. Section four proposes the adaptive test case ranking and selection algorithm based on the S-CRM. Section five describes an experiment by applying the S-CRM and MAT to a WSGT environment, and analyzes the experiment result. Section six concludes this paper.

4 Coverage Relationship Model (CRM)

4.1 Motivation

For a sample set of applications S, after applying two test cases (TC) A and B respectively, A generates two output sets A_C and A_I. A_C denotes the correct output set, while A_I denotes the incorrect output set. Likewise, B generates a correct output set B_C and an incorrect output set B_I. Each set of artifacts is defined as a state. For example, if the software artifact generates the output A_C for a given test case, then the artifact is in state A_C.

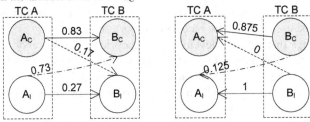

Fig. 1. an example of overlap probability

For the artifacts in set A_C, they may be in set B_C or B_I when B is applied. The number on the arch from denotes the *Coverage Probability* $\vec{P}_{s1 \to s2}$ from set s1 to set s2. For example, from set A_C to B_C, the coverage probability $\vec{P}_{Ac \to Bc}$ is 0.83, which denotes that 83% artifacts in A_C will be in B_C when TC B is applied. The left part of Fig. 1. shows the coverage probability from TC A to TC B. Similarly, from TC B to TC A, the coverage probability can also be calculated as shown in the right part of Fig. 1..

Note that the coverage probability from one state S1 to another state S2 $\vec{P}_{s1 \to s2}$ does not necessarily be equal to $\vec{P}_{s2 \to s1}$. For example, if the size of A_C is 10, the size of B_C is 5, and the size of the intersection set between A_C and B_C is 4, then $\vec{P}_{Ac \to Bc} = 4/10 = 0.4$, while $\vec{P}_{Bc \to Ac} = 4/5 = 0.8$.

4.2 Coverage Relationship Model and Potency

4.2.1 Coverage Relationship Model

Consider a more complex situation, where multiple TC exists and each TC has one correct set and multiple incorrect sets, as shown in Fig. 2..

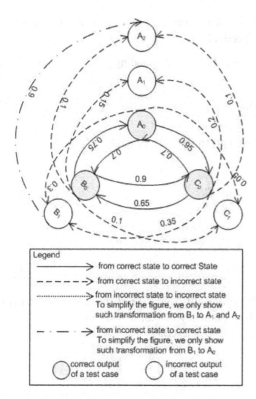

Fig. 2. An example of test case Markov chain model

In the CRM, let

$C = \{c_1, c_2, \ldots c_m\}$ be the set of software artifacts that implement the same specification, where m is the size of the artifacts set.

$T = \{t_1, t_2, \ldots t_n\}$ be the set of test cases, where n is the size of the test case set. For each t_i, let

$V_i = \{v_{i,0}, v_{i,1}, \ldots, v_{i,k}\}$,

be the different output values after applying t_i to C, where $(k+1)$ is the number of different output values.

Let $s_{i,j}$ denotes the subset of C that generates the same output value $v_{i,j}$ for t_i, thus C can be represented as S_i after t_i is applied

$S_i = \{\{s_{i,0}\}, \{s_{i,1}\}, \ldots, \{s_{i,k}\}\}$,

Because for a given input, there is one correct output (or a range of correct answers) and multiple incorrect outputs (or multiple ranges of incorrect answers), let $v_{i,0}$ be the correct output value, and $v_{i,1}, v_{i,2}, \ldots, v_{i,k}$ denote various incorrect output values. Thus, $s_{i,0}$ denotes the correct output set of C that generates the correct output value $v_{i,0}$, and $s_{i,1},s_{i,2},...,s_{i,k}$ denotes the incorrect output sets that generate those incorrect values $v_{i,1}$, $v_{i,2},...,v_{i,k}$, respectively.

- let $q_{i,j}$ be the size of the set $s_{i,j}$, thus S_i has a corresponding Q_i

$$Q_i=\{q_{i,0}, q_{i,1}, ..., q_{i,k}\},$$

- let $p_{i,j}$ denotes the probability that a given test case generates the $s_{i,j}$,

$$p_{i,j}= \frac{q_{i,j}}{m}$$

4.2.2 Potency

The potency of a test case is that probability that the test case can detect a fault [21]. For example, if a test case has a potency of 0.5, it will fail half of the versions. Thus, a potency of test case t_i can be defined as

$$Pot_i=1-p_{i,0}= 1- \frac{q_{i,0}}{\sum_0^k q_{i,k}} = \frac{\sum_1^k q_{i,k}}{\sum_0^k q_{i,k}}$$

- For any two set of output $s_{i,\alpha}$ and $s_{j,\beta}$, where $i\neq j$, the *Coverage* ty $\vec{P}$ from $s_{i,\alpha}$ to $s_{j,\beta}$ is defined as

$$\vec{P} s_{i,\alpha\rightarrow}s_{j,\beta} = sizeof(s_{i,\alpha}\cap s_{j,\beta})/q_{i,\alpha}$$

The value on the edges of the CRM represents the Coverage Probability.

- use $\Delta(t_1,t_2)$ to denote if the aspects of software that test case t_1 can test covers that of test case t_2, or simply say t_1 covers t_2; and use $\not\Delta (t_1,t_2)$ to denote if t_1 does not cover t_2;
- use the notation "+" to denote the overall testing domain of multiple test cases. For example, $\Delta(t_1+t_2+t_3+ ... + t_n, t_{n+1})$ means that the overall testing domain of t_1, t_2, t_3 ... and t_n covers that of t_{n+1};

Lemma 1: For any two set $s_{i,\alpha}$ and $s_{j,\beta}$, if $i=j$ then $s_{i,\alpha}\cap s_{j,\beta}=\varnothing$.

Proof: Because for any artifact, it cannot generate the correct output and incorrect output for a given TC at the same time.

Lemma 1 indicates that there is no coverage probability between two sets that belong to the same test case.

4.2.3 An Example

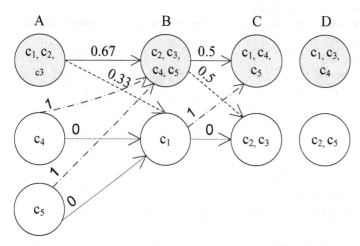

Fig. 3. An Example of CRM consisting of 4 test cases and 5 versions

Fig. 3. shows an example CRM consisting of four test cases and five versions, and shows the $\vec{P}$ from test case A to B, and the $\vec{P}$ from test case B to C. As can been seen from Fig. 3. , for test case A, there is:

$$S_A=\{\{c_1, c_2, c_3\}, \{c_4\}, \{c_5\}\},$$

and the potency of test case A is:

$$Pot_A=3/5=0.6$$

For test case B, there is

$$S_B=\{\{c_2, c_3, c_4, c_5\}, \{c_1\}\},$$

Thus, from the correct set of test case A to that of test case B, the transition probability is

$$\vec{P} = sizeof(\{c_1, c_2, c_3\} \cap \{c_2, c_3, c_4, c_5\})/sizeof\{c_1, c_2, c_3\}=2/3\approx0.67$$

4.3 CRM Construction

Table 1. shows an algorithm of construction the CRM. This algorithm uses a table data structure "CoverageProbalitilyMap" to store the coverage probability from one set to another set. Note that the arch in the map is bidirectional because the coverage relationship is bidirectional as shown in Fig. 1..

Table 1. the Algorithm of Constructing the CRM

Input: $C=\{c_1,c_2...,c_m\}$;
   $T=\{t_1,t_2...,t_n\}$;
//1st Step: Create all sets
foreach (t_i in T)
Begin
  $V_i\leftarrow\{v_{i,0}\}$;
  $S_i\leftarrow\{\varnothing\}$;
  foreach (c_j in C)
  Begin
    Output=apply t_i to c_j;
    if (output is NOT in V_i)
    Begin
      V_i.addNewValue(Ouput);
      S_i.addNewSet(c_j);
    End
    else S_i.addComponentToSet(c_j);
  End
End
//2nd Step: Calculate Coverage Probability
foreach (S_j in S)
  foreach(S_j in S where $i\neq j$)
  Begin
    foreach ($s_{i,\alpha}$ in S_i)
      foreach($s_{j,\beta}$ in S_j)
      Begin
        $\vec{P}_{s_{i,\alpha}\to s_{j,\beta}} \leftarrow sizeof(s_{i,\alpha}\cap s_{j,\beta})/ sizeof(s_{i,\alpha})$
        CoverageProbalitilyMap.addEdge($s_{i,\alpha}$, $s_{j,\beta}$, $\vec{P}$);
    End
End

5 Simplified Coverage Relationship Model Analysis

It is expensive to construct the full CRM. Suppose on average each test case has k different outputs, the computational effort of calculating the coverage probability consisting of n test cases is $n*(n-1)*k^2$. Most times may only concerns about two sets: correct set and incorrect set, unless further study is needed to analyze the coverage relationship between different incorrect sets. Thus, this paper proposes the Simplified Coverage Relationship Model (S-CRM) to reduce the computational complexity of constructing the full CRM. In S-CRM, each t_i has only two sets, a correct set $s_{i,C}$ and an incorrect set $s_{i,I}$, the incorrect set $s_{i,I}$ combines all the incorrect sets from the full CRM into one incorrect set by simply using the union operation, i.e.,

$S_i = \{\{ s_{i,C} \}, \{ s_{i,I} \}\}$,

where $s_{i,I} = \bigcup_{j=1}^{k} s_{i,j}$. Correspondingly,

- $q_{i,C}$ and $q_{i,I}$ denote the size of the set $s_{i,C}$, and $s_{i,I}$, respectively;
- $p_{i,C}$ and $p_{i,I}$ denote the probability that a given test case generates the $s_{i,C}$ and $s_{i,I}$, respectively.

S-CRM can reduce the computational effort from $n*(n-1)*k^2$ to $n*(n-1)*4$. Hereinafter, the discussion will be based on the S-CRM.

5.1 S-CRM Analysis Preparation

In S-CRM, for two test cases, four types of coverage probability exist: from correct set to correct set (C→C), from correct set to incorrect set (C→I), from incorrect set to correct set (I→C), and from incorrect set to incorrect set (I→I), as shown in Fig. 4. :

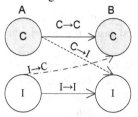

Fig. 4. A S-CRM example

For simplicity purpose, in the following analysis we will always calculate $\vec{P}$ from test case A to test case B, so in the subscript of $\vec{P}$ we will omit A and B. For example, $\vec{P}_{A,I \to B,I}$ is referred to as $\vec{P}_{I \to I}$.

The coverage probability from the any set is 1, thus we can have equation (1) and (2):

$$\vec{P}_{C \to C} + \vec{P}_{C \to I} = 1 \qquad (1)$$

$$\vec{P}_{I \to C} + \vec{P}_{I \to I} = 1 \qquad (2)$$

Since p is the potency of test cases, thus we can have equation (3) and (4)

$$1 - Pot_B = (1 - Pot_A) * \vec{P}_{C \to C} + Pot_A * \vec{P}_{I \to C} \qquad (3)$$

$$Pot_B = (1 - Pot_A) * \vec{P}_{C \to I} + Pot_A * \vec{P}_{I \to I} \qquad (4)$$

Let $\vec{P}_H$ be the pre-defined high bound threshold on coverage probability, e.g., $\vec{P}_H = 0.99$.

Let $\vec{P}_L$ be the pre-defined low bound threshold on coverage probability, e.g., $\vec{P}_L = 0.01$.

Let Pot_H be the pre-defined high bound threshold on potency, e.g., $Pot_H = 0.98$.

Let Pot_L be the pre-defined low bound threshold on potency, e.g., $Pot_L = 0.02$.

Rule 1: Coverage relationship is not symmetric and in fact, for any two test cases t_a and t_b, if $\Delta(t_a, t_b)$, then $\Delta (t_b, t_a)$

Lemma 2: If $Pot_b < Pot_a$, then $\Delta(t_b, t_a)$; if $\Delta(t_a, t_b)$, then $Pot_b < Pot_a$.

Proof:

Let

A_C and B_C be the correct set of t_a and t_b respectively, and

The $\vec{P}_{t_b,C \to t_a,C} = sizeof(A_C \cap B_C)/sizeof(B_C)$

The $\vec{P}_{t_a,C \to t_b, C} = sizeof(A_C \cap B_C)/sizeof(A_C)$

$Pot_b < Pot_a \Rightarrow q_{a,I} > q_{b,I}$

$$\Rightarrow \vec{P}_{t_a,C \to t_b, C} > \vec{P}_{t_b,C \to t_a,C}$$

If $\vec{P}_{t_b,C \to t_a,C} > \vec{P}_H$, then also $\vec{P}_{t_a,C \to t_b,C} > \vec{P}_H$. In this case, $\Delta(t_a, t_b)$ instead of $\Delta(t_b, t_a)$, because the coverage relationship is not mutual according to rule 1.

Lemma 2 indicates that less potent test cases never cover more potent test cases. If a coverage relationship exists between any two test cases, it must be that the more potent test case covers the less potent test case.

Lemma 2 implies an optimization method to further reduce the effort of constructing the S-CRM. If all test cases are ranked in terms of their potencies, then those test cases in low rank do not cover the highly ranked test case. For example, if test case t_a ranks higher than test case t_b, one only needs to determine if t_a cover t_b by using $\vec{P}_{C \to C}$ or $\vec{P}_{C \to I}$ from t_a to t_b, or using $\vec{P}_{I \to C}$ or $\vec{P}_{I \to I}$ from t_b to t_a. Therefore, one only needs to calculate the coverage probability from the current test case to all test cases after it. Thus, the computational effort of construing the S-CRM can be further reduced from $n*(n-1)$ to $n*(n-1)/2$.

Lemma 3: for any two test cases t_a and t_b, and any test case set T, if $\Delta(t_a, t_b)$, then $\Delta(T+ t_a, T+t_b)$

Proof:

Because $\Delta(t_a, t_b) => \vec{P}_{t_a,C \to t_b,C} = \text{sizeof}(A_C \cap B_C)/\text{sizeof}(A_C) \geq \vec{P}_H$

$\vec{P}_{(T+t_a),C \to (T+t_b),C} = \text{sizeof}(T_C \cup (A_C \cap B_C))/\text{sizeof}(T_C \cup A_C)$

$\qquad \geq \text{sizeof}(A_C \cap B_C)/\text{sizeof}(A_C)$

$\qquad = \vec{P}_{t_a,C \to t_b,C} \geq \vec{P}_H$

When $T_C \subseteq A_C \cap B_C$,

$\text{sizeof}(T_C \cup (A_C \cap B_C))/\text{sizeof}(T_C \cup A_C) = \text{sizeof}(A_C \cap B_C)/\text{sizeof}(A_C)$

Otherwise,

$\text{sizeof}(T_C \cup (A_C \cap B_C))/\text{sizeof}(T_C \cup A_C) > \text{sizeof}(A_C \cap B_C)/\text{sizeof}(A_C)$

Thus, $\Delta(T+ t_a, T+t_b)$

5.1.1 From Correct Set to Correct Set (C→C)

Two cases may happen to $\vec{P}_{C \to C}$:

- $\vec{P}_{C \to C} > \vec{P}_H$
- Analysis: According to equation (1), one can have

$\vec{P}_{C \to I} < 1 - \vec{P}_H$

This case indicates that for those versions that test case A cannot detect the fault, test case B is very unlikely to detect the fault as well. Therefore, test case A covers B, and applying test case B is almost in vain if test case A cannot detect the fault.

  - Conclusion: $\Delta(A,B)$
  - Recommendation: eliminate B and use A only

- $\vec{P}_{C \to C} < \vec{P}_L$

  - Analysis: According to equation (1) and (4), one can have

$Pot_B = (1-P_A)*(1- \vec{P}_{C \to C}) + p_A * \vec{P}_{I \to I} \approx 1- p_A * \vec{P}_{I \to C}$ (5)

This case indicates that, given a fixed $\vec{P}_{I \to C}$, the less possibly the test case A can detect the fault, the more possibly that test case B can detect the fault. Thus, test case A does not cover test case B, and one should calculate $\vec{P}_{C \to C}$ from B to A to see if $\Delta(B,A)$.

  - Conclusion: Δ (A,B)
  - Recommendation: Calculate $\vec{P}_{C \to C}$ from B to A to see if $\Delta(B,A)$

5.1.2 From Correct Set to Incorrect Set (C→I)

This is the contrary case as C→C. Because according to equation (1), the larger the $\vec{P}_{C\to C}$ is, the smaller the $\vec{P}_{C\to I}$. Thus, the contrary rules in C→C can apply. Two cases may happen to $\vec{P}_{C\to I}$:

- $\vec{P}_{C\to I} > \vec{P}_H$

    - Analysis: This case indicates that $\vec{P}_{C\to C} < \vec{P}_L$
    - Conclusion: $\triangleq$ (A,B)
    - Recommendation: Calculate $\vec{P}_{C\to I}$ from B to A to see if Δ(B,A)

- $\vec{P}_{C\to I} < \vec{P}_L$

    - Analysis: This case indicates $\vec{P}_{C\to C} > \vec{P}_H$
    - Conclusion: Δ(A,B)
    - Recommendation: eliminate B and use A only

5.1.3 From Incorrect Set to Correct Set (I→C)

Two cases may happen to $\vec{P}_{I\to C}$:

- $\vec{P}_{I\to C} > \vec{P}_H$

    - This case indicates that for those versions that have been failed by test case A, it is very unlikely that test case can detect the fault. Thus, test case B does not cover test case A.
    - Conclusion: $\triangleq$ (B,A)
    - Recommendation: Calculate $\vec{P}_{I\to C}$ from B to A to see if Δ(A,B)

- $\vec{P}_{I\to C} < \vec{P}_L$

    - This case indicates that if for those versions that have been failed by test case A, it is very likely that test case B can fail them as well. Thus, test case B covers test case A.
    - Conclusion: Δ(B,A)
    - Recommendation: eliminate A, and use B only

5.1.4 From Incorrect Set to Incorrect Set (I→I)

This is the contrary case as I→C. Because according to equation (2), the larger the $\vec{P}_{I\rightarrow C}$ is, the smaller the $\vec{P}_{I\rightarrow I}$ is. Thus, the contrary rules in I→C can apply to I→I. Two cases may happen to $\vec{P}_{I\rightarrow I}$:

- $\vec{P}_{I\rightarrow I} > \vec{P}_H$

    - Analysis: This case indicates that $\vec{P}_{I\rightarrow C} < \vec{P}_L$
    - Conclusion: Δ(B,A)
    - Recommendation: eliminate A, and use B only

- $\vec{P}_{I\rightarrow I} < \vec{P}_L$

    - Analysis: This case indicates $\vec{P}_{I\rightarrow C} > \vec{P}_H$
    - Conclusion: ≙ (B,A)
    - Recommendation: Calculate $\vec{P}_{I\rightarrow I}$ from B to A to see if Δ(A,B)

Table 2. Summary of the Coverage Probability Analysis

From Test Cases A to B	$\vec{P} < \vec{P}_L$	$\vec{P}_L < \vec{P} < \vec{P}_H$	$\vec{P}_H < \vec{P}$
C→C	Conclusion: ≙ (A,B) Recommendation: Calculate $\vec{P}_{C\rightarrow C}$ from B to A to see if Δ(B,A)	Conclusion: A covers B to some extent, Recommendation: Calculate $\vec{P}_{C\rightarrow C}$ from B to A to see if Δ(B,A).	Conclusion: Δ(A,B) Recommendation: eliminate B and use A only
C→I	Conclusion: Δ(A,B) Recommendation: eliminate B and use A only	Conclusion: A covers B to some extent, Recommendation: Calculate $\vec{P}_{C\rightarrow I}$ from B to A to see if Δ(B,A)	Conclusion: ≙ (A,B) Recommendation: Calculate $\vec{P}_{C\rightarrow I}$ from B to A to see if Δ(B,A)
I→C	Conclusion: Δ(B,A) Recommendation: eliminate A, and use B only	Conclusion: B covers A to some extent, Recommendation: Calculate $\vec{P}_{I\rightarrow C}$ from B to A to see if Δ(A,B)	Conclusion: ≙ (B,A) Recommendation: Calculate $\vec{P}_{I\rightarrow C}$ from B to A to see if Δ(A,B)
I→I	Conclusion: ≙ (B,A) Recommendation: Calculate $\vec{P}_{I\rightarrow I}$ from B to A to see if Δ(A,B)	Conclusion: B covers A to some extent, Recommendation: Calculate $\vec{P}_{I\rightarrow I}$ from B to A to see if Δ(A,B)	Conclusion: Δ(B,A) Recommendation: eliminate A and use B only

5.2 Summary Table

Table 2 summarizes the four ways to analyze the coverage relationship for S-CRM: $\vec{P}_{C\to C}$, $\vec{P}_{C\to I}$, $\vec{P}_{I\to C}$, and $\vec{P}_{I\to I}$. According to equation (1) and (2): $\vec{P}_{C\to C}$ and $\vec{P}_{C\to I}$ are interchangeable, and $\vec{P}_{I\to C}$ and $\vec{P}_{I\to I}$ are also interchangeable, thus these four parameters can be categorized into two groups in terms of their source sets: the source set $\vec{P}$ is correct set ($\vec{P}_{C\to C}$ and $\vec{P}_{C\to I}$), and the source set of $\vec{P}$ is incorrect set ($\vec{P}_{I\to C}$ and $\vec{P}_{I\to I}$). This paper uses $\vec{P}_{C\to C}$ and $\vec{P}_{I\to C}$ to delegate each group respectively to explain the difference.

In most cases, both $\vec{P}_{C\to C}$ and $\vec{P}_{I\to C}$ can find the coverage relationship between two test cases. However, in the following cases, choosing $\vec{P}_{C\to C}$ or $\vec{P}_{I\to C}$ to calculate the coverage probability from test cases t_A to t_B is a tradeoff between accuracy and efficiency.

- When the potency of both test cases is very small, e.g., $Pot_A < Pot_L$ and $Pot_B < Pot_L$

    - Analysis:
      For example, for a set C consisting of one hundred and two components, if t_A fails 101th application only, and t_B fails 100th application only, then from t_A to t_B: $\vec{P}_{C\to C} = 99\% >= \vec{P}_H$, which indicates t_A covers t_B, and t_B should be eliminated. However, the reason that $\vec{P}_{C\to C}$ reaches a large value is because the correct sets of both test cases are large, thus it does not necessarily indicate t_A cover t_B. On the contrary, from $\vec{P}_{I\to C} = 100\%$ one can conclude $\triangle$ (t_B, t_A), and both t_A and t_B should be kept for further testing. Thus, in this case $\vec{P}_{I\to C}$ is more accurate than $\vec{P}_{C\to C}$. On the other hand, compared to $\vec{P}_{I\to C}$, $\vec{P}_{C\to C}$ is more efficient in terms of test cases selection, because $\vec{P}_{C\to C}$ will eliminate ineffective test cases even if they are not covered by other test cases(e.g., t_B).

    - Conclusion: In this case, $\vec{P}_{C\to C}$ misses some ineffective test cases if they are not covered by other test cases, which can lead to a compact but potent test case set; On the contrary, $\vec{P}_{I\to C}$ keeps any ineffective test cases even if they only add a little new coverage to the existing test case set T, which may lead an accurate but large test cases set. $\vec{P}_{C\to C}$ trades accuracy for efficiency, while $\vec{P}_{I\to C}$ trades efficiency for accuracy.

    - Countermeasure: If accuracy is more important than efficiency, two alternative countermeasures can be used to increase the accuracy:

Use $\vec{P}_{I\to C}$ instead of $\vec{P}_{C\to C}$

If still use $\vec{P}_{C\to C}$, increase the threshold $\vec{P}_H$, make $\vec{P}_H > 1 - p_L$.

- When the potency of both test cases is very large, e.g., $Pot_A > Pot_H$ and $Pot_B > Pot_H$

  – Analysis:
    For example, for a set C consisting of one hundred and two components, if t_A fails all components except the 101th, and t_B fails all components except the 100th, then from t_A to t_B: $\vec{P}_{I \to C} = 1\%$, which indicates $\Delta(t_B, t_A)$, and t_A should be eliminated. However, the reason that $\vec{P}_{I \to C}$ reaches a large value is because the incorrect sets of both test cases are large, thus it does not necessarily indicate t_B cover t_A. On the contrary, from $\vec{P}_{C \to C} = 0\% < \vec{P}_L$ one can conclude $\Delta(t_A, t_B)$, and both t_A and t_B should be kept for further testing. Thus, in this case $\vec{P}_{C \to C}$ is more accurate than $\vec{P}_{I \to C}$. On the other hand, compared to $\vec{P}_{C \to C}$, $\vec{P}_{I \to C}$ is more efficient in terms of test cases selection, because $\vec{P}_{I \to C}$ will eliminate the test cases if they are cannot detect much more fault than other test cases. (e.g., t_A).

  – Conclusion: In this case, $\vec{P}_{I \to C}$ misses those test cases that only add a little new coverage than the existing test case set T, which can lead to a compact but still potent test case set; On the contrary, $\vec{P}_{C \to C}$ keeps any test cases as long as if they can add new coverage than the existing test case set T, which may lead an accurate but large test cases set. $\vec{P}_{I \to C}$ trades accuracy for efficiency, while $\vec{P}_{C \to C}$ trades efficiency for accuracy.

  – Countermeasure: If accuracy is more important than efficiency, two alternative countermeasures can be used to increase the accuracy:

Use $\vec{P}_{C \to C}$ instead of $\vec{P}_{I \to C}$

If still use $\vec{P}_{I \to C}$, decrease the threshold $\vec{P}_L$, make $\vec{P}_L < 1 - Pot_H$.

Since any of the four types of coverage probability ($\vec{P}_{C \to C}$, $\vec{P}_{C \to I}$, $\vec{P}_{I \to C}$, $\vec{P}_{I \to I}$) can be used to analyze the coverage relationship, one can use only one to construct the S-CRM. Thus, the computational effort of constructing the S-CRM can be further reduced from n*(n-1)*4 to n*(n-1).

6 Adaptive Test Cases Ranking Algorithm

This section proposes two adaptive test case ranking algorithms. Both algorithms rank test cases according to their potency and CRM. The higher the potency of a test case is, the higher its rank is. The purpose is to apply the test cases with the highest probability to detect failures first to reduce test cost by ruling out failed versions as soon as possible. However, ranking by potency alone is not the optimal way of test case selection, as two potent test cases may cover the same aspects of the software. Thus, ranking by potency may subject the software to be penalized by the same mistakes multiple times.

One way to address the problem is to analyze how test cases are developed. Specifically, if two test cases were developed to evaluate the same aspects of software, e.g., control flow or data flow, and on the same segments of software, then these two test cases have almost identical coverage. This paper takes another approach, instead of by evaluation of how test cases are derived, it evaluates the test case coverage by the earlier results obtained. If test cases A and B fail the same set of versions, their coverage is highly correlated. If they fail completely different set of versions, they have almost no overlap in their coverage.

While analyzing how test cases are derived may yield accurate results, assigning coverage relationship by examining test cases have several distinct advantages:

- The entire process of identifying coverage relationship among test cases can be automated, and this can eliminate many human errors;
- There is no need to track and record the derivation or rational of test cases; and
- The resulting coverage is purely results driven. Specifically, two test cases derived from the same testing techniques and on the same software segment may still identify faults in two completely different sets of versions. In other words, an identical testing process applied to the same code segments may still produce test cases that detect different kinds of faults. For example, one of two control flow test cases may detect the incorrect action within a path, while the other may detect a fault in a decision in the same path. However, the CRM approach is completely results driven based on data collected.

Note that because the CRM is totally based on test results, thus two test cases derived from two different testing techniques and address two completely different code segments, may still have identical coverage in the CRM. This does not imply that the two test cases have the same coverage, it implies only that the people who made the first mistakes also made the second mistake in another part of the code by accident. As more data will be collected during the process, test cases developed using different techniques will eventually detect different sets of versions.

The proposed test case selection is thus based on a) test case potency; b) the CRM obtained. The CRM overwrites the potency criterion, i.e..,, for a set of existing test case T, and two new test cases $t_a \notin T$ and $t_b \notin T$, even if $p_{a,I} > p_{b,I}$, but if $\Delta(T + t_b, T + t_a)$, then t_b should rank higher than t_a.

Two adaptive ranking algorithms are given in Table 3. and Table 4. respectively. Table 3. describes a C→C algorithm for adaptive test cases ranking by using $\vec{P}_{C \to C}$. Table 4. presents an I→I algorithm for test case ranking by using $\vec{P}_{I \to I}$.

Table 3. The C→C Algorithm

Initialize component set $C=\{c_1,c_2...,c_m\}$;

Initialize test case ranking $T=\{t_1,t_2...,t_n\}$ according to their potency

TestCase* $t=t_1$; $\vec{P}_{C\rightarrow C}=0$;

While (t!=null)

Begin

foreach(t_i that ti.rank<t.rank)

Begin

$\vec{P}_{C\rightarrow C}$←calculate the coverage probability $\vec{P}_{C\rightarrow C}$ from t to t_i;

if ($\vec{P}_{C\rightarrow C}>=\vec{P}_H$) then delete ($t_i$);

else if ($\vec{P}_{C\rightarrow C}<=\vec{P}_L$);
// one can customize the operation if t does not cover t_i.

else;// one can customize the operation if t covers t_i
to some extent, for e.g., move t_i to the end of the rank

End

t.ranked=true;

t=t→next;

End

Table 4. The I→I Algorithm

Initialize component set $C=\{c_1,c_2...,c_m\}$;

Initialize test case ranking $T=\{t_1,t_2...,t_n\}$ according to their potency

TestCase* $t=t_1$; $\vec{P}_{I\rightarrow I}=0$;

While (t!=null)

Begin

foreach(t_i that ti.rank<t.rank)

Begin

$\vec{P}_{I\rightarrow I}$←calculate the coverage probability $\vec{P}_{I\rightarrow I}$ from t_i to t;

if ($\vec{P}_{I\rightarrow I}>=\vec{P}_H$) then delete ($t_i$);

else if ($\vec{P}_{I\rightarrow I}<=\vec{P}_L$);

// one can customize the operation if t does not cover t_i.

else ;// one can customize the operation if t covers t_i
to some extent, for e.g., move t_i to the end of the rank

End

t.ranked=true;

t=t→next;

End

Note that the algorithm based on $\vec{P}_{I \to I}$ is slightly different from that of $\vec{P}_{C \to C}$ in that the direction of calculating the coverage probability is opposition, i.e., the direction of calculating $\vec{P}_{C \to C}$ is from t to t_i, while the direction of ing $\vec{P}_{I \to I}$ is from t_i to t. According to equation (1) and (2), one can apply the same algorithms by replacing $\vec{P}_{C \to C}$ with 1- $\vec{P}_{C \to I}$ in Table 3. and replace $\vec{P}_{I \to I}$ with1- $\vec{P}_{I \to C}$ in Table 4. respectively.

Table 5. The adaptive algorithm

Step1: using the C→C algorithm or I→I algorithm to rank existing test case set T.

Step2: Rank newly added test case t.

While (t!=null)

Begin

t.Pot←t.calculatePotency(C); //C is the component set.

Foreach(t_i in the ranked test case list T)

Begin

if (t_i.Pot>=t.Pot)

Begin

$\vec{P}_{I \to I}$←calculate the coverage probability $\vec{P}_{I \to I}$ from t to t_i;

if ($\vec{P}_{I \to I}$ >= $\vec{P}_H$) then exit; //t_i covers t, just delete t.

End

else

Begin

$\vec{P}_{I \to I}$←calculate the coverage probability $\vec{P}_{I \to I}$ from t_i to t;

if ($\vec{P}_{I \to I}$ >= $\vec{P}_H$) then replate(t, t_i); //t covers t_i, just replace t_i with t.

End

End

End

These algorithms are adaptive because the test case can be re-ranked whenever new data arrive, in this way, test cases are constantly being ranked as the test is being performed, and only the most potent test cases that has least coverage relationship with already applied test cases will be selected for test execution. A two-step adaptive algorithm is listed in Table 5. . When a new test case t is added into the test case set, its potency is calculated and its result sets are established by performing testing on the component set C. For all test cases that are more potent than t, the coverage relationship is calculated to check if t is covered by these test cases; for all test cases that are less potent than t, the coverage relationship is calculated to check if t covers these test cases.

7 Experiment Studies

This section demonstrates an experiment of applying S-CRM to web services group testing [21]. A Web service is an instance or implementation of the Web service specification. Such a specification can be a Web Services Description Language (WSDL) [26] file, or a Web Ontology Language for Service (OWL-S) [18] file. WSDL file presents the required interface of a function. Web service client, which is typically a local application, can invoke any external Web Services that implement the WSDL file. There might be multiple Web service vendors implementing the same interface according to the WSDL or OWL-S but with different algorithms. Specifically, WSDL does not specify the algorithm to be used. Instead, it specifies only the input-output relationships. Thus, potentially different algorithms can be used if they achieve the same functionality. The OWL-S specifications are different as they may specify the high-level algorithms to be used. In that case, a service developer may have less freedom in choosing different algorithms. The proposed techniques can be used to evaluate multiple implementations of the same service specifications. For this experimental study, sixty services have been independently developed and they have been evaluated using thirty-two test cases. All the services and test cases can be obtained by contacting the authors.

7.1 Experiments Results Analysis

Table 6. shows that the test cases are ranked by their potencies after the experiment. The result is divided into to two rows because of page size limitation. The TC3 ranks first with the largest potency, while TC30 ranks last because it has the smallest potency.

Table 6. The test case ranking according to the potency

TC ID	3	4	2	1	10	11	9	12	16	6	7	13	14	5	8	15
potency	0.4	0.37	0.35	0.3	0.23	0.23	0.22	0.22	0.18	0.17	0.17	0.17	0.17	0.15	0.15	0.15
TC ID	18	20	21	22	23	24	25	26	27	28	29	31	32	17	19	30
potency	0.05	0.05	0.05	0.05	0.05	0.05	0.05	0.05	0.05	0.05	0.05	0.05	0.05	0.03	0.03	0.03

As can be observed from Table 6. , all test cases with have a potency Pot<Pot$_H$. Thus, from the explanation in section 3.2, one can conclude that calculating $\vec{P}_{I \to I}$ or $\vec{P}_{I \to C}$ can lead to an accurate test case set. Table 7. shows the test case rank af-

ter applying the I→I algorithm with $\vec{P}_{\text{H}}$=0.95. The $\vec{P}_{\text{I}\to\text{I}}$ from TC3 to TC4 is 0.55.

Table 7. Select and rank the test cases by using the I→I algorithm

TC	3	4	2	1	10	11	9	12	16	6	7	13	14	8	15	18
$\vec{P}_{\text{I}\to\text{I}}$		0.55	0.33	0.72	0.79	0.93	0.92	0.92	0.64	0.8	0.9	0.8	0.9	0.89	0.89	0

From the explanation in section 3.2, one can conclude that calculating $\vec{P}_{\text{C}\to\text{C}}$ or $\vec{P}_{\text{C}\to\text{I}}$ can lead to a compact but might inaccurate test case set. Table 7. shows the test case rank after applying the C→C algorithm with $\vec{P}_{\text{H}}$=0.95. The $\vec{P}_{\text{C}\to\text{C}}$ from TC3 to TC4 is 0.72.

Table 8. Select and rank the test cases by using the C→C algorithm

TC	3	4	2	1	10	16	7	18
$\vec{P}_{\text{C}\to\text{C}}$	0.72	0.63	0.87	0.93	0.93	0.94	0.94	

Compared with Table 7. and Table 8. , one can find that all test cases retained by the C→C algorithm can be found in the test cases retained by the I→I algorithm. This conclusion supports the analysis in section 3.2: when the potency of test cases is very small, C→C algorithm trades accuracy for efficiency, while I→I algorithm trades efficiency for accuracy. In this experiment, I→I algorithm eliminates 50% test cases (16/32), and C→C algorithm eliminates 75% test cases (24/32),

Compared Table 6. with Table 7. , one can see the relationship between the number of eliminated test cases and the rank of the test cases. The top 10 ranked test case in Table 6. are retained in Table 7. after applying the I→I algorithm. Only one test case from 11th to 15th in Table 6. is eliminated, and the total number of eliminated test cases increases to 4, 9 and 16 for top 20, top 25 and all test cases in Table 6. . Fig. 5. shows the number of eliminated test cases increases if these test cases have low ranks.

7.2 Test Case Effectiveness Analysis

While the proposed CRM saves testing efforts by eliminating redundant test cases, it still keeps the effectiveness of the remained test cases. This section provides the effectiveness of CRM by using experimental data.

The test result is shown in Fig. 6. . The most left column is the sixty web services, and the first show denotes the thirty-two test cases. The test cases and web services are organized and numbered. A white cell in the figure denotes a correct output, while a black cell denotes an incorrect output. The right three columns show the number of test cases in total thirty-two test cases, the sixteen test cases selected by the I→I algorithm, and the eight test cases selected by the C→C algorithm respectively, that fail a given web services. If the total thirty-two test cases set can detect the error for a given web services, the test case set selected by the I→I algorithm or C→C algorithm can detect the error as well. Therefore, in this experiment, the I→I algorithm and C→C algorithm do not lose any effective test cases.

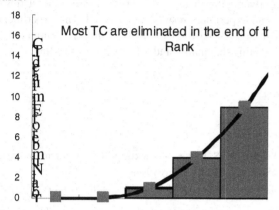

Fig. 5. The relationship between the number of eliminated test cases and the rank of those test cases.

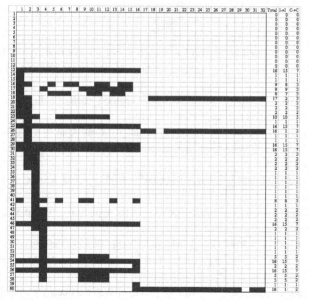

Fig. 6. Compare the coverage of total test case set, the test case set selected by I→I and C→C algorithm

8 Conclusions

This chapter presents a Model-based Adaptive Testing (MAT) for multi-versioned software based the CRM. The CRM can be used to select and rank test cases, and can identify and eliminate those duplicate test cases or those test cases that cover the same aspects. In addition, two adaptive test cases ranking algorithms are given by using the coverage probability. Experiments are conducted using the proposed techniques, and experiment results are analyzed. The experiment results indicate that the CRM-based test case selection algorithm can eliminate redundant test cases while maintaining the quality and effectiveness of testing.

References

[1]   A. Bar-Noy, F. Hwang, H. Kessler, and S. Kutten. A new competitive algorithm for group testing. Discrete Applied Mathematics, 52:29--38, July 1994.

[2]   L. Baresi, and E. Di Nitto, Test and Analysis of Web Services, Springer, 1st edition, November, 2007

[3]   A. Bertolino, L. Frantzen, A. Polini, and J. Tretmans. Audition of web services for testing conformance to open specified protocols. In Architecting Systems with Trustworthy Components, No. 3938 in LNCS. Springer-Verlag, 2006.

[4]   P.A. Bonatti, P. Festa, "On Optimal Service Selection", Proc. of the International World Wide Web Conference (WWW), 2005, pp.530-538.

[5]   Kai-Yuan Cai, Yong-Chao Li, Ke Liu, "Optimal and adaptive testing for software reliability assessment," Information & Software Technologies, volume 46, December 2004, pp. 989-1000.

[6]   G. Canfora and M. Di Penta, "Testing Services and Service-centric Systems, Challenges and Opportunities," IT Professional, vol. 8, no. 2, 2006, pp. 10-17.

[7]   Liming Chen; A. Avizienis, N-Version Programming: a Fault-Tolerance Approach to Reliability of Software Operation, Twenty-Fifth International Symposium on Fault-Tolerant Computing, 1995, pp. 113-119.

[8]   B. De, "Web Services - Challenges and Solutions", WIPRO white paper, 2003, http://www.wipro.com.

[9]   D. Z. Du and F. Hwang, Combinatorial Group Testing And Its Applications, World Scientific, 2nd edition, 2000

[10] J. Garcia-Fanjul, J. Tuya, C. de la Riva. Generating test cases specifications for bpel compositions of web services using spin, International Workshop on Web Services Modeling and Testing (WSMaTe), 2006.

[11] Heckel, R. and Mariani, L., Automatic conformance testing of Web Services, Proceedings of FASE 05: 34-48.

[12] Andrew B. Kahng, Sherief Reda, Combinatorial group testing methods for the BIST diagnosis problem, Proceedings of the 2004 conference on Asia South Pacific design automation: electronic design and solution fair, pp. 113 – 116, Yokohama, Japan, 2004

[13] J. Koehler, B. Srivastava, "Web Service Composition: Current Solutions and Open Problems", ICAPS 2003 Workshop on Planning for Web Services, pp. 28-35.

[14] N. Milanovic, M. Malek, "Current Solutions for Web Service Composition", IEEE Internet Computing, Nov/Dec 2004, Volume: 8, Issue: 6. pp. 51- 59.

[15] S. Narayanan and S. McIlraith, "Simulation, verification and automated composition of web services", In Proc. WWW, 2002.

[16] Dmitri Nevedrov, Using JMeter to Performance Test Web Services, http://dev2dev.bea.com/pub/a/2006/08/jmeter-performance-testing.html

[17] OASIS: Business Process Execution Language for Web Services (BPEL4WS), 2003. http://xml.coverpages.org/bpel4ws.html

[18] OWL-S, http://www.daml.org/services/owl-s/

[19] William N. Robinson, "A requirements monitoring framework for enterprise systems," Requirements Engineering Journal, 11 (2006): 17-41.

[20] W.T Tsai, X. Bai, Y. Chen, X. Zhou, "Web Service Group Testing with Windowing Mechanisms," IEEE International Workshop on Service-Oriented System Engineering (SOSE), Beijing October 2005, 213-218.

[21] W.T. Tsai, Y. Chen, R. Paul, H. Huang, X. Zhou, X. Wei, "Adaptive Testing, Oracle Generation, and Test Script Ranking for Web Services," 29th IEEE Annual International Computer Software and Applications Conference (COMPSAC), Edinburgh, July 2005, pp.101-106.

[22] Web Services Policy 1.2 - Framework (WS-Policy) W3C Member Submission 25 April 2006, available at http://www.w3.org/Submission/2006/06/

[23] J. A. Whittaker and M. G. Thomason. AMarkov chain model for statistical software testing. IEEE Trans. on Software Engineering,20(10):812–824, Oct. 1994.

[24] W3C, the World Wide Web Consortium, www.w3.org/

[25] Web 2.0, Wikipedia, http://en.wikipedia.org/wiki/Web_2

[26] WSDL, available at http://www.w3.org/TR/wsdl

[27] Pulei Xiong, Robert L. Probert, Bernard Stepien, An Efficient Formal Testing Approach for Web Service with TTCN-3 , In Proceedings of the 13th International Conference on Software, Telecommunications and Computer Networks (SoftCOM 2005), Split, Croatia, 2005.

[28] Yongyan Zheng, Jiong Zhou, P. Krause, A model checking based test case generation framework for Web services, 4th International Conference on Information Technology New Generations, 2007.

[29] Hong Zhu, A Framework for Service-Oriented Testing of Web Services, 30th Annual International Computer Software and Applications Conference, 2006.

About the Editors

Jing Dong received his B.S. in computer science from Peking University and Ph.D. in computer science from the University of Waterloo. He is currently an Assistant Professor of Computer Science at the University of Texas at Dallas. His research interests are services computing, high-assurance system engineering, formal methods, software engineering, model driven architecture, design pattern, and software architecture. He has been a guest editor of IEEE Computer and Program Co-Chair of IEEE Symposium on High Assurance System Engineering. He is a member of the ACM and the IEEE. Contact him at jdong@utdallas.edu.

Raymond A. Paul serves in command and control (C2) Policy and manages network enabled command and control systems engineering development in the Department of Defense. His current research focus is on high assurance system engineering, software engineering, C2 networks, dynamic environment decision making, and sensor network. Paul holds a doctorate in software engineering and is an active "Fellow" member of the IEEE Computer Society and member of the ACM. Contact him at raymond.paul@osd.mil.

Liang-Jie Zhang is a research staff member and program manager of application architectures and realization at the IBM T.J. Watson Research Center. His technical interests include services computing, Internet media, and software engineering. He is the founding chair of the Services Computing Professional Interest Community at IBM Research. Dr. Zhang is the editor-in-chief of IEEE Transactions on Services Computing. Zhang has a PhD in pattern recognition and intelligent control from Tsinghua University. Contact him at zhanglj@ieee.org.

J. Dong et al. (eds.), *High Assurance Services Computing*,
DOI 10.1007/978-0-387-87658-0_BM2, © Springer Science+Business Media, LLC 2009

About the Authors

Nasser Alaeddine received a B.E. degree in Computer and Telecommunication Engineering from American University of Beirut, Lebanon in 1993, and M.S. degree in Software Engineering from Southern Methodist University, and a Ph.D. degree in Computer Science from Southern Methodist University expected in May 2009. Since 2001, he has been working for Verizon, Dallas, Texas, now as a senior manager for IT product development. He worked for SAPTriversity, Toronto, Canada and AJB Software Design, Toronto, Canada as a software engineer between 1998 and 2001. He also worked as a network engineer between 1993 and 1998. His current research interests include software testing, quality assurance, software reliability, and software process.

Xiaoying Bai is an Associate professor in the Department of Computer Science and Technology at Tsinghua University, China. Her research interests include software engineering, software testing and service-oriented architectures. She received her PhD from Arizona State University. Her email is baixy@tsinghua.edu.cn.

Farokh B. Bastani received the BTech degree in electrical engineering from the Indian Institute of Technology, Bombay, and the MS and PhD degrees in computer science from the University of California, Berkeley. He is currently a professor of computer science at the University of Texas at Dallas. His research interests are in the areas of relational programs, high-assurance hardware/software systems engineering, hardware/software reliability assessment, self-stabilizing systems, inherent fault tolerance, and high-performance modular parallel programs. Dr. Bastani was the Editor-in-Chief of the IEEE Transactions on Knowledge and Data Engineering and is on the editorial boards of the International Journal of Artificial

Intelligence Tools, the Journal of Knowledge and Information Systems (KAIS), and the Springer-Verlag book series on Knowledge and Information Management (KAIM). He has been the program chair/co-chair and the PC member of many conferences.

Jay S. Bayne received his B.Sc (70), M.Sc.(71), and Ph.D. (76) degrees in electrical engineering and computer science from the University of California at Santa Barbara. He was Professor of Computer Science at California Polytechnic State University from 1973-1984. He is presently CEO of Meta Command Systems, Inc. and Executive Director of the Milwaukee Institute. Additionally, he is Adjunct Professor of Computer Science at the University of Wisconsin-Milwaukee and a consultant to the Office of the Assistant Secretary of Defense (OSD/NII).

Ramesh Bharadwaj is currently a member of the Software Engineering Section of NRL's Center for High Assurance Computer Systems. He also served as an Adjunct Associate Professor of Computer Science at George Washington University.

Alenka Brown is a Senior Research Fellow for the National Defense University-CTNSP; Special Advisor for Human Interactions to the Deputy to the Assistant Secretary of Defense, Networks & Information Integration/ Department of Defense Chief Information Office (ASD(NII)/DoD CIO) for National Leadership Command Capabilities Office, and the Director to the Integrated Information & Communications Technology Support (IIS) Directorate. Dr. Brown as a Senior Advisor to the Defense Agencies and Intelligence Community, and is Director of Human System Development under the National Security Directorate at DoE-Oak Ridge National Laboratory. Dr. Brown earned a Ph.D. in Human Factors Engineering (emphasis in Cognitive Engineering); M.S. in Electrical Engineering, and a B.S. in Computer Science. She is a Certified Human Factors Professional, Lead of the "Human Interoperability Enterprise," Program, and considered one of the foremost experts of behavioral communications in cross-cultural pattern recognition. Dr. Brown's field of knowledge and publications topics range from human interoperability dynamics of human networks, traditional human factors and /virtual/nuclear/display environments, instrumentation and controls, command and control, micro behavioral language, trust and mistrust indicators, rapid trust for hastily formed networks, neural-linguistics of human (social) networks, cognitive-behavior cross cultural analysis, psycho-physiological assessments of special targets of interests, information operational assessments of underground facilities, human system integration, and other topics of US interests.

Chun Cao received his B.Sc., M.Sc. and Ph.D. degrees in Computer Science from the Nanjing University. He is now a lecturer in the Department of Computer Science and Technology at Nanjing University. His research interests include software engineering, access control and service-oriented computing.

Yinong Chen is with the Computer Science and Engineering Department at Arizona State University. His research interests include fault-tolerant computing, reliability modeling, and Web services testing. He received his PhD from University of Karlsruhe, Germany. His email is yinong.chen@asu.edu.

S.C. Cheung received his M.Sc. and Ph.D. degrees in Computing from the Imperial College London. He is an Associate Professor in the Department of Computer Science and Engineering at the Hong Kong University of Science and Technology. He participates actively in the research communities of software engineering and service-oriented computing. He serves on the executive committee of the ACM SIGSOFT, the editorial boards of the IEEE Transactions on Software Engineering (TSE), the Journal of Computer Science and Technology (JCST), and the International Journal of RF Technologies: Research and Application. His research interests include context-aware computing, service-oriented computing, software testing, fault localization, RFID, and wireless sensor network systems.

Paolo Falcarin is research assistant in the Software Engineering Group at Politecnico di Torino, where he received his PhD in software engineering in 2004. He was task leader of service creation environment activities in IST-SPICE project. His current research interests include automated software engineering, telecom service oriented architectures, software modeling.

Zhenghua Fu is a research staff member at IBM T.J. Watson research center in Hawthorne, New York. He received Ph.D in Computer Science from UCLA in 2004, and joined IBM in 2006. Dr. Fu's research interests include composition, sharing and collaboration of digital media.

Arif Ghafoor is currently a Professor in the School of Electrical and Computer Engineering, at Purdue University, West Lafayette, IN, and is the Director of Distributed Multimedia Systems Laboratory. He has been actively engaged in research areas related to multimedia information systems, database security, and parallel and distributed computing. He has published numerous papers in these areas. Dr. Ghafoor has served on the editorial boards of various journals including ACM/Springer Multimedia Systems Journal, the Journal of Parallel and Distributed Databases, and the International Journal on Computer Networks. He has served as a Guest/Co-Guest Editor for various special issues of numerous journals including ACM/Springer Multimedia Systems Journal, the Journal of Parallel and Distributed Computing, International Journal on Multimedia Tools and Applications, IEEE Journal on the Selected Areas in Communications and IEEE Transactions on Knowledge and Data Engineering. He has co-edited a book entitled "Multimedia Document Systems in Perspectives" and has co-authored a book entitled "Semantic Models for Multimedia Database Searching and Browsing" (Kluwer Academic Publishers, 2000). He has been consultant to numerous organizations including UNDP, US Dept. of Defense, Bell Labs, and GE. Dr. Ghafoor is a Fellow of the IEEE. He has received the IEEE Computer Society 2000 Technical Achievement Award for his research contributions in the area of multimedia systems. In 2007 he has received an IEEE Technical Achievement Award in Bioinformtics.

LiGuo Huang is currently an Assistant Professor of Computer Science and Engineering Department at the Southern Methodist University. She received both her Ph.D. and M.S. from the Computer Science Department at the University of Southern California (USC). Her research centers around software process modeling and improvement, process data/text mining, software economics/value-based software engineering, software metrics and modeling, software quality, and high dependability computing. Previously she had been intensively involved in originating the principles of value-based software engineering and published related papers in IEEE Computer and IEEE Software. She is currently a member of the IEEE.

Jun-Jang (JJ) Jeng is a Research Staff Member at the Thomas J. Watson Research Center. He received a B. S. degree in Chemical Engineering from National Taiwan University, and M. S. and Ph. D. degrees in Computer Science from the Michigan State University. His research interests include Business Process Management, Formal Methods, Software Engineering, Cloud Computing, Green Computing, Cyber-Physical Systems, Real-Time Systems, and Agent Technology. Dr. Jeng is an IEEE senior member.

Chao Liang received his B.Engr. and M.Engr. degrees from Department of Electronic and Information Engineering, Huazhong University of Science & Technology (HUST), China, in 2000 and 2002, respectively. He is currently a Ph.D. candidate at the Department of Electrical and Computer Engineering, Polytechnic University, Brooklyn, New York. His research interests include network optimization in overlay and wireless networks, corresponding algorithm and protocol design.

Hui Lei is a Research Staff Member at the IBM T. J. Watson Research Center, where he manages the Messaging Systems department. He received a Ph.D. from Columbia University, an M.S. from Courant Institute, New York University, and a B.S. from Sun Yat-sen University; all in Computer Science. Prior to his doctoral career, he was a Senior Software Engineer at Syncsort Inc. Hui Lei's research has spanned the areas of application messaging, mobile computing, business process management.

Jian Lu received his B.Sc., M.Sc. and Ph.D. degrees in Computer Science from Nanjing University, P.R. China. He is currently a Professor in the Department of Computer Science and Technology and the Director of the State Key Laboratory for Novel Software at Nanjing University. Prof. Lu serves on the Board of the International Institute for Software Technology of the United Nations University. He also serves as the director of the Software Engineering Technical Committee of the China Computer Federation. His research interests include software methodologies, software automation, software agents, and middleware systems.

Xiaoxing Ma received his M.Sc. and Ph.D. degrees in Computer Science from the Nanjing University, P.R. China. He is an Associate Professor in the Department of Computer Science and Technology. His research interests include service-oriented computing, self-adaptive computing and component-based software engineering.

Miroslaw Malek received the M.Sc. degree in Electrical Engineering (Electronics) and the Ph.D. degree in Computer Science in 1975, both from the Technical University of Wroclaw, Poland. He is professor and holder of the Chair in Computer Architecture and Communication at Humboldt University in Berlin since 1994. In 1977, he was a visiting scholar at the Department of Systems Design at the University of Waterloo, Ontario, Canada, then Assistant, Associate, and Full Professor at the University of Texas at Austin where he was also a holder of the Bettie Margaret Smith and the Southwestern Bell Professorships in Engineering.

Supratik Mukhopadhyay is currently a faculty member at the Utah State University. He has extensive experience in research and education in the areas of software engineering, service-oriented computing, and formal methods.

Suku Nair is a Professor and Chair in the Computer Science and Engineering Department at the Southern Methodist University at Dallas where he held a J. Lindsay Embrey Trustee Professorship in Engineering. He is also the director of HACNet (High Assurance Computing and Networking) Lab., which drives the NSA Center of Excellence in Information Assurance at SMU. He received his M.S. and Ph.D. in Electrical and Computer Engineering from the University of Illinois at Urbana in 1988 and 1990, respectively. He is a member of the IEEE, and Epsilon Pi Epsilon.

Jianwei Niu received the BSc degree in computer science from Jilin University, Changchun, China, and the PhD degree in Computer Science from the University of Waterloo in 2005. She has been an assistant professor in the Department of Computer Science at the University of Texas at San Antonio since 2005. Her research interests include formal methods, software modeling, and computing security. She is a member of ACM.

Manuel Peralta is currently a PhD student in the Utah State University

Mark Robinson received his BS in Computer Science at Trinity University in 1993. He founded Fulgent Corporation, a software engineering firm in 2004 and is currently serving as the company's president. He received his MS in Computer

Science from the University of Texas at San Antonio in 2006 and is currently a PhD student in Computer Science.

Hui Shen is a PhD student in the Department of Computer Science at the University of Texas at San Antonio. She received the B.E degree in Software Engineering from Beijing Institute of Technology, China, in 2006. Her current research interests include formal methods and requirements engineering.

Michael F. Siok received his Bachelor's of Engineering Technology Degree (with a second major in Music) from Southwest State University in Marshall, MN USA in 1985, a Master's of Science in Engineering Management from Southern Methodist University (SMU) in Dallas, TX USA in 1995, and his Doctorate of Engineering in Engineering Management in 2008, also from SMU. Michael works for Lockheed Martin Aeronautics Company in Fort Worth, TX as a software systems engineer developing avionics and test systems and software for advanced fighter aircraft. His current work and research interests include topics in software reliability, software safety, testing, and the application of engineering techniques and models to company business problems. Michael is a member of the IEEE, the ACM, and the INCOSE and is a Certified Systems Engineering Professional. He is a registered Professional Engineer in Texas in the field of Software Engineering.

Vladimir Stantchev is a senior scientist at the Berlin Institute of Technology where he heads the Public Services and SOA Group. In 2008 he was a visiting postdoctoral scholar - Fellow at the University of California, Berkeley and at the International Computer Science Institute in Berkeley. He holds a Ph. D. in Computer Science from the Berlin Institute of Technology.

Longji Tang received ME in Computer Science & Engineering and MA in Application Mathematics from Penn State University in 1995. He is a PhD candidate in Software Engineering at the University of Texas at Dallas. His research interests include software architecture and design, service-oriented architecture, service-oriented computing and application, system modeling and formalism. He is also a senior technical advisor at FedEx IT as well as leader/architect in several critical eCommerce projects.

Jeff (Jianhui) Tian received a B.S. degree in Electrical Engineering from Xi'an Jiaotong University in 1982, an M.S. degree in Engineering Science from Harvard University in 1986, and a Ph.D. degree in Computer Science from the University of Maryland in 1992. He worked for the IBM Software Solutions Toronto Laboratory between 1992 and 1995 as a software quality and process analyst. Since 1995, he has been with Southern Methodist University, Dallas, Texas, now as an Associate Professor of Computer Science and Engineering, with joint appointment at the Dept of Engineering Management, Information and Systems. His current research interests include software testing and quality assurance, measurement, analysis and improvement of software reliability, safety, dependability, and complexity, risk identification and management, and applications in net-centric, commercial, web-based, service-oriented, telecommunication, and embedded software and systems. He is a member of IEEE, ACM, and ASQ Software Division.

W. T. Tsai is a professor in the Computer science and Engineering Department and director of the Software Research Laboratory at Arizona State University. His research interests include software engineering and Web services testing and verification. He received his PhD from University of California at Berkeley. His email is wtsai@asu.edu.

Mohammad Gias Uddin received his B.Sc. in Computer Science and Engineering from Bangladesh University of Engineering and Technology in 2004. He received his M.Sc. degree from the Electrical and Computer Engineering Department of Queen's University, Kingston, Canada in 2008. He is currently a software developer at Recognia Inc., Ottawa, Canada.

Feng Xu received his B.S. and M.S. degrees from Hohai University in 1997 and 2000, respectively. He received his Ph.D. degree from Nanjing University in 2003. He is an Associate Professor of Computer Science at Nanjing University. His research interests include trust management, trusted computing, software reliability.

I-Ling Yen received her BS degree from Tsing-Hua University, Taiwan, and her MS and PhD degrees in Computer Science from the University of Houston. She is currently a Professor of Computer Science at the University of Texas at Dallas. Dr. Yen's research interests include fault-tolerant computing, secure and survivable systems, parallel and distributed systems, grid and peer-to-peer computing, and component-based design of distributed adaptive systems. She had published over 150 technical papers and received many research awards in these research areas. She has served as Program Chair/Co-Chair for the IEEE Symposium on Reliable Distributed Systems, IEEE High Assurance Systems Engineering Symposium, IEEE International Computer Software and Applications Conference, IEEE International Symposium on Autonomous Decentralized Systems, etc. She has served on the Program Committee of many conferences.

Kang Zhang is Professor of Computer Science Department, Adjunct Professor of University of Electronic Science and Technology and Soochow University. Prior to joining UTD, he held academic positions in the UK and Australia. Dr. Zhang's current research interests are in the areas of information visualization, visual programming and visual languages, and Web engineering; and has published over 170 papers in these areas. Home page: www.utdallas.edu/~kzhang

Chunying Zhao received the BEng and MEng in computer engineering from Nankai University, China, in 2002 and 2005, respectively. She is currently a Ph.D.

candidate in the University of Texas at Dallas. Her current research areas include software engineering, visual languages, service-oriented architecture, and information visualization.

Yajing Zhao received the MS degree in Computer Science from the University of Texas at Dallas in 2007. She is a Ph.D. candidate at the University of Texas at Dallas, majoring in Software Engineering. Her research interests include software architecture and design, service-oriented architecture, semantic web services, system modeling, and model transformation.

Xinyu Zhou received his PhD from Arizona State University where he worked on Web services design, testing, and implementation. Email: xinyu.zhou@asu.edu.

Mohammad Zulkernine is a faculty member of the School of Computing of Queen's University, Canada, and the leader of the Queen's Reliable Software Technology (QRST) research group. He received his Ph.D. from the University of Waterloo, Canada in 2003, where he belonged to the university's Bell Canada Software Reliability Laboratory. Dr. Zulkernine's research focuses on software reliability and security (automatic software monitoring and intrusion detection, methods and tools for reliable and secure software). His research work are funded by a number of provincial and federal research organizations of Canada, while he is having an industry research partnership with Bell Canada. He is a senior member of the IEEE and a member of the ACM. Dr. Zulkernine is also cross-appointed in the Department of Electrical and Computer Engineering of Queen's University, and a licensed professional engineer of the province of Ontario, Canada.

Index

A

Actuality, 116
Adaptive Testing, 285
agent, 149
architectural translucency, 2
assessment, 19
availability, 24

B

bandwidth, 264
BPEL, 167, *See* Business Process
  Execution Language
Business Process Execution Language, 219

C

Capability, 116
cognitive engineering, 72
component diversity, 193
  dependability attribute perspective,
    193, 199, 214
  environmental perspective, 193, 196,
    214
  internal perspective, 193, 204, 214
  value perspective, 193, 209, 214
Conformance Checking, 133
continuation, 156
coordination, 166
Credibility, 24
cybernetics, 106
Cyberphysical systems, 103, 104
cyberspace, 105, 106, 108, 113, 114

cyberspatial objects, 105, 108, 115
cyberspatial reference model, 103, 104

D

data envelopment analysis (DEA), 193,
  199, 201, 214
decision making, 74
dependability, 193, 194
dependability attribute, 194, 200, 210
dependable, 20, 165
digital earth reference model, 108
distributable thread, 113
distributed enterprises, 68
Distributed Hash Table, 262
dynamic reconfigurations, 175

E

enterprise operating system, 112
Enterprise Service-Oriented Architecture,
  241
events, 151
experimental computer science, 5
Extensible Markup Language, 222

F

failure, 195
fault, 195
fault-failure mapping, 206
federated systems, 104

G

geospace, 105, 110, 117
graph grammar, 129

group testing, 285

H

human interoperability, 66

I

infospace, 105, 110, 115
interaction, 46
Internet Video On-Demand, 261

L

Latency, 116

M

Modeling, 230
monitoring, 46

N

net-centric system, 19
non functional properties, 95
nonfunctional properties, 2

O

ontology, 22, 179
operational profile (OP), 196
OWL-S, 167

P

peer-assisted video streaming, 261
Performance, 116
performance measurement framework, 103
Potential, 116
Productivity, 116

R

recommendation, 47
reconfiguratio, 148
regression testing, 285
reliability, 23, 193, 200
replication, 3, 4
REST, 243

S

Safety, 24
security, 24, 45, 195
semantic web services, 92
sequence diagrams, 230
service access points, 108, 110, 121
service composition, 90
Service Creation Environment, 90
service engineering, 90

service level agreement, 2, 103, 113, 269
service systems, 103, 104, 105, 106
service-based software, 45
service-oriented architecture, 1, 127
Simple Object Access Protocol, 221
situation awareness, 74
SOAP. *See* Simple Object Access Protocol
sociospace, 105, 110, 115
SOL, 152
Spatial Graph Grammar, 135
Spread, 147
State machines, 238
static type system, 146
statistical testing, 285
synchronous programming, 146
Synchrony Hypothesis, 152

T

test case selection and ranking, 285
time-utility function, 113, 115
trading protocols, 106
Trust, 46
trust rules, 46
trustworthiness, 19

U

UML. *See* Unified Modeling Language
Unified Modeling Language, 219
utility accrual scheduling, 113

V

value propositions, 103, 104, 105, 106,
    110, 116, 120
VEGGIE, 135
viable systems model, 106
video streaming, 261
Visual languages, 134

W

Web Service Definition Language, 222
Web services, 1, 130, 219, 285
Web-Oriented Architecture, 241
WSDL. *See* Web Service Definition
    Language

X

XML. *See* Extensible Markup Language